FROM DENG XIAOPING TO JIANG ZEMIN

Two Decades of Political Reform in the People's Republic of China

Yiu-chung Wong

University Press of America,® Inc.
Lanham · Boulder · New York · Toronto · Oxford

**Copyright © 2005 by
University Press of America,® Inc.**
4501 Forbes Boulevard
Suite 200
Lanham, Maryland 20706
UPA Acquisitions Department (301) 459-3366

PO Box 317
Oxford
OX2 9RU, UK

Library of Congress Control Number: 2004114175
ISBN 0-7618-3074-X (paperback : alk. ppr.)

To My Aunt Who Taught Me

the First Chinese Character

To Anita, Cyelle, Samuel and Cedric

with Affection

CONTENTS

LISTS OF TABLE

ABBREVIATIONS

Beida	—	Peking University
CAC	—	Central Advisory Committee
CASS	—	Chinese Academy of Social Sciences
CC	—	Central Committee
CCP	—	Chinese Communist Party
CDIC	—	Central Discipline Inspection Commission
CMC	—	Central Military Commission
CPPCC	—	Chinese People's Political Consultative Conference
CR	—	Cultural Revolution
CS	—	Central Secretariat
GMD	—	Guomindang (Nationalist Party)
GLF	—	Great Leap Forward
NPC	—	National People's Congress
PLA	—	People's Liberation Army
PRC	—	People's Republic of China
SC	—	Standing Committee
SEZs	—	Special Economic Zones
SSRC	—	Committee on the Studies of Comparative Politics of Social Sciences Research Council

ACKNOWLEDGEMENTS

The book is developed from my Ph.D thesis on China's political reform submitted to the University of Queensland in 1996. However, two new chapters were added to the book and the other chapters have been extensively revised. In writing this book, I owe a great debt to a number of people without whose help and support the completion of this book would have been impossible.

First of all, I would like to thank Professor C.L. Chiou, my Ph.D. thesis supervisor at the Department of Government, University of Queensland (Australia) for his generous and invaluable comments on my thesis some of which have been absorbed into this book. Next, I would like to extend my thanks to the following people: Dr Don Flecher, Reader of the Department of Government, the University of Queensland; Professor Beatrice Leung, Professor Brian Bridges and Professor Peter Baehr, and Dr Chan Che-po, my colleagues at the Lingnan University (Hong Kong); Dr Pun Kwok-hung, Associate Professor at the University of Hong Kong; Dr Lai Chi-kong, Senior Lecturer of the History Department, the University of Queensland; Dr Anita Y.K. Poon at the Baptist University (Hong Kong) and Willy Lam Wo-lap, senior analyst of Chinese affairs at CNN, all of whom have read parts of the manuscripts of my original draft and their invaluable suggestions and comments are most appreciated. It goes without saying that all the faults are mine.

I would also like to thank Lingnan University, which has granted me a six months study leave that enabled me to complete the book. My thanks go to my Research Assistant Mr Wilson W.Y.Lau whose diligence and the punctuality in completing the tasks I assigned were rare among young men. Last but not least, I would like to thank the editorial board of the University Press of America. Their patience and continuous support in the project is much appreciated.

INTRODUCTION

In the Deng Xiaoping and Jiang Zemin era, it is indisputable to say that no political event was more significant than the outbreak and subsequent suppression of the Tiananmen pro-democracy movement in 1989. It marked the end of the hopeful decade of the 1980s and began the woeful stagnation of the 1990s. The tragic events of June 4 1989 in the People's Republic of China (PRC) shocked the world. Unexpectedly, the sudden death of a former general secretary of the Chinese Communist Party (CCP) triggered the largest social movement since the founding of the PRC in 1949. Beijing, the capital, was surrounded by more than 300,000 People's Liberation Army (PLA). Millions of people around the world viewed the tanks and armored personnel carriers of the PLA rolling over Beijing's Changan Avenue, crushing whatever was in their way. Ordinary citizens, including teenagers, workers, students, and women were gunned down. The visual image of a white-shirted young man standing before a row of tanks symbolized the helpless and desperate Chinese masses vis-a-vis the powerful coercive Party/state machinery.[1] It is incredibly hard to believe that a government that claims to represent the interests of the people and, in particular, the working class could suppress so brutally a spontaneous social movement initiated mainly by university students and participated in by nearly all walks of life in China. To this date, the total number of victims remains a mystery and the extent of the atrocity has become a taboo in China.[2]

In the past two decades, no issue has attracted more attention from students of Chinese politics than the issue of democratization of Chinese polity which certainly is a key issue in the political reform/ political structural reform program launched by the Chinese leadership.[3] Democratization is invariably an indispensable part of any book concerning China's political development since 1949.[4]

In fact, the goals of the pro-democracy movement in 1989 were completely in line with the political reform program proposed by the CCP in the 1980s. By and large, the movement has sided with the establishment and overthrowing the CCP governance has never been the principal objective. It is especially disheartening that the massacre took place at a time when the world community anticipated that China's road towards democracy had become nearly irreversible after ten years of modernization push. Almost in a single day, China was propelled out of a hopeful era of reform. The crackdown or the bloody clash between the social-political forces unleashed by reforms and the CCP hardliners was a consequence of the ten years of interaction between economic and political structural reform prior to 1989. The Tiananmen massacre seems to have been inevitable with the fierce power and ideological struggles within the CCP ruling hierachy (Ruan Ming 1994; Wu Jiang 1995). The political structural reform was a key component of the comprehensive reform strategy initiated by Deng in the late 1970s when China turned away from Mao's autarkic policy.

The 1990s became a much different epoch than the previous decade. Fearing the outbreak of another June 4, the CCP was never comfortable with socio-political forces that it could not control. Alternatively, intellectuals with liberal inclinations were targets of political harassment and surveillance.   Ideological monitoring and control was tightened more than ever. Despite the increasing marketization of the economy and even its accession to the World Trade Organization (WTO) at the beginning of 21st century, political suppression was brutal, as in the cases of the Democratic Party and Falun Gong. Non-governmental organizations were severely restricted and "public space" for genuine intellectual debate was curtailed. As John Burns, a Hong Kong political scientist, has said, "After 50 years of revolutionary transformation and uneven consolidation, and a generation of economic re-structuring, the political institutions of the People's Republic of China remain essentially Leninist.... China's constitution continues to legitimize a monist political system....the Party continues to repress all attempts to organize challenges to its authority".[5]

In the Third Plenum of the Eleventh Central Committee (CC) in December, 1978, the CCP abandoned the political line of "class struggles as the key link" and "politics take command" and shifted its focus to economic development and modernization. For the first time since 1949, the CCP members "from the central down to local levels are now concentrating their energy and attention on socialist modernization" (CCCCP 1981:100-101). This is easier said than done. As later events unfolded, perhaps except at the end of the 1970s and beginning of the 1980s, the CCP has never been as "solid as a block". Intra-party struggles and debates had characterized the CCP political development in the reform era, even at the zenith of Deng's power. Jiang's authority was repeatedly challenged by the Party's orthodox fundamentalists in the early 1990s.

The economic reform began initially in the agricultural sector after the Third Plenum of the Eleventh CC. A system of responsibility and contract was introduced to the peasant households, attempting to bolster production enthusiasm of the peasantry. In 1984, economic reform was introduced to the urban industrial sector (CCCCP 1984). As the economic reform went into full swing, Deng Xiaoping, then China's *de facto* supreme leader after his third rehabilitation in 1977, also pronounced a series of reform measures in polity. In his seminal speech on political structural reform, "On the Reform of the System of Party and State Leadership" in August 1980 (Deng 1984:302-325), Deng strongly criticised the bloated and inefficient Party/state structure, and called for a sweeping reform of the Party cadre and leadership system.

Broadly, his state and leadership reform package touched two kinds of relations, namely Party/state relations and state/society relations (Burns 1989a). Contrary to most of the pundits who argue that there has not been much reform in politics, I would argue that the 1980s saw the most liberalized regime in China and the Chinese intellectuals enjoying most freedom since 1949. Political regression took place in the 1990s. As I shall show, the twenty years of economic and political reforms produced profound repercussions in Chinese polity and society. From the very beginning, the political reform process was full of twists and turns. It was resisted by the Party ideological fundamentalists and conservatives, while the reformists tried to push the reform as far as they could. The intense conflicts between the conservatives and the reform-minded leaders ultimately led to the downfall of two general secretaries, Hu Yaobang and Zhao Ziyang, respectively in 1987 and 1989. Despite the constraints, Deng's role in the reform process was pivotal and it was always he who ultimately decided the outcome of the policy controversies and intra-Party power struggles. He personally embodies the two inherently contradictory trends in the Chinese reform process: hard-politics and soft-economics.[6]

This book attempts to explore and examine the background, origins, dynamics, policies, processes, and consequences of the macro political structural reform in the PRC in the decades of Deng Xiaoping and Jiang Zemin by applying a theoretical approach that was developed in the modernization theories. It is an integrated approach that attempts to study the political development of developing countries holistically. Detailed discussion will be provided in chapter 1. The book covers roughly the period from 1979 to the end of the twentieth century. It seeks to depict and outline the pattern of political development in China in the same period, and intends to understand the 1989 pro-democracy movement, in particular, in the light of the political structural reform carried out in the previous ten years. Emphasis will be placed on the restructuring of the Party/state apparatus.

The book does not intend to analyse economic reform *per se* in detail, but in so far as it is related to political structural reform, economic issues will be dealt with. Within the structural limits of the Chinese political system and cultural context, the role of Deng Xiaoping and Chen Yun in the reform era will be analysed. Lastly, the political structural reform programmes put forward in the 1990s by the CCP headed by Jiang Zemin, who was handpicked by Deng Xiaoping to replace Zhao Ziyang in the Fourth Plenum of the Thirteenth CC in June 1989, will be examined and analysed. In the last chapter, I shall examine the democratic prospects in China.

The book is divided into eight chapters. The first chapter attempts to set up a theoretical framework that can be used to analyse China's political structural reform in the 1980s and 1990s. The "crisis and sequence" approach is used in this book as an orienting framework. Guiding hypotheses will be derived from this approach and applied to the analysis of the polity of contemporary China. Rationale and justifications are put forward to explain why the particular modernization framework is used in the context of the evolution of development studies in the past several decades. The second chapter aims to explore the origins of the political structural reform. The nature of the CCP Party/state since the founding of the PRC will be briefly discussed, and the Maoist legacy inherited by the reformist period will be analysed. The history of the PRC will be reviewed in the light of the concepts borrowed from the "crisis and sequence" approach.

The third chapter examines the policies on reforming the Party/state polity in the 1980s. In addition, the power bases of the factional groups associated with the policies will be analysed. The fourth chapter attempts to outline the process of the political structural reform in the 1980s and tries to throw light on the socio-political forces that rallied behind the policies. In addition, cyclical process of *shou* (tightening) and *fang* (liberating) of the reform process will be identified a and analysed.[7] Chapter five deals with the consequences of the reform and the CCP's subsequent brutal suppression of the movement. In relation to the political structural reform, the concept of "civil society" will be critically examined. Moreover, some general theoretical issues about marketization, liberalization, and democratization will be discussed. Chapter six reviews the political development and attempts a survey of the political reform measures in the 1990s. Chapter seven is more theoretical and analysis will be on the relationships between marketization, liberalization and democratization in the context of present social science literature. Lastly, in chapter eight, the democratic prospects for the post-Deng-Jiang era will be explored. The conclusion will summarize the main themes of the entire book and assess the possible contribution of the book to the study of this field.

Notes

[1] The *Time* Weekly picked the Chinese young man to be one of the twenty most influential political figures in the twentieth century. As the author said, " With a single act of defiance, a lone Chinese hero revived the world's image of courage." See *Time* (1998).

[2] In a press conference on 6 June 1989, Yuan Mu, the official State Council spokesman, disclosed that only 23 university students were killed in the massacre. The total number of deaths was about 300, including soldiers and ordinary citizens. The total number of casualties was about 8,000. In a report to the Standing Committee (SC) of the National People's Congress (NPC) at the end of June, Chen Xitong (1989), the mayor of Beijing, said that about 200 people died, including 36 university students, and 6,000 soldiers and security men and 3,000 ordinary citizens were injured. The International Amnesty estimated that at least 1,300 people were killed in the incident (Li Kwok-shing 1992:506). The foreign news agencies had different estimates of people being killed: CNN (1,400), BBC (2,000), ABC (2,000), Reuters (1,000), Agence France (1,400). According to one Hong Kong source (*Cheng Ming*, July 1989:10), the number of deaths on June 4 (from mid-night to seven o'clock in the morning) was 8,720. From June 3 to 9, the number of casualties was 28,790. Nicolas Kristof and Sheryl Wudunn, the two New York Times reporters based in Beijing from 1988 to 1993, estimated that (1994:90) only 400 to 800 people were killed in the crackdown. The Chinese Red Cross told foreign news agencies that a survey of Beijing hospitals after the 4 June found that 2,600 people died in the government assault (Schell 1994:166). Ding Zilin (1994a, 1994b), an associate professor of Beijing's People University, was able to locate the names of 96 deaths and 49 casualties after five years of searching and investigation. She has been continuously harassed by the Chinese authorities ever since. A Chinese scholar Liu Xiaobo (1992), who was on hunger strike in Tiananman Square, and was one of the last ones to retreat from the Square, said that he saw no one being killed in the Square. He may well be right. Now it is widely believed that the most heavy killings took place in the East Changan Avenue (Shen Tong 1990). Unless the victims are rehabilitated, the true figures may never be known.

[3] In this book, I will use the concepts *zhengzhi gaige* (political reform)and *zhengzhi tizhi gaige* (political structural reform) interchangebly. I am aware that political reform is often used by students of Chinese politics outside China and very often the term denotes an element of "multi-party" politics. On the contrary, the Chinese leadership since the mid-1980s has never used political reform but always political structural reform. For more details, see chapter 3.
[4] The two recent examples are Zhao Suisheng. (Ed.)(2000) and Wong Yiu-chung, (Ed.)(2000).
[5] John Burns (1999). The People's Republic of China at 50: National Political Reform. In *China Quarterly*, no.159, September, pp.580-581.
[6]It is almost a norm that scholars of China classify Chinese leadership since 1978 into a conservative-reformist dichotomous schema. Personally, I do not object to such classification provided one does not take such a view too mechanically. When labelling Chinese leadership conservative or reformist, one should not lose sight of the significant issues involved. The labels are meaningful only in relation to the issues. For example, two or three years after the downfall of the "Gang of Four", Chen Yun, who died in April 1995, is now generally considered to be the chief protagonist of the conservative camp in the 1980s, but he was a reformist at the end of the 1970s (Harding 1987:43-44). Likewise, Deng Xiaoping, the architect of the reform, was not a reformist at all in the June 4 events. Instead, he was the arch conservative. In 1992, in the course of his "imperial tour" to the Southern coastal provinces, Deng suddenly became a great reformist again, fighting back the conservative retrenchment policies set in after June 4 (Deng, 1993:376-378; Shambaugh, 1993a).
[7] It is strange that the studies on the policy cyclical process in the PRC was a fad in the 1980s. However, the studies completely disappear in the 1990s. Academic studies do have fashions. For details, see chapter 4.

CHAPTER ONE

THEORETICAL FRAMEWORK – BACK TO MODERNISATION THEORY

This chapter intends to introduce a theoretical framework which is used in the analysis of the political structural reform in the PRC in the 1980s and 1990s. It starts with a literature review in which some recent works on China's political structural reform, both in English and Chinese, are discussed. The "crisis and sequence" approach is used in this book, which is a sub-theory of modernization theory in general.[1] Before proceeding to the discussion of the justifications and rationale of using this approach throughout the book, a general discussion on the rise and fall of the two major developmental paradigms (Kuhn 1970) in the past several decades is put forward, which serves as the background to comprehend the approach more substantially. Then a detailed examination of the approach is provided, with specific guiding hypotheses derived from the approach that will become the orienting focus of the book.

Literature Review

A variety of Western and Chinese overseas academic works have been published on the political development of the CCP Party/state in the 1980s and 1990s, with emphases on state bureaucracy decision-making process and policy implementation (Lampton 1987; Lieberthal and Lampton 1992; Lieberthal and Oksenberg 1988; Shirk 1993; Wu Guoguang 1997), Party/state-society relations (An Chen 1999; Friedman, Pickowicz, and Selden 1991; Goodman and Hooper 1994; McCormick 1990; Shue 1988; Stavis 1988; Tsou 1986), policy output (David Chang 1989; Harding 1987; O'Brien 1990; Rosenbaum 1992), elitist politics and cadre system (Baum 1994; Burns 1989c; Fewsmith 2001; Willy Lam 1995,1999; Lee Hong Yun 1991; Nathan and Gilley 2002), cultural and ideological development (Brugger and Kelly 1990), and the post-Tiananmen crisis discourse (Black and Munro 1993; Dittmer 1993; Han Minzhu 1990; Hicks 1990; Ogden, Hartford, and Zweig 1992; Perry and Wasserstrom 1992; Gordon White 1991; Womack 1991a; Unger 1991) and China's democratization (Zhao Suisheng 2000). However, no predominant paradigm on the China's political development has emerged, let alone political structural reform.[2]

To date, works on the political structural reform on China in the 1980s and 1990s are numerous, but most of them are either edited works (Baum 1991; Rosenbaum 1992; Gordon White 1991) or single articles (Burns 1989a, 1999; Gao Fang 1988; Ma Min 1993; Su Shaozhi 1990; Wang Ruowang 1988; Wong, Yiu-Chung 2000b). Furthermore, most of the works treat economics and politics together (David Chang 1989; Chen Ziming 1992; Harding 1987; Shirk 1993; Gordon White 1993a). Brugger and Kelly (1990), Chen Ruisheng (1992), McCormick (1990), O'Brien (1990), Stavis (1988), Wong, Yiu-Chung (2000a) variously concentrate on the themes of the political structural reform. There has not been a systematic work on the reform in politics as a whole.

Chen Ruisheng's book (1992) represents the official view of the CCP leadership and obviously cannot deviate from the Party standpoint. Published in the aftermath of the 4 June massacre, the book tried to justify and legitimize the reversing political reform programme under the name of orthodox Marxism. The result is a work that appears to be incoherent and contradictory. The name of Zhao Ziyang, who was purged in the Fourth Plenum of the Thirteenth CC, was not even mentioned. McCormick's book (1990) concentrates on political participation in the early reformist China, in particular the county level elections in the early 1980s. Borrowing the notion of the Leninist state and Weberian concepts of charismatic, rational-legal, traditional or patrimonial, and charismatic rulership, McCormick interpreted the post-Mao political structural reform as an attempt to change from charismatic authority to rational-legal authority from top down. He (1990:6-8) argued that the relatively autonomous Leninist state has become a major obstacle in limiting change.

Stavis's book (1988) is an "interim report" on China's political structural reform in 1986/87, especially in the analysis of the socio-political context in which the 1986/87 student demonstrations broke out. Though numerous sources of materials are used, the book looks like a piece of journalistic reporting rather than serious academic writing. Brugger and Kelly's book (1990) is a work on China's ideological-cultural development, particularly Marxism, in the early 1980s. In fact, the focus of the study is quite narrow, i.e. on the debate over the "socialist alienation" in 1982/83.[3]   It is a pity that the "culture fever" in 1988, culminating in the filming and broadcasting of the television series *He Shang* (River Elegy), was not even mentioned. Furthermore, academic debates seldom manifest for the sake of debate in CCP China. They invariably carry political intonations and consequences. Brugger and Kelly seem to be missing this essential point. Harding's work (1987) covers the period from 1978 to the mid-1980s. His notion of "consultative authoritarianism" is enlightening and his analysis of the reform policies is thorough. However, it is questionable that his "radical-moderate reformer" schema is theoretically more fruitful than the schema of the "reformist-conservative" dichotomy. In fact, in a crisis situation, opinions very often tend to polarize and only two camps can be distinguished; on the other hand, policies undergo periodic fluctuation. When important issues come to a decision, the "moderate-radical" schema cannot be applied.

O'Brien (1990) produced the most comprehensive book on the reform of China's NPC in the 1980s. He argued that legislative development is a component of political change. "Throughout its history, the NPC has been a window in evolving Party/society and Party/state relations that has shed light on the broad character of the Chinese polity" (1990:4). Gordon White's book (1993a) is succinct and his contribution lies in the able treatment of the interlinkages between the economic and political reform. He further explored the relationship between marketization and democratization in China. In analysing China's democratic prospects, his analysis turns from critical to normative. White (1993a:248-255) suggested that China's road to democracy can take two steps: first, from totalitarianism to authoritarianism; second, from authoritarianism to full-fledged democracy. Without outlining the institutional bases of his arguments, his suggestions remain abstract.

Tsou's book (1986) is in fact a collection of essays that span more than eighteen years. He tackled China's political structural reform from an historical perspective, putting the reformist era in the context of the modernization movement since the May-Fourth Movement in 1919. He provided insights into the nature and vicissitude of the communist movement since its birth in 1921. His characterization of the Maoist regime as a system of "totalism" (1991:271) is widely used by many Chinese political scientists, (e.g. Yan Jiaqi 1990). Shirk's book (1993) is admirable in terms of the scope of study. She attempted to explore the decision-making mechanism, institutional features and processes in devising the economic reform policies within the CCP Party/state structure. By comparing China's success and the Soviet failure in economic reform, Shirk tried to show that successful economic reform can be achieved without changing the basic communist Party/state structure. Nonetheless, her argument that "Deng Xiaoping took cautious approach of introducing economic reform without political reform" (1993:333) is not tenable. Despite periodic retrenchment in ideological-political arenas, genuine political structural reform was introduced.

Chen Zimin (1992), one of the most famous Chinese dissidents, who was charged by the Chinese government to be one of the "black hands" behind the 1989 prodemocracy movement, has written one of the best works on the reformist period in the 1980s in prison. Being an insider in the CCP core power centre during the reign of Hu Yaobang and Zhao Ziyang, Chen is able to provide insights into the decision-making process at the critical juncture in that period.

Wu Guoguang's (1997) book is devoted wholly to the theme of political reform but, in fact, he only provides the decision-making process of political reform by the power groups within the CCP in the short period leading to the CCP Thirteenth Party Congress in October 1987. An Chen (1999) analysed how the "one party democracy" emerged as a result of the political reform launched in the 1980s and 1990s.There was indeed an element of institutional "checks and balances" inherent in the CCP party/state structure after two decades of reform.

Several factors may contribute to the academic poverty in this area. Firstly, the Chinese economic and political structural reforms are too intimately linked. It is extremely difficult or almost futile to isolate intellectually the two dimensions. Consequently the reformist policies in economic and political arenas are very often examined together. Secondly, the term political structural reform seems too all-embracing. In his political report (1987b) in the Thirteenth CCP Congress, Zhao Ziyang listed seven broad areas under the subsection of political reform, namely 1) separating the Party and government; 2) delegating state power and authority to provincial levels; 3) reforming government bureaucracy; 4) reforming the cadre system; 5) establishing a system of political dialogue and consultation between the Party and the people; 6) enhancing the monitoring roles of representative assemblies and mass organizations; and 7) strengthening the socialist legal system. Works published on the political structural reform in China (Li Shengping 1989; Li Yongchun and Luo Jian 1987; Li Yongchun, Shi Yuanqin and Guo Xiuzhi 1987; ZGZXP 1987) always include these aspects. It is extremely difficult to handle such vast complicated subjects in a single study.

Thirdly, students of Chinese politics have not made sufficient use of the theories and concepts developed in political science in general and applied them to the studies of contemporary China. Among the above-mentioned works, McCormick (1990) used the notions of the autonomous Leninist state and Weberian typology of authority in analysing the political structural reform in the 1980s. O'Brien (1990) borrowed the functional-structural method and applied it to the analysis of China's NPC. Works by Brugger and Kelly (1990), David Chang (1989) Harding (1987), Shirk (1993), and Gordon White (1993a) are all more descriptive than theoretical.

The above works have thrown light on the elitist politics, institutional development, ideological flux, and political participation in contemporary China. But a macro view of the integrated political development, political structural reform in the 1980s in particular is urgently needed. My book attempts to make use of existing social science theory, such as modernization theory, in the study of contemporary China, hopefully to throw new light on the interpretations of China's political structural reform in the past two decades. Before proceeding to the discussion of the "crisis-sequence" approach, a background on the rise, fall and rejuvenation of modernization theory is outlined.

Modernization Theory versus Dependency Theory

After the Second World War, a host of colonies began to shrug off the shackles of colonialism and strive for national independence. The task of modernization and economic development naturally became the centre of national commitment. The development and prosperity of the Western industrialized countries, the United States of America in particular, attracted the attention of the ruling elites in the post-colonial states and became the object of simulation. Amidst the world-wide trend of imitating the West, modernization theory emerged in the late 1950s and early 1960s in the development literature.[4]

Heavily drawing upon the theoretical heritage of the nineteenth century Durkheimian evolutionary theory and Talcott Parsons' structural functionalism, modernization theory builds around the notions of progress and modernization in the process of development, especially in the developing countries in the 1950s. The modernizationists share several basic assumptions. Firstly, societal change is evolutionary and unidirectional. The society moves irreversibly from a primitive stage to a more advanced stage. Secondly, modernization is a transformative process in which traditional or backward societies become modernized or developed societies. The modernization theorists postulate a pair of dichotomous societal units: traditional and modern societies. Both are conceived to be incompatible and exclusive. Thirdly, the theorists further assume that the USA and Western Europe would be the developmental models for the developing countries. In other words, the institutions of the West should be and could be transplanted to the Third World countries in order that modernization would be achieved. Fourthly, the modernization theorists are extremely optimistic over the development of the developing countries. Alternatively, they assume that Western values and institutions could be easily transplanted to indigenous communities (Evans and Stephens 1988:740-743; So 1990:33-36).

In the mid-1960s, Coleman (1971), an American political scientist, proposed one of the most widely-used models in the study of political development, the well-known "differentiation-equality-capacity" model (So 1990:31-32). According to him, political modernization means the process of differentiation of political structure, secularization of political culture, and the increasing capacity of the political system. Coleman argued that differentiation of political structure and the quest for equality are the dominant trends in the process of political development. Ultimately, the process of differentiation and acquisition of equality ethos would lead to the enhancement of extractive and regulative abilities of the political system. He also suggested that in the process of development, the developing countries may encounter six "system-development problems" or "crises" which the developing countries must resolve in the modernization process in one way or the other. The six "crises" of modernization are as follows:[5] 1) the crisis of national identity during the transfer of loyalty from primordial groups to the new-born nation; 2) the crisis of political legitimacy for the new state; 3) the crisis of penetration, i.e. the difficulty of implementing policy throughout the country by the central government; 4) the crisis of participation (a lack of political participatory institutions to channel mass demands to the state); 5) the crisis of integrating of various divisive social and political groups; 6) the crisis of distribution, i.e. the   state is unable to bring about economic growth and distribute sufficient goods, services, and values to satisfy mass expectations.[6]

The modernization school dominated the academic community in the studies of development in the 1950s. However, in the early 1960s a new school began to gain adherents in development literature. Dependency theorists attacked the fundamental assumptions of the modernization school. The new approach attracted numerous followers and academics in the developing countries. It gained increasing popularity among elites because of the failure of development in the Latin American countries (So 1990:91-92). By the early 1960s, despite two decades of governmental efforts to modernize, the Latin American countries had been plagued by high rates of unemployment, spiral inflation, currency devaluation, high national deficit, declining terms of trade, and the increasing gap between the wealthy and the poor.

The concept of dependency was employed to analyse the phenomena of economic stagnation, increasing poverty, and runaway inflation in the backward countries, and furthermore, the tremendous gap between the developed countries, such as the USA and Western Europe, and Third World countries. According to the dependency thinkers, the industrialized countries were the exploiting countries while the developing countries were being exploited.

The dependency school accused the modernization theorists of being theoretically imperialist and hegemonic, and of overlooking the changing historical context between developing countries and advanced industrialized countries, with the consequence that they ignored the idea that there might be an alternative path of development. Furthermore, the modernizationists' belief that Western institutions and values could be transplanted was naive and unsubstantiated. In short, the modernization school was criticised as being ahistorical and "ethnocentric".

The theoretical heritage of the dependency school can be traced back to Marxism-Leninism, in particular Lenin's theory of imperialism (Tucker 1975:211-218). Lenin argued that in the late nineteenth century competitive capitalism was transformed structurally into monopoly capitalism, and the process was characterized by the infusion of banking and finance capital. In order to ensure the supply of raw materials to the advanced industrialized countries and markets for the manufactured goods from the West, the political conquest of foreign land became a necessity. Thus, two sets of nations were distinguished: the conquering countries and the conquered countries. Applying the Leninist assumption of political polarization to the post-colonial context after the Second World War, the dependency thinkers postulated that the development of the industrialized countries and underdevelopment of the Third World countries are structurally related. They are "two sides of the same coin". Methodologically, dependency thinkers take the international context as the primary variable in accounting for the internal structure of the developing countries, while the domestic forces are taken as the secondary variable (Evans 1979:16-25). However, theoretical assumptions of the dependency school would be eclipsed by the emergent reality.

The Demise of Dependency Theory

One of the earliest exponents of the dependency school was Paul Baran, who advanced the "impossibility" thesis of development in the Third World countries in the late 1950s (Palma 1978:886). He argued that the only way to break off the economic stagnation is to launch a "socialist revolution", which will break up the grip of the foreign capital and release the capital necessary for genuine development. Following Baran, Frank (1979:95) furthered the explication that in the absence of a socialist revolution and within the world capitalist economy, the developing countries would not have genuine development.

However, the "impossibility" thesis on the part of the developing countries was rebuked by reality. The development of some Third World countries, especially the rise of the East Asian Newly Industrialized Countries (NICs)[7] since the late 1960s and early 1970s, has challenged the fundamental assumptions of the dependency school. The rapid development of the East Asian NICs does not fit the theory (Evans 1987). Nevertheless, the most important theoretical challenge to the dependency school was posed by Bill Warren, who, in fact, came from the same school. Observing the tremendous strides in industrialization made by the developing countries since the late 1960s, Warren (1973:3) argued that the industrialization prospect for quite a number of developing countries was optimistic and in fact substantial progress in economic development had already been achieved. Using manufacturing output as an indicator of industrialization, Warren (1973:5-7) pointed out that the peripheral countries as a whole had made significant progress in industrialization since the Second World War. For example, in 1937, the industrialized countries accounted for about nine times the manufacturing output of the Third World countries, and by 1959, the ratio had been reduced to seven to one. In the 1960s, the average annual growth rates of the Third World countries were 7 percent, whilst that of the Western nations were only 6 percent. Warren attacked the dependency thinkers for applying a set of utopian criteria to measure the industrialization process in the developing countries. He (1973:4) argued,

> The "development" concept, understood not simply as a retardation, but as distribution of economic development, suffers from the fact that, apart possibly from the USA, England and France, there has never been a so called "normal" development of industrial capitalism in any country and the distortion referred to appears to be judged so against an unstated ideal criterion.

Furthermore, Warren (1973:16) strongly attacked the ambiguity of the notion of "dependence":

> When faced with the fact that a measure of industrialization in the Third World has taken place, socialist writers have argued this merely results in a different style of dependence, i.e. that independent industrialization (or economic development) is impossible....What happens with this approach is that, either explicitly or implicitly, a somewhat utopian ideal is advanced under the banner of an "independent economic development" that lacks any specific class connotation. Obviously, the actual capitalist development cannot match up to this ideal (full employment, diversified industry and agriculture, adequate housing, relatively egalitarian income distribution, etc.) So it is happily concluded that only socialism provides a solution. In this process the problem of what the actual developments are and how conducive they may be to developing capitalism is ignored. Thus many revolutionaries live in a happy world in which capitalist development never comes up to the left's requirement, and so can be regarded as a failure.

The Warrenite criticism of the utopian dependency criteria for economic development was devastating, especially as it came from a convert rather than an enemy. The dependency thinking was further eroded by the developmental experience of the East Asian NICs. The early dependency thinkers were forced to revise and refine the concept of "dependence". In the late 1970s, sophisticated dependency scholars such as Cardoso and Falleto (1979) and Evans (1979) introduced the notion of "comprehensive analysis of development", in which a holistic "structural-historical" approach was used. While still using "dependency" as their focus of arguments, the phenomena of development were admitted and taken for analysis.

The early dependency theorists defined "dependency" in such a way that a backward country was subjected to the exploitation of the industrialized countries through foreign investment and trade. Therefore, development was impossible as the exploiting countries remitted the profits back home. In the hands of refined dependency thinkers, the concept was used not as a "formal theory", but as a "methodology for the analysis of concrete situations of underdevelopment", (Palma 1978:909). The meaning of "dependency" was simply redefined as: "from the economic point of view a system is dependent when the accumulation and expansion of capital cannot find its essential dynamic component inside the system" (Cardoso 1979:XX). The centre of economic dynamics still lies outside the developing countries, but development is not excluded. Commenting on the falsifying evidences by the East Asian NICs experiences upon the dependency perspective, Evans (1987:220-221) tried to rescue the theory by arguing that if the dependency thinkers "confront the East Asian experience with historical-structural or Cardosian version of the dependency approach.....results for that approach are confirmatory. Work by Latin Americanists has clear heuristic value in suggesting ways of analysing East Asian outcomes". What Evans meant was that the mechanistic version of the dependency approach may well have been falsified but the more sophisticated Cardosian version was not.

If a refined dependency thinker such as Evans can still find some "heuristic value" for the early dependency analysis of development, the modernization theorist Almond (1987:454) characterized the whole dependency movement as a "propaganda fragment of an ideology, a polemic against mainstream development theory", and some of the dependency literature as "guerrilla-intellectual work" (1987:450). Becker (Almond 1987:467) gave the most succinct criticism of the whole dependency movement in the mid-1980s:

> Deficient in explanatory power and unable to stand up to empirical test, "theory" of dependencia as a systemic outcome of relations with international capitalism is, in reality, an ideology. Dependencista ideology has been useful to political and economic elites striving to free themselves and their nations from subjugation to neocolonialism. That goal has been largely attained. Now the task is to focus on the national basis of elitism and domination, which an ideology that blames all evil in the Third World on the metropoli cannot do. The ideology depreciates the drive to institute local participatory democracy and to extend it beyond formal politics; one searches in vain for a dependencista appreciation that democracy is the only meaningful check on elite power. Accordingly, dependencismo no longer furthers, as it once did, the cause of general human liberation. It is time, therefore, for progressives to lay it to rest.

Consequently, at the end of the 1980s, the dependency school was far less important than in the 1960s (Overholt 1993:226). Despite the severe criticism of the dependency approach, Almond, however, found that the dependency movement could have positive impact on development studies. Two of the significant contributions by dependency thinkers on political development studies are their analytical focus on the international and economic variables. Almond admitted that the early modernization studies tended to be confined to internal national and political arenas. The international and inter-linkages with the economics were very often ignored (Almond 1987:456) in these early studies.

It is interesting to compare the two editions of comparative politics by Almond and Powell (1966, 1978). The second edition "is not a marginally revised edition. It has been rewritten from first to last" (Almond and Powell, 1978:V). The book adopts a three-level approach, namely system, process, and policy. Most notably, the authors add a whole chapter on "the political economy of development" which the 1968 edition lacks. Therefore, it would not be wide of the mark to hypothesize that despite his criticism of the dependency school, Almond himself was influenced by their ideas. The reciprocal influence on both schools has made a new approach possible, an approach which Evans & D. Stephen (1988:740) called "the new comparative historical political economy".

Though Almond gave some credit to the positive influences of the dependency school, I would argue that on the whole, he overlooked the essential differences between dependency theory and modernization theory. Firstly, the dependency approach originated from Marxism and Leninism, while modernization theory is from the nineteenth century mainstream sociological theories. Secondly, dependency theory looks at society as an entity full of conflicts, while modernization theory takes society as an entity in functional equilibrium. Thirdly, dependency theory, following the Marxist tradition, places primacy on infrastructure, i.e. structure and relations of production, while modernization theory sees society constituted by separate yet interdependent variables. Fourthly, dependency theory is economic-deterministic, while modernization theory takes economics, politics, culture, religion, etc. as equally important elements. Modernization theory and dependency theory are, in fact, two theoretical paradigms, in Kuhnian sense, in development studies.

The Revival of Modernization Theory

The decline of the dependency theory was not only made possible by the diminishing radicalization of the academic community, but politically further aggravated by the Gorbachevian and Dengist reforms in the former Soviet Union and post-Mao China. In both countries, orthodox socialist ideology was subjected to reinterpretation and the Stalinist notion of collectivist command economy was totally rejected. The reforms in both countries have proved that the dependency advocation of a so-called "independent development" — development insulated from the world capitalist economy — is illusory. By the end of the 1980s, the perception of the role of multinationals and direct foreign investments by the state socialist states and Third World countries had gone through a dramatic reversal. In contrast to the revolutionary 1960s, the links with the advanced industrialized nations were not seen as sources of backwardness but   important channels that could promote economic development for the country. Foreign investments were now eagerly sought throughout the state socialist countries, including China, Cuba, and Vietnam. By the end of 1990s, with the crumble of the Soviet Union and China's accession to the WTO, capitalism had won the battle over socialism. Fukayama even pronounced it as "the end of history". Entering the twenty-first century, the trend of globalization seems unstoppable (David Held, et als, 1999).

In the absence of a satisfactory explanatory developmental paradigm and disastrous socialist practice in   Eastern Europe and Maoist China, modernization theory re-emerged as the only viable explanatory framework. Undoubtedly, early modernization theory has the defect of a mechanistic view of dualistic traditional and modern societies. But the most significant stimulus to modernization studies is the rise of the East Asian NICS. Hong Kong, Singapore, South Korea, and Taiwan have come to be known as the "Four Little Dragons" in the Asia Pacific region. Their economic growth in the past three decades before the Asian financial meltdown in 1997 has been astonishing, surpassing the economic performance of the major industrialized powers (Berger and Hsiao 1988:27-43; Wade 1990:34-51).

Modernization theory comes to be viewed as a legitimate theory to account for the development of the East Asian NICs. In addition, along with economic development, social structure of the East Asian NICs began to resemble that of the industrialized nations. Differentiation of occupational structure has occurred, consequently increasing social mobility. Literacy has spread and mass educational standards have been raised. Most important of all, more political participatory mechanisms have been established and have allowed people to be involved in governmental decision-making processes. So, after all, the fundamental assumptions of modernizationist unidirectional and linear development might be correct. Methodologically, the modernizationists have become more sophisticated. Not only unidirectional and linear developments are not taken as apriori assumptions, they are seen as the guiding themes in the research agenda, to be verified in the concrete studies of each case. Two of the well known examples are provided by Wong Siu-lun (1988) on the "entrepreneurial familism" of Hong Kong enterprises and Davis's (1987) study on the relationship between religion and development in general and the role of religion in Japanese modernization in particular.

Wong's starting point is that Chinese traditional values (mainly Confucian values) and kinship are not incompatible with economic development, i.e. modernization. They might even facilitate development. He traced the influence of the traditional family on the internal organization of the Chinese enterprises in Hong Kong. He argued that traditional family structure, in fact, has a positive impact on development. On the paternalistic management in the enterprises, he found that the patron-client relationship between employers and employees helps to retain the workers in the highly fluctuating production industries, and also to retard the growth of class consciousness among workers, which contributes to social stability. The practice of nepotism is also functional in that, in the small firms, family members provide a reliable and cheap labour force which tends to enhance the competitiveness of the firms during economic recession.

Lastly, Wong estimated that in 1978, about 60 percent of small industries in Hong Kong were family-owned. He (1988:142) pointed out that the corporate kinship structure is conducive to the management of economic resources which again enhances the competitive strength of the Chinese family firms. Instead of counterposing traditional and modern values, Wong's studies show that traditionalism could serve as a positive element in modernization. Wong discarded the early modernizationists' notion that traditional and modern societies are incompatible.

Weber's book *Protestant Ethic and the Rise of Capitalism* (1985) has become one of the important sources of intellectual heritage of modernization theory. It has formed a book of reference in the developmental studies, especially on East Asian NICs.[8] According to Davis (1987:222-223), Weber's treatment of the "rise of capitalism" could be characterized as a theory of hurdles, which sees development as though it were an obstacle race between traditional and modern societies. In this race, the fastest runners, i.e. developed countries which succeed in surmounting the hurdles, are rewarded with modern civilization. Weberian theory requires that traditional societies must overcome several hurdles before they become modern countries. The obstacles or hurdles include: the institution of legal framework, the replacement of patrimony, the emergence of a free labour market, the rejection of magic, the establishment of a rational administration organization and most important of all, the existence of a spiritual ethos of achievement.

Weber's view, in fact, Davis criticises, represented the vantage point of the aggressors and the developed nations. His theory of barricades views development and religion from the standpoint of traditional societies: how they set up barricades to protect themselves from the disruptive advancement of the capitalist values and institutions. What traditional societies most fear is not progress or development but social disintegration and moral degradation caused by the acculturation of Western penetration. Davis (1987:230-231) postulated that traditional societies were constituted by three concentric rings: an inner one representing economy and its values (such as achievement and universalism); an outer one representing society, its existing status, and power relations; and finally, the middle ring standing for "immunological barrier" that traditional societies erect to block expanding economy, or rather to resist anarchy created by an unrestricted market. From this point of view, economic development takes place not just when a developer or modernizer invades traditional society, but when the barriers of the traditional society themselves fail to fend off the attacks. The porousness of the religious barricades has allowed the economy and its values to expand and penetrate the domain of society itself, i.e. the inner ring expanding into the outer ring with the middle ring contracting.

Davis's theory of barricades helps to correct what would be a one-sided interpretation of the role of religion in the development of European capitalism. In his view, economic development occurred not only because "hot Protestants" filled the markets with the "zeal of God", as Weberians argued, but because Christians failed to resist market infiltration. Equipped with this theory and applying it to studies on the relationship between religions (Confucianism, Taoism, Buddhism, Shintoism, and popular myths) and economic development in Japan, Davis examined the negative enablements (failure to obstruct change) and positive enablements (promotion of change) of religions. He (1987:268-269) came up with the following conclusion,

> While not denying the possibility that religion may sometimes have a positive, stimulating effect on social change and economic development, I have emphasized the importance of its functional role, and the ways in which that role itself has changed in order to accommodate development....I would suggest that more attention be paid to the religious attitudes which appear while development is taking place".

In this aspect, Davis has offered new light on modernization studies.

The early modernization theorists were criticised as being ahistorical and intellectually naive by positing a simple mutually exclusive dichotomy of tradition. The refined modernization theorists such as Davis and Wong have instead concentrated on concrete studies, examining the relationships among traditional values, social structure, economic development, and religions. Their studies have successfully brought "history back in" and "tradition back in" (So 1990:86). The new modernization studies have avoided using simplistic statements or presenting single-variable analyses. Instead, they now pay attention to multi-variable analyses and are alert to multilinear paths of development, and the interaction between internal and external factors. Most important of all, now the notion of historical inevitability towards progress inherent in early modernization theory begins to fade. Historical development is taken as the result of a combination of both internal and external factors.[9]

The "Crisis and Sequence" Approach and Its Application

In the light of these new studies and methodologies, the modernization approach has gained a new intellectual vigour. Bearing this in mind, it is therefore extremely useful to apply some of the methods, theories or concepts in this approach developed in the 1960s and 1970s to the study of contemporary developing countries. The "crisis and sequence" approach is one of the most influential approaches expounded in that period. In this book, I shall use this theoretical framework in the study of the political reform in China during the 1980s and 1990s.[10] In line with the functional theory of political development expounded by James Coleman, the "crisis and sequence" theory was initiated by the SSRC of which Coleman was a member in the United States of America in the late 1960s and early 1970s. Having observed a spate of new post-colonial nations gaining independence after the Second World War in the Third World countries, the SSRC decided to embark on a project of conferences and publications, intending to bring together all existing knowledge and expertise about development problems and patterns in post-independence countries (Almond 1987).

The SSRC also aimed to test a theory of political development -- the "crisis and sequence" theory. In their book (Binder et al. 1971), Binder, Coleman, LaPalombara, Pye, Verba, and Weiner proposed that patterns of political development could be explained by the ways in which nations and societies encounter and solve a common set of state-nation-building crises or problems. The form that these problems take, and the sequence in which these "crises" occur, would constrain or determine the structural development of the political system. Five crises or problem-areas are identified by the SSRC. They are: national identity, legitimacy, participation, penetration, and distribution.[11] The list is by no means exhaustive but they constitute genuine problems that developing countries encounter in the modernization process, in which the ideas of capacity, differentiation, and equality are central in the meaning of modernity (Binder 1971:21-22).

The five crises or problem-areas are all, in fact, related to the government decision-making power. They can be redefined as follows: a) the identity crisis refers to the definition of the set of individuals within the decision-making scope of the government; b) the legitimacy problem refers to the basis on which and the degree to which the decisions of the government are accepted by the citizens of a society because of the belief as to the "rightness" of the ways in which governmental decisions are made; c) the participation crisis is the crisis of who takes part and who has some influence over the making of government decisions; d) the penetration crisis is the crisis of how much effective control the central government has; e) the distribution crisis refers to the decisions of the government over the allocation of resources. The five crises or problem-areas could be conceived of as having a close relationship to the process by which government makes and enforces decisions (Verba 1971:299).

Presumably, the new independent country may encounter the crises in "sequence". For a newborn nation, the most urgent task is to implant a sense of nationhood on the members of the political community. Next comes the establishment of the legitimacy of the state apparatus. Subsequently, the state can exercise various forms of governmental capacities.[12] The resolution of the participation crisis is essential, for it gives citizens formal channels to be involved in the important government decisions, thus enhancing the legitimacy of the government. The performance in the penetration crisis consolidates the political basis of the new state. Lastly, the survival of the new regime relies almost entirely on the resolution of the distribution crisis, i.e. providing a decent living standard for all members of society.

However, in using the approach in the study of developing countries, one must be aware of its limitations. Basically, the approach is a theoretical approach that focuses on macro historical and societal change. The time period under study may range from a few decades to several hundred years (Grew 1978). My book on the political structural reform of China covers two decades from 1978 to the end of the 1990s, a relatively short time span. The PRC regime is relatively new, but China as a social-political-cultural entity has a long history. It goes without saying that, in the course of state-building process, the PRC has met profound legitimacy, participation, penetration, and distribution crises. Moreover, it should be pointed out that the notions of participation, penetration and distribution are too general. In applying these concepts to specific and concrete analysis, a more precise delineation is required.

Besides, the term "sequence" would also easily give rise to ambiguities. The merit of using "sequential model" of development lies in the fact that it "can give order to historical understanding of change and development by providing a framework within which causal statements can be made about development patterns that extend over a long period of time" (Verba 1971:285). It is characterized by the logical form: B event is preceded by A event; C event is preceded by B event. A, B, and C could become both independent and dependent variables. They need not be deterministic, but they do constitute a causal model in which political development becomes intelligible.

The term "sequence" does not imply that the five crises would appear in sequential order in political development. In fact, this mechanical view of "sequence" has been rejected outright by the SSRC members and other scholars (Binder 1971:64-65; Grew 1978:28; Verba 1971:297). The crises are not mutually exclusive. Therefore, they may exist simultaneously at any point of time. In some cases the crises may recur, and in others the crises may never be resolved. At times, the effort to resolve one crisis breeds another crisis. Indeed, it is the dialectical nature of this approach that brings out the complexity of political development. Discussing the notion of "development syndrome", Coleman (1971:100) captured the insight of this approach by saying:

> From the evolutionary perspective the process of political development is neither linear in pattern nor temporal in sequence; rather, it is the consequence of the evolving dialectic among the three dimensions of the development syndromes. Some long-established contemporary politics may cease to develop and become arrested at a level of differentiation, equality, and capacity which no significant further development can occur, some of the newer politics, on the other hand, possessed of a high evolutionary potential, may make quantum "leapfrogging" advances. What are certain are the main elements in the dialectics; what are not certain are the forms of the outcome.

The dialectical relationship can be seen from the following table:

Table 1.1
The Relationship between the Five Crises or Problem-areas

Performance Area To Government	Facilitative Inputs	Secondary Demands for Performance Triggered
Identity	legitimacy	participation (distribution)
Legitimacy	extraction penetration	
Penetration	legitimacy extraction	distribution (participation?)
Participation	legitimacy	distribution (identity?)
Distribution	legitimacy	participation penetration (identity?)

Source: Verba 1971:311

The table shows the relationships between the five crises or problem-areas in terms of demands triggered and facilitative inputs generated. The relationships show how successful performance in one area would facilitate performance in another. For example, performance by the government to resolve identity crisis would obviously enhance the legitimacy of the regime, but it would simultaneously trigger the demand of the population for participation, which aggravates the participation crisis. Similarly, enhancing penetration would increase the government's capacity to resolve legitimacy and extraction problems, but it would trigger demand for distribution or participation. Further resolving the participation crisis would enhance the distributive demand. Finally, resolving distribution crisis would facilitate solving legitimacy crisis but it would trigger participation and penetration demands. In general, institutionalized performance on the crises at the top of the table facilitates performance on the crises listed below in the table. Identity directly affects legitimacy which in turn affects others below it. Therefore, the creation of institutionalized capacity to generate a sense of national identity facilitates the institutionalization of legitimacy, and legitimacy, in turn, facilitates participation, penetration, and distribution, etc.

Alternatively, from the table it may be argued that the five crises are linked in such a way that in the long run there will be some kind of balanced growth in the institutionalized performance in all five problem-areas. There are two reasons for this holistic balanced growth in resolving the crises. Firstly, if performance in one area lagged behind, another performance area would be adversely affected. For instance, poor performance in legitimacy would affect performance in the other four areas. Secondly, to speak positively, institutional performance in any one area is always facilitated by performance in other areas. The resolution of legitimacy crisis would facilitate performance in other areas. Consequently, unless performance in all areas keeps at the more or less same pace, performance in any particular one area will slow down. For instance, systems may be unable to reach certain levels of distributive performance if legitimacy lags too far behind and successful performance on the distributive area, such as leading to higher physical welfare and education, may generate pressure for performance in other areas, such as participation (Verba 1971:310). Therefore, it can be seen that the five problem-areas or crises are closely related.

Despite its merits, the conceptual framework can serve only as a guiding device and the five crises or problem-areas are only orienting concepts. As Binder (1971:67) summarized succinctly:

> They (the five crises) are not stated as empirical events nor as complex process,....they are the functional requisites, i.e. the historical process by which these ubiquitous modern political phenomena manifest themselves in particular countries, are the phenomena to be described, operationalized, measured, tested for continuity and change, and predicted. When these things have been accomplished in a sufficient number of cases, maybe then we can hazard a general theory of political development. In the meantime, the crucial test will be whether

historians can recognize and agree on the characterization of these processes in the countries they know.

Thus, my study of the political structural reform of contemporary China may constitute one of the cases that may serve to enrich the approach. As China has embarked on a process towards modernity, leaving behind an autarkic Maoist regime, the adoption of this theoretical approach seems to be most appropriate. Specific hypotheses deriving from this general framework will be formulated in the last section of this chapter. An analysis on the traditionalist nature of the CCP regime in the Maoist epoch has been attempted to serve as a background for the understanding of China's political modernization after the death of Mao.

China as a Neo-Traditional Polity

China is a developing country, as the Chinese government always claims it to be.[13] It has more than two thousand years of centralized imperial rule, with the largest bureaucratic organization in the world. Since the unification by the First Emperor Qin Shi Huangdi in 221 B.C., China had been ruled by imperial despotism until 1911. With the overthrow of the Qing dynasty, republicanism was established by Dr. Sun Yat-sen. Chiang Kai-shek unified the country in 1927 and ruled it until 1949. Mao Zedong became one of the founders of the CCP and PLA and founded the PRC in 1949, along with other veteran revolutionaries.

From 1949 to 1976, adopting the Marxist-Leninist-Stalinist communist ideologies, Mao tried to materialize the utopian socialist paradise in China, plunging millions of Chinese into brutal class struggles and launching endless political campaigns, most notably the Great Leap Forward (GLF) and the Cultural Revolution (CR). With the concentration of political power and Party control of mass media, the CCP tried to shape a generation of socialist "new man". Paradoxically, the revival of imperial behavioural practices during the Cultural Revolution demonstrated that the "feudal" past was deeply embedded in China's contemporary political culture. Extreme fanaticism in the cult of Mao, the so-called "loyalty dance", the ten-thousand-year long live slogans, and complete subordination of a nation of 800 million to one dictator remind people that, despite several decades of tumultuous social and political change, China still has not shaken off its imperial past.

The elements of "feudal" past have been noted and analysed by both Western and Chinese academics (Chiou 1995; Friedman, Pickowicz, and Selden 1991; Jin Guantao and Liu Qingfeng 1990; Li Zehou 1987;

Lieberthal 1995; McCormick 1990;   Sun Longji 1990; Tao Hai, Zheng Yide, and Dai Qing 1989; Teiwes 1984; Tsou Tang 1986; Walder 1986; Yan Jiaqi 1990). Many of them in fact argued that the Communist revolution has reinforced the "feudal" elements in spite of the CCP's claims to eradicate China's feudalism. Socially, the CR strengthened the traditional Chinese practices of *guanxi* (network of relations). Economic disarray and social chaos caused by the CR forced the ordinary Chinese to revert more than ever to *guanxi* practices. Most important of all, Mao and Deng reigned like imperial emperors (Li Zhisui 1994; Ruan Ming 1994; Salisbury 1992).

Undeniably, the PRC has undergone tremendous social, political, cultural, and ideological transformation since 1949. The CCP has been ruling the country ever since through its expanding cadre system and a huge PLA. The economic system has changed from the command system to a mixed system in the last 18 years. Entering the 1990s, the CCP declared the establishment of a socialist market system (CCCCP 1993). However, patrimonism, nepotism, and the patron-client relationships in the Party/state bureaucracy persist. With its residual "feudal" influences on the political culture of contemporary China, the enmeshing of traditional and modern elements can hardly be denied. Therefore, it could well be called a neo-traditional society.[14]

Pushing for faster economic development and improving the living standard of the people were the original main goals of the CCP communist revolution. But very soon the goals were sidestepped by Mao and his radical associates. It was not until the mid-1970s Zhou Enlai raised the slogan of "four modernizations" in the Fifth NPC in 1975. While the modernization of agriculture, industry, national defence, and science and technology were seen as necessary to propel China into a modern nation, China saw itself as having a political system more advanced than democratic capitalism. Subsequently, there was no need for political modernization.

However, amidst the struggles between the two political lines, the slogan was left unused and it was heavily criticised by the "Gang of Four". It was not until the death of Mao and the rehabilitation of Deng Xiaoping in 1977 that the slogan began to resurface. The Third Plenum of the Eleventh CC in December 1978 marked a turning point in the history of the PRC. Four modernizations were given the most prominent position in the party documents (Liao Gailong 1991:338-339). After more than twenty years of political turmoil and economic stagnation, the CCP was finally prepared to commit to the betterment of people's standard of living.

Deng Xiaoping launched reform and open-door policy in the same Plenum (Liao Gailong 1991:339-340). The Dengist reform since 1978 has been characterized as the second revolution (Harding 1987; Deng Xiaoping 1993:81-82). Since then, sweeping changes have been introduced. Four modernizations are still the goals of the reform. Political modernization was not mentioned officially due to ideological constraint, but political reform was introduced as an essential component of the reform programme. I would argue that political reform is, in fact, political modernization (Li Shengping 1989:53; Womack 1984; Yan Jiaqi 1990). For the first time since 1949, the CCP top leadership admitted that its political system was backward and at times even "feudal" (Deng Xiaoping 1983:294-296; Hu Yaobang 1982; Zhao Ziyang 1987b). The application of the "crisis and sequence" approach is, therefore, most relevant in this context, though one must be aware of its limitations. China's political institutions need to be modernized and this has become a consensus among the most prominent intellectuals, such as Fang Lizhi, Li Honglin, Su Shaozhi, Yan Jiaqi, Yu Haocheng, Bao Zunxin, Liu Binyan, Wang Ruoshui, Wang Ruowang. As Binder (1971:53) defined the concept of political modernization:

> The political path to modernity involves critical changes of identity from the religious to the ethnic and from the parochial to the societal. It involves critical changes in legitimacy from transcendental to immanent sources. It involves critical changes in political participation from elite to masses and from family to group. It involves critical changes of distribution from status and privileges to ability, achievement, and the control and management of capital. And it involves critical changes in the degree of administration and legal penetration into social structure and out to the remote regions of the country.

The strategic change in development strategy in 1978 brought tumultuous repercussions to China's socio-political structure. China re-entered the world community after thirty years of autarky under Mao. The Dengist reform made modernization possible. It is the aim of this book to explore the complexities of these changes, especially in the political arena, by using the "crisis and sequence" approach.

The Formulation of Guiding Hypotheses

As has been discussed in the previous sections, the five crises or problem areas serve only as orienting concepts and remain at the level of abstraction. Specific hypotheses must be derived from the general theory and put to empirical observation. In this study, the hypotheses will be applied to the Chinese context. Before proceeding to formulate the specific hypotheses pertinent to China's political structural reform, it will be methodologically appropriate to provide an overall picture of the reform in the 1980s.

China's initial reform policies began in the agricultural sector. The communique of the Third Plenum of the Eleventh CC affirmed that "the private plots of the peasantry, family sideline productions, and village fairs are necessary adjuncts of the socialist economy" (ZZWY 1987:8). Then People's communes were dismantled in 1980 and a responsibility system was introduced, which allowed the peasants to use the land for a certain period of time. Notwithstanding the government taxes, they could keep the surplus (ZZWY 1987:272-274), but private selling of the land was still prohibited. The reform in agriculture instantly boosted the productivity and morale of the farmers. The successful implementation of the agricultural reform laid the foundation for further reform in the urban area, which involved intertwining sectors, such as pricing, enterprise management, taxation, labour, finance, and foreign trade. In 1984, the CCP introduced reform to the industrial sectors with the aim of setting up a "planned commodity economy based on public ownership" (CCCCP 1984:13). In 1992, the CCP pledged to establish a socialist market system regardless of the type of ownership involved in the Fourteenth CCP Congress. After eighteen years of reform, the economic system has gone through tremendous structural change.

Five Special Economic Zones (SEZs) were set up and an intimate relationship with the world capitalist economy was forged. Foreign trade increased enormously and China became an integral part of world economy. Hundreds of cities have opened up and foreign direct investment has been eagerly sought. Numerous private enterprises have sprung up. Joint ventures with foreign companies are common. After the 4 June massacre in 1989, individual enterprises were again suppressed. However, during his "southern tour" in early 1992, Deng (1993:375) called for a faster development strategy and urged the current leadership headed by Jiang Zemin to seize opportunities to develop. Individual enterprises bounced back. Marketization of China's economy seems to have quickened again with its goal of establishing a socialist market system.

By the 1990s, the structural components of China's economy had gone through substantial changes. The scope and extent of control over the economy by the central authorities had greatly shrunk, except in some key heavy and defence industries. Public ownership and state sector in the national economy had declined. Various types of joint ventures or even wholly-owned foreign enterprises flourished. The range of goods available for free markets expanded greatly. The overall economic structure did not change very much in terms of quantitative shares of industrial and agricultural output in GNP, but the ratio of distribution of labour force shifted as people moved into labour-intensive and service industries in both urban and rural areas.

The significant changes in the economy also brought about tremendous social changes. The ideological control exerted by the CCP relaxed. Freedom to move became possible as the household registration system was gradually eliminated. Open criticism of the CCP's major foreign and domestic policies is still not possible, but there have been genuine debates in the press on the direction of economic reform. Moreover, people have freedom to keep silent. Mass media are basically still controlled by the Party/state. "Public sphere" does not exist. Dissidents have been ceaselessly harassed, but non-political groups have flourished, particularly business organizations.

It is worthwhile to examine the interrelationships between marketization of the economy (distribution problem-area), liberalization of social life (penetration problem-area), and democratization of the political system (participation problem-area), using China as a case study. The relationships between marketization, liberalization, and democratization, can, in fact, be reformulated by using the terminology of the "crisis and sequence" approach. Distribution means the management of economic resources with a goal to achieving better living standard in a particular country. It involves more rational allocation of resources and increased production. In Chinese context, the economic reform initiated by Deng Xiaoping was to overhaul the Stalinist command system which had become a fetter to increased productivity. Democracy means the institutional involvement of the largest possible section of population in the national governmental decision-making processes. The post-Mao political reform was, though limited, a process of political democratization. Penetration means that the public conform the government policies voluntarily. In Post-Mao era, a process of social liberalization occurred. There had been an outpouring of mass enthusiasm on the reform programmes in the late 1970s and early 1980s. The CCP Party/state exhibited unprecedented penetrative ability over the population.

With reference to table 1.1, the five crises or problem-areas could be hypothesized in the following way:

First,
performance in *Identity* would trigger demand in *Participation.*

Second,
performance in *Penetration* would trigger demand in *Distribution.*

Third,
performance in *Participation* would trigger demand in *Distribution.*

Fourth,
performance in *Distribution* would trigger demand in *Participation.*

Fifth,
performance in *Legitimacy* would aid the performance in all problem-areas and vice versa.

   This book also aims to examine the interrelationships of marketization, liberalization, and democratization, with particular emphasis on the exploration of the hypotheses outlined above. However, among the five crises or problem-areas, the *second, third,* and *fourth* hypotheses would be more important in the Chinese socio-political context. The fifth hypothesis is almost a truism, as no government can rule in the long run without a sufficient degree of legitimacy. The ruling elite cannot possibly rely on physical coercion alone. Legitimacy always enhances the government's decision-making power to resolve other crises (Pye 1971b:137).
   The first hypothesis involves the problem of identity, which is complex. From Pye's discourse (1971a:110-111) on identity crisis, two types of identity can be classified. The first one is the national identity crisis in which the populace fail to identify itself with national community or ethnic race. The second type is the political identity in which the political system or government is the object of identification. In contemporary China, political identity crisis occurs from time to time, such as in the aftermath of the 4 June massacre (Goldman, Link, and Su Wei 1993), but the national identity crisis seldom manifests itself. Pye's standpoint on identity crisis is ambiguous, but in view of the "crisis and sequence" approach used by the SSRC, there is no doubt that it is the national identity crisis in its mind. Friedman (1995:25-43) argued very strongly for the emergence of a new nationalism in southern China and in the minorities autonomous regions, due to separate development in the south and north. I would argue that Friedman has, in fact, confused

national identity problem with the political identity problem. Notwithstanding the fashion trends, social tastes, and even levels of living standard, it is questionable that the southern provinces and the minorities would seek national independence.[15] Indeed, by the mid-1990s, *difang zhuyi* (regionalism) had increasingly become a political force to be reckoned with (Chang Hsia 1992; Willy Lam 1999: 219-228). However, the central government still holds the trump cards in the political manoeuvre between the provinces and the centre. The centrifugal forces of the peripherals have been exaggerated. Therefore, throughout the thesis, I shall not take the national identity crisis as a unit for analysis. Having set a theoretical framework. I shall proceed to the analysis of the political structural reform in China in the 1980s and 1990s.

Notes

[1]Modernization theory is a broad term embracing social, economic, and political development. The "crisis and sequence" approach is a specific framework that is used in analysing political development of a particular country (So 1990:18-32).
[2] It is impossible to come to grips with all the studies on China's political development. The works listed here is based on my personal reading. Halpern (1993:124-128) has argued that a predominant paradigm on the studies of Chinese politics is emerging. The focus of the paradigm is on the institutions or structure which shape the interest, intention, and resources of the political actors. The theoretical fruitfulness has yet to be demonstrated and even if it was, it was an approach of study on Chinese politics in general, not solely on the political reform.
[3]More details of the debate, see chapter 4.
[4]The discussion of modernization theory and dependency theory is mainly based on Palma (1978), Almond (1987), Evans and Sephens (1988), and So (1990). So's book is a succinct study of the three major development frameworks, namely modernization, dependency, and world system.
[5]It is interesting to note that, in developing the "crisis and sequence" model, the Committee on Comparative Politics of the Social Research Council (SSRC), in which Coleman was a member, deleted the crisis of integration. Presumably, the integration crisis could be incorporated into the penetration crisis. (Binder et al. 1971; Grew 1978).
[6]According to the SSRC, the term "distribution" does not only mean the conventional distribution of goods and services. It has a broader connotation that is equivalent to economic management of a country.
[7]Under increasing pressure from the PRC, the United Nations changed the name of NICs to NIEs (Newly Industrialized Economies) in July 1988. China's

displeasure over the label is understandable, since it still claims sovereignty over Taiwan and Hong Kong. Here and throughout the thesis, I shall use the more familiar term "NICs". A good introduction to the achievement of the East Asian NICs and analytical studies behind their success story can be found in Berger and Hsiao (1988), Deyo (1987), and Wade (1990).

[8]In his book, Weber (1985:170-2)argued that the Protestant ethic -- Lutheran branch—has given to the "Rise of Capitalism", because they have "spiritual affinity". In his studies of Chinese religion (including Confucianism), Weber categorically denied that Confucianism has any positive elements to the economic development of China. However, since the rise of the East Asian NICs, there have been pundits calling for the re-evaluation of the role of Confucianism in economic development (King 1992:128-167). They argued that the East Asian NICs are all situated within the Confucian-influenced zones, their economic development could be attributed to Confucianism. I could not deal with this topic in detail here due to lack of space, but I would like to make two points. Firstly, the meaning of Confucianism has never been clarified. In Chinese history, there have been many versions of Confucianism. Furthermore, to Western and Chinese scholars, Confucianism seems to have different meanings. Secondly, entering the 1990s, the fifth and sixth dragons have been emerging (Taber 1992). Malaysia, Indonesia (both are predominately Muslims), Thailand (a Buddhist country), and the Philippines (a Catholic country) are all catching up very fast with the East Asian NICs. Therefore, the impetus to economic development must be sought elsewhere. China's economic growth has been phenomenal in the past fifteen years. How could one explain the fact that rapid economic growth occurs in a country which claims to have eradicated the influence of Confucianism?

[9]Personally, I do not agree with Wong's thesis, despite his sophisticated arguments. The goal of Wong's study is to correct the naivety of early modernizationists that tradition and modernity are incompatible. While this point is well taken, it remains arguable that Confucianism could act as a positive enablement to economic development. In fact, Wong's discussion of Confucian values is selective. The traditional closed-knit family structure may have acted as a positive element to economic development. There are core Confucian values which are definitely detrimental to economic growth, such as the lack of entrepreneurial spirit, looking down on commercial activities, and disdain of manual labour. On Davis' study on the relationship between religion and economic development, it seems to me that his theory of hurdles is not necessarily incompatible with the Weberian thesis. Weber emphasized that the existence of a body of value, i.e. Protestant Ethic, is the prerequisite of the rise of capitalism. What he stressed is the necessary condition of economic development. There are other conditions, such as the existence of contract law, the development of a market, the separation of business from households, the development of rational book-keeping, the existence of wage-labourers, and the development of Western cities (Weber 1985:7-8).

[10]About the application of this theory to the study of contemporary political development, see also Ng Yu-shan (1993).

[11]Three meanings of crisis could be denoted as: 1) the existence of a political problem, whether or not perceived by the governing elites; 2) a problem so great as to constitute a threat to the survival of the state or party, unless it is solved by institutional rejuvenation; 3) a turning point in the history of the political system (Grew 1978:44). The meaning of (1) seems too general. It would be difficult to imagine a system without political problems. (3) is, in fact, the consequence of (2). Therefore, (2) is the meaning I am using in this thesis. (2) implies (1).

[12]A political system has four kinds of capacities, namely extractive, distributive, regulative, and symbolic capacities (Almond and Powell 1978:289-321).

[13]In terms of per capita income, according to the popular perception, China is one of the poorest countries in the world, with an average income of about US$380 in 1993 (*Time* May 1993:33). However the International Monetary Fund has estimated that, using a new purchasing power method, China had become the world's third largest economy by the early 1990s in terms of GNP and in fact, China's per capita income was US$1,450 in 1991 (Overholt 1993:20). Western countries had previously underestimated the economic strength of the PRC.

[14]The concept of "neo-traditionalism" was first developed by Jowittt (1978, 1983) in his study of the former Soviet Union. It was used and expanded by Walder (1986) on the study of China's industrial authority on the pre-reform period. Tsou Tang has termed the Maoist regime as "feudal totalitarianism" (1986:144). He used the term neo-traditionism in the analysis of Chinese politics as early as 1968 (1986:11), but he lacked elaboration. Lipton has described the communists as "tilial communists" (Robert Litfton 1961:386). Li Honglin, former vice-president of Fu Kien Academy of Social Sciences, has pointed out that the present CCP regime is the combination of a revolutionary tradition and feudal peasantry tradition. (Tau Hai, Thy Yide and Dailly, 1989:124-125).

[15]To the CCP leadership, perhaps there are national identity crises in Tibet and Taiwan. Independence is one of the stated goals in the party platform of the ruling Democratic Progressive Party in Taiwan. In 1999, the former president Lee Teng-hui announced the two state theory in the cross strait relationships. In 2002, the incumbent president Chen Shui-bien proposed the "one side, one country" theory. Tibetans' continuous struggle for genuine autonomy has been crushed by the PRC government.

CHAPTER TWO

THE MAOIST LEGACY – ORIGINS OF THE POLITICAL STRUCTURAL REFORM

This chapter deals with the issues of the origins of political structural reform initiated by the post-Mao leaders in the late 1970s. First, a discussion on the paradigmatic shift of Western scholarship on the studies of contemporary China is provided. The discussion attempts to illustrate that an analysis of China's political structural reform is meaningful only in the light of modernization theories which include the component of political modernization. Under the previous paradigms, the issue of political structural reform did not even exist. Then followed by an examination of the rationale and justifications behind Deng Xiaoping's modernization program. I shall also discuss the legacy of Maoist rule at the dawn of the reformist era. A review of PRC history will be conducted in light of the modernization concepts of participation, distribution, penetration, and legitimacy crises.

Mao had ruled the PRC for twenty-seven years when he died in September 1976. He had been the most dominant leader of the CCP for forty-one years after he was elected the chairman of the Military Affairs Commission at the Zunyi Conference in 1935. Beginning in 1949, he had controlled the Party as well as the military machine. From 1959 to 1969, Mao conceded unwillingly his state post to Liu Shaoqi. To eliminate his political opposition, Mao engineered the Cultural Revolution (CR) in 1966 and Liu was banished from his zenith of power. The post was practically abolished and was formally scrapped in 1969. The post was not revived until 1983 when Li Xiannian was elected the president in the Sixth NPC. Mao nearly dominated the CCP Party/state political process.[1] It is worthwhile, therefore, to review the nature of the CCP governance before proceeding to the discussion of the political structural reform. Maoist China serves as the background or stage on which the Dengist reform program could be comprehended.

I would argue that, in the light of modernization theory, what the PRC inherited from Maoist rule is that the CCP encountered four crises at the time of Mao's death, namely legitimacy, participation, penetration, and distribution, except perhaps the national identity crisis. Many developing countries had been ruled by tribal groups before European colonization and it is difficult to implant a sense of national identity even after years of colonial rule. However, China has been a cultural entity for almost three thousand years and it has never been totally conquered and occupied by any single foreign power, notwithstanding the Western enclaves in the major Chinese cities such as Shanghai and Tianjin, enjoying extra-territoriality. The sense of ethnic "Chineseness" is deeply rooted in the consciousness of every Chinese. Nowadays, Chinese identity, in most parts of China, has never been challenged. Nationalism or patriotism is still a powerful cohesive force (CCCCP 1994).[2] It is skillfully manipulated by the CCP to preserve its ruling status (Willy Lam 1999: 270-276).

Participation, Distribution, Penetration and Legitimacy

Political participation means the involvement of the ordinary people in the major governmental decision-making process.[3] Since 1949, China has been ruled by the CCP which is an ideologically- motivated and revolutionary vanguard party. The CCP is organized upon the model of Lenin's Bolshevik Party with the principle of "democratic centralism" which should presumably combine democratic consultation with centralized decision-making power. But the principle was perverted from the very beginning when the Soviet Union was established by Lenin. Lenin's dictatorship inevitably led to the totalitarian dictatorship of Stalin.[4] Political power is monopolized by the CCP. Major policies have been made from the top. In the early1950s, Mao was the first among equals. Basically, collective leadership was the norm. As years went by, Mao became more despotic. In the period of the CR, "the 'dictator' was substituted for the Central Committee." The Party organizational structure was practically disbanded and Mao's utterings and mutterings (his little red book) replaced laws and Party rules and were hailed across the whole of China. To be sure, the CCP policies required mass followers. Instead of voluntary political participation, the masses were mobilized to support the Party/state policies. From time to time, there were crises of participation in the history of the PRC, but in the last years of Mao's rule, it worsened.

Distribution crisis occurred mainly because, particularly in the aftermath of the CR, China's industrial sectors were in chaos and the economy as a whole was stagnant. The standard of living remained unchanged for two decades. The distribution problem has two dimensions: first, finding the ways and means of producing more material goods, and secondly, regardless of the quantities of material goods produced, changing the bases on which material goods were distributed among the members of society (LaPalombara 1971b:236). The first problem was the growth problem and the second one the problem of equality. The first problem was much more serious that the first one. Apparently, at the end of Mao's reign, China's economic development had reached a crisis point within the command economy. Evidently, economic reform engineered by Deng at the late 1970s involved both dimensions.

The penetration problem also has two dimensions: geographic and social-psychological. The first aspect refers to the effective control or jurisdiction of the central government concerning a piece of territory over which it claims to have sovereignty. The second is concerned with the public's conformance to the policies of the central government. It can either mean that the government imposes what it wants regardless of the views and attitudes of the population or the extent to which the population accurately receives the information about the policies and wishes to conform to these policies voluntarily (LaPalombrara 1971a: 207-209). The first one refers to the actual control exercised over the particular territory by the government, while the second is closely related to the problem of legitimacy.

Since the founding of the PRC, the CCP has been in effective control over the country except in the era of CR when most of the country was in chaos. Therefore it could hardly be said that there was a crisis on the first dimension. At the end of the 1970s, despite the disputes over the controversial claims over territories along the Sino-Russian border and South Pacific islands and even a border war with India in 1962, the CCP, backed up by the powerful PLA, basically exercised effective control over Chinese territories. The crisis occurred in the second dimension and it is intimately related to the legitimacy crisis. The first Tiananmen incident in 1976 clearly show that Mao's 'mandate of heaven" was at his end. At the end of Maoist era, the participation, distribution and penetration crises were so serious that the CCP encountered one of the most profound legitimacy crises since the establishment of the PRC (Pye 1971b:136). Unmistakably, the legitimacy crisis was the end product of the failure to resolve the above crises.

The Paradigmatic Shifts

The Western paradigmatic perception of the Maoist regime can be classified into three phases. The first period was in the 1950s. Engaging in the cold war confrontation with the former USSR, the United States primarily perceived communist China as a satellite state of the Soviet Union. The predominant paradigm in the studies of the Soviet Union was the model of "totalitarianism", which was employed to interpret Soviet politics in the 1950s (Bunce and John Echols III 1986). Since China was also a communist country, thus, by implication, China was a totalitarian country too. The characteristics outlined by Sovietologists were applicable to China as well,

> (Totalitarianism) may be defined as a commitment to the total mobilization of a society's resources to accomplish the goals and programs decided by the totalitarian leadership or by the dictator himself. In essence, some would define it as a new form of "oriental" despotism with a control over human beings, material resources, and commitments greater than ever achieved before.....It destroys and creates social classes; it arrests, jails, tortures, shoots, expels, exiles, or declares "unpersons" those it suspects of disloyalty; it controls what is said over the radio, printed in the press, seen on television, expressed in the classroom, depicted in the novels, painted on canvas. It and it alone determines what the correct party line is and decides who (or what nation) is anti-party or unMarxist. Absolute power and control over the population is its first concern...."(Field 1967:197-198).

As development strategy, the ruling Communist Party of the Soviet Union (CPSU) performed two major roles: first, setting national goals and monitoring the implementation of these goals; secondly, mobilizing the Soviet society in achieving these goals. The official guiding thought was Marxism-Leninism which constituted the overt political culture of the nation. The education system was state-controlled. The writers and artists were government employees. Their function was to publicize government policies. The people received a comprehensive set of beliefs and values regarding political process through centrally-controlled mass media.

In a similar vein, the political institutions and processes delineated by students of Chinese politics in China were analogous, albeit the term "totalitarianism" was rarely used. Exploring China's social control mechanism in the 1950s, Vogel (1967) asked one delicate question: "How can the CCP regime minimize discontent while making the people do what they don't like to do?" The Chinese authorities did not use direct coercion, and the methods of control were more subtle and effective than direct compulsion. Vogel described a mechanism of an interactive process that finally ended in the submission of individuals to the Party/state. Firstly, the government tried to persuade those citizens who were reluctant to volunteer. The citizens were first presented with rational arguments, If that approach was inefficient, the government would resort to patriotism, stressing why the regime needed volunteers. The use of penalty was not mentioned but that the regime intended to penalize those non-volunteers who did not respond to the calls of the government was known to everyone. The people would face criticism from peers in the discussion meetings and the cadres would come to their home and tried to "understand" what they were thinking. Furthermore, the people's records were kept in a dossier which would follow them wherever they went. Any "unpatriotic" record would be preserved for life and would have great impact for their future working life. Finally, the non-volunteers gradually built up anxiety about what penalties they might face. When the anxiety became too great, they at last gave up and volunteered (Vogel 1967:172).

In a compelling study on "brain washing" in the PRC in the early 1950s, Lifton (1961) detailed the psychological processes and subtle mechanism through which a man's personality was transformed and mind set changed. The psychological transformation consisted of eight stages which constituted what Lifton called "ideological totalism".[5] The key to this "brain-washing" process was control of the environment and human communication with the external world, isolating individuals concerned in entirety, filling them with a sense of guilt, reducing the victims to a hopeless situation. The totalists would then appear as moral superiors and the victims would surrender unconditionally (Lifton 1961:419-437). In these discussions, the term "totalitarianism" was never mentioned but the image they conveyed was crystal clear. "Totalitarianism" implies both psychological and institutional aspects.

Institutionally, the "totalitarianism" thesis postulates that only two classes exist: the ruler and the ruled and the two classes are in constant opposition. It further assumes that the ruling elite is a monolithic whole. It was Krushchev, the Soviet leader from 1954 to 1964, who caused the gradual decline of the "totalitarianism" thesis (Bunce and Echols III 1986:319). As in the evolution of natural science depicted by Thomas Kuhn, when the old paradigm fails to account for the new phenomena, producing anomaly, a new paradigm would emerge (Kuhn 1970). The model was criticized as failing to take into consideration the conflicting political forces within the monolithic leadership in the 1960s. The overt consensus, in fact, covers up the potential conflicts within the ruling elite.

The secret speech denouncing the crimes of Stalin by Krushchev at the Twenty-second CPSU Congress in 1956 marked the turning point of the Sino-Soviet relationship. The ideological war between the two communist giants later escalated into a border war in 1969. In 1957, Mao launched the GLF movement which resulted in millions of deaths. The GLF also marked a radical shift away from the Soviet developmental model that had guided China's national economic reconstruction in the First Five-year Plan (1952-1957). The GLF underlined four themes of Maoist strategy of development which were to dominate Chinese political economy in the following twenty years until the inception of the reformist period. First, the CCP proclaimed China's ability to catch up to the Western industrialized countries in a short time with zealous optimism. Second, mass line and human will were glorified in the production process and national construction. Third, the "politics takes command" thesis asserted that correct political consciousness was more important than other factors of production. Finally, the CCP believed that advances in all fronts, such as economics, politics, culture, and ideology, were possible (Towsend and Womack 1986:119-120).

All these themes would reappear in the era of the CR. A brief retrenchment period (1962-1965) set in and the CCP pragmatic leaders headed by Liu Shaoqi and Deng Xiaoping revised the radical policies of the GLF and implemented the policies of adjustment and restructuring. They succeeded in bringing back the economy from the verge of collapse.

The GLF and onset of the CR signified a new phase of studies on contemporary China, as the CCP turned away from the simulation of the Soviet development model. The characteristics of this stage are that the ways and means by which the monolithic leadership exercise control over the population are ignored, and instead, focus is put on China's socialist development strategy in contradistinction to the Stalinist model in the Soviet Union. Under the influence of the spread of socialist thoughts in the 1960s, radicalization of the Western intellectuals, institutional decay of the USA and widespread opposition to the American involvement in Vietnam, the perception of Maoist China changed. A new "revolutionary state" thesis emerged, which took the CCP propaganda materials at face value. The proponents of this paradigm believed that China had realized a socialist paradise without class struggles. Production is not for profit but for the benefit of whole society (Sweezy 1975). Exploitation had disappeared and absolute equality was achieved. Maoist China was hailed as the only viable developmental model for the Third World countries. A spate of literature praising Mao's role in unifying China and raising people's living standard by socialist ideology was published. Globally, the Dependency theory was the predominant paradigm in the developmental studies, attacking the metropoli-peripheral exploitative trade relationships imposed by the hegemonic powers of the West, hailing the autarkic policies of socialist states. The "new revolutionary state" thesis is obviously a distant cousin of the Dependency school of thought.

In a study of Mao's economic strategies from the GLF to the CR, after dismissing four approaches that were prevalent at the time,[6] Wheelwright and McFarlane (1970:214-215) offered a fifth approach:

> We believe that a genuine attempt is being made in
> China to construct a new morality, a new moral basis

> for living in socialist society, and on a scale
> unprecedented in the whole of human history....CR
> was not the more narrow revolt of the peasantry
> against, but a broader and more general conflict
> between revolutionaries and technocrats over the kind
> of society desirable for China. That is the CR is not
> just a crossroad on China's path to industrialization,
> but a crucial turning point on the Chinese road to
> socialism.

Further, they suggested (1970:221-222) that Mao had enriched traditional socialist thought, for Maoism emphasized not only material production but also the purification of the human soul. Maoism intended to change human nature:

> A fundamental axiom of Maoist thought is that public
> ownership is only a technical condition for solving
> the problems of Chinese society. In a deeper sense,
> the goal of Chinese socialism involves vast changes in
> human nature, in the way people relate to each other,
> to their work, and to society. The struggle to change
> material condition,....requires the struggle to change
> people....Maoism is also a revolt against the
> imperatives of a more technological and industrial
> way of life.

Equally emphasizing the Maoist ideology of changing human nature and creation of a "new socialist man", Gurley (1976:6-7) argued that Maoist China had created an alternative path to economic development, thereby challenging the fundamental axioms of Western economic development theories:

> The Maoists believe that economic development can
> best be promoted by breaking down specialization, by
> dismantling bureaucracies that give rise to experts,
> technicians, authorities, and bureaucrats....The
> proletarian world view....stresses that only through
> struggle can progress be made;.... that active
> participation by the "masses" in decision-making will
> provide them with the knowledge to channel their
> energy most productively; and that the elimination of
> specialization will not only increase workers' and

> peasants' willingness to work hard for the various
> goals of society but will also increase their ability to
> do this by adding to their knowledge and awareness
> of the world around them.

Maoist practice not only revolutionalized traditional development theory, but also posed a threat to the Soviet model of building socialism.[7] Mao was seen as a prophet who saw the evils inherent in Western industrialized societies and had devised an alternative path of development without these evils.

In that phase, Western social scientists no longer talked about the ways that the CCP manipulated people and its means of indoctrination. The "totalitarianism" image gave way to a regime which had been plagued by horrendous developmental problems, yet endeavored to solve them. China was seen as a country unified by Mao who had eliminated poverty, solving the problems of food, clothing, and housing for seven hundred million people. Furthermore, China's practice of socialism was more advanced than that of the Soviet Union. This was indeed a paradigmatic shift.[8]

The death of Mao and the arrest of the "Gang of Four" signaled another landmark on the study of contemporary China. It gave birth to a new interpretative framework that tried to accommodate new sources of data and information withheld during the Maoist era. The primary sources and statistics on Maoist reign released by the CCP leadership after the death of Mao revealed the tremendous human sacrifices in the pre-reform era. The "socialist new man" was a fake. The equality admired by so many was in fact equality of poverty, and yet behind the poverty the governing elite led a luxurious life comparable to the emperors of Chinese feudal dynasties. The paradigm of "revolutionary state" collapsed totally. The shift was made possible foremost by the CCP ruling elite themselves. From the vantage point of 1980s, having studied the three generations of Western scholarship on China, Harding (1984:299) pointed out that

> Western scholars took over the political standpoint of
> the Maoists as well as their data and their models of
> Chinese politics. That is, much second-generation
> scholarship on China was characterized by an
> idealism about the CR that occasionally verged on
> apology.

In the course of the CR, the CCP ruling elite, backed and approved by Mao, developed a theoretical framework to legitimize the purge of the senior cadres and dismantling of the Party apparatuses. Mao's theory of "continued revolution under the dictatorship of proletariat" came to dominate the domestic politics of China (CCCCP 1981:33). The radicals argued that contradictions would not disappear in a socialist society which was still characterized by class struggles. Since the collectivization of agriculture and socialization of industries in 1956, China had been plagued by "two-line struggle" with Mao and Liu Shaoqi representing the proletarian and bourgeois headquarters respectively. If the bourgeois line was in power, then capitalism in China would be restored, just as capitalism had been restored in the Soviet Union, the Maoists asserted. The breakout of the CR was precisely to eliminate the bourgeois line inside the CCP. Mao's two lieutenants Zhang Chunqiao (1975) and Yao Wenyuan (1975) elaborated Mao's theory and attempted to legitimatize the outbreak of the CR in orthodox Marxist tradition.

Zhang's article spearheaded the attack on the notion of bourgeois rights.[9] He called for the restriction and ultimately the elimination of these rights and the curbing of the remaining elements of privileges and inequality of income. This would lead to the elimination of the three great differences, namely between agriculture and industry, city and countryside, and mental labor and manual labor. Yao argued (1975:14-5) that China was practicing the commodity system which would always breed bourgeois rights in exchange and distribution system. Consequently, a new bourgeoisie would emerge. Therefore the task of the dictatorship of the proletariat is to restrain the enlargement of bourgeois rights and to destroy the newly-created bourgeoisie.

The self-legitimized theory attracted widespread admiration of leftist intellectuals in the Western countries, but inside China, it was held in contempt by intellectuals and their articles were perceived as nothing but trying to appeal to Mao. The debate camouflaged the personal power struggles between Mao and Lin Biao, his anointed successor.[10] Writing in the mid-1980s, Walder (1987:156) argued that Maoism as the Western scholars saw it, in fact, had never actually existed in China

> To a large extent, our understanding of Mao's 'theory ofcontinuing the revolution under the

> dictatorship of the proletariat — with its almost
> exclusive emphasis on populist and egalitarianism
> themes — is a rationalized, heavily edited
> reconstruction by Western scholars for Western
> consumption designed to appeal to Western
> sensibilities.

The following themes were conceived by the West as the essence of Maoism: revolt against the Soviet developmental model, elimination of economic and social inequality, opposition to bureaucratism and corruption, idealization of a frugal life style, denial of selfishness, a demand for mass participation in the administration, and a theory of how a new ruling class emerged within the CCP. Walder contends (1987:158) that these themes were highly selective and most meaningful to the Western audience:

> But what themes are left out in the distillation? Here
> are a few: a paranoid political world view that sees
> Chinese society as riddled with hidden conspirators
> and traitors; a mentality that can brand someone
> traitor for unguarded utterance or insufficient
> enthusiasm in the worship of Mao; a mentality that
> encourages the treatment of "enemies" as non-
> humans subject to any form of humiliation or torture;
> a notion of rebellion that is for the purpose only of
> enforcing ever more slavish conformity to a single
> dictator's vision; a notion of democracy that clearly
> means total unanimity and conformity to the will of
> the Great Leaders.

The death of Mao and the downfall of his followers marked the end of an era in which China's search for socialism was a total failure (Jin Guantao and Liu Qingfeng 1990; Friedman, Pickowicz, and Selden 1991). Mao's revolutionary flavor faded and it was as if people awoke from a nightmare. A new phase of study on the PRC also emerged. The thesis of totalitarianism came back, and, this time, in the aftermath of the CR, a new element was emphasized: China's traditional and feudal remnants in the political culture and behavior of contemporary China.

Tsou Tang's articles (1986) first raised the notion of "feudal totalitarianism". He examined the Chinese totalitarian phenomena from a historical perspective. Taking the totalitarianism thesis as a working paradigm, Tsou tried to answer the question: Why did the totalitarian tendencies manifest themselves with accelerated speed after 1949 and culminate with the Maoist regime? He argued (1986:181-182) that because modern China encountered a total crisis, involving politics, economics, culture, and society, therefore it required a total response. The total response contained two elements that made it into a totalitarian movement and regime: the decisive and central role of political power and the use of violence used by a tightly organized elite that regarded itself as the vanguard of the working class. The CCP tried to resolve the total crisis by capturing total power by trying to establish effective political authority in order to bring about a fundamental transformation of the social structure, and by instituting a new economic system and a new society.

Tsou Tang's approach was to account for the origins of totalitarianism in China historically and situate it in the context of political crises China faced in the waves of Western imperialism.[11] Sharing the same paradigm, but using different terminology, Walder (1986) focused on the study of China's industrial working class *per se* and its relationship with the political authority. He called the type of authority that the Chinese working class had to live with "neo-traditional", which was the integration of the patrimonial and patriarchal rule and modern bureaucratic form. Moreover, the relationship of the working class and political order is explored. Walder came out with a new term: "organized dependence".[12] By exploring the informal and formal aspects of the work groups in the factory and the institutional culture inside it, Walder seems to provide us an image of China that combines political totalitarianism, patrimonial feudal industrial authority, and modern bucreaucracy.

The book of Friedman, Pickowicz, and Selden (1991) is a case study of the failure of the CCP regime to uproot historically unresolved problems in a North China county. In their words, the triumph of socialism in 1949 did not eliminate poverty, but instead "built a system" that strengthened some of the least humane aspects of the culture and failed to resolve historically rooted problems, leaving China's people trapped in a painful and humiliating dilemma." (1991:XIII) The authors (1991:282) basically shared the feudal-totalitarian thesis of Chinese politics and accepted the fact that the Maoists had created an unprecedented disaster for China:[13]

> There were no institutional checks on arbitrariness, coercison, and abuse of power. By joining a Marxist logic of progress through class struggle, a Leninist belief that the democratic centralism of the party-state embodied higher forms of democracy, and Stalinist institutions and policies, the party-in-power-taking-the-socialist-road rendered patriotic supporters in the countryside victims of an unmitigated disaster.

It is important to note that the reformist leadership seemed to share this image of Chinese politics in Mao's era and was eager to improve upon it. Political structural reform was put in the reformist agenda as soon as Deng seized political power from Hua Guofeng. The following is detailed analysis of the crises that the PRC encountered at the time Mao died.

Participation Crisis

The notion of participation can be understood, as I have mentioned, as the problem of involving people in the major governmental decision-making processes. In this respect, the CCP has ruled the PRC by excluding all other societal-political forces. Any other organized force would be seen as a threat to its grip of total power. Inheriting the Leninist organizational principle of "democratic centralism", the CCP has concentrated the administrative, military, and ideological power in a political elite (at times even in the single hand of Mao) and exercised control over society. This is a unified system of Party/state/military/ideological power (Su Shaozhi 1990:56).

Before 1949, when Mao and his colleagues were in the wilderness of Yenan and vowed to overthrow the despotic Guomindang (GMD) regime and the so-called three "big mountains" -- imperialism, feudalism, and bureaucratic capitalism, their political blueprint for a new China was impregnated with idealism and the vision attracted numerous idealistic intellectuals. In 1945, Mao announced that once the CCP became the governing party, it would turn China into an independent, free, democratic, united, and wealthy new country. A free and democratic China would be one in which all levels of government, local and central, were created by elections by universal franchise and the officials would only be accountable to the people who elected them (Su Shaozhi 1990:57).

The GMD regime had become increasingly incompetent and corrupt, and civil war broke out immediately after Japan surrendered in 1945. Then with inflation rampant, official abuse of government power widespread, and soldiers demoralized, CCP victory over the GMD seemed imminent. In an important speech on the eve of the founding of the PRC, Mao (1975 V.4:417) called upon the people to unite and elect their own government. But by then, Mao (1975 V. IV:418) had begun to redefine the rights of the people and "reactionaries"

> Democracy is practised within the ranks of the people, who enjoy the rights of freedom, of speech, assembly, association and so on. The right to vote only belongs to the people, not to the reactionaries. The combination of these two aspects, democracy for the people and dictatorship over the reactionaries, is the people's democratic dictatorship.

It was soon discovered that by the sheer "dialectics" of the united front tactics people were turned easily into enemies, thereby subject to the dictatorship of the proletariat. In the CR, the veteran revolutionaries of the CCP were turned into enemies and suffered intolerable humiliation and torture. Indeed the meaning of the people was completely and arbitrarily decided by the Marxist ideologues in accordance with the needs of revolutionary expediency (Steve Chin 1976:89-90).

After seizing power, the CCP started to reshape the political and economic institutions. Economically, a large-scale land reform movement was launched from 1949 to 1952 and then the First Five-year Plan based on the Soviet model was also designed. With Marxism-Leninism as its ideological guide, the CCP, after the land reform movement, began to collectivize the capitalist enterprises and the peasantry according to its socialist project. Initially, the CCP leadership envisaged the completion of the socialization and collectivization of industries and peasantry in three five-year plans, i.e. fifteen years (Mao 1977:87). Mao, however, took a radical turn and the process was completed instead in 1956 (Liao Gailong 1991:256). After that, Mao turned the national bourgeoisie, initially categorized as a rallying force in the united front tactics in the stage of new-democratic revolution, into class enemies meant to be suppressed (Mao 1977:65).

In the pre-reform epoch, there occurred several participation crises (Wong Yiu-chung 1990). The first participation crisis emerged in 1956. The First Five-year plan was near its completion. The Korean war had already come to an end, this was the first time in a century that China had fought a war without losing it. Influenced by the relative liberalization in the Soviet Union and Hungary at that time and confident of its ability to govern in the new regime, Mao decided to launch the "let hundred flowers bloom, let hundred schools of thought contend" campaign in February 1957. The initial goal of the campaign was to encourage the people, in particular the intellectuals, to speak up and raise criticism concerning the work style of the CCP. By July, the criticism became sharper and demonstrations occurred in the elitist universities, such as Peking (Beida) and Tsinghua Universities. The CCP found the situation uncontrollable.   Mao became furious and turned the rectification movement into the Anti-Rightist campaign that ultimately silenced a whole generation of intellectuals for three decades.[14]

Among the critics, two of the most active university students were Lin Xiling and Tan Tianrong (they became rightists). Lin (SUCU 1982:6) criticized the CCP's pseudo-socialism:

> We don't have a bourgeois democratic tradition. I don't think our socialism is a genuine one. Genuine socialism should be democratic, but we don't have democracy. Our socialism is established on feudal tradition and therefore is not true socialism. We must fight to realize the authentic socialism.[15]

Tan (SUCU 1982:2) criticised the dictatorial work style of the CCP:

> Since 1953, we have been ruled by the bureaucratized members of the CCP, from central levels to local levels. They are despotic and always trash human rights.

Many intellectuals also criticized the governing style of the CCP and most importantly they questioned the political legitimacy of the CCP.   They wanted to be involved in the decision-making process of major national policies. For example, Chu Anping, the editor-in-chief of *Brightness Daily*, pointed out that "the political monopoly by the CCP is the origin of factionalism." Luo Rongji, one of the leaders of the biggest democratic party, the Democratic League of China, rejected the thought reform movement of the CCP and charged that people should be allowed to debate openly about the future of China.[16] Mao felt that the ruling status of the CCP was threatened and he responded by changing the nature of the campaign to purge the dissenting intellectuals. Obviously, the participation crisis had not been solved and it was only suppressed by coercion. In the short run, coercion seemed to be a very effective way to deal with the crisis.

The consequences of the Anti-Rightist campaign were that on the one hand, it "led the authorities to denounce as rightists 552,877 of China's boldest patriots" (Kristof and Wudunn 1994:66);[17] on the other hand, Mao was able to silence the intellectual dissent so completely that all the democratic parties would not dare to challenge him any more. Then, Mao turned his target of struggle to his colleagues by elaborating the theory of class struggle under socialism.

The catastrophic consequences created by the GLF forced Mao to back off from the limelight of China's domestic politics. He retreated to the backstage of the political scene. Mao gave his presidency of the PRC to Liu Shaoqi in the First Session of the Second NPC held in April 1959. Liu and his moderate CCP Politburo members brought in a series of pragmatic measures to correct leftist tendencies of Mao's policies and revive the battered economy. Under Liu's leadership, economic development became the top priority of the party and the pragmatic measures he introduced included: first, the reintroduction of material incentives, such as free markets and private plots, in order to spur agricultural productivity; second, enterprises were to be evaluated on efficiency and profit criteria; third, "expertise" was placed in precedence over "redness", ideologues were to ignored and intellectuals were emphasized; fourth, provincial authorities were to be given more power to set production quota and price (Townsend and Womack 1986:119-120).

The political report by Liu Shaoqi in the Eighth CCP Congress, held in September 1956, defined the main contradiction in China as the contradiction between an "advanced social system" and "backward productive force". Mao's diagnosis of the contradictions between the proletariat and national bourgeoisie was sidetracked and the explicit reference to Mao's thought was deleted.[18] Mao was reluctant to be ignored. He called for continuing class struggles in the Tenth Plenum of the Eighth CC in September 1962. The communique of the Tenth Plenum wrote that "class struggle will be inevitably reflected in the Party. The influences of foreign imperialism and bourgeoisie are the social origins of revisionism inside the Party" (Liao Gailong 1991:292). At the end of 1965, he started the CR to purge the moderate leadership.

The debut of the CR was the publication of Yao Wenyuan's article "Commentary on the Newly Revised Historical Play *Hai Rui Dismissed from Office*" in *Wen Hui Bao* in Shanghai on 16 May 1965. The CCP Politburo sent a circular to the whole Party on 16 May 1966, formally launching the movement. In August, the Eleventh Plenum of the Eighth CC rectified the decision of the Politburo dominated by Mao. The Ninth CCP Congress was convened in April 1969. A new CCP Constitution was adopted. Lin Biao was designated as the successor of Mao and Marxism-Leninism-Mao Zedong Thought upheld as the theoretical basis of the CCP's policies.[19]

Amidst the chaotic situation during the CR, there appeared an influential *Dazibao* in Guanzhou by Li Yizhe (a pen name used by three people, namely Li Zhengtian, Chen Yiyang, and Wang Xizhe). The article was entitled "On Socialist Democracy and the Legal System", which received widespread attention.[20] It was copied and recopied and passed from hand to hand. What made this article so popular was that, in the days of lawlessness and "fascist dictatorship", it was the first article since the outbreak of the CR that discussed the problems of democracy and the rule of law. The acceptance and spread of this article, in fact, reflected a major participation crisis.

Nominally, Li's big-character poster lauded Mao's launching of the CR and his general direction for the party/state was correct. In fact, it was a calculated move to undercut the red banner by raising the red banner. Li criticized the so-called "Lin Biao system" and hoped that the coming Fourth NPC in 1975 would put the rule of law into its agenda. Making use of Mao's "theory of continuing revolution under the dictatorship of the proletariat", Li explored the process in which the capitalist roader in the CCP who had transformed from "servant of the people" to "master of the people" (Anita Chan et al. 1985:36). Li argued that Mao's revolutionary line had never been dominant in the

CR, instead China was dominated by the "Lin Biao system", which was a fascist dictatorship rooted upon the feudal mentality of Party members. They called for the establishment of a legal system that could enforce the rule of law, thus protecting the rights of the people. In Li's view, the most important task of the deputies of the coming Fourth NPC was the problem of supervising and eliminating the privileges of the senior party members.

> Our cadres should not become officials and behave like lords, but should be the servants of the people. But power can corrupt people most easily. When a person's status changes, it is most effective to test whether he is working for the interests of the majority or of the minority. Whether he can maintain his spirit to serve the people depends, apart from his own diligence, mainly on the revolutionary supervision of the masses (Anita Chan et al. 1985:80).

Moreover, the Fourth NPC should enact, in black and white, clauses limiting special privileges of the Party members. As later events unfolded, the Fourth NPC failed to respond to calls and the three members of Li Yizhe group were taken to struggle meetings for criticism. Li Xiannian, then a Politburo member, declared the article a counterrevolutionary document and Jiang Qing reportedly said that the poster was "the most reactionary article yet since liberation." (Anita Chan et al. 1985:12) Numerous struggle meetings were held to condemn the Li Yizhe group between January and March 1975. Without doubt, the participation crisis revealed by the Li Yizhe *Dazibao* was once again suppressed by the ideologically ossified power-holders.

Instead of introducing more democratic elements, as urged by the Li Yizhe group, the Fourth NPC tightened its grip on the state apparatus. The Fourth NPC passed a new state constitution and some provisions were either amended or added: first, the post of the state presidency was abrogated; second, it was explicitly stated that the NPC was the highest power organ under "the leadership of the CCP"; third, the chairman of the CC of the CCP commanded the national armed forces; fourth, the procuratorate was abolished and its function was taken over by the public security offices (PRC 1975).

The only positive sign in the Fourth NPC was that Zhou Enlai (1976:234) proclaimed in his government report that China must realize the four modernizations (modernization of agriculture, industry, national defense, and science and technology) in the twentieth century. However, the slogans of striving for four modernizations were soon to be buried by the *pi Lin, pi Kong* (criticize Lin Biao, criticize Confucius) campaign, engineered by the "Gang of Four" with the tacit support of Mao.

By 1974, Zhou Enlai had been suffering from cancer and the need for a successor to run state affairs seemed imminent. Mao rehabilitated Deng in 1973 for the second time.[21] In 1974, Deng was promoted to the membership of the CCP Politburo and effectively replaced Zhou as the head of the government bureaucracy. But his work was constantly hampered by the radicals backed by Mao. The intra-party struggles were fierce and Mao seemed to hold the balance.

The Chinese people had long been extremely dissatisfied with the ultra-leftist policies of Mao. The death of Zhou ignited the third participation crisis since 1949. Zhou died from cancer on 8 January 1976 and he was perceived as a symbol of order and pragmatism during the tumultuous period of the CR. He had protected a large group of veteran bureaucrats from being physically exterminated. His death sparked the largest spontaneous social movement during the reign of the CCP. In the three months from February to April, thousands of people laid wreaths on the Monument of People's Heroes and hundreds of poems and essays were pasted on the Monument to praise his diligence, loyalty, and perseverance. One of the most cited poems read (Tong Huaizhou 1978:11) as follows,

> In my grief I hear demons shriek; I weep while wolves and jackals laugh. Though tears I shed to mourn a hero, with head raised high, I draw my sword.[22]

Another poem (Tong Huaizhou 1978:282) revealed completely the awakening of the participatory consciousness of the people:

> China is no longer the China of the past, People are no longer foolish as before; the feudal society of the First Emperor has long gone. We believe in genuine

> Marxism-Leninism. Let those who distort the true
> Marxism-Leninism go to hell!

On 5 April the Beijing Municipal authorities dispatched thousands of urban militia and public security men to disperse the crowd by using clubs and arrested hundreds of citizens. The authorities labeled the movement as "counterrevolutionary". Deng Xiaoping was alleged to have masterminded the incident and was subsequently removed from all his posts by an expanded CCP Politburo meeting hosted by Mao. The spontaneous social movement was crushed by the violent suppression by the radicals within the CCP, including Mao.

Mao died on 9 September 1976. Hua Guofeng succeeded him as the chairman of the CCP. Soon afterwards the "Gang of Four" was arrested by the special security forces of 8341 under the personal command of Politburo member Wang Dongxing.[23] Deng Xiaoping was rehabilitated and restored to his former position in the Third Plenum of the Tenth CC held in July 1977. In the Third Plenum of the Eleventh CC, Deng stroke a decisive victory over Hua's faction and succeeded in setting up his own political line. Politically and ideologically, the Third Plenum of the Eleventh CC held in December 1978 had already achieved a radical break with Maoist rule (Liao Gailong 1991:338-340). With Deng as the de facto top leader, the CCP could now push for full modernization wholeheartedly.

The "Beijing Spring" pro-democracy movement broke out in a time when Deng was engaging in power struggles with Hua's "whateverist" faction. In the aftermath of the rehabilitation of Tiananmen incident in November 1978, the students in Beida and Tsinghua University began to paste big-character posters inside the universities, criticizing Hua's conservative policies, in particular his obstruction of Deng's return. They had the initial support of Deng who saw the popular protest as a rallying force in his struggles with Hua. With his implicit support, soon the posters began to appear on Xidan Wall in November 1978. For the next year or so, the wall became known as Xidan Democracy Wall and it became a rallying point for democratic activists. The big-character posters discussed all the sensitive issues that one could not see in the official media (Fraser 1980).

On 5 April 1979, the *People's Daily* published an editorial calling for the upholding of the four cardinal principles, namely the socialist road, the people's democratic dictatorship, the leadership of the CCP, and Marxism-Leninism-Mao Zedong Thought (Deng Xiaoping 1983:149-151).[24] It was a public signal that the government was going to turn hard on the pro-democracy movement. Soon the municipal authorities began to crack down and Wei Jingsheng was the first among democratic activists to be arrested and imprisoned. On 8 December 1979, the Beijing municipal government forbade the pasting of posters onto Xidan Wall.

But the movement continued in other cities. It was estimated that hundreds of magazines, journals, and pamphlets were published all over China. According to one account (SUCU 1982:480), in 1979 and 1980, at least 127 magazines and journals were published by the democratic activists without the censorship of the CCP. The issues discussed by the activists were wide-ranging, such as the problems of democracy, special privileges of the cadres, whether China was a Marxist state, the meaning of dictatorship of the proletariat, problems of modernization, and the evaluation of Mao, etc. However, among the contending thought, there were mainly two streams of thoughts among the activists. The first one is what I call the "human rights" faction, represented by Wei Jingsheng, and the second is the "democratic socialist" faction represented, by Wang Xizhe (Wong Yiu-chung 1990:55). They both share the consensus that the democratization of Chinese society was necessary and hat the CCP could no longer represent the people. Wang's analysis still sticks to some fundamental assumptions of Marxism, while Wei emphasizes the importance of Western democratic tradition and institutions. He (SUCU 1982:173) argued that

> If Chinese want to achieve modernization, we must first practice democracy and modernize our social structure.....Democracy, in fact, is the prerequisite and condition of industrialization. Without these prerequisites and conditions, we cannot even preserve our existing achievement, not to mention further development.

Furthermore, Wei (SUCU 1982:195) warned that, amidst the applause heaped upon Deng's modernization drive, people could not trust Deng unconditionally and had to be beware of him becoming a dictator. He argued:

> Historical experience tells that we must not trust any
> politician unconditionally. The question is whom we
> should trust and more importantly, how to monitor
> them so as to execute the will of the majority. We
> can only trust those who are accountable to us and
> those representatives who are not appointed from the
> above..... Anyone who rejects the supervision of the
> people and who infringes the democratic rights of the
> people are the enemies of the people.[25]

In a similar vein, Wang also called for the supervision of the cadres
and urged the establishment of objective criteria that could serve as the
monitoring mechanism over the government officials (SUCU 1982:318).
Unlike Wei, who borrowed Western ideas of democracy, Wang's
criticism of the CCP was based on what he believed be to true
socialism, thus avoiding posing a direct challenge to the PRC. He
believed that Maoist Marxism was distorted and the task then for the
CCP was to go back to original Marxism (Wong Yiu-chung 1981).

The "Beijing Spring" democracy movement lasted for only two and
a half years, starting from the first appearance of the big-character
posters on Xidan Wall until the complete suppression of all democratic
activists. After April 1981, the movement totally vanished and the
activists were either imprisoned, such as Wang Xizhe and Wei
Jingsheng, or silenced. All the prominent activists, besides Wang and
Wei, such as Fu Shenqi, Xu Wenli, Ren Wanding, Liu Qing, and He
Qiu, were to receive various prison terms. But it was Wei Jingsheng
who received the heaviest penalty of all.[26]

In the late 1970s, Deng and his lieutenants would probably have
agreed with what the democratic activists had criticized about the CCP
regime. What they hated to see was that the activists had been engaging
in political activities outside the official-sanctioned channels, thus
constituting a challenge to the CCP's monopoly of political power.
While cracking down on the democracy movement, Deng launched what
I called the "official democracy movement".[27] Having launched the
economic reform, Deng realized that without some elements of political
reform, the economic reform would be a fiasco and subsequently
modernization could not be achieved. By introducing political reform,
Deng's move was unprecedented in CCP history. The previous
participation crises were all resolved by violent suppression. On the
contrary, Deng faced this crisis head on and tried to resolve it by

institutional rejuvenation. He believed that the Maoist China had to be substantially changed. It will be seen that in the reform era, the crisis of participation will not be totally resolved. This crisis reached its zenith after the violent crackdown on the 1989 pro-democracy movement.

Distribution Crisis

Distribution crisis is a crisis of resource management and therefore it is, in fact, a crisis of economy. As discussed before, the crisis has two dimensions: first, the government would try to find ways and means to increase production of goods for the population; second the government would try to change the redistribution mechanism of the available goods. The first dimension deals with the problem of economic growth and the second with the problem of redistribution in the conventional sense. Certainly, the two dimensions are intimately related. In the Chinese context, the Maoist regime had been characterized by an extreme form of egalitarianism (Riskin 1987:223-256). However, if the economy goes derailed and even the subsistence level of the population cannot be maintained, then the problem of redistribution is irrelevant as in the case of GLF movement in which millions of people died of starvation.

Maoist China suffered two great economic setbacks in the pre-reform era, which resulted from Mao's utopian socialist projects and cost the nation dearly. For the first three years after they seized power from the GMD, the CCP struggled to bring the widely disrupted economy into order. After eight years of Japanese invasion and four years of civil war, the CCP undertook to restore production plants, communication and transportation facilities. Rampant inflation could not be allowed to continue and government revenue had to be ensured. The CCP tackled the problem of farmland which had existed for thousands of years in traditional China. It launched a land reform program which had been implemented sporadically in the CCP-controlled areas before 1949. A set of Agrarian Reform Laws were promulgated in June 1950 which stated that the reform would begin by stages in the areas newly-acquired by the CCP. By early 1952, the land reform had basically been completed. Approximately 300 million land-less and land-poor peasants were allocated 700 million *mu* (1 *mu* = 0.0667 hectare) of land. By implementing the land reform, the CCP successfully eradicated the landowning class in China, thereby restructuring the social classes (Liao Gailong 1991:231).

The initial economic reconstruction was completed in 1952. The government started the First Five-year Plan in 1953. The Plan relied heavily on the Soviet aid. The chief task was to concentrate efforts on the construction of 694 large and medium-sized industrial projects with 156 projects assisted by Soviet aid as its core projects. The Plan laid the foundation for China's socialist industrialization. It also aimed to collectivize agricultural producers' co-operatives and handicraft producers' co-operatives, thereby laying the preliminary foundation for the socialist transformation of agriculture and handicrafts. The regime tried to place the capitalist industries in the form of state capitalism, which is a transitional stage to socialism, thus laying the foundations for the socialist transformation of private industries and commerce (Mao Zedong 1977:98-100). The 1950s was the golden age of the CCP reign. For the first time in modern Chinese history, the CCP brought about an independent China, free from war, foreign invasion, and domestic turmoil. Economic development proceeded rapidly. The total state investment in capital construction, agriculture, education, transport, and energy amounted to 76.6 billion yuan (renminbi) in the first Five-year Plan (Riskin 1987:56). The actual results of the Plan surpassed the estimated targets, with industrial production growing by an average annual rate of 18 percent and annual agricultural growth rates of 4.5 percent (Riskin 1987:57-58).

In 1958, the CCP suffered the first great economic setback. The Sino-Soviet debates and conflicts became public. Mao contemplated moving away from the Soviet model of socialist development. The Second Plenum of the Eighth CC in May 1958 adopted the political line of "going all out, aiming high and achieving greater, faster, better and more economical results to build socialism". The Politburo of the CCP met at Beidaihe in August to adopt the resolution to establish People's Communes in the rural areas. The policies soon brought a tide of upsurge in the GLF and People's Commune movement all over China. Following the instructions from Mao to catch up to Britain in steel production in 15 years, the whole nation was mobilized and engaged in the production of pig iron at the backyard furnace. The operations of thousands of primitive blast furnaces exhausted the labour supply, and farmland was left uncultivated. The radical policies, coupled with natural calamities and the withdrawal of Soviet aid, brought the Chinese people untold suffering and millions of people died of starvation.[28]

The gross industrial value fell from 165 billion yuan in 1960 to 85 billion yuan in 1962. The gross agricultural value only reached 40.5 billion yuan in 1961, which was less than the value of 1951. Grain production fell from 195.05 million tons in 1957 to 143.50 million tons in 1960, thus per capita food grain was reduced from 620 *jin* (1 *jin* =0.5 kg) in 1956 to 430 *jin* in 1960 (ZTN 1984:167).   The supply of edible oil was reduced from 1.22 million tons in 1956 to 0.39 million tons in 1962, the per capita 16.4 *jin* in 1956 was reduced to 6.0 *jin* in 1960, but the population had increased by 50 million. The annual production of pigs was 154 million in 1957, but in 1961 the production was halved. The supply of pork, beef, and lamb reached 3.985 million tons in 1956, but the supply was only 1.94 million tons in 1962 (ZTN 1984:160). The supply of sugar was rare and the production was only 0.64 million tons, only one-third of the normal annual supply.

The economic disaster was revealed in the demographic catastrophe during the three years from 1959 to 1961. Officially, the disaster was attributed to several factors. One was the withdrawal of Soviet experts and aid because of the row over the ideological orthodoxy of socialism. The unilateral action disrupted China's core industrial projects. However, Soviet aid was mainly for industrial projects, primarily situated in urban areas, while it was the countryside that was devastated and where the population was decimated. The second was the natural disasters. China is a vast country with recurrent natural disasters. From 1959 to 1962, China was hit by drought but the cultivation areas affected were not particularly widespread compared with the previous years. The reduction of food grain in these years was abnormally heavy. Grain production fell from 200 million tons in 1958 to 170 million in 1959, a reduction of 30 million tons. In 1960, it was further reduced to 143.5 million tons. In these two years, the reduction was almost one-third of the annual production (ZTN 1983:158).

The CCP policies of import and export made things worse. In the years of starvation, instead of increasing importation of grain, on the contrary, the CCP reduced the importation and increased the export of grain. In 1959, the importation of grain was a bare 2 thousand tons, while the export was raised to 4.16 million tons which was almost double that of 1958. Even in 1960, the import of grain was still at the minimum level of 66,000 tons (ZTN 1983:422,438). Neither the withdrawal of Soviet aid nor natural disaster factors can account sufficiently for the economic fiasco of the GLF. In fact, the radical policies of Mao were the principal cause of the disasters (Li Zhisui 1994:306-312).

The second major distribution crisis in the PRC was in the period of the CR. Unlike the GLP, the impact of the CR was mainly on the urban areas rather than rural sectors. Further, the GLF movement lasted for about four years and in the early 1960s the moderate leaders adopted the retrenchment policies of "adjustment, restructuring, consolidating, and improving" to restore the economy. The CR lasted for about thirteen years from 1966 to 1978 when Deng Xiaoping launched economic reform. Thirdly, in the course of the CR, the economy was disrupted by factional struggles and intra-party conflicts, while in the GLF the radical policies directly hit the economy. Fourthly, the impact of the CR involved aspects of culture, education, and arts, and the intellectuals were especially hard hit, while the effect of the GLF was largely limited to the economy. Peng Dehuai, the Defense Minister, was purged after he raised strong objections to the GLF radical policies. However, on the whole, the CCP stood by Mao.

In the CR, industrial output suffered the greatest loss in 1967 and 1968. The combined industrial loss in those two years was 30 billion yuan in value. The production of crude steel fell from 15 million tons in 1966 to 9.04 million tons in 1968 and the production of crude iron fell from 13 million tons in 1966 to 8.5 million tons in 1968. In 1967 and 1968, the industrial and agricultural sectors lost 10 percent and 4 percent of annual output value (ZTN 1983:9-10). The second political comeback of Deng Xiaoping in 1975 boosted the economic growth rate to 11.1 percent, unprecedented in the era of the CR, but when Deng was dismissed from office in the wake of the Tiananmen incident in 1976, the growth rate fell to 1.7 percent. In the ten-year period from 1966 to 1976, the population increased from 745.42 million to 937.17 million, an increase of almost of 200 million (ZTN 1984:81) which became a heavy burden on the development of the economy.[29]

When Mao died in 1976, a revolutionary and mobilizational era finally was laid to rest, but it took two more years for the pragmatic CCP leadership headed by Deng to reorient the country towards the modernization process. Hua Guofeng basically preserved the radical line unchanged, but he emphasized more on economic priorities.[30] The economic program of the Ten-year Plan (1976-85) he proposed in the First Session of the Fifth NPC was too ambitious. The Plan proposed the construction of 120 giant industrial projects by the end of 1985. Hua underestimated the seriousness of the imbalance of China's national economy and the Plan was simply unrealistic. After the Third Plenum of the Eleventh CC, the Plan was simply scrapped and Hua was criticised as ultra-leftist (CCCCP 1981:49).

When Deng embarked on his reform in 1978, he inherited a Stalinist command economy in which the enterprises had to seek approval from the Central government for nearly everything. The state exercised control through mandatory procurement and allocation of key agricultural and industrial products, and by setting the price and quota of goods. The growth rates in Maoist China were fairly impressive. But one of the most important defects of the command economy is the emphasis on quantity of output rather than quality and efficiency. Certainly, in terms of quantity, the CCP has achieved a certain measure of success. In 1949, the total value of industrial and agricultural output was 55.7 billion yuan. By 1978, it reached 684.6 billion yuan (ZTN 1984:20). However, the efficiency of the state sectors remained a problem. Despite Mao's efforts to move away from the Soviet model of economic development and his attempt to put in the elements of voluntarism and egalitarianism, he never completely discarded the Stalinist model of socialism and the central characteristics of the command economy (Harding 1987:19).

Deng ushered in his reformist policies amidst a profound distribution crisis. In the urban areas, the standard of living for millions of people had remained stagnant for more than two decades, as can be shown in the following table:

Table 2.1
Average Per Capita Income in Urban China, 1957 and 1977

	1957	1977
Urban Population(millions)	99.0	115
Percentage employed	30	50
Employed urban population(millions)	29.7	55.2
Average industrial wage(yuan/yr)	690	632
Average real industrial wage(yuan/yr)	690	542
Real per capita income(yuan/yr)	207	259

Source: Walder 1986:197

During the two decades (1957-1977) the average real income declined considerably from 690 yuan to 542 yuan. The per capita real income appeared to have increased by 25 percent, a modest annual increase of 1.25 percent. However, the improvement was entirely due to a 60 percent rise in the labor participation rate in the urban force. In 1957, only 30 percent of urban residents were employed; by 1977, 50 percent were employed. Similarly, the standard of living for a family is shown in the following table:

Table 2.2
**Average Per Capita Income of Wage-earning Families, 1957 and
1977**

	1957	1977
Average family size	4.37	4.30
Average no. employeed family members	1.33	2.20
Dependent per wage earner	2.29	1.10
Average nominal wage(yuan/yr)	690	632
Average real wage(1950 yuan)	545	440
Average per capita income	166	218

Source: Walder 1986:188

Again, the average nominal wage and real wage declined
considerably. But in terms of per capita income, it still increased by
about 45 percent between 1957-1977 or an average annual increase of
2.25 percent, largely because more people in the family were employed.
Looking at the state sector of industry, it conveys the same message.
From 1957 to 1977, average real wages in state industry declined by
19.4 percent. The decline in real wages in the state industry was 16.5
percent if measured from the pre-Cultural Revolution peak in 1964. The
decline was so great that the average real wage in 1977 was even less
than it had been in 1952. It started to climb back only in 1978 and
afterwards when the economic reform went into full swing.

Penetration Crisis

The social-psychological control of the CCP over Chinese society
was extremely rigid and powerful. It exerted its mobilizational abilities
by two methods: thought and organizational control. In 1951, the CCP
promulgated *Regulations Regarding the Punishment of Counter-
Revolutionaries*, launching a nationwide campaign to eliminate the

GMD counterrevolutionaries but, in fact, destroying social forces that it saw disloyal to the new regime. In the same year, an ideological rectification campaign to criticize Hu Shih, a famous May-Fourth scholar, and Hu Feng, a party literary critic, was launched. A study movement of thought remoulding was carried out among teachers, writers, and intellectuals in general, calling on them to be reeducated through criticism and self-criticism (Lifton 1961:246-248).

Administratively and organizationally, the CCP broke with the GMD tradition. The whole structure of the GMD administration was declared invalid and a new structure was created from bottom up, but the securities apparatus remained basically continuous (Schurman 1968:371-372). The process of organizing the population proceeded in two directions. On the one hand, it went from top to bottom by expanding the existing civil administration functions of public security forces; on the other hand, it proceeded from bottom up through the mass organizations. In the early 1950s, residents committeess or neighborhood committee were formed. They were not part of the CCP formal structure, but they monitored the activities very closely and persist to this day (Kristof and Wudunn 1994). The other channel by which urban population was organized was through the units of production where the people worked. As Shurman (1968:LII) said, Maoist China was "a China of organization".

The control mechanisms of the CCP in the three decades prior to the reformist era were rigid. During the CR, though the Party was disbanded and cadres imprisoned, the ideological control was as tight as ever. All literature was prohibited except a few novels. Across the vast country, only eight films were allowed to be shown. Schools and universities were suspended for several years. Production was discontinued and red guards would enter the residence of anyone at will searching for anything they thought was anti-Mao. Anyone could be branded as counter-revolutionaries. China was like an army barracks and formal mechanisms of control were unnecessary.[31] Writing in the early 1980s, Butterfield (1982:322) pointed out:

> Foreigners who visited China often came away
> saying proudly that they were able to walk wherever
> they wanted, poking down old lanes, looking into
> people's houses, without being followed. China
> really isn't a police state after all, they concluded.

> But an American who has lived in Peking since
> before 1949 scoffed at their naivete. The control
> system operates the other way around, he explained,
> from the inside out, for the government has
> organized society as security system as much as it is a
> social or economic system. It is built on three
> overlapping and mutually reinforcing components:
> the *danwei* or workplace, the street committee, and
> the "small group" where political study sessions are
> held. The Communists have created such a thorough
> organization, it is like radar; it picks up wherever
> you go.

The reform has not shaken the overall control by the CCP over the
population but it certainly has corroded the extent of its grip. The
control mechanism was still terrifying as told by Kristof and Wudunn
(1994:49-50), when they were writing at the end of 1980s

> The most distinctive feature of China today is the
> social control that it employs. The Communist Party
> relies upon an ingenious "iron triangle": the
> residence permit, which limits where you live; the
> secret personnel file, which records your sins and
> political reliability; and the work unit, which
> supervises every aspect of your life. This triangle
> controls your life.[32]

In the 1950s, the prestige of the CCP was at its zenith and after
overthrowing the corrupted GMD regime, it was regarded by the nation
as its savior. China had been bullied by the Western powers for over a
century. The country had been torn by rebellions, revolutions,
warlordism, and invasion and finally, here came a revolutionary party
which seemed wholly devoted to the cause of national salvation. The
CCP unified the country, restored the economy, drove away the foreign
imperialists, and banished the extra-territories of the foreign residents.
The people genuinely felt proud when Mao proclaimed on 1 October
1949 "the Chinese people have stood up". No sooner had the regime
consolidated power than it launched numerous political campaigns. But
the intellectuals participated in these campaigns voluntarily. Amidst the
"brain-washing" movements, they believed that they should remould

themselves to adjust to the demands of the new regime. Liu Binyan (1990:39), the scathing author, recalls

> As soon as the civil war ended, the new regime launched several political campaigns involving millions of people. The campaigns of Resist-America-Aid-Korea and suppression of the counter-revolutionaries were launched at the same time. On the one hand, numerous youth wished to join the army to fight Americans; on the other hand, former GMD officials reported to the public security office to confess their crimes. The urban mass reported to the new regime those enemies who had not been exposed. People participated in these activities wholeheartedly. People were overjoyed with the independent status China has and the advent of a new era (inflation halted, living standard raised gradually and social order restored). People attributed all these achievements to the CCP and they would do whatever it told them.

Times change. After three decades of Maoist rule, people were disillusioned. Intellectuals were alienated in 1957 in the Anti-Rightist campaign which was initially launched to solicit their opinions on national issues, but later the campaign turned out to be a frame-up. The campaign silenced thousands of intellectuals. In the era of CR, though the ultimate target was the so called "capitalist roader"-the power-holders within the party, Mao began his purge in the cultural arena and the intellectuals again became the targets of persecution. Wu Han, a former university professor and vice-major of Beijing, was the scapegoat of the intra-party power struggle for writing the play *Hai Rui Dismissed from Office* (Li Zhisui 1994:441-442). Numerous intellectuals committed suicide, including Lao She, a prominent author; Jian Bozan, a Beida historian, and Fu Lei, an essayist. In the era of the CR, nearly one hundred million people were victimized.[33] By launching the CR, the Maoist regime completely alienated the whole nation and faced a profound legitimacy crisis. After Mao's death, the crisis loomed larger and could no longer be suppressed. As one young woman told Butterfield (1982:309):

> Before the Cultural Revolution, we Chinese lived
> under a great illusion. We believed the Communists
> could save China and make it prosperous and strong
> again. People were very idealistic and hardworking.
> Now people have seen through this, and they have
> suffered a terrible loss of faith.

The girl was one of the approximately sixteen million "sent-down youth" who, in the course of ten years, went to the countryside to learn revolution from the peasantry. The red guards and young students were sent down to the rural areas and that was supposedly to gain a cleansing experience but it had unintended effects. The youth discovered that after twenty years after the liberation, the Chinese, particularly the peasants, still lived in extreme poverty and were subject to the tyranny of local party cadres. After they returned home, they found the education system in chaos and could not find employment. Most important of all, they found that they had lost ten years and they were no longer young. Subsequently, they were completely disillusioned. At the end of the 1970s, there emerged a current of *sanxin weiji* (three beliefs crisis): *xinyang weiji* (crisis of faith), *xinxin weiji* (crisis of confidence), and *xinren weiji* (crisis of trust) (Butterfield 1982).

When Deng Xiaoping was restored to his powerful positions in 1977, China was facing a multiple crisis situation. The economy was in shambles, and the Party bureaucracy was in disarray. However, veteran cadres were rehabilitated and returned to previous rankings, but they were too old to take on the Herculean task of modernization. China was in a period of uncertainty. The ideological straightjacket was gradually loosened but the Mao adulation was still widespread and a movement to cleanse his remnant influence was yet to be waged.

With the back-up of returned veterans and intellectuals, Deng was determined to change the radical policies of Mao. He knew that modernization requires the alliance of the whole nation. Different classes must be rallied. The Maoist ideology of dividing the nation into class enemies could no longer be tolerated. Unlike Mao who categorized the intellectuals into the "stinking ninth" class, Deng saw intellectuals as an important source of productive force. Modernization could not be achieved without their contribution. Against this background, Deng embarked on his grand design of modernization of economics and politics in China in the late 1970s.

Notes

[1] Domination does not, of course, mean that Mao was involved in the minutest details or concrete implementation of the Party/state policies. The domination of Mao's personality on contemporary Chinese politics is vividly depicted by Dr Li Zhisui (1994) who had been Mao's personal physician for twenty-two years from 1954 to 1976. I would argue that Li's memoir is perhaps the most important book on Mao since he died in 1976.

[2] Some social scientists have argued that, in the course of economic reform, there emerged several kinds of identities, namely regional, national, and global in the coastal provinces, such as Guangdong (Lynn White and Li Cheng 1993:154-193). I believe that the definition of the term "identity" has been too vague. These identities are not incompatible with the common cultural "Chineseness" identity.

[3] In a more vigorous definition of political participation, Weiner (1971:164) stated as follows: any voluntary action, successful or unsuccessful, organized, episodic or continuous, employing legitimate or illegitimate methods, intended to influence the choice of public policies, the administration of public affairs, or the choice of political leaders at any level of government, local or national.

[4] In a prophetic statement, Trotsky contended that the methods used by Lenin in the revolutionary struggles would, "lead....to this: the party organization is substituted for the party, the Central Committee is substituted for the party organization, and finally the 'dictator' is substituted for the Central Committee" (Tucker 1975).

[5] What Lifton means is a psychological process through which a person totally lost his or her original identity, replaced by another new personality make-up. Later on, Tsou Tang, an American-Chinese political scientist, employed the term "totalism" to mean "a socio-political system in which there are no moral or ideological limits to the extension of state functions into any sphere of social life, except such limits as its top leaders adopt and hence can change at any moment."(1991:271)

[6] The four approaches were: first, the "power struggle" approach which saw the policy differences of the ruling elites as devices to legitimate their struggles for personal power; second, the "Chinese culture" approach which saw the rule of the CCP as merely a short interlude in the development of Chinese civilization; third, the "political aberration" approach which held that Maoist China was a political aberration of true Marxism, since

according to traditional socialism, only countries with high productive power can become socialist; fourthly, the "peasant anarchism" approach which saw the CR as a rejection of Marxism and a re-emergence of Chinese peasant anarchism (Wheelwright and McFarlane 1970:212-215).

[7] Sweezy (1980:85-95) argued that the Maoist contribution to the development of socialist thought was in two areas: first, the breakaway from the Soviet developmental model, second, the notion of class struggle as manifested in the CR.

[8] There were certainly some dissenting voices, one of them was Simon Leys who revealed the true reality of China in the wake of the CR in the early 1970s. He (1978:201) strongly criticised the Maoist apologetics that "Western ideologues now use Maoist China just as the eighteenth-century philosophers used Confucian China: as a myth, an abstract ideal projection, a utopia which allows them to denounce everything that is bad in the West without taking the trouble to think for themselves. We stifle in the miasma of industrial civilization, our cities rot, our roads are blocked by the insane proliferation of cars, et cetera. So they hurry to celebrate the People's Republic, where population, delinquency, and traffic problems are nonexistent. One might as well praise an amputee because his feet aren't dirty."

[9] This is a special Marxian term. It means that in class societies, such as capitalist society, different human beings endowed with different abilities would produce different amounts of labour. Ultimately the inequality in labour would lead to class inequalities. In a classless society, these rights would vanish.

[10] After the expulsion of Liu Shaoqi from the CCP in the Twelfth Plenum of the Eighth CC in October, 1968, the struggles between Mao and Lin Biao soon began. Lin pushed for the restoration of the post of the president of the PRC but Mao favoured abandoning it. There emerged a series of plots and counterplots, which finally resulted in the defection of Lin to the Soviet Union, but the plane crashed in Mongolia (Li Zhisui 1994:535-541).

[11] Fairbank (1983:part II) provides a concise account on China's modern history and the invasion of Western powers.

[12] Walder himself explicitly states that the neo-traditional image of communist society differs fundamentally from the image of totalitarianism. However, he also conceded (1986:5) that "The neo-traditional image shares with the totalitarian one a focus on the distinctive communist institutions that foster organized political control." I would argue that what he called "organized dependence" is in fact a variant of the totalitarianism model. The

[21] Deng Xiaoping's first downfall in his political career was in the 1930s (Evans 1995:64-65).

[22] The poem was translated in Black and Munro (1993:24).

[23] According to Li Zhisui (1994:631-636), Hua Guofeng and Wang Dongxing had long wanted to arrest Jiang Qing, but they waited for the right moment. After the death of Mao, together with Marshall Ye Jianying, they took action. Li's book provides an insider account of the arrest of the "Gang of Four".

[24] The editorial, in fact, was an elaboration of Deng's speech in the Theoretical Work Conference on 31 March 1979.

[25] It was said that when a friend recommended that Wei tried to arrange an audience with Deng Xiaoping, Wei snapped back, "Why? He has no legal status to talk to me, he wasn't elected by the people" (Black and Munro 1993:50).

[26] Black and Munro (1993) portray the rise and fall of the "Beijing Spring" democracy movement, in particular from the democratic activists' point of view.

[27] I would call the political structural reform programmes introduced by Deng as a kind of "democracy movement" in an official sense. It has often been argued that the difference between the Chinese model of reform and the Soviet one was that Deng launched economic reform without simultaneously launching political reform (Shirk 1993; Overholt 1993). This is obviously not true. As I shall argue in this book, there have been genuine political structural reform programmes during the Dengist era especially in the early 1980s. Limited by structural constraints, Deng was cautious to see that these measures did not lead to a multi-party system. For more details, see chapter 3.

[28] There are different estimates of the number of people starved to death in the GLF. The figures range from 15 million to 43 million (Southerland 1994). Despite the problems of the accuracy of the statistics, the official figures point to a demographic disaster during 1959 to 1960 (ZTN 1983:103).

[29] Due to the lack of accurate statistics, the number of victims who died in the CR is still unknown. Hu Yaobang, the former CCP general secretary, openly admitted that one million people died in the factional fightings (Southerland 1994). According to one Chinese author, Zheng Yi, cannibalism was openly practised in Guangxi Province in the CR and "thousands participated in the cannibalism and at least many hundreds were eaten" (Mirsky 1995).

[30] On 7 February 1977, the *People's Daily*, *Red Flag* and *Liberation Army Daily* published a joint editorial entitled "Learn the documents and grasp the key link". The editorial said that "Whatever Chairman Mao's decision, we must resolutely uphold it; whatever Chairman Mao's instruction, we must consistently obey". Hua and his lieutenants were later labelled as "whateverists" (Deng Xiaoping 1983:35-36).

[31]For that I have some personal experience. At the end of 1971 when I was a university student, I went to Shanghai to visit my aunt. Her room was too small and she asked one of her young neighbours to accommodate me. That night we slept on the same bed. Later my aunt told me that he reported, after that night, to the public security office immediately what I said during the night. Fortunately, having sensed the tense mood in the city, I was reluctant to chat. On the way in Guangzhou, I bought four volumes of Mao's selected works. I was considered a "progressive" young man by the public security men and I returned to Hong Kong safely.

[32]Kristof and Wudunn (1994:94-98) recounted a case of how the power of the residence committee can determine the life and death of a person. China was bidding for the hosting of the Olympics 2000 and the International Olympic Committee prepared an inspection tour of Beijing on 7 March 1993. Two days before the inspection, in an alley at the southern part of Beijing, Zhang Guiying, a deputy head of the street committee, came to the house of Wang Choru, a forty-one-year-old slightly retarded man, with a policeman. They had no arrest/detention warrant and wanted to take him away. Wang had committed no offence, but the authorities considered the fact that Wang might cause embarrassment in case the Olympic inspectors whizzed by their alley by car. They took Wang by force. The next day the policemen came to Wang's parents, telling them their son was dead. No reason was given. On the day of cremation, they were given 5000 yuan compensation.

[33]A moving account of how one was persecuted in the CR is in Cheng Nien's book (1986). Cheng was kept in solitary confinement for six years by the Chinese authorities. Only after her release in 1974 did she know that her daughter had jumped from a building and died instantly.

CHAPTER THREE

RESTRUCTURING THE PARTY/STATE POLITY IN THE 1980s

This chapter deals with the political structural reform policies introduced or initiated by the reformists within the CCP starting in the late 1970s until the 4 June brutal crackdown in 1989. Without going into details about the political structural reform process which will be discussed in the fourth chapter, I shall discuss, first, the evolution of the notion of political structural reform in the first half of the 1980s within the CCP ruling elite. [1] Second, I shall discuss the rationale behind the political structural reform as perceived by the Party reformists headed by Deng Xiaoping. On this I shall be brief, as chapter 2 has been devoted to the discussion. Third, I shall delineate the substance of the political structural reform policies and the implications of these policies on the socio-political arenas. Finally, the limitations of these reform measures will be analysed. The reform measures will be broadly categorized into five areas that will become the focus of this chapter: a) democratizing the Party/state apparatus and political process; b) arranging for smooth succession; c) streamlining the Party/state bureaucracy; d) strengthening the NPC; e) liberalizing intellectual life.

The Notion of the Political Structural Reform

The Third Plenum of the Eleventh CC was a turning point in the history of the PRC. It marked the prevalence of Deng Xiaoping's politics of modernization. With the death of Mao and the collapse of the radical clique in the Party in 1976, China was geared towards a new era. Deng himself was rehabilitated for the third time in 1977. Hua Guofeng was briefly at the helm. From his rehabilitation to the opening of the Third Plenum at the end of 1978, Deng was able to manoeuvre to corrode the power base of Hua Guofeng. By the time the Third Plenum was held, though Hua still occupied the three key posts in the Party/state, namely chairman of the CCP, chairman of the CCP Central Military Commission (CMC), and state premier, his capacity to shape the political agenda of the Party had drastically diminished.

The communique of the Third Plenum endorsed the decision of shifting the focus of the CCP work to socialist modernization. The Plenum called on

> the whole Party, the army and the people of all nationalities to work with one heart and one mind, enhance political stability and unity, mobilize themselves....pool their wisdom and efforts and carry out the new Long March to make China a modern, powerful socialist country before the end of this century (ZZWY 1987:5).

The Plenum discussed the need to free one's mind from *benben zhuyi* (dogmatism or fundamentalism), to seek truth from facts and to correct the erroneous Party decisions made in the CR. It urged the whole Party to implement the genuine system of "democratic centralism", so that open discussions on important issues between Party senior cadres and the rank-and-file would become possible. In the areas of economic and industrial management, the Plenum criticised the phenomena of bureaucratism and the overlapping roles of the Party cadres and government officials. Subsequently, these suggestions were incorporated, two years later, into the political structural reform package enunciated by Deng to be implemented in the 1980s.

However, the term political structural reform was not mentioned in the Third Plenum and the communique used the term *shangceng jianzhu de gaige* (reform in the superstructure) (ZZWY 1987:4). The CCP at that time was still in the shackles of Maoist ideocracy. Marxist and Maoist terminology still dominated political discussions. Soon afterwards, the CCP shifted to a more precise term that denoted the wide-ranging issues that popped up in the reform process. The term *gaige he wanshan shehui zhuyi zhengzhi zhidu* (reform and perfecting socialist political system) was used on different occasions by Ye Jianying (1979), Hu Yaobang (1981), and Deng Xiaoping (1983:180). In his seminal speech on the political structural reform in August 1980 (Deng Xiaoping 1984:302-325), which was widely regarded as the most comprehensive political reform blueprint in the 1980s, Deng used the term *gaige dang he guojia lingdao zhidu* (reform of the Party and state leadership system). In a speech addressing the issues of reform on a forum of the CCP Central Military Commission in 1982, Deng used another term to denote the sweeping reform process that was going on at that time. The term he used was *tizhi gaige* (structural reform) (Deng Xiaoping 1984:386). In an important speech on Labour Day in 1985, Hu Qili, then a member of the Standing Committee (SC) of the CCP Politburo, used a more comprehensive term *zhengzhi gaige* (political reform) (Li Yongchun, Si Yuanqin, and Guo Xiuzhi 1987:6). It was not until the second half of 1986 that the CCP gradually converged on the usage of the term *zhengzhi tizhi gaige* (political structural reform). In a series of meetings with foreign dignitaries in 1986, Deng (1993:176-180) was the first senior leader who raised the notion of political structural reform. From then on, the whole CCP leadership adopted the same term in all the official announcements and Party documents. Zhao Ziyang's *Government Work Report* in 1987 adopted the term and his political report delivered, in the capacity of the acting general secretary of the CCP, in the Thirteenth CCP Congress devoted a whole section on the "reform in the political structure" (1987b). Li Peng replaced Zhao Ziyang as premier in the First Session of the Seventh National People's Congress (NPC) in 1988. In his first *Government Work Report* (1989), Li Peng used the same term. In his *Government Work Report* in 1990, Li Peng did not discard the term even after the suppression of the pro-democracy movement in 1989, but the political structural reform policies, in the aftermath of colossal shake up of the CCP hierarchy as well as in personnel aspects, had been drastically altered. The term has since been used in major government and Party occasions, but over the past two decades, new substances have been continuously added (Jiang 1992, 1997, 2002; Zhu Rongji 1999, 2000, 2002).

Unlike the economic reform, particularly that in the urban sectors, which lacks a comprehensive plan, the reformists seemed to have a general idea of what the political structural reform covers but they lacked a common term to denote what they had in mind in the late 1970s and early 1980s. The political references have been quite consistent since the Third Plenum of the Eleventh CC. Basically, the scope of political structure reform includes the following aspects: a) to improve the Party and state leadership style; b) to improve the state structure; c) to reform the administrative and management system; d) to reform the cadre personnel management system; e) to democratize political and legal institutions; f) to strengthen the Party/state monitoring mechanisms; g) to democratize the Party's decision-making process (Li Yongchun, Shi

Yuanqin, Guo Xiuzhi 1987:7). In sum, the aim of the political structural reform in the 1980s was to restructure or reorganize the Party/state polity. Even in the 21st centruy, the emphasis of the political structural reform is shifting. Depending on the political situation, but the aims and objectives remain more less the same, that is, to reform the Party/state polity under one Party supremacy.

The Rationale of the Political Structural Reform

As I argued in the second chapter, the Dengists encountered a multiple crisis situation after the death of Mao and the downfall of the "Gang of Four". The consequence of the participation, distribution and penetration crises was the serious erosion of legitimacy for the CCP Party/state. More than once Deng (1983:352) said that without reform, the CCP and PRC would have perished. The economic and political reforms were aimed at rescuing the Party from becoming irrelevant to national political life, to prevent the country from disintegration, and to enhance the prestige and the governing capacities of the Party, thereby restoring the authority or legitimacy of the Party/state. This is the CCP's "self-rejuvenating" thesis which basically argues that the introduction of political reform is to strengthen and improve the socialist political system. This is a view that was prevalent at the beginning of the reform era. However, as economic reform deepened, the CCP leadership increasingly adopted an 'utilitarian' point, which saw political structural reform as a means to an end, i.e. economic reform. Alternatively, the ultimate value of the political structural reform lies in the facilitation or promotion of economic reform. This view has dominated the CCP leadership since the Tiananmen crackdown. Hu Angang, one of the active members of the think-tank of the CCP leadership, stated very clearly on this view, "China takes reform, including political reform, as one of the means for development. Any measure that can facilitate development, we'll do it; any measure that can not facilitate development, we'll be cautious....we are for quickening economic reform and social progress....Political democratization is not the same as political reform....Political reform may not be starting from political democratization, it can start from the political decision making apparatus"(1999b).

There is third thesis that argues for the necessity or inevitability of the political reform. The "economic-reform-induced" thesis argues that as economic reform deepens, the complementary political reform must proceed in tandem. Nonetheless, the thesis recognizes the political structural reform as an end in itself. On the contrary, according to this view, economic reform serves to facilitate political structural reform. The aims of the political structural reform are the protection of human rights and democratization of the political system. This view is shared widely by both Western and Chinese academics on Chinese politics (An Chen 1999;Chen Ziming 1992; Gordon White 1993a; Harding 1987; Li Shengping 1989; Su Shaozhi 1982; Wong Yiu-chung 2000b; Yan Jiaqi 1992a; Zhao Suisheng 2000).[2] However, the official media totally reject this view.

After the initial success in the countryside, the economic (distribution) reform was extended to the urban sectors or industrial sectors in 1984 (CCCCP 1984). It was then that the reform process became more complex and necessitated the corresponding restructuring of the Party and government apparatus which had, until then, controlled all the educational institutes, factories, enterprises, production plants and other social organizations. The most authoritative argument of this view was put forward by Zhao Ziyang who was considered to be the chief engineer of China's reform decade before his downfall (Deng Xiaoping was to be the chief architect). He argued (1994):

> In practice, I increasingly feel that the economic reform and political reform should be launched more or less in tandem. If the political reform lags too behind, the economic reform can hardly go on and that would give rise to many socio-political problems. Initially, I thought that if the standard of living for the people is raised, people would be satisfied. Society then would be stable. In their political participatory consciousness would be heightened as well. If the political institutions fail to catch up, society would not be stable.[3]

However, I would argue that these two theses were applicable to different periods of the political structural reform in the 1980s. There were two tides of political structural reform measures from the late 1970s to the end of the 1980s. The 'self-rejuvenating' thesis was the dominant theme in the first tide of the political reform in 1981/82, while the 'utilitarian' thesis was applicable in the second tide of the reform in 1986/87. The third thesis has never been dominated in the reform era. I would argue that for the first tide, Deng's emphasis was on the institutionalization of the CCP political and legal institutions, a reform move that was necessary to prevent the cult of Mao from happening; while the second tide reform was more economics-related, which means the political structural reform measures were envisaged in order to deepen economic reform.[4] This chapter would discuss the policies from a holistic point of view.

The Political Structural Reform Policies

Deng's widely-known speech on the reform of the Party and state leadership in an expanded CCP Politburo meeting in 1980 laid out the causes, problems, and measures of the political reform for the CCP Party/state structure. From 1980 to the Thirteenth CCP Congress in 1987, the reformists attempted to implement the measures outlined in Deng's speech. In his speech, Deng outlined the goals of the political reform and attacked the grave defects of the CCP Party/state polity, probing as well into the causes of these defects. According to Deng (1984:304), the long term goal of the political reform is to realize the superiority of the socialist system and speed up China's modernization. Three objectives must be achieved in order to realize this goal. First, in the economic arena, productive force must be rapidly developed so as to improve the standard of living of the common people. Second, in the political arena, socialist democracy must be practised and the rights of political participation of the people must be protected, thus their rights to manage state affairs are ensured. A political system marked by stability and unity must be created, without which, Deng stressed, four modernizations cannot be materialized. Third, in the organizational arena, a large number of young and energetic cadres must be trained and brought to the key positions in the modernization process.

Deng singled out the problem of bureaucratism for his most scathing remarks. He also heavily criticised the phenomena of over-concentration of power, patrimonialism, nepotism, life tenure system and special privileges of the cadres. In a widely-quoted paragraph, Deng (1984:310) listed the problem of bureaucratism as manifested in the following aspects:

> Standing above the masses, abusing power; divorcing oneself from reality and the masses; indulging in empty talks; sticking to a rigid way of thinking; being hidebound by convention; overstaffing administrative organs; being dilatory, inefficiency and irresponsible; failing to keep one's word; circulating documents endlessly without solving

problems; shifting responsibility to others;....suppressing democracy, deceiving superiors and subordinates, being arbitrary and despotic, practising favouritism, offering bribes, participating in corrupt practice in violation of the law, and so on.

The political structural reform was meant to cure these defects. However, Deng (1984:317) admitted that the problem of bureaucratism was intimately connected with the Party's highly centralized management system, which the CCP regarded as essential in a socialist political and economic system, and the remnant influences of China's traditional highly bureaucratized political structure. The reformists accepted the fact that China's three-thousand-year old feudalist elements still exercised a powerful impact over contemporary China.[5]

Deng (1984:311) also attacked the indiscriminate concentration of political power over the Party committees in the name of strengthening the Party leadership in the past three decades, especially in the era of the CR. Very often the over-concentration of power in the Party committees was turned into personal dictatorship that completely ruined intra-Party democracy and distorted the principle of collective leadership and individual responsibilities. The life tenure system was attributed to the Soviet model of socialist development, and the warring political environment in which the CCP seized power. The first generation of revolutionary veterans were in their 40s and 50s when they established the PRC.[6] They were busy consolidating their power base, and to think of retirement was certainly unrealistic. By the 1960s, the succession crisis began to unfold, and in fact, one of the goals of the CR for Mao was to breed loyal and competent successors to the revolutionary regime he created. He brought into the core of the CCP leadership some of the younger members, such as Wang Hongwen and Yao Wenyuan, who became the vice-chairman and CCP Politburo member respectively. The post-Mao reform dethroned Mao's line and imprisoned his radical supporters. Deng understood entirely that the succession crisis had loomed larger than ever when he returned to power the third time in 1977. One of the key components of his reform initiatives was to resolve the succession crisis and to arrange a smooth transition.

Haunted by the personal experiences of victimization and arbitrary political persecution during the CR, the main thrust of Deng's speech was on the institutionalization of the post-Mao reform. This was shown clearly in Deng's answer to a question posed by the Italian journalist Oriana

Fallaci as how to prevent the repetition of the CR. Deng's definitive answer (1984:330) fell unequivocally onto the restructuring of the Party/state institutions and establishment of a "sound system". Deng (1984:316) argued:

> It is true that the errors we made in the past were partly attributable to the way of thinking and style of work of some leaders. But they were even more attributable to the problems in our organizational and working systems. If the systems are sound, they can place restrains on the actions of bad people; if they are unsound, they may hamper the efforts of good people or indeed, in certain cases, may push them in the wrong direction. Even so great a man as comrade Mao Zedong was influenced to a serious degree by certain unsound systems and institutions, which resulted in grave misfortune for the Party....Stalin gravely damaged socialist legality, doing things....would have been impossible in the Western countries like Britain, France and the United States.

In pointing out that the Western institutionalized polity would not have produced the CR-style disaster, Deng attached a particular importance to the institutionalized factors. As pointed out earlier, the primary focus of the first wave of the political reform in the early 1980s was to establish strong or sound *zhidu* (institution or system) or *zhiduhua* (institutionalization).[7] A wide range of measures were taken in the 1980s, in particular in the early leadership of Hu Yaobang, i.e. before 1983. I shall investigate the measures in the following five aspects:

a)   Democratizing the Party/state Apparatus and Political Process

One of the most important participation reform measures in reducing the power of the CCP and democratizing the political machinery, thereby loosening its grip over the government apparatus, is to separate the functions and responsibilities of the Party cadres and government officials. China has been a one-party dictatorship country since 1949. Despite occasional relaxation of the totalistic control over society in the past five decades, in particular in the post-Mao reform era, the domination of the CCP over domestic politics is not questioned, and indeed can not be challenged. Whether the CCP exercises control in the name of "proletarian dictatorship" as in the CR or "people's dictatorship" as in the

1950s, 1980s and 1990s, is relatively unimportant. The CCP controls the country through the government ideological and coercive apparatus. Therefore, there exist, in fact, "two governments" in the PRC (Li Shengping 1989:32-35). The dual structures exist side-by-side, with the government institutions totally subordinated to the Party machinery. In the tumultuous period of the CR, the two sets of apparatuses were virtually paralysed, with most of the senior party leaders being purged. Mao ruled the whole country and gave his instructions through the PLA and extra-constitutional institutions such as the Central Cultural Revolution Group, headed by Kang Sheng, with his wife Jiang Qing as the deputy. Lin Biao, the defence minister, became the second in command in the Party/state. His successor status was even enshrined in the Party constitution.

Moreover, a PRC government unit or department is subjected to two kinds of leadership in the PRC political system: a higher hierarchical government unit or department and the Party committee of the equivalent rank. Alternatively, the government apparatus is always subordinated to the Party structure (Pu Xingzu 1999). Subsequently, the dual structures have bred bureaucratic confusion, wasteful spending and red tape. In launching the modernization drive, the CCP cannot afford to preserve things as they are. On the one hand, as Deng criticized, the substitution for or replacement of the government functions by the Party has made the government apparatus redundant; on the other hand, the Party leaders have been immersed in running day-to-day affairs, neglecting the general direction of the Party/state. Bureaucratism and inefficiency have blemished the authority of the CCP and have caused the inevitable expansion of bureaucracy (Deng Xiaoping 1984:303-304).

A series of measures were introduced to implement Deng's grand design of the political structural reform. The foremost priority was to separate the functions of the Party/state. The separation of the functions of the Party and government involved several aspects. First, the activities of the CCP members would be placed within the laws of the state. The privileges of the Party members could not be tolerated, and they had to be treated as ordinary people. Alternatively, the CCP members did not have extra-legal power and they had to comply with the state Constitution. The *Certain Regulations about the Political Life Within the Party* passed on the Fifth Plenum of the Eleventh CC in February 1982 specifically stipulated that "Before the Party rules and state law, everyone is equal, the Party will not allow any Party members to go beyond the law and Party rules" (ZZWY 1987:180). Second, in Deng's view (1984:346) it was essential to delimit and clarify the responsibilities and obligations of the

Party officials, so that the Party cadres would not be involved in mundane affairs of daily administration. Instead, they had to concentrate on the planning of the strategic developmental goals of the Party. Deng (1984:323) issued the following directive to the Party:

> From now on, all matters within the competence of the government will be discussed and decided upon and the relevant documents issues, by the State Council and the local governments concerned. The Central Committee and local committees of the Party will no longer issue directives or the decisions in such matters.

Third, the leadership style of the Party cadres had to be changed. The separation of the Party and the government means that the Party cannot exercise direct control over the government apparatus. Only by indirect ways can it assert the leadership of the CCP over the country. Controlling or monopolizing the nominations of the important government posts is one of the mechanisms. Moreover, the reformist leaders called on the Party members to set an example for the people and exercise leadership through examplary influence (Hu Yaobang 1981).[8] The diminishing role of the Party in the government apparatus entails a drastic reduction of Party personnel in the government units, which necessitates the reshuffling of the Party/state cadres. The separation of the Party and government ha been manifested in the cancellation of the Party Committees in various organizations, such as factories, scientific research institutes, education institutes, and enterprises, etc.[9]

Furthermore, the CCP started to decentralize the grip of its total power. The leading cadres of the Party/state were advised not to hold too many concurrent posts, and the number of deputy posts was sharply cut. In the Third Session of the Fifth NPC in 1980, Zhao Ziyang replaced Hua Guofeng, who was occupying three key Party/state posts at the same time, as the premier of the State Council. In the same session, the number of vice-premiers was slashed from 17 to 12. The number of vice-premiers was further reduced to 4 in the First Session of the Sixth NPC in 1983.[10] After 1980, the Party secretary or the first secretary would not hold any government post, thereby changing the tradition of holding the secretary post and administrative head simultaneously. From 1980 to 1983, the reform of separating the Party and the government functionaries reached the level of cities and counties (ZGZXP 1987:281-283). In the political report by Zhao Ziyang (1987b) in the Thirteenth CCP Congress in 1987, the separation of the government and Party functions was still listed as the top priority in the political reform agenda.

To avoid the disaster of the concentration of power in the hands of a few individuals or even in one person as in the Maoist era, the reformist leadership decided to reinstitute the Central Secretariat (CS) under the leadership of the CCP Politburo in the Fifth Plenum of the Eleventh CC in February 1980. Hu Yaobang was elected as the general secretary of the CS. [11] Formally, the Central Secretariat was a working organization responsible for the implementation of the major policies led by the Politburo, the SC of the Politburo in particular. The real objective was to devolve the power of the Standing Committee of the Politburo. It was a rejection of Mao's personal dictatorship in the pre-reform times and one of the ways to build up collective leadership.

To supervise or monitor the activities of the Party members, to regularize the intra-party political life, and to introduce the element of checks and balances, a Central Discipline Inspection Commission (CDIC) was established headed by veteran leader Chen Yun in the Third Plenum of Eleventh CC in 1978. The Commission was seen as a mechanism that could counter the power of the powerful individual Party members including the top leaders. The Commission was led by Chen Yun whose status in the reformist era was second only to Deng Xiaoping, and it turned out to have considerable political clout, for it directly reported to the CCP Central Committee. In its first nationwide conference in 1983, the Commission disclosed the total number of cases investigated for discipline violation committed by the Party members was 380,000 (*Ming Pao* 14 August 1983). In the province of Guangdong alone, over 500 Party officials were expelled from the Party for various economic crimes such as smuggling and embezzlement of public funds (*Ming Pao* 8 August 1983). However, as later events show, the CDIC became a powerful conservative weapon against reformist officials.

Mao had been the chairman of the CCP for thirty-one years (1945-1976) and the post was tainted with charismatic authority. [12] To further sweep away the authoritarian residues left over by the post and secondarily, to drive out Hua Guofeng from the political scene, the reformist leadership abolished the post of the CCP chairmanship altogether in 1982. Instead the post of general secretary of the CS was restored. Before the CR, the general secretary was the administrative head of the CS which was in charge of implementing policy decisions made in the Politburo. Deng was elected as the general secretary of the CS in 1956 and held the post until the outbreak of the CR. Now the post of the Party chairman was abolished and the general secretary became the top leader in the CCP, at least in formal terms, but in reality it was regarded as only the first among equals. Hu Yaobang was again elected the general secretary in the First Plenum of the Twelfth CC in 1982, while Hua Guofeng was downgraded to be a member of the CC. Hu (1982) declared that a system of collective leadership would be built. Policies would be widely consulted before they were implemented. Hu warned that the past mistakes in the CR must not be repeated, for the destruction of intra-party democracy is too costly.

The new state Constitution passed in the Fifth Session of the Fifth NPC in 1982 was the fourth Constitution in the history of the PRC. It was widely claimed to be the most comprehensive and thoughtful one among the four PRC Constitutions (Byron Weng 1984, 1987). A new Party Constitution was also passed at the Twelfth CCP Congress in the same year. Both constitutions contained important new provisions about the Party/state. [13] The 1982 Party Constitution (CCCCP 1982 General Programme) stipulated that the CCP

> leads the people in promoting socialist democracy, perfecting the social legal system....the Party must conduct its activities within the limits permitted by the constitution and the laws of the state.

The new state Constitution was equally emphatic on the predictability of the national political life. It (PRC 1982:Preamble) stipulated:

> The people of all nationalities, all state organs, the armed forces, all political parties and public organizations and all enterprises and undertakings in the country must take the constitution as the basic norm of conduct, and they have the duty to uphold the dignity of the constitution and ensure its implementation.

It further emphasized (Article 5):

> All state organs, the armed forces, all political parties and public organizations and all enterprises and undertakings must abide by the constitution and the law. All acts in violation of the constitution and the law must be looked into.

> No organization or individual may enjoy the privilege of
> being above the constitution and the law.

An editorial in the *People's Daily* (5 December 1982) on the new state Constitution noted explicitly that the term "all" means "there can be no exception whatsoever" and that "our Party, like all other parties, groups, and organizations must conduct its activities within the limits permitted by the constitution and the law".

In one of the most significant moves to restore Party/state legitimacy, the reformist leadership introduced direct elections and multi-candidacy elections to the county level of the People's Congress. The NPC passed the Election Law, the Organic Law of the local People's Congress and the local People's Government in the Second Session of the Fifth NPC in June 1979. The Laws changed the election procedures of the local People's Congress and the structure of the local government. The NPC abolished the administrative structure of the "revolutionary committee" established during the period of the CR. The NPC reinstituted a government structure that was similar to that in the 1950s but new elements were added in the Election Law.

The 1953 Election Law and the 1954 state Constitution (Article 56) set up a four-level hierarchical system of the People's Congress, first, township or commune; second, county (this level does not only include county, but also smaller cities without administrative districts or administrative districts that are divisions of a large city, or some autonomous regions where the majority are ethnic minorities); third, provinces, autonomous regions or cities directly administered by the central government, and finally the NPC. In the 1950s and 1960s (before the CR), only the deputies of the lowest level of the People's Congress were directly elected. The deputies of other levels of the People's Congress were elected by the lower levels of the deputies. The new Election Law and the state Constitution extended direct elections by universal franchise to the county level. The 1980/81 county elections were not only universal popular elections since the outbreak of the CR in 1966, but they, in fact, became the first nation-wide elections above the lowest level of the government units since China became a republic in 1912 (Nathan 1985:196).[14] The directly-elected deputies serve a term of three years, while the indirectly-elected deputies of the NPC and the provinces, autonomous provinces and centrally administered cities serve a term of five years (Pu Xingzu 1999).

The introduction of the multi-candidacy elections, i.e. more candidates than the vacancies to be filled, is also significant in that this gives the electorate at least a degree of freedom of choice. In spite of the pre-election consultations among the members, the fact that nominations were equal to the number of post to be elected gave the voters no choice at all.[15] There were other important changes besides the introduction of the county-level direct elections and competitive elections. First, the new Election and Organic Laws guarantee the use of secret ballot throughout the country, while previously secret ballot was used only in the elections of the urban areas. In rural areas, the voters cast their votes simply by a show of hands. Second, the new Laws reaffirm the right of the deputies to query the executive branch and submit motions to the Congress. Third, the new Laws reaffirm the rights of citizens to nominate candidates for the deputy positions at the county level, while in the previous decade, the Party totally controlled the nomination list. The new Laws were implemented in the 1980/81, 1984, and 1987 elections.[16]

Even more significant was the introduction of competitive elections into the Party structure by secret ballot. According to the new Party Constitution (Article 11), the Party committees at all levels and the delegates to the higher Party levels should be decided by the Party members. Two methods could be used. The first method was to produce a candidate list by a preliminary election and put it into the second round voting. The second method was to suggest a list of candidates that exceed the vacancies and after deliberation, put to it to a vote. Aside from the competitive elections in the Party/state political apparatus, competitive elections were also held in the workplaces, such as production plants, research institutes, and enterprises. The significance of the impact of direct elections could not be minimized and one of the consequences of the direct elections at various work units was the shrinking of political power of the Party/state (Womack 1984).

The reformist CCP leadership also began to lift the veil of secrecy on the decision-making processes and mechanisms (Feng Jian and Zeng Jianhuai 1983). Under the slogans "making decision-making process transparent and scientific", the leadership regularized the NPC and CCP Congresses. The NPC meets every year and beginning in the second half of the 1980s, the meetings usually take place in March. The Party constitution stipulates that the CCP Congress should be convened every five years. Notwithstanding the irregularities of the CC meetings, the dates and the agenda of the meeting were usually announced some weeks before. The communiques were published after the meetings. This was in stark contrast to the practices during the CR. In the name of national security and because of the highly abrupt change of leadership, the official press announced the opening and closing of meetings after meetings were well over.[17]

In a speech addressing the participants of a forum on "soft science", Wan Li (1986), the influential vice-premier, emphasized that to introducing scientific methods into the decision-making process and the democratization of it were a key part of the political structural reform. He criticised that the traditional CCP decision-making process was dictated by personal likes and dislikes of leading cadres. He argued that modern society had become so complex that the decision mechanisms must be rationalized. It was impossible to make decisions based on limited sources of information. Instead, quantitative methods must be utilized. In addition, democratic consultations with those affected by the policy decisions must be carried out. In a stroke reminscient of the critical spirit of the May-Fourth movement, he argued forcefully:

> In a modern society, science and democracy cannot be separated. Without democracy, science cannot develop and vice versa. To facilitate scientific decision-making, we have to democratize the process. Without democratic consultation, people cannot participate in the discussion and without their participation, science cannot develop. Conversely, to democratize the decision-making you must utilize scientific methods.

Moreover, to solve problems arising from economic and political reforms, the reformist leadership, the State Council under Zhao Ziyang in particular, introduced the think-tank system into the central decision-making process. The State Council set up several research institutes in the early 1980s, namely the Centre of Economic Research, the Centre of Technology and Economics, the Centre of Economic Law Research, the Centre of Price Reform, and the Centre of Political Reform that carried out studies on the emergent issues pertaining to the reform. Later the research institutes were reorganized. Zhao Ziyang came to depend on his so-called "three institutes and one association", namely the Research Institute on the Reform of Economic Structure, the Research Institute on Agricultural Development, the Research Institute on International Problems of China International Trade and Investment Corporation, and the Association of the Young Economists in Beijing. Hundreds of academics were co-opted into the process (Feng Jian and Zeng Jianhuai

1983; Li Yongchun and Luo Jian 1987:146-147; Yan Jiaqi 1992a; Zhu Jiamin 1995). To gain expertise in various fields of specialization, famous scientists and economists were invited to give lectures to the CCP top leaders in Zhongnanhai to make them acquainted with the issues in the course of modernization.

b) Arranging for smooth succession

China's *ganbu zhidu* (cadre system) is a nomenklatura system.[18] Strict hierarchical ranking is preserved and privileges are allocated based on ranking and status. Because of the Party/state structure of the PRC, nearly all the *guojia ganbu* (state cadre) are Party members, and in fact only Party members can become senior government officials. The CCP is the largest political organization in the world, in terms of membership. As of 1989, it had a membership about 66 million, a fifteenfold increase over the membership of the early 1950s. It constituted 5% of the whole population in China. (*Ta Kung Pao* 7 November 2002).[19] The system was basically copied from the former Soviet Union. While in the early 1950s, the PRC looked like a coalition government. One of the vice-presidents of the PRC was Soong Chingling, the widow of the late Dr Sun Yat-sen, founder of the Republic of China. Among the cabinet ministers, 42 out of 93 were non CCP members (Pu Xingzu 1999). By the early 1960s, the CCP totally filled up the cadre system. During the CR, the CCP Party/state structure was completely paralysed and the Organization Department of the Central Committee, which was responsible for appointments, promotions, transfers, and removals of the senior cadres, was not even mentioned in the press between 1967 to 1972. Its head was not identified until 1975 (Burns 1987:37).

After the return of Deng in 1977, efforts were made to rehabilitate a large number of veteran leaders purged during the CR. As head of the CCP Organization Department from 1978 to 1980, Hu Yaobang, withstanding the pressure of the "whateverist" faction, eradicated the radical personnel policies, and made the return of the veterans possible. However, the return of the senior leaders made the succession crisis more serious, as younger radicals fell to disgrace after the CR. As I mentioned before, the first generation veteran revolutionaries were in their 40s or 50s when they seized political power from the Chiang Kai-shek regime in 1949. As Marxist idealists, they were more eager to impose their socialist utopia upon a "semi-feudal" and "semi-colonial" China rather than thinking of institutionalizing or routinizing the Party/state succession procedures.

The CCP leadership became aware of the recruitment problem in the highest echelon of leadership by the late 1950s. When Liu Shaoqi was elected as the president of the PRC in 1959, it was generally assumed that he was groomed to succeed Mao as the top leader of the CCP, notwithstanding the fact their age gap was a mere five years. The outbreak of the CR not only ruined the succession arrangement, but almost destroyed the Party/state apparatus. Liu was condemned as a "GMD spy, traitor, revisionist", and was tortured to death. Instead, Lin Biao, the "mentally unsound" defence minister (Li Zhisui 1994:454), was picked by Mao, and his status of successor was even enshrined in the Party Constitution in the Ninth CCP Congress in 1969. Lin Biao's defection and subsequent death and the ill-health of Zhou Enlai pressured Mao to rehabilitate Deng Xiaoping to run the State Council. After the Tiananmen Incident in 1976, Deng was discredited and Hua Guofeng ascended to the peak of his political power.

During Mao's reign, choosing the successor was always based on doctrinal purity and ideological commitment. A debate on "redness versus expertness" ran through the PRC history. Mao always won and his hostilities towards intellectuals were well-known. The intellectuals were always the objects of purge in the numerous political campaigns culminating in the CR. Writing in 1972, Leys (1978:118-119) pinpointed the seriousness of the problem:

> The regime is a gerontocracy: of the twenty men who ruled China in 1972, half were very old men-two nearly ninety, two past eighty, six past or nearly seventy; and in that small group of patriarchs, three or four were senile or chronic invalids. Since the regime knows no retirements or age limit for its higher personnel, there is no honourable and decent choice between absolute power and total disgrace, which explains the keenness and energy with which decrepit disabled gouty old men cling to their seats in the Politburo.

When the CCP reformist leadership launched the modernization programme in 1978, they were confronted with three kinds of problems in the management of the cadre system. The first was the overage of the Party cadres at all levels of the hierarchy, in particular the top leadership. The collapse of the radical policies and the rehabilitation of the purged senior leaders made the return of thousands of the middle-ranking cadres possible. The second problem was the lack of expertise and ability in economic development. During Mao's era, "politics takes command". People learning skills and reading books were very often accused of being "revisionist" or even "counter-revolutionary". The Party cadres were totally unprepared for the advent of a new era which emphasized knowledge, expertise, and administrative abilities.

According to one source (Li Yongchun and Luo Jian 1987:101), among the 20 million Party cadres in 1983, the college-educated only accounted for 19%. 40% of the cadres were below the level of junior middle school. As of 1982, among the 4,000 county Party secretaries, college-educated cadres accounted for only 4% and 69% were below the level of junior middle school. As Deng (1984:213-214) emphasized again and again, "The line and principles adopted for the modernization programme are correct, but the problem-and it is a serious one-is a lack of trained personnel necessary to carry them out....Without a great many qualified people, we will not achieve our goal." The third problem, comparatively easier to tackle, was the problem of eliminating Maoist remnants and followers of Hua's "whateverist" faction. Hua and his followers were phased out in two years and, paradoxically, the resolution of this problem aggravated the first and second problems, as a large pool of pre-CR cadres were restored to their former positions.

Selecting younger and politically reliable successors became one of the key components of Deng's political structural reform package. He was aware that the pre-reform cadre system was detrimental to the resolution of the recruitment and succession crises. He (1984:309) attacked strongly that

> The problem facing us is that....the existing organizational
> system also works against the selection and use of the trained
> persons who are so badly needed for China's modernizations.
> We hope that Party committees and organizational
> departments at all levels will make major changes in this area,
> resolutely emancipate their minds, overcome all obstacles,
> break with old conventions and have the courage to reform
> outmoded organizations and personnel.

In a speech commemorating the thirtieth anniversary of the establishment of the PRC, Ye Jianying (1979) stated the three criteria for choosing political successors at all levels. First, they must support wholeheartedly modernization and the reformist political line and policies. Second, they must be selfless, obedient to the Party rules and state laws. Third, they must have a strong sense of responsibility and outstanding administrative abilities. Chen Yun (ZZWY 1987:289) proposed that the leading cadres must combine the qualities of socialist commitment and administrative abilities. But it was Deng (1984:308,396) who laid out the four authoritative criteria, namely *geminghua, nianqinghua, zhishihua, and zhuanyehua* (upholding the hegemony of the CCP leadership and the socialist road, younger in average age, better educated, and professionally more competent).

Hu Yaobang incorporated the criteria into the political report he delivered in the Twelfth CCP Congress in 1982. The four criteria were written into the new Party Constitution (Article 34). In line with the spirit of the political structural reform in the early 1980s, Deng (1984:219) further called for the institutionalization of the selection process and mechanisms without which, he claimed, a complete solution to the problem was impossible.

Two pieces of significant policy in the cadre management system were the introduction of the mandatory retirement system and fixed term tenure for the Party/state senior leaders. The Party Constitution (Article 37) stipulated explicitly that the cadres, whether democratically elected or appointed, would not have a life-tenure job. If the old cadres were unfit for work, they should retire or *lixiu* (leave and rest at home). The 1982 state Constitution restricted the following posts to at most two consecutive terms, i.e. ten years: chairman and vice chairmen of the SC of the NPC (SCNPC), the president and vice-presidents of the PRC, the premier and vice-premiers, state councillors, the president of the Supreme People's Court, and the procurator-general of the Supreme People's Procuratorates.[20]

The CCP passed a *Decision Concerning the System of the Retirement for the Old Cadres* in 1982. The *Decision* stipulated that senior cadres holding cabinet ministerial and vice-ministerial posts, Party secretary and deputy secretary posts, governorship and vice governorship in the provinces and autonomous areas, leading cadres of the Supreme People's Court and Supreme People's Procuratorates should not exceed 65 years of age. Those holding assistant posts should not exceed 60 years of age (ZZWY 1987:414). "when we have regulations explicitly stating the retirement age for cadres of different levels and departments, everyone will know when he is supposed to retire." (Deng Xiaoping 1984:219) To mollify the old cadres, a Central Advisory Commission (CAC) was established, together with the provincial levels of the Advisory Commission.[21] The Party Constitution (Article 22) stipulated that the

Commission served "as political assistant and consultant to the Central Committee." The membership was limited to senior cadres who have at least forty years of Party experience. Their status would be the same as the Central Committee members and they could attend the Central Committee meetings. The vice-directors and the SC members could even attend the CCP Politburo meetings. Their salaries and privileges would be kept, including superior housing, cars, drivers and access to the best hospitals and food stores.[22]

The reformist leadership decided to devise a three-echelon strategy in order to quicken the process of age rejuvenation. At every level of Party leadership, the core group was instructed to be composed of cadres from three age cohorts, roughly in their 40s, 50s, and 60s. The leaders exhorted breaking the old habits of sticking to seniority, urging talented young people be promoted regardless of their family background.[23] From 1982 to 1985, 469 thousand younger cadres were recruited to the leadership positions of the county departmental level, and 1.25 million old cadres resigned. One hundred and thirty one senior cadres resigned from the CC, CAC, and the CDIC at the CCP national conference in 1985 (*People's Daily* 9 February 1986). The average age of the leading cadres in the provinces, municipal, and county was lowered from 62, 56, and 49 in 1982 to 53, 49, and 44 respectively in 1985. The college-educated cadres reached 62%, 55%, and 54% in the provinces, municipal and county respectively in 1985, up 45% on average from 1982 (*People's Daily* 26 June 1986). An organizational reshuffle at the ministerial and provincial levels in 1984/85 succeeded in lowering the average age from 61.5 and 57 to 56.5 and 53 respectively (Li Shengping 1989:143).

An analysis of the Central Committee membership in the Eleventh, Twelfth, and Thirteenth CCP Congresses, which cover eleven years, underlines the tremendous personnel transformation in the PRC in the 1980s. The following tables (3.1 to 3.5) show the average age, education level, and ratio of specialists of the CC members and the CCP Politburo members (all tables are taken from Li Cheng and Lynn White 1988).

Table 3.1
Average Age of CC Members

CC	Year held	Average Age
11th	1977	64.6
12th	1982	62
13th	1987	55.2

Table 3.2
Average Age of the CCP Leadership Core

Level	12th	13th
SC of The Politburo	73.75	63.6
Politburo	71.8	64
Secretariat	63.7	56.2

Table 3.3
Percentage of College Educated in CC

CC	Percentage
11th	25.7
12th	55.4
13th	73.3

Table 3.4
Percentage of Specialists in CC

CC	Number	Percentage
11th	9	2.7
12th	59	17
13th	57	20

Table 3.5
Change in Educational Level of Poliburo Member

Level	11th	12th	13th
None	4(15.4%)	3(10.7%)	0(0%)
Pri.school	5(19.2%)	10(35.7%)	0(0%)
Middle school	6(23.0%)	3(10.7%)	5(27.7%)
Military school	5(19.2%)	3(10.7%)	1(5.6%)
College	6(23.0%)	9(32.1%)	12(66.6%)
Total	26(100%)	28(100%)	18(100%)

The average age of the CC members was reduced from 64.6 in the Eleventh Congress to 55.2 in the Thirteenth Congress, a reduction of 9 years. The average age of the Politburo members was lowered from 71.8 in the Twelfth Congress to 64 in the Thirteenth Congress. The percentage of the college-educated CC members was raised from 25.7 in the Eleventh Congress to 73.3 in the Thirteenth Congress. The ratio more than tripled. With hindsight, the Twelfth CCP Congress was perhaps the most important one among the three CCP Congresses held in 1977, 1982, and 1987. Certainly, it had transitional characters. Basically, it rectified the reform measures initiated and implemented since the Third Plenum of the Eleventh CC in 1978. In view of the emergent issues, it intensified the reform process and introduced new points of departure. The Eleventh CCP Congress in 1977 was still dominated by Maoist remnants and Mao's theory of the continued revolution under the dictatorship of the proletariat was still unchallenged. In fact, Hua Guofeng's chairmanship of the CCP was not confirmed until that Congress. In the five years between the Eleventh and Twelfth CCP Congresses, China had undergone a "second revolution", in which the radical policies were completely overhauled, and Mao Zedong Thought was subject to new interpretation. Politics of modernization took precedence. Most importantly, the Twelfth CCP Congress was used by Dengist reformers "to begin the replacement of the revolutionary elite generation by the technocratic elite generation" (Mills 1983:19). It was really a replacement from "mobilizers to managers" (Li Cheng and Lynn White 1988:371). As Lee Hong Yung (1991:284-285) argued

> The bureaucratic reforms succeeded in replacing the revolutionary cadres with bureaucratic technocrats who are qualitatively different from their predecessors in terms of political experience, socialization, and value orientation. This rise of technical experts marks an end to the Maoist era associated with the former revolutionaries.... It also signals an end to the Maoist practice of selecting political leaders for their revolutionary potential rather than for the expertise needed to develop a modern society.

Admittedly, the replacement in 1982 had only a limited impact at the highest level of the CCP leadership. The membership of the SC of the Politburo remained largely in the hands of the septuagenarians and octogenarians. The exclusion of Hua Guofeng from the core of the political power became confirmed and he was demoted to the CC. The old guard such as Li Xiannian, Ye Jianying, Nie Rongzhen, and Xu Xiangqian retained their full membership of the Politburo. The addition of Hu Qiaomu [24] and Yang Shangkun, both of whom were Deng's strong supporters, gave the average age of the Politburo members as 71.8. Astutely, Deng was able to inject new blood into the CS. Six new members were added, including the CCP General Office Director Hu Qili, Hebei first Secretary Chen Pixian, and Minister of Textile Hao Jianxiu, all of whom were former subordinates of Hu Yaobang when he was the first Party Secretary of the Communist Youth League.

The addition of some young members gave the mean age of 63.7. There were 210 full members in the Twelfth CC. 99 were new members and 111 were re-elected from the Eleventh Congress. The change was more dramatic than that at the Tenth and Eleventh Congresses. The Tenth Congress had dropped one-third of the Ninth CC members and the Eleventh Congress 40% of the Tenth CC members. The Twelfth Congress dumped 45% of the Eleventh CC members. In all, over 60% of the Twelfth Congress membership were new (Li Kwok-shing 1990:142-143). The accelerating rate of personnel turnover testified to the tremendous political transition, in particular the generational change in the 1980s in the CCP power hierarchy. The Twelfth CCP Congress was transitional in nature in the sense that the injection of new blood was effected below the highest level—the Politburo, in particular the military leadership. [25] However, the elite transformation indicates the broad trends of change in Chinese society. In analysing the structural change of the Thirteenth CCP Congress, Li Cheng and Lynn White (1988:371) argued that

> The history of the CCP indicates that changes in the leadership composition often reflect broad social, economic, and political changes in the country at large....But more important, (the new Central Committee) represents a new kind of political elite-managers and technocrats-who are qualitatively different from the old revolutionary veterans-mobilizers and ideologues-in terms of political experience, ideological outlook, administrative ability, and value orientation. This elite transformation, which started in the early 1980s and reached its peak in the Thirteenth Party Congress in October 1987 has been part of a wider and more fundamental change, a move from revolution to reform in the Chinese society.

c) Streamlining the Party/state Bureaucracy

The problem of bureaucratism so vociferously criticised by Deng Xiaoping is closely associated with the centralized features of the CCP Party/state bureaucracy. China is the most populous country in the world, with a population of 1.3 billion in the end of 1990s. To exercise control over such a huge population and vast territory, a stalwart government apparatus is required. Two thousand years of centralized despotism makes matters worse. The CCP has established the world's largest bureaucracy since 1949. There were about 8 million state cadres in China in 1958 (Wang, C.F. 1995:145). Burns (1989b:120) estimated that there were 27 million Party and state cadres in China in 1985.[26] Now, the "dual structures" of the Party/state bureaucracy have made the problem of bureaucratism intolerable. When the PRC was founded in 1949, the Administrative Council (later changed to State Council) had only 35 ministries and 4 special committees, namely the Politics and Law Committee, Culture and Education Committee, Finance and Economics Committee, and People's Supervision Committee. The State Council was reorganized in 1954. Four special committees were cancelled and 64 ministries and 8 offices were established (Pu Xingzu 1999). The number of ministries was cut to 60 in 1959, but increased to 79 in 1964. At the time of the CR, it was reduced to 32. From 1977 to 1981, the State Council restored and newly established 48 ministries and offices. The total number of approved establishments in the State Council reached 100 in 1981, the highest in the history of the PRC (Pu Xingzu 1999). From 1979 to 1982, though the number of vice-premiers in State Council decreased from 18 to 13, the number of ministers increased from 83 to 99, and vice-ministers from 800 to 900. The total number of staff in the State Council reached 49,000 (ZGZXP 1987:181).[27]

Deng appealed to the whole Party that the reduction of redundant personnel in the central government and streamlining the Party/state bureaucracy was a matter of upmost importance, even life and death for the CCP. In fact, "it constitutes a revolution" (Deng 1984:374):

> If we don't carry out this revolution but let the old and ailing stand in the way of young people who are energetic and able, not only will the four modernizations fail, but the Party and state will face a mortal trial and perhaps perish.

Deng (1984:375) called for the trimming of five million Party/state cadres in the revamping of the Party/state bureaucracy. The 1982 Party Constitution formally incorporated the four formal criteria for picking successors who must be revolutionary (defined as keeping in line with the politics of modernization since the Third Plenum of the Eleventh CCP Congress), younger in average age, better educated, and professionally more competent (Article 34).

The CCP issued *Certain Principles Concerning the Organizational Make-up at the Provincial Level* in 1982, in which the Party suggested that the organizational structure must comply with the four criteria. It imposed the maximum number of vacancies for the following posts: Party secretary, deputy Party secretaries, Party standing committee members; governor, vice-governors; director, deputy-directors of the provincial Advisory Committee; secretary and deputy-secretaries of the provincial CDI; chairman and vice-chairmen of the provincial People's Congress; chairman and vice-chairmen of the Chinese People's Political Consultative Conference (CPPCC). It stipulated that the number of Party secretary and deputy secretaries should not exceed 4 for small provinces, 5 for normal provinces, and 6 for large provinces or autonomous regions. The number of vice-governors should be within the range of 3 to 5. The number of deputy-directors and standing committee members of the provincial Advisory Committee should be 2 to 3 and 9 to 15 respectively. The number of the deputy-secretaries and standing committee members of the CDI should be 2 to 3 and 7 to 9 respectively. Finally, the number of vice-chairmen of the provincial CPPCC should be 9 to 15 (ZGZXP 1987:278-279).

The streamlining and trimming based on the four criteria went into full force from October 1982 to March 1983. The 100 ministries and offices were cut to 60, and staff reduced by one-third. According to a survey compiled by the 38 ministries and committees, the number of the post of ministers, vice-ministers, directors, deputy-directors were reduced by 67%. The average age for the ministers and directors in the 41 ministries and committees/departments was lowered from 65.7 to 59.5 at the end of 1983. The percentage of college-educated ministers was raised from 38% to 50%. In the CCP directly affiliated working organs, the personnel structure had changed significantly. Based on the statistics on 13 departments and committees, the number of posts for the ministers, vice-ministers, directors, deputy-directors was reduced by 40%. The average age was lowered from 65.9 to 62.8. The college-educated percentage was raised from 43% to 53.5% (ZGZXP 1987:278).

At the provincial level, similar reorganization took place. The number of posts of Party secretaries, deputy secretaries, governors, vice-governors, standing committee members, etc, was reduced by 35%. At the same time, senior cadres holding concurrent Party and government posts were axed by 63.8%. The average age was lowered from 62.2 to 55.5. The number of college-educated cadres rose from 20% to 42%. 71% of the newly promoted leading cadres were college-educated (ZGZXP 1987:280-281). Instructions were issued to the Party leaders at the municipal, county, and town levels, urging them to launch the same reshuffling (ZGZXP 1987:190-191). The leading cadres at the municipal, district, and county levels were reduced by 36%, 29%, and 25% respectively in the 1982/84 reorganization (Lee Hong Yung 1991:255).

Despite the herculean effort by the CCP reformist leadership, the long term effect of the streamlining of bureaucracy remained elusive. By the end of 1986, the number of ministries and committees climbed back to 71. By 1988, the number reached 76 (Li Kwok-shing 1990:274). It looked like China's bureaucracy was caught in what Zhao Ziyang (1987b) described as an endless cycle of "streamlining-swelling-restreamlining-reswelling". In the political report delivered in the Thirteenth CCP Congress in 1987, Zhao Ziyang emphasized that the leadership tried to "work out a plan for restructuring the organs of the central government." Zhao envisaged the establishment of a new civil service system to resolve the problems of bureaucratism and political succession completely. Nonetheless, no sooner had the proposal been put forward than China was plunged into the most serious economic crisis in the reformist era. The leadership turned its attention to readjusting and restructuring economic priorities. In a compromise gesture between the reformists and the conservatives after the dismissal of Hu Yaobang, Li Peng replaced Zhao Ziyang as the premier of the State Council in the First Session of the Seventh NPC in 1988. Then came the brutal crackdown of the pro-democracy movement in 1989. It was not until 1992 that the idea of organizational reform was revived and implemented on an experimental basis. In the political report delivered in the Fourteenth CCP Congress in 1992, Jiang Zemin emphasized that:

> At present the Party/state apparatus are overstaffed and overlapping. Many organs lack efficiency and are detached from the masses. This inhibits the changing of the function of the economic units. The situation must be changed....Organizational reform and streamlining the bureaucracy is an extremely difficult task.

Unless the structural factors are identified and drastic measures taken, the problems of China's bloated bureaucracy will not go away.[28]

d) Strengthening the NPC

The restructuring of the Party/state bureaucracy was in tandem with the reform of the NPC. When asked to describe the basic characteristics of the PRC political system, the standard answer one gets from the CCP leaders is that the system of the people's congress is the basic system of the PRC (Chen Ruisheng 1992:84, Pu Xingzu 1999:66; Jiang Zemin 1991; Zhao Ziyang 1987b;). This standard characterization underscores the importance of the NPC. The NPC is defined as the "highest organ of state power" in the PRC Constitutions (PRC 1954 Article 21; 1978 Article 20; 1982 Article 57). The 1954 Constitution even deemed it the "only legislative authority in the country" (Article 22). Nevertheless, this "highest organ of state power" was reduced to less than a "rubber stamp" in the pre-reform epoch. During the CR, the existence of the NPC became a mere formality and it did not have a session from 1964 to 1975. In its first twenty-four years of establishment, no session was held in thirteen years. During the CR, 60 of the 115 members of the SCNPC were charged with being spies, traitors, counterrevolutionaries, and capitalist roaders (O'Brien 1990:56).

After years of neglect, the CCP reformist leadership began to revive the People's Congress as they embarked on the modernization drive. O'Brien (1990) argued that four motives prompted the CCP leadership to reform the NPC. First, the CCP aimed to enhance popular acceptance through institutionalized legitimacy. The legitimacy problem was particularly acute in the deep crisis of faith and belief in the aftermath of Mao's death. Second, the CCP tried to create a political environment conducive to economic reform. Third, the legislative reform would most probably enhance the efficiency of the bureaucracy, thus strengthening the Party leadership. Fourth, a stronger legislature would guarantee reform and contribute to political stability. Nevertheless, O'Brien missed two essential points. First, as I argue in the beginning of this chapter, the legislative reform is, in fact, a part of the legal modernization programme conceived by the CCP reformist leadership to institutionalize the legal framework left in havoc in the era of the CR. The leadership has stressed over and over again that the state of lawlessness must not recur and *renzhi* (the rule by man) must be abolished. By strengthening the NPC, the leadership set out to regularize national political life.

By reviving and strengthening the NPC, the leadership made political life more predictable. Determined to avoid the past mistakes of over-concentration of power in one person, the legal restraints set by the NPC would set up a checks and balance mechanism, albeit the Chinese way, within the political structure dominated by the CCP. Second, the economic imperative was essential. As China's economic reform spread from rural areas to the urban metropolis area, in particular the establishment of the four SEZs in 1980 and the opening of the 14 cities in the coastal areas in 1984, the shortage of capital became apparent. To attract foreign capital requires a stable legal code. The enormous amount of economic activity necessitates massive legislation in regulating commercial transactions. The revived NPC must bear the responsibility of formulating bills and laws. In fact, the strengthened NPC and its Standing Committee passed eighty-eight laws, amended and revised twenty laws, and made forty-five legal decisions from 1979 to 1989 (O'Brien 1990:158).

The other reform measure concerning the NPC was the enormous formal power vested in its SCNPC by the 1982 new state Constitution that recognizes the "National People's Congress is the highest organ of state power" (Article 57). The 1975 state Constitution (Article 16) qualifying phrase "under the leadership of the Communist Party" was dropped. Also omitted was the statement of Article 2 of both 1975 and 1978 state Constitutions "the Chinese Communist Party is the core of leadership of the whole Chinese people". In formalistic terms, the NPC is the sovereign power of the PRC. It has been given a wide range of powers and functions (PRC 1982 Articles 62-64), especially the SCNPC. In view of the mammoth size of the NPC and the consequent difficulty of convening meetings (the Sixth NPC in 1983 had 2884 deputies and the Seventh in 1988 had 2883 deputies), the SCNPC could easily substitute for the NPC. It is indeed "a legislature within a legislature" (O'Brien 1990:148).

To reform the SCNPC, the size of the SC was reduced from 196 to 155 with the aim of enhancing participatory ratio and convening lengthy plenary meetings (Peng Zhen 1982). In addition, to strengthen the backup support to the SCNPC, six permanent committees were set up, namely Law and Nationalities; Finance and Economics; Education, Science, culture and Public Health; Foreign Affairs; and Overseas Chinese. In 1988, a new Internal Judiciary Committee was established. These Committees have enormous power and authority to investigate or study any issues that fall under the scope of jurisdiction of the SCNPC. In the second half of the 1980s, the membership of the Committees increased from about a dozen to a range of 17 to 30. By 1990, 80% of the members of the SCNPC served on the Committees (Chen Ruisheng 1992:48).

Furthermore, the members of the SCNPC were prohibited to hold full-time state administrative posts to allow them more time for legislative activities.[29] A chairmanship core composed of the SCNPC chairman, vice chairmen, and secretary general was set up. With a membership of about 20 to 25 people, the group could have more flexibility in holding long meetings. To delegate more legislative power to the regions, the SC (PRC 1982 Article 96) in the provincial and county People's Congress was established. Subsequently, the power of legislation at the provincial and county levels vis-a-vis the NPC was enhanced. The supervisory function over the local people's government was also strengthened (Li Yongchun and Luo Jian 1987:129; Pu Xingzu 1999).

The introduction of competitive elections, both in direct and indirect elections at the provincial and county levels improved the deputies' quality markedly. At the Sixth NPC in 1983, the percentage of the college-educated deputies was raised to 44.5%, and 41.5% of the deputies were engaged in professional or technical work. 76.5% deputies were new and the average age of these newcomers was 53 at the time of their election. In the Seventh NPC in 1988, 76% of the deputies were under 60, and their average age was less than 53, and 56% were college-educated (O'Brien 1990:132). The improvement, however, was not made at the level of the SCNPC. The average age of the members of the SCNPC was 69.3 years old. Even worse was the case of the vice-chairmen whose average age reached 74. Despite robust health, the SCNPC chairman Peng Zhen was 81 at the time of his election. Fortunately, he retired in 1988 and was replaced by Wan Li, a 72 year old reformist.

To improve the quality of the deputies and gain legitimacy for the NPC as an institution, competitive election to the SCNPC was introduced. In the Sixth NPC in 1983, the CCP still controlled the nomination of the SCNPC and vice-chairmen. In the Seventh NPC in 1988, nevertheless, competitive election, was introduced into the SCNPC. Nine of 144 candidates were eliminated but their names were not revealed. The number of votes received by the elected chairman and vice chairmen were, however, announced. Wan Li, the elected chairman, received 64 against votes and 11 abstention votes. Chen Muhua, a former Politburo member, received 313 against votes and 45 abstentions. The new vice president Wang Zhen received 212 against votes and 77 abstentions votes. Even the elected president of the PRC Yang Shangkun received 124 against votes and 34 abstentions. Li Guixian, one of the state councillors, received as many as 404 against votes and 29 abstentions.[30] The Seventh NPC was regarded as the most open and democratic congress the PRC had ever had.

e) Liberalizing Intellectual Life

Liberalizing intellectual life can be an important measure to ameliorate the penetration crisis. Intellectuals were denounced as "stinking ninth category" in Mao's reign. Famous writers and prestigious academics were often the objects of repeated attacks during numerous political campaigns in the pre-reform period (Ye Yonglie 1992). Many committed suicide and some were tortured to death in the CR. The reformist CCP leadership realized that the success of the four modernizations relied on the contributions of intellectuals. The Dengists set out to redefine the role of the intellectuals in the era of rapid development and gave them a new status in light of the modernization drive. In an attempt to show adherence to Marxist orthodox and rally the intellectuals, Deng quoted Marxist and Leninist classics to argue that scientists and technological personnel were an integral part of the productive force, the promotion of which was now the chief task of the Party. Deng (1984:104) claimed that intellectuals were scholars, not capitalists. The nature and status of the intellectuals depend on whom they serve. "Mental workers who serve socialism are part of the working people" (Deng 1984:105). The intellectuals were thus reclassified as part of the working class. The reinterpretation relieved the intellectuals of their psychological fear that had overwhelmed them since the Anti-Rightists movement in the late 1950s.

In a speech commemorating the centenary of Marx's death, Hu Yaobang (1983) forcefully argued that

> In the new era of modernization, the intellectuals play a particularly important role....The intellectuals are indispensable intellectual factors for modernization. They are the treasures of the whole country....and improving their working and living conditions should be considered as part of the infrastructural construction.

To boost the morale of intellectuals, the leadership introduced a system of professional titles for the intellectuals working in scientific, social sciences, and higher education fields in January 1986. The system was designed to institutionalize and regularize the promotion criteria which now began to emphasize the importance of professional competence and administrative ability. The system was first put into implementation on a trial basis in the Academies of Science and Social Sciences, State Education Commission and the ministries of agriculture, health, and mineral resources.[31]

Once the ideological straightjacket of Maoism was removed and Mao Zedong Thought was interpreted as a collective effort jointly produced by the whole CCP veteran revolutionaries (CCCCP 1981, 1982), the demise of Maoist ideocracy emboldened the intellectuals to assert their own power. They were eager to expand the realm of intellectual inquiry. Yan Jiaqi, then director of the Institute of Political Science of Chinese Academy of Social Sciences (CASS), publicly argued that "in scientific research, there should not be 'forbidden zones'....Science is a world of three 'withouts': without forbidden zones, without icons, and without final truth" (1988:139). The pursuit of truth and beauty should take precedence over ideological commitment and no doctrine should be exempted from the critical analysis of social scientists. The implication of these messages was that Marxism-Leninism -- the ruling ideology of the CCP -- should not be a forbidden zone of critical intellectual inquiry.

Fang Lizhi, the outspoken vice-president of the University of Science and Technology in Anhui Province before his expulsion from the CCP in early 1987, made the most damaging remarks about the CCP and Marxism-Leninism. In a lecturing tour to several universities, he publicly castrated Marxism, claiming Marxism had already been obsolete (1987:3). Engels' book on natural dialectics could no longer become the guide of scientific research (1987:95). He argued that no socialist state in the post-World War II period had been successful. "I am here to tell you that the socialist movement, from Marx and Lenin to Stalin and Mao Zedong, has been a failure....Complete Westernization is the only way to modernize" (1987:183-4).[32] Jin Guantao, a research fellow at the CASS, argued that socialist practice in China faced a tragic dilemma and socialist practice met with total failure (Jin Guantao and Liu Qingfeng 1990:22). Su Shaozhi (1988; 1992), then director of CASS's Institute of Marxism, Leninism, and Mao Zedong Thought, called for the re-conceptualization and re-evaluation of socialism, Marxism, and capitalism. The productive force of advanced capitalism, he claimed, in fact, was far superior to that of the state socialist countries. Yu Haocheng vehemently criticised the grave defects in China's legal system such as the privileges of the senior cadres and the massive abuse of power among the leaders (*Cheng Ming* September 1985:50-51). Wang Ruowang criticised that the devising of the so-called third-echelon strategy was similar to the succession arrangement in feudal dynasties (*Cheng Ming* December 1985:6-7). Li Honglin (1986) emphasized that without a highly democratized polity, socialist modernization could not be accomplished.

A young scholar Ma Ding (pen name) published an article entitled "The Ten Changes in the Research of Economics in Contemporary China" in *Gongren Ribao* (*Worker Daily*) on 2 November 1985. He argued that Marx's *Capital* could not provide answers to the problems of economic development in China nowadays. He urged the application of Western economic methods to the study of China's economic problems. Another young scholar Deng Weizhi was even bolder than Ma Ding and he pointed out bluntly that Marxism had been invalidated by the development of contemporary China (*People's Daily* 14 March 1986). Hu Sheng, president of the CASS, conceded that scholars should have the right to publish works that did not employ Marxist method of analysis. He even admitted that some of these works were beneficial to the people (*Cheng Ming* June 1986:9). In an article called "Theory and Practice" by a special commentator in the *People's Daily* on 7 December 1984, the author boldly charged that Marxism could not solve the problems of China's development, since the works by Marx and Engels had been written a hundred years ago.[33]

The new liberal Party propaganda chief Zhu Houze addressed a conference on the reform of the political structure at the Central Party School in Beijing in July 1986. He reiterated that young cadres should study, clarify, and even absorb relevant Western non-Marxist political thoughts. He urged that Party/state administrators should not intervene in the academic debates (*Cheng Ming* October 1986:20). In responding to Zhu's call, some political theorists began to articulate unorthodox views about political reform. Yan Jiaqi suggested that China should seriously study parliamentary forms of government, and Su Shaozhi even recommended the introduction of political pluralism and multi-party competition (*Cheng Ming* October 1986:29). Yu Guangyuan, a CCP veteran economist, argued that Marx's *Capital* could explain the inevitability of the socialist revolution, but it was certainly inadequate in accounting for socialist modernization (*Cheng Ming* April 1985:25).

Intellectuals engaged in artistic creation were also affected by the outspoken demands of the social scientists. They began to demand "freedom of creative writing". As early as 1979, in the immediate aftermath of the Third Plenum of the Eleventh CC, in an address to the Fourth Congress of Chinese Writers and Artists, Deng (1984:205-206) declared that CCP leadership in artistic circles

> doesn't mean handing out administrative orders and demanding that literature and art serve immediate, short-range political goals. It means understanding the special characteristics of literature and art and the law of their development and creating conditions for them to flourish....It is essential that writers and artists follow their own creative spirit.

Writers and artists were urged to choose their own topics and methods of expression. Deng did not mention the notion of "freedom of creation", and he still insisted on the leadership of the CCP in the literary enclave but in a way different from that in the Maoist era. In a speech to the Fourth Congress of the Chinese Writers' Association in December 1984, Hu Qili (*People's Daily* 30 December 1984), a member of the SC of the CCP Politburo, noted explicitly:

> Creation must be free, that is to say, authors must use their own brains to think and that they must have full liberty in choosing topics, themes and modes of expression....the Party, government and different social organizations must resolutely protect such creative freedom of the writers.

Though Hu still stated that creative writing should serve the cause of socialist modernization and the people, this is the first time since 1949 that one of the top CCP leaders coined the term of "freedom of creative writing". Wang Meng, a liberal author, who became the minister of culture in the Fourth Session of the Sixth NPC in 1986, pointed out that the Party should not engage in particular intellectual controversies but should pay more attention to the financing and maintenance of the cultural institutions (*People's Daily* 13 July 1986). Hu Jiwei, a former editor-in-chief and director of the *People's Daily*, made a similar appeal for creative writing at a meeting of journalists and scholars held in Shanghai in April 1985. Hu in fact was entrusted by the NPC to draft legislation about various issues in journalism, including freedom of the press (*Cheng Ming* May 1985:41). By 1985, intellectuals had experienced the most relaxed political and intellectual atmosphere since 1949. Their support of the CCP reform policies seemed genuine. The social liberalization had gradually established a relatively private realm that was not closely monitored by the CCP Party/state.

However, the intellectual thaw in the mid-1980s did not last long. Obviously the liberal leadership was handcuffed by the conservative forces within the Party. The standpatters were waiting for a chance to strike back. That chance came when the university students started to parade on the streets of Anhui Province and spread to a number of large cities. The student turmoil caused the resignation of Hu Yaobang in early January 1987. Together with Hu, three outspoken critics of the CCP, namely Fang Lizhi, Liu Binyan, and Wang Ruowang, were expelled from the Party, thus arresting the liberalization process of the intellectuals.

The Changing Socio-political Structure

Throughout the 1980s, Deng was the undisputed leader of the CCP. He claimed himself to be the core of the second generation of the CCP leadership since the founding of the PRC. The economic and political structural reforms initiated by him have changed the Chinese Party/state polity significantly. The ideological flavour of the regime has receded. The Party fundamentalists conceded step by step to the reformist pressures and failed to preserve a Maoist orthodox line. The state has become less interfering, thanks to the establishment of an economic sphere that was relatively independent of CCP control. A legal code has emerged and the Party/state began to take the rights of the citizens more seriously. There were lawsuits against local government for pecuniary compensation by common folks in social issues. The economic reform enabled individuals to have opportunities to seek wealth, thus developing personal potentialities. One of the seven aspects of the political structural reform in Zhao Ziyang's political report in the Thirteenth CCP Congress was the establishment of a system of consultative dialogue between the Party/state and societal groups. Accepting the necessity of resolving conflicting interests peacefully, the CCP realized that the economic and political reforms had transformed the social structure of the PRC. Divergent social interest groups have emerged.

Before the suppression of the pro-democracy movement in 1989, China's political scene was the most relaxed and rational-legal in value orientation, especially for intellectuals, since 1949. Many of them were co-opted into the government decision-making mechanisms of the State Council headed by Zhao Ziyang (Zhu Jiamin 1995). The political life of the Party was enlivened as the principle of "democratic centralism" was reinterpreted with more emphasis being put on the democratic aspect. In the Party/state bureaucracy, the removal, transfer, and promotion of the cadres have been more institutionalized and the responsibilities of the Party/state functionaries more clearly defined. However, the basic gist of the political system has remained unchanged. The political system of the Dengist reformist era has been variously characterized as "consultative authoritarianism" (Harding 1987:200), "market Leninism" (Kristoff and WuDunn 1994:431), "Leninism without Marx" (Brugger and Kelly 1990:174), and "market Stalinism" (Gordon White 1993a:50). All of these characterizations convey the same message: soft economics and hard politics.

Despite ten years of political structural reform and Hu-Zhao's determination to restructure the CCP Party/state, the reform definitely has limitations, as shown in the crackdown of Tiananmen pro-democracy movement in 1989. The limitations can be analysed from two perspectives: the personality element and the ideological-political dimension. In terms of life experience, Deng and his peer groups such as Chen Yun, Yang Shangkun, and Peng Zhen, belong to the first generation of leaders of the CCP who had struggled their entire lives in revolutionizing the Chinese state and society. In their view, the socio-political system they built in 1949 had functioned quite effectively for a long period of time and had achieved great success in national prestige until the outbreak of the CR. The system was perverted by the increasingly dictatorial work style of Mao Zedong. To them, the basic system was sound. Obviously, they would not attempt to push reform to such an extent that this basic system would be completely overhauled. The condemnation and rejection of the Western notion of "division of power" was not accidental (Deng 1993:195, 307).

Among the gerontocrats, Deng was perhaps the most liberal.[34] He did see the Stalinist command economy had failed to deliver the goods to the people. The Soviet model of development had become obsolete.[35] The perverted principles of socialism had be reinterpreted and the mistaken policies in the CR corrected, but the fundamentals of the system had to be preserved. Meanwhile, the economic management system must be reformed to keep in line with the modernization drive. This was precisely the position of Deng when he began the "second revolution". Maintaining a precarious balance between the will to uphold the hegemony of the CCP and the determination to modernize the economy, Deng was walking on a tightrope. He was engaged in a "two front" battle. He was neither a leftist nor a rightist. He was both a reformist as well as a conservative. In fact, in a talk with George Schultz, a former Secretary of State of the United States of America, Deng (1993:209) frankly admitted that

> In China, nobody is totally opposed to reform. Some people overseas take me as a reformist; take others as conservatives. I am a reformist; this is correct. If you say upholding the four cardinal principles is conservative, then I am a conservative as well. To be more exact, I am a *shishi qiushi pai* (pragmatist).

In the concluding speech to the Party's Theoretical Work Conference on 30 March 1979, Deng raised the slogan of upholding four cardinal principles, namely the socialist road, the hegemony of the CCP, the dictatorship of people's democracy, and Marxism-Leninism-Mao Zedong Thought. He argued that the upholding of the four cardinal principles was the prerequisites of China's four modernizations. Ideologically, on the one hand, he attacked the "phony, ultra-left socialism" and "feudal fascism" of the "Gang of Four"; on the other, he (1984:172-174) also warned a handful of people who were spreading ideas against the four cardinal principles, and the CCP must "struggle unremittingly against these currents of thoughts." The speech vividly demonstrated Deng's two-front battle: against ultra-leftism and bourgeois liberalization. This inherent instability of Deng's ideological mindset explains why the reform process was moving like a pendulum. This also explains why the reform policies always fell half way. The Maoist remnants in the Party, including Deng himself, constituted structural obstacles to the political reform. Trying to avoid confrontation with the Party conservatives, the reformists conceded whenever strong resistance occurred. As Gordon White (1993a:197) observed, the reform era has created a "struggle between two parties within the Party."[36]

The separation of the Party and government functionaries was easier said than done. According to the reform plan, the Party leaders were supposed to decide the general orientations and directions of the policies. They should only exercise leadership over ideological and political work, not meddle with the daily administration of the government. In reality, it is extremely difficult, if not impossible, to distinguish political work from administrative work. With the principle of the monistic leadership of the CCP enshrined in the state Constitution, there is no guarantee that the Party officials exercise power only over the general direction of the Party and national policies. It is up to cadres to exercise self-restraint not to interfere with state affairs. Besides, the government officials who reject and resist the intervention of the Party cadres could easily be labelled as engaging in "anti-Party" activities.

Furthermore, is it possible for someone to have power and not to use it? The answer is negative. The functioning of Western democracy is based on the assumption that power should not be concentrated in one person or a group of people. There must be checks and balances. "Absolute power corrupts absolutely" as Lord Acton said. The reformist intellectuals realized this and they introduced Western political theories to the Chinese audience gradually (Li Shengping 1989). The separation of the functions of the Party and government has not been ensured by constitutional means; rather it was outlined by the Party and the oscillation of the policies is too just obvious. In addition, in announcing the separation of the Party and government functions, the CCP also called for the strengthening of Party leadership. For the cadres, to strengthen means to control and have more power. The CCP policies, in fact, involved two inherently contradictory elements.

The introduction of the direct elections of the People's Congress at the county level may have improved the quality of the deputies, in terms of educational background and age cohort, but it has had little effect upon the national political system as a whole. In fact, there occurred various kinds of difficulties at the level of implementation. Many middle-level cadres did not comply with the Election Law. Some increased the government representation to more than that allowed by the law. Some failed to provide more candidates than the posts to be filled. Some intervened in the nomination process and some even halted the entire election process in midway (McCormick1990:145-156). [37] The competitive elections were only extended, at the highest level, to the SCNPC and CCP Central Committee. The method of electing the chairman and vice-chairmen of the NPC, the president and the vice-presidents of the PRC, the members of the CS, Politburo, and Standing Committee of the Politburo remains unchanged. The chairmanship of the CCP Central Military Commission and the state CMC has been occupied by the same person and in contrast to other key government posts, the term of service for the chairman of the state Central Military Commission is not stated in the new state Constitution.

The arrangement of the political succession to the top Party post derailed when the two general secretaries Hu Yaobang and Zhao Ziyang were dismissed. In fact, since the founding of the PRC, the succession arrangement has never been solved. Liu Shaoqi and Lin Biao, the two successors anointed by Mao, met with tragic death. Hua Guofeng's reign was short-lived and he became a victim of political and ideological struggles. After his third ascendance to power in the late 1970s, Deng realized the urgency of the problem. He was a 74 year-old man when the Third Plenum of the Eleventh CC was held. Hu and Zhao were staunch reformists and they were Party veterans. Hu had been closely associated with Deng since the 1930s. He became the first secretary of the Communist Youth League in the 1950s. In the course of the CR, he was purged along with Deng. He was first restored to the position of the head of the important CCP Organization Department, a key position that was in charge of all the personnel change in the CCP nomenclatura system. He held the concurrent post of the CCP Propaganda Department in June 1979. Under his leadership, a large number of old guards had been rehabilitated and three million cases of persecution had been reassessed (*People's Daily* 1 June 1989). He was elected the general secretary of the newly reinstituted Central Secretariat in the Fifth Plenum of the Eleventh CC in 1982, becoming therefore the nominal top man in the Party/state structure. It turned out that Deng's support was indispensable. He was accused of being lax in combating bourgeois liberalization and ignoring the four cardinal principles, which culminated in the student demonstrations in 1986. He was forced to resign.

Zhao was less intimate with Deng and his power basis was principally in Guangdong Province where he served as the first Party secretary before and after the CR. He was transferred to Sichuan Province in December 1975, where he started to implement the agricultural responsibility system, together with Wan Li in Anhui Province (Lin Yan 1993). Zhao was so successful in his endeavour that there was a saying circulating in China in the late 1970s, "if you want foodgrain, look for Ziyang." He was picked by Deng and moved to the central government. Zhao replaced Hua Guofeng as the premier of the State Council in the Third Session of the Fifth NPC in 1980. When Hu resigned, Zhao succeeded as the acting general secretary. He was confirmed as the general secretary in the Thirteenth CCP Congress in 1987.[38] Zhao was extremely unwilling to take up the top post. He repeatedly said that it was more appropriate for him to be the premier than the general secretary. In an interview with a Japanese journalist, he prophesied that he would be *zai jie nan tao* (he could not escape the fate of being purged) (*Ta Kung Pao* 28 February 1988).[39] Prophetically, he was charged with splitting the Party in handling the 1989 pro-democracy movement. Zhao (1994) defended his position but to no avail. He was dismissed from all Party/state posts except for his membership in an expanded CCP Politburo meeting in June 1989.[40] The notion of "third echelon" was not mentioned by the official press after 1987.

Despite the attempts at reducing the Party/state personnel in the 1980s, the problem of over-staffing remained serious. As of 1987, only 16% of the Party/state cadres were college-educated (He Bochuan 1988:359). According to the government figures (Chen Ruisheng 1992:101), the administrative expenditure in 1990 was 2.5 times that of 1980. In Gansu Province alone, the number of administrative staff expanded from 200,000 in 1980 to 660,000 in 1990. There were 2 million redundant staff in the county Party/state apparatus over the whole country. In the Central government, the total number of ministries and committees had gone up to 85 in 1992. The State Council was contemplating another round of administrative streamlining in 1993 (Li Peng 1993). Again, the Chinese bureaucracy seemed to fall into the vicious circle of "swelling-streamlining-reswelling-restreamlining". Structural incentives are inherent in the Party/state. Unless the structural elements are identified, the problem of over-expansion will not go away.

In every country, power begets opportunities. In China, political power is monopolized by the CCP which means the monopoly of opportunities or avenues of social mobility. In the reformist period, individuals could seek wealth through self enterprising efforts but the Party/state officials still wield enormous power. In a country permeated by paternalism, neopotism and back-door *guanxi*, the political power of the officials gives them access to special privileges. The loss of political power may mean the loss of everything. The structural incentives in the enlistment of Party/state functionaries are almost unlimited. In the reformist era, the political opportunities have been transformed into economic opportunities (Hu Angang 2001).[41]

The four cardinal principles were asserted in the 1982 state Constitution (Preamble). Among the four principles, Peng Zhen (1982) said that upholding the leadership of the CCP was the most important one. The strengthening of the NPC was construed as a means to contribute to the collective leadership dominated by the CCP. It was not envisaged to become an independent political machinery. This "highest state authority" is under the leadership of the Party. In a political crisis, it was simply cast aside. The case of Hu Jiwei, a former member of the SCNPC, is a case in point. Hu was a liberal and had been an editor-in-chief of the *People's Daily* in the early 1980s. In the debates on "socialist alienation",[42] he was criticised. He was elected as a member of the SCNPC in 1988. In line with the power conferred by the Constitution as a SCNPC member, he called for an emergency meeting to discuss the political situation during the 1989 pro-democracy movement. His appeal was joined by another 56 SCNPC members. After the crackdown, he was criticised for acting improperly and was dismissed from the SCNPC and the vice-directorship of the SCNPC's Education, Science, literacy, and Health Committee in 1993.

    In retrospect, the mid-1980s seemed to be the prime time for the outspoken intellectuals. Many expressed unorthodox views about the political system and Marxism. More importantly, the reformist leadership was sympathetic to their views. Having been classified as part of the working class and an important component of the productive force, intellectuals received more respect. At one time, leading academics were invited to give lectures to the leaders in Zhongnanhai. But the CCP leadership seemed to divide the intellectuals into two types: one technical and technological; the other liberal-humanistic. The leaders were never at ease with the latter. The 1980s saw the interspersing of political campaigns against the liberal-humanistic intellectuals. The campaign criticising Bai Hua, an army writer, was launched in 1981. Then the debates on "socialist alienation" ended as a number of key proponents lost their jobs. Hu Jiwei was one of them. Wang Ruoshui lost his post of deputy editor-in-chief of the *People's Daily*. The anti-bourgeois liberalization movement resulted in the expulsion of Fang Lizhi, Liu Binyan, and Wang Ruowang in 1987. The 1989 crackdown on intellectuals was the most severe one, resulting in the imprisonment of hundreds of intellectuals.

    In sum, ten years of reform have loosened Chinese polity and society considerably. Social liberalization has taken place. Social structure has differentiated and the occupational system has diversified. Popular culture has emerged and the privileges of the leading cadres have been broken to some extent. By the mid-1980s, the combined economic and political reform measures were able to ameliorate the participation, distribution, penetration, and legitimacy crises to some extent.

Notes

[1]It is difficult to distinguish different meanings conveyed by the term "political structural reform". The malleability and subtlety of the Chinese language also allow different interpretations in different contexts even using the same term (Baum 1994:12-14). It is important to take into consideration the overall political context in which the Chinese official announcements are made or the documents are issued. Very often one has to read "beyond the lines" in order to understand the actual references. The term "political structural reform" is a case in point. For Western sinologists, political structural reform always leads to a system of multi-party politics. Anything short of this would be discounted (Overholt 1993; Shirk 1993). But the Chinese reformists consider that any measures changing the Maoist system and facilitating modernization could be called political structural reform. It does not have to lead to pluralistic politics. In fact, nearly all the CCP top leaders, regardless of reformist or conservative, emphasize the inappropriateness of the transplant of the Western Political system to Chinese soil (Deng Xiaoping 1993; Hu Yaobang 1982; Jiang Zemin 1992; Zhao Ziyang 1987b).

[2]The relationship between economic marketization and political democratization is a complicated problem. In our terminology, this is the relationship between distribution and participation. I shall deal with this problem in detail in chapter 5.

[3]The true identity of this speech has not yet been established. The speech is said to have been delivered by Zhao Ziyang in the Fourth Plenum of the Thirteenth CC held on 23/24 June 1989 in defense of his handling of the June 4 pro-democracy movement. The same Plenum stripped Zhao of all his Party posts including the posts of general secretary of the CCP and the first vice-chairman of the CCP Central Military Commission. The Shanghai Party chief Jiang Zemin was elevated to the post of general secretary. Judging from the contents of the speech, I personally believe that it may well have been written by Zhao but it is extremely unlikely that the CCP leadership would let Zhao deliver the speech in a CC meeting, after Zhao was declared to have committed "serious mistakes". A controversy broke out as regarding the author of the speech in Hong Kong after its publication in *Economic Journal* on 4 June 1994 (*Open Magazine* July 1994:15-16).

[4]Though Harding (1987) argued, correctly, that two waves of political structural reform occurred in the 1980s, he failed to distinguish the essential difference between these two waves.

[5]It is interesting to observe the CCP's stance on feudalism and capitalism. In the course of the ten-year reform in the 1980s, the reformists very often took feudalism as an object of attack when they introduced political reform, as Deng's

speech in 1980 and Zhao Ziyang's political report in 1987. In both speeches, feudalistic remnants were attacked and listed as two of the main causes that contributed to the formation of bureaucratism in the CCP Party/structure (the other factor being the war time influence during the 1930s and 1940s). The conservatives' counter-offensives often took the form of attacking "bourgeois liberalization", as in 1983, 1987, and 1989. In Western countries, "left" symbolises the progressive and anti-establishment attitude, while "right" supports the status quo. On the contrary, being a Marxist-Leninist regime, leftists in China struggle to preserve the existing political structure, while rightists try to shake up the system, both economically and politically. Thus, paradoxically, leftist becomes rightist and vice versa. Indeed, the concepts of right and left in politics are as relative as they are in spatial position. About the meaning of "left" and right, see also Tsou Tang (1986:XI-XLI).

[6]The age of the leaders in 1949 was as follows: Mao, 56; Liu Shaoqi, 51; Deng Xiaoping, 45; Zhou Enlai, 51; Zhu De, 63; Chen Yun, 53; Peng Zhen, 47; Ye Jianying, 52 Yang Shangkun, 42; Peng Dehuai, 51; He Long 53; Chen Yi, 48; Lin Biao, 43; Liu Bocheng 57; Li Xiannian, 40. They would have been septuagenarians or octagenarians, if still alive, by the end of the 1970s.

[7]According to modernization theory, institutionalization is defined as "a process by which organizations and procedures acquire value and stability." The level of any political system can be measured by the adaptability, complexity, autonomy, and coherence of the organizations and procedures (Hungtinton 1968:12).

[8]I would argue that separating the Party and government functions is the most important single piece of reform measure in the political structural reform. Since the June 4 and the Fifteenth CCP Congress in 1992, the Jiang Zemin regime, as a step to re-concentrate power, has established a system of so called "cross-office holding" of the Party top officials (Willy Lam 1999 214-218).

[9]The "totalitarian" nature of the CCP regime would be much more concrete if expressed in terms of organizational structure: there is a Party committee in every organization, making major decisions about that organization. Non-Party members are excluded. In Maoist China, the family was perhaps the only institution in which the Party committee did not exist, therefore beyond the direct control of the CCP. To Andrew Walder's "organized dependence" thesis(1986), certainly a great deal of family functions were replaced by the work units.

[10]At the time of his struggles with Hua Guofeng, Deng's reform programme of separating the Party and the government had the objective effect of forcing Hua to give up his crucial posts he inherited from Mao after 1976 and thereby weakening his political basis considerably (MacFarquhar 1993b:326). Hua was replaced by Hu Yaobang and Deng Xiaoping as the chairman of the CCP and the CCP Central Military Commission in the Sixth Plenum of the Eleventh CCP Congress in June 1981.

[11]According to Ruan Ming (1994), after the post of the chairman of the CCP was abolished, Hu became the nominal head of the Party. But his power was circumscribed as he has power to convene a Politburo meeting but cannot host it. This move was to prevent Hu from concentrating too much power.

[12]The much publicized Zunyi Conference in 1935 during the Long March, in fact, only established Mao's leadership in military affairs but not in the Party organization. The expanded Politburo meeting at Zunyi elected Zhang Wentian to be the general secretary, the top post in the Party. Mao was elected as the chairman of the Military Affairs Commission, while the former chairman Zhou Enlai was demoted to the post of deputy chairman. It was only in 1945 that Mao was elected as the chairman of the CCP. However, it must be pointed out that by taking over the chairmanship of the Military Affairs Commission, Mao became the most powerful man in the CCP.

[13]The English translation of both Constitutions is based on *Beijing Review* N.52, 27 December 1982, pp10-52 (state Constitution) and N.38, 20 September 1982, pp8-21 (Party Constitution).

[14]The 1975 state Constitution provided no provisions on the elections of the local People's Congress. The 1978 state Constitution (Article 35) stated that the election of the deputies would be conducted by secret ballots on the principle of universal franchise, but it must be preceded by a process of "democratic consultation" among the voters.

[15]Under the 1979 Election Law the number of candidates for the county-level deputies was to exceed the number of positions by 50% to 100%. In the revisions to the Election Law in 1986, the ratio was reduced to 33% to 100% (Pu Zingsu 1999).

[16]Cheng Zihua, minister of civil affairs at the time of the first county level elections, stated that in the future, direct elections would be extended to higher levels (Womack 1982), But direct elections had been extended only to a few municipalities by the early 1990s. The most dramatic democratization experiment in the 1980s in China took place in Shekou-8.2 sq.km zone inside the Shenzhen SEZ. The entire Shekou administrative committee was popularly elected by the zone's 1200 cadres in 1985. It was the first time that a Chinese executive branch of government was elected by its staff (*The Mirror* November 1986:26-30). It was not a direct election by universal franchise, but its impact spread far beyond its border. By the end of the 1980s, before the 1989 crackdown, Shenzhen was the most advanced city in China, both economically and politically.

[17]The highly irregular pattern of meetings can be seen from the following facts: the Seventh CCP Congress was held in 1945, but the Eighth CCP Congress was held in 1958, and it was held twice in the same year. The Ninth CCP Congress was held in 1969, after an interruption of eleven years. The Tenth CCP

Congress was held in 1975 and the Eleventh CCP Congress in 1977. The NPC was suspended throughout the CR and the deputies were largely purged.

[18]This can be defined as "a list of positions, arranged in order of seniority, including a description of the duties of each office. Its political importance comes from the fact that the Party's nomenklatura--and it alone--contains the most important leading positions in all organized activities of social life" (Burns 1987:36).

[19]By contrast, the membership of the eight so-called democratic parties, as of the late 1990s, was only about 460,000. The eight democratic parties are as follows: the Revolutionary Committee of the Nationalist Party, the Chinese Association for Promoting Democracy, the China Democratic National Construction Association, the Democratic League of China, the Chinese Peasants and Workers Democratic Party, the China Zhi Gong Party, the September 3 Society, and Taiwan Democratic Self-Government League (Pu Xingzu 1999:862-869).

[20]The important omission was the post of the chairman of the CMC (PRC 1982 Article 94). As later events show, the omission was not an oversight. Deng was elected the chairman of the newly created state CMC. The CCP regime "grows from gun barrel". It is understandable that, despite his old age, Deng still clang on to the military power. He resigned in 1989 but his enormous power in the army remained. Emulating Deng, Jiang Zemin kept his CMC chairmanship after the resignation of the general secretary in November 2002.

[21]In 1982, Deng (1984:393) stated that the Central Advisory Commission would be transitional. It was a preliminary step towards abolishing the life-tenure system. The Commission was formally disbanded in the Fourteenth CCP Congress in 1992 (CCCCP 1992:138).

[22]The CAC turned out to be a powerful institution within the CCP, though it was not supposed to be a decision-making body. The amalgamation of so many veterans with so much revolutionary experience exerted tremendous influence over the decision-making process. It was instrumental in forcing Hu Yaobang to resign in early 1987 when the student demonstrations spread throughout the country. It also played an important part in causing Zhao Ziyang's downfall during the 1989 pro-democracy movement.

[23]The most celebrated case in recruiting young people to senior Party rank in the 1980s was Wang Zhaoguo (Cha, 1984). Then Wang was the Party secretary in a factory and he was picked by Deng who was making a tour of the factory. Wang was soon promoted to the CS. He is now a vice-chairman of the SCNPC.

[24]Hu turned out to be a powerful conservative after the Third Plenum of the Eleventh CCP Congress (Ruan Ming 1994; Wu Jiang 1995).

[25]Deng was elected the chairman of the CMC and the three veteran marshals Ye Jianying, Nie Rongzhen, and Xu Xiangqian were elected vice chairmen of the CMC. Ye resigned in 1985 and Nie and Xu in 1987. Deng passed the

chairmanship to Jiang Zemin only at the Fifth Plenum of the Thirteenth CC in November 1989.

[26]In a speech in Shanghai in April 1986, Hu Qili disclosed that the number of cadres had increased from 19 million in 1980 to 26.5 million in 1985 (Li Shengping 1989:146), a figure not too far away from Burns' estimation.

[27] Two small examples will suffice to show how cumbersome Chinese bureaucracy is. First, in a city, the management of a factory decided to build a toilet in the factory. It had to obtain 96 chops of approval from various governments and offices (Chen Ruisheng 1992:191). Second, a municipality wished to build a foodstuff factory. The preparatory committee obtained 427 chops of approval, but still, unfortunately, it did not succeed (He Bochuan 1988:355).

[28]For more details on the trimming of the CCP bureaucracy in the 1990s, see chapter 6.

[29] This legislation was very often ignored. Some members of the SCNPC continued to hold state posts. One of the notable examples is Zhou Nan, former director of the Hong Kong Xinhua News Agency which is a ministerial post. Zhou retired in 1997 after China's resumption of sovereignty over Hong Kong. He was elected a member of SCNPC in the Eighth NPC in 1993.

[30]I would argue that the announcement of the number of votes received by the chairman and vice-chairmen of the NPC, the president and vice-presidents of the PRC could be taken as a breakthrough on the part of Chinese political culture in which old age and seniority are often respected or even awed. The genrontocracy considers the low election votes a public humiliation.

[31]Despite the praise heaped upon the intellectuals, improvement of their living and working conditions remained elusive. The intellectuals still suffered "three heavies and two neglects", namely heavy family burden, heavy responsibility, and heavy pressure at work; inadequate remuneration and meager living condition (*Ming Pao* 6 March 1983). For that, I have again some personal experience. I went to visit Wen Yuankai, one of the boldest reformists at that time, in Shanghai in 1982. Wen was an associate professor in the Department of Biochemistry at the University of Science and Technology in Anhui Province. He was having a vacation of about ten days in Shanghai during the Chinese Lunar New Year. His Shanghai home was a mere 80 sq.ft. room with a double bed, a dinner table, a writing table, a book shelf, with several chairs crammed into one room.

[32]A succinct comparison of the ideas of Fang and Yan on China's political structural reform can be found in Chiou's book (1995:36-51). More details on their ideas, see also chapter 4.

[33]In China's Party/state controlled mass media, usually the article by a special commentator in the *People's Daily* carries special significance. Apparently, the impact of that article was too much for the conservatives to bear. To mollify the

conservatives, the next day, the editorial board retracted the sentence in question, and claimed that it should have read "Marxism-Leninist works could not solve *all* of today's problems".

[34]Even in Yenan period, Deng was the first senior Party leader to advocate the diminution of Party power (Willy Lam 1995:240).

[35] In launching the modernization drive, Deng could not fail to notice the emergence of the East Asian NIEs in China's peripheries. In each of these dragons, market forces play a very important role in their respective economic development (Berger and Hsiao, Michael 1988).

[36]For details of the cyclical nature of the reform process, see chapter 4.

[37]Taking one district from Nanjing as an example, McCormick (1990:130-156) provides an excellent case study on the problems emerging at the implementation level during the direct election at the county level. In fact, the student demonstrations at the end of 1986 started as a protest to the cadre's abuse of power in the nomination stage in the county election (Tsang Wai-yin 1989).

[38]According to Wu Jiang (1995:128-9), Zhao's political orientation was different from Hu Yaobang's. In fact, the political line of "anti-leftist in economic arena, anti-rightist in political-ideological arena" was first proposed by Zhao in 1978 when he was still in Sichuan.

[39]In Chinese, the four characters mean that the misfortune would definitely fall on me. In the political context in which the interview was conducted, what Zhao really meant was that the fate of being purged could not be avoided.

[40]Since 1935, the expanded CCP Politburo meeting has become an extremely important venue in making major Party decisions. Here are some examples. Mao was elected the chairman of the Military Affairs Commission in Zunyi Conference in 1935. The CCP made the decision to establish the People's Commune to accelerate the collectivization process in 1958. Peng Dehuai was purged in 1959. Mao circulated the 5.16 notice, announcing the beginning of the CR in 1966. Deng was dismissed by Mao in 1976. Hua Guofeng agreed to resign from the Party chairman post in 1980. Deng delivered the seminal speech on the political reform in 1980. Finally the resignation of Hu in 1987 and the dismissal of Zhao in 1989. All these important decisions were made in the expanded CCP Politburo meetings. It could be argued that the expanded Politburo meetings could co-opt more non-Politburo members in the discussion process. But it could be argued the other way round, at the time of crisis, very often the formal mechanisms would be brushed aside and non Politburo members could exercise powerful influence over the decisions. The facts testify to the institutional weaknesses and unpredictability of the political process within the CCP and the lack of the Party's formal crisis-resolving mechanisms.

[41]The off-spring of the old veterans have been doing business in Hong Kong and becoming billionaires, for instance, Deng Zhifang, the younger son of Deng Xiaoping; Wan Chongchang, son of Wan Li; Wu Jianchang, son-in-law of

Deng; Chen Weili, daughter of Chen Yun; Ye Xinfu, son of Ye Xuanping, etc. For autobiographical sketches of other princelings, see He Ping and Gao Xin (1995). Similarly, the sons of Jiang Zemin and Li Peng have all became extremely rich men (*SCMP* 10 January 2002).

[42]About the details of the debates, see chapter 4.

CHAPTER FOUR

THE CYCLICAL PROCESS OF POLITICAL STRUCTURAL REFORM

Having analysed the contents of the political structural reform, I shall now proceed to examine the process of political structural reform. The reform process, whether economic or political, seems to be moving like a cycle in the 1980s. The phenomenon has been depicted by many students of Chinese politics (Baum 1993, 1994; Dittmer 1990a; Gold 1990a, 1990b; Harding 1987; Lam Willy 1995; Lieberthal 1995; Ruan Ming 1994; Schell 1994; Tsou Tang 1986).[1] But the precise nature of the cycles has never been fully explored. I shall attempt to analyze the nature of the cyclical process, with a delineation of the exact number of the cycles. Concomitantly, their causes and consequences will be investigated. Finally, the role of Deng Xiaoping and Chen Yun in the 1980s and their relationships to the cyclical process will be examined. It is interesting to see that the cyclical process seemed to have lost its momentum in the 1990s and incidentally, students of Chinese politics suddenly lost their enthusiasm in the concept. The studies on the policy cycles suddenly disappeared overnight.[2]

In the reformist period, the role of Chen Yun is significant in the sense that apparently his power basis was as strong as Deng's and more importantly, his idea of "cage economy" represented a "non-Maoist alternative" as far back as the 1950s (Lardy and Lieberthal 1983). One of the essential political-ideological differences between the Dengist era and the Maoist reign is precisely that Deng, though widely perceived as the "paramount leader" of the CCP, alone could not dictate the CCP political agenda. Their role in the 1980s will be critically examined. What Harding (1987:200) described as "consultative authoritarianism", Gordon White (1993a:20) as "shadow pluralism" and Lieberthal and Oksenberg (1988:169) as "fragmented authoritarianism" points to the fact that there have been at least two more or less equally powerful factional groups within the CCP. Certainly the groups have similarities in preserving the political hegemony of the CCP but their political-ideological gap is almost unbridgeable. In fact, their struggles for the domination of the CCP political agenda in the 1980s could largely account for the cyclical nature of the reform process.[3]

The Nature and Dynamics of the Reform Cycles

The cyclical nature of the reform cycles is not something novel in the Dengist era. Such cycles existed in the 1950s and 1960s. In their classic studies on the relationship between the CCP and the peasantry in the pre-reform period, Skinner and Winckler (1980) argued that a pattern of cyclical interaction marked by a five-stage policy changes occurred in these years. They identified a total of eight cycles of radicalization-deterioration-de-radicalization in policies at the national level from 1949 to 1969.

The cyclical process is marked by the alternating phases of authoritarian control and liberalization. They are characterized by the *fang* (loosening) and *shou* (tightening) of the policies on the part of the CCP. Organizationally, the cycle is made possible by two structural pre-requisites. First, the CCP is still a fairly effective and coherent organization or institution. Since its founding in 1921, the CCP has been a revolutionary Leninist-type political party that emphasizes iron discipline and complete subordination of the individual members to the Party centre (CCCCP 1982). In the Maoist era, discipline of the Party was reinforced by ideological fanaticism and political theocracy. The ceaseless "two-line" struggles within the CCP in the pre-reform era were always engineered by Mao himself. The conflicts between the so-called revolutionary line and the "revisionist line" constituted intra-Party struggles. As I argued in chapter 2, popular resistance to the CCP rule was crushed in the Anti-Rightists movement in 1957.

The onset of the reformist era diluted the complete control of the CCP, and there emerged for the first time since the founding of the PRC semi-autonomous social forces. These semi-autonomous social forces, such as the student movements of 1986/87 and 1989, began to question the governability of the reform CCP leadership. Nevertheless, the CCP remained the only viable political force that could organize and govern China. Its monopoly of political power was still fairly extensive and no other socio-political force was capable of replacing its ruling status. In the course of the economic reform, the limited social mobility and economic opportunities available to individuals and groups have undermined the totalistic control of the Party but its political strength is still formidable.

Second, there has been a lack of sufficiently strong popular resistance to the authority of the CCP. This point is related to the first structural trait, but they are not identical. After 1949, the elimination of the divergent social-political forces was so complete that the CCP remained the only viable political force that could launch "revolution from above".[4] The domination of society by the Party/state was so overwhelming that the budding civil society simply disappeared after 1949.[5] The Dengist reform has seen dramatic social and economic changes such as the reduction in the state's tight control of social and economic activities, the decline of ideology, the development of privatized sectors of the economy, the growth of contractual family farming in the rural areas, the increasing use of market forces in the allocation of goods and services, the emergence of the *nouvel riche*, increased exposure to international influence, incorporation into the world economy, and some degree of political relaxation. All these have produced semi-autonomous societal forces, but still the monopoly of the political power of the CCP could not be challenged. The fact that the CCP could exercise loosening and tightening policies at will indicates that countervailing socio-political forces still have not become a reality. The CCP could change its course of action as it sees appropriate.

In sum, the reform cycle can be defined as the alternating phases of the policy output of the CCP, in which either authoritarian control or liberalization in political-ideological-economic domains was emphasized. The structural postulates must be that, first, the ruling Party must be fairly coherent and consolidated so that the center could command the compliance of the bona fide members and, second, the non-existence of autonomous social forces.[6]

Viewing macroscopically over the reform decade from 1978 to 1989, one could easily observe that there were two kinds of reform cycles: economic and political-ideological. Shirk (Baum 1994:7) and Dittmer (1999:419-422) rightly pinpointed the existence of these two reform cycles but they were wrong to argue that these cycles were essentially "synchronous". Shirk delimited that *fang* (expansion) predominated in 1979-80, 1984, 1986-87, and 1988, while *shou* (contraction) predominated in 1981, 1985-86, 1987, and 1988-89. Dittmer identified three boom and bust economic cycles in the 1980s. The boom years were 1978-80, 1982-85, 1986-88, while the bust years were 1980-81, 1985-86, and 1988-90.[7] Disagreeing with Shirk, Baum (1994:5-9) argued that in fact the economic, political, and ideological trends have not always coincided or co-varied. The pattern of the cyclical flux has been quite irregular and asynchronous. He quoted as one example the fact that the anti-bourgeois-liberalization backlash of spring 1987 in the aftermath of the student demonstration in Chinese colleges was not accompanied by any significant contraction of economic reform measures. I would argue that Shirk's and Dittmer's observation of the pattern of the reform cycles was superficial. On the other hand, Baum argued rightly the non-synchrous nature of economic and political-ideological cycles.

The relationship between economic and political-ideological cycles is complicated. Economic and political-ideological cycles, together with *fang* and *shou,* constitute four variables in the analysis. Logically, the four variables could have four types of arrangement:

> First, economic *fang* and political-ideological *fang*;
> Second, economic *fang* and political-ideological *shou*;
> Third, economic *shou* and political-ideological *fang*;
> Fourth, economic *shou* and political-ideological *shou.*

In fact, all these logical pairs have empirical correspondence in the reform period. The first type occurred in 1979/80 at the time when the CCP put forward a variety of economic and political structural reform measures. The fourth type occurred in 1989/90 in the wake of the crackdown of the pro-democracy movement when the hard-liners, with the support of Deng Xiaoping, purged the reformists inside the Party. Economically, Li Peng's retrenchment program halted the marketization reform and individual enterprises were condemned by the new boss Jiang Zemin. The second type occurred in 1984 and 1992 after Deng's "southern trip". In 1984, the CCP opened 14 cities and passed the *Decision on the Reform of the Economic Structure*, while ideologically the anti-spiritual pollution was in full force. Deng's trip to southern China in early 1992 re-ignited the reform fire, and it was instrumental in effecting the decision to establish a socialist market system by the CCP in the Fourteenth Party Congress in October 1992. The third type occurred in late 1988 when Li Peng's austerity program was in full swing, but Zhao Ziyang was slowly but firmly pushing for administrative reform in the central government and the intellectuals exhibited unprecedented boldness in articulating their criticism of the CCP Party/state.

However, Shirk, Dittmer and Baum, and, indeed, other scholars, such as Harding and Gordon White, have missed the most important characteristics about the reform cycles. My argument is that despite the turns and twists, the economic cycles were basically progressive. That is to say, despite repeated retrenchments over the decade, the cycles moved upward: the Chinese economy became more open and more marketized. The setting up of the Special Economic Zones (SEZs), the opening of hundreds of cities for foreign direct investment, the increasing participation in world trade, the reform of the financial system, the cancellation of the household registration system, the reform of the labour market, and the marketization of hundreds of goods and services – all these culminated in the CCP's avowed claim to establish a socialist market system by the end of this century. The progressive nature of the economic cycles is evident.

Conversely, the political-ideological cycle is, however, regressive. In other words, Deng Xiaoping was more politically reactionary at the end of the 1980s than at the end of the 1970s. In hindsight, as noted in chapter 3, there were two political reform tides in the 1980s, but the basic thrust of the two reform tides was essentially different. The first tide emphasized the institutionalization of the CCP political institutions, with the ultimate goal of establishing a system of socialist democracy. Democracy was taken as a goal (Liao Gailong 1980). The second tide was economics-oriented. By the mid-1980s, the reforms had produced intractable problems, such as *guandao* (official racketeering), inflation, mass psychological insecurity, and widespread bribery. The will to reform the totalistic political organization of the CCP was long forgotten. The ensuing problems engendered during the reform process occupied Deng's mind. His reform attempts were further curtailed by strong resistance from the military and orthodox Marxists within the CCP (Ruan Ming 1994).

Looking back, Deng's speech on the "Party and State Leadership" delivered in 1980 at the expanded CCP Politburo meeting was still the most radical political structural reform package of the 1980s. In dealing with the dissidents outside the Party, Deng was relentless. For example, Wei Jingsheng was imprisoned for fifteen years for allegedly "leaking state secrets" in 1979.[8] Most of the democratic activists in the Beijing spring were rounded up and put into jail. Bai Hua, a writer in the army, was criticized in 1981 for writing a film script in which a controversial statement was cited, "You love your motherland, but does your motherland love you?" The statement was attacked for having an adverse social effect on the audience. It was alleged to have encouraged national nihilism. Bai Hua was criticized, but not penalized. In the anti-spiritual pollution campaign in 1983, Wang Ruoshui and Zhou Yang, two of the most prominent exponents of the "socialist alienation" theory, received different treatment. Zhou was forced to recant in public and Wang was removed from his post as the deputy editor-in-chief of the *People's Daily*. Hu Jiwei, the editor-in-chief, was also removed for publishing articles with politically "incorrect" views in the *People's Daily*.

In the campaign against "bourgeois liberalization" in early 1987, three prominent intellectuals, Fan Lizhi, Liu Binyan, and Wang Ruowang, were expelled from the CCP.[9] The general secretary Hu Yaobang fell to the conservative backlash over the campus revolt at the end of 1986. The line of the victims of Deng's hard-line measures moved upward until it reached the nominal top man in the Party hierarchy. The political suppression culminated in the 4 June bloodbath. As chairman of the CMC, Deng surrounded Beijing with regiments of PLA and suppressed the pro-democracy movement most brutally with tanks and machine guns.[10] Zhao Ziyang was forced to resign and a massive clean-up movement followed. In the political-ideological *fang/shou* cycles, their increasingly oppressive and violent nature was shown. In the economic sphere, with Deng's "southern trip", the hesitant and ambivalent Jiang Zemin decided to side with Deng and hastened economic reform. Political structural reform has never been the focus of the CCP since 1989. Conversely, an iron grip was exercised over the dissidents, and the control over the mass media was unprecedented.

In analyzing the dynamics of the cyclical flux, three elements must be included. First, the role of Deng Xiaoping. Notwithstanding his undisputable position in the CCP, he was not, however, as omnipotent as Mao. Mao was a charismatic leader, while Deng was not. There was a whole generation of veteran revolutionaries who were as experienced as him. I shall deal with this aspect in more detail in the last section of this chapter. The second factor is the factional alignments within the CCP in the post-Mao period. It was commonly agreed that a broad reform coalition united by the victimization experiences of the CR was formed in the struggles against the "whateverists" headed by Hua Guofeng (Baum 1994; Chen Ziming 1992; Harding 1987; Lieberthal 1995; Ruan Ming 1994; Wu Jiang 1995). The split began to show only after the triumph of the reformist political line in the Third Plenum of the Eleventh CC. The third factor is the unforeseen external forces or events that were basically unrelated to the reform process itself, but impinged upon the process and changed its course drastically. Examples are the so-called "self-defence" war against Vietnam, the Polish crisis in 1980/81, the Asian democratization movement in South Korea and the Philippine's "people power" revolution in 1985 and 1986, Gorbachevian reform in the former Soviet Union in 1986/87, the sudden death of Hu Yaobang in 1987, the collapse of Eastern Europe communist regimes in 1989/90, and the dismemberment of the Soviet Union itself in 1991. All these events had far-reaching effects on the evolution of reform cycles in China. This is perhaps one of the reasons that caused the irregularity of the cyclical movement of reform. The relatively peaceful international environment in the 1990s perhaps contributed to the disappearance of the dramatic pendulum-type switching of policies domestically.

The Cyclical Flux

There are significant differences of opinion over the exact number of ideological-political reform cycles in the 1980s. Writing in the early 1980s, Tsou Tang failed to locate the number of cycles in his insightful work (1986), although he had observed and noted the multiphase repetitions of policies in the course of political structural reform within a short period of time. Baum (1993:341) pointed out that there were three complete cycles in the 1980s. However, since his work began at the Twelfth CCP Congress in 1982 and stopped in 1989. Later, he modified the number of cycles from three to six in another work dealing with Chinese politics in Deng's era published in 1994. Writing in 1990, Dittmer (1990a:422) argued that three cycles occurred in the 1980s, and Shirk (Baum 1994:7) argued that there were four. I would argue that both Dittmer and Shirk represented a misreading of the political events in China. For instance, Shirk took 1979-80 as one of the periods that was *fang*. Economically, this might be true, but not political-ideologically. Since Shirk considered that economic and political-ideological cycles were synchronous, her observation overlooked the debate on "practice is the sole criterion of testing truth", which took place between May to December 1978. This was an extremely important debate, for, as Wang Ruoshui claimed, "the debate greatly liberated people's thought, broadening the intellectual horizon, and it laid the ideological foundation for the future reform" (Tao Hai 1989:186).

The debate should certainly be regarded as one of the key events in the *fang* cycle. Dittmer grouped the time from Mao's death in September 1976, to December 1979, as the first cycle of *fang*. He blurred the essential differences between Maoist era and Dengist epoch. Despite the arrest of the "Gang of Four" and its ensuing criticism campaign, the two years before the Third Plenum in December 1978 was still dominated by

Mao's theocracy. Hua Guofeng still adhered to the Maoist line, emphasizing the predominance of class struggles. The focus of the CCP's work still had not shifted from "politics takes command" to economic modernization. The period from the time Mao died to August 1977 when Deng was politically resurrected for the third time could hardly be called a *fang* period.

Paradoxically, The most detailed and largely accurate picture of the cyclical flux of political development was provided by the arch conservative Marxist theoretician Deng Liqun. He deduced a model of cycles from 1978 to 1987. According to his interpretation, the model represented the struggles between revolutionary political line and implicated implicitly that Deng, the new Helmsman, was the instigator of "bourgeois liberalization" (Ruan Ming 1994:171). The following table shows his model:

Table 4.1
Deng Liqun's Cyclical Model from 1978 to 1987

Year/phase	Key events
First round:1978-79	
1978 (*fang*)	"criterion of truth" debate
	Democracy Wall
	Third Plenum of Eleventh CCP Congress
1979 (*shou*)	Wei Jingsheng arrested
	Four cardinal principles
Second round:1980-81	
1980 (*fang*)	Gengshen reform
	Local elections
1981 (*shou*)	Economic readjustment
	Bai Hua criticized
Third round:1982-83	
1982 (*fang*)	Constitution revised
	"Humanism" and "alienation" debate

1983 (*shou*)	Anti-spiritual pollution campaign

Fourth round: 1984-85

1984 (*fang*)	Urban reform and "open cities"
	Cultural and artistic freedom
1985 (*shou*)	Economic retrenchment
	Critique of "bourgeois liberalization"

Fifth round: 1986-87

1986 (*fang*)	Revival of Gengshen reforms
	Student demonstrations
1987 (*shou*)	Hu Yaobang dismissed
	Campaign against "bourgeois liberalization"

Sixth round: 1988-89

1988 (*fang*)	Neo-authoritarianism debate (late 1987)
	administrative reform
1989 (*shou*)	Economic reform frozen (late 1988)
	Tiananmen crackdown

Sources: Ruan Ming 1994:168-171 and the sixth round of cycles is deduced by Baum (1994:6)

Deng Liqun's model serves better than any other models to illustrate the multiple phases in which reform cycles took place. I shall base my analysis principally on Deng's model in this chapter, but, unlike Deng, we must bear in mind the progressive and regressive nature of the economic/ideological-political cycles. According to Deng's model, the proactive pressures for "bourgeois liberalization" were strongest in even-numbered years, while what was called the revolutionary line reasserted itself in odd-numbered years. Deng Xiaoping supported the "bourgeois liberalization" in even-numbered years, and the revolutionary camp in odd-numbered years (Ruan Ming 1994:171).

The First Cycle (1978-79)

It could be argued that the post-Mao reform cycles were a continuation of the Maoist policy cycles.[11] Nevertheless, I would argue that in the late Mao period, it would be difficult to deduce any political-ideological cycles. The visit of the American president Richard Nixon to China in February 1972 marked the turning point in the post-1949 Sino-American relationship. A *fang* occurred in the diplomatic front, but it was not accompanied by similar loosening in domestic policies. It was not until the second political revival of Deng Xiaoping in January 1975 that the domestic policies turned *fang*. Deng began to tackle various problems immediately after his restoration of power, such as strengthening the Party leadership, rectifying the Party's work style, consolidating the army and imposing strict discipline with a view to end the chaotic situation in the railway and industrial production plants (Deng Xiaoping 1984: 11-50).

Meanwhile, the "Gang of Four" controlled the propaganda apparatus with the support of Mao. As the apparachiks knew from the very beginning, the *pi Lin pi Kong* (criticize Lin, criticize Confucius) ideological purification campaign in 1974 was targeted at Zhou Enlai. The "Gang of Four" chose dozens of scholars and experts from Tsinghua University and Beida to set up a writing team using a pseudonym of *Liang Xiao* (two schools) to write articles relating historical analogies to the current political struggles. According to their interpretation, the theme of "two-line" struggles had been running through Chinese history for three thousand years. The reactionary line represented by Confucius and his followers had striven to restore the old order, while the revolutionary line symbolized by the *fajia* (Legalists) was relentless in consolidating the new order. The fierce struggles had persisted until the time of the PRC. The political implication of the campaign was to warn the Party/state officials against reverting to a "revisionist line" represented by Zhou Enlai. Mao stood by the side. Instead of a political-ideological cycle, Mao seemed to be walking in the "middle road" (Tsou Tang 1986:255-256). His middle position was vividly demonstrated when he appointed Hua Guofeng to be the acting premier after Zhou Enlai died in April 1976. The "Gang of Four" was said to be angry with Mao's choice, while others praised Mao's smart move (Li Zhisui 1994:610-611). One did not find cyclical flux, but rather the simultaneous *fang* and *shou*, though in different arenas, all masterminded by Mao alone.

Mao died in October 1976. The Third Plenum of the Tenth CC in August 1977 passed the resolution to restore Deng Xiaoping to his former portfolio: vice-chairman of the CCP, vice-chairman of the CMC, PLA chief of staff and vice-premier. The Eleventh CCP Congress in October 1977 formally pronounced the end of the disastrous ten-year CR. The political report delivered by Hua Guofeng contained the contradictory elements of "class struggles" and economic development. On the one hand, it hailed Mao as the greatest contemporary Marxist, and his theory of the continued revolution under the dictatorship of the proletariat as the " most productive theoretical work" (CCCCP 1977:19) in contemporary Marxism; on the other hand, the people were urged to create order and raise productivity amidst chaos. The report prophesized that socialist modernization would be achieved by the end of this century (CCCCP 1977:7), but the Maoist ideological residues were evident.

The pragmatist faction led by Deng Xiaoping was certainly uncomfortable with this temporary yet contradictory synthesis. The "whateverists" were willing to accept economic modernization as their chief goal, but they saw the Maoist method of rule and mass mobilization through class struggles as correct. The pragmatist camp saw, on the contrary, that Mao's method of governance was basically faulty and that the Maoist theory of continued revolution under socialism was incompatible with the goal of economic modernization. The CR had plunged China into the most profound participation, distribution, penetration, and legitimacy crises since 1949. The reformists believed that only by abandoning the Maoist belief system and mobilizational tactics could the CCP regain popular support and ruling legitimacy.

Thus, the post-Mao coalition under the nominal leadership of Hua Guofeng was inherently unstable.[12] In a joint editorial of *People's Daily*, *Red Flag*, and *Liberation Army Daily*, on 7 February 1977, the two "whatever" instructions were published. Hua reiterated the same policy in the Central Work Conference in March. However, the pressures for Deng's return were so great that Hua was unable to resist. Chen Yun was particularly active in persuading Hua to restore Deng's status. Once the rehabilitation of Deng became formalized in the Eleventh CCP Congress, it became a loophole in the floodgate. Mao personally purged Deng in the wake of the Tiananmen Incident in 1976. Now the verdict was reversed. Once the "taboo" was thrown open and the sacred became secular, the trend could not be stopped. Deng lost no time in attacking Hua's policies. Deng saw Hua as legitimized only by Mao's statement: "With you in charge, I am at ease." An attack on Mao's personality cult inevitably corroded the authority of Hua. By doing so, Deng achieved dual purposes: undercutting Hua's most important source of power and removing ideological constraints on the four modernizations.

The movement of the "emancipation of mind" was needed in order to set free people's minds from Maoist fundamentalism. After years of mass political indoctrination, Marxism-Leninism-Mao Zedong Thought had become so pervasive that cadres and people would not think and act beyond the sanctions of the Party. Modernization and economic development need a different type of mentality. The ideological breakthrough came from the publication of an article entitled "Practice is the Sole Criterion of Testing Truth" in *Brightness Daily* on 11 May 1978 by a "special commentator".[13] The article asked the question: "What is the criterion of testing truth?", and then it answered categorically that "practice is not only the criterion of testing truth, but it is the sole criterion" (GRSC 1978). It argued that Marxism as a body of truth was "the consequence of long term practice by people". Similarly, the correctness of the political lines of revolutionary parties and the international communist movement "must be decided by social practice". It strongly pledged to shake off the mental handcuffs imposed by the "Gang of Four", and insisted that the truth and falsehood of any theories must be tested by continuous practice.[14] The political implication of the article was crystal clear. It means that any ideas and policies, including those endorsed by Mao, should not be accepted as truth if they do not work, or if they fail to produce positive results. Deng's call "to seek truth from facts" saw the beginning of the end of Maoist dominant ideology.[15]

The article had far-reaching repercussions. Understanding the political implication of the statement perfectly well, the "whateverists", therefore, refused to endorse the new ideological formula. On the contrary, Deng was more in touch with the political situation, and he saw the necessity of the new legitimation within the CCP. During the second half of 1978, many PLA leaders and provincial Party leaders registered their support for the new ideological line. Deng's triumph was completed when the Third Plenum of the Eleventh CC held in December 1978 highly

> evaluated the discussion of whether practice is the sole criterion for testing truth. Noting that this is of far-reaching historic significance in encouraging comrades of the whole Party and the people of the whole country to emancipate their minds and follow the correct ideological line (Tao Hai 1989:97).

Deng's personal assessment of the debate was even higher. For him, the debate was concerned with the "destiny of the Party". He (1984:154) pointed out the importance of the debate:

> It is clear that....When everything has to be done by the book, when thinking turns rigid and blind faith is the fashion, it is impossible for a party or a nation to make progress. Its life will cease and that party or nation will perish....In this sense....the debate is really a debate about ideological line, about politics, about the future and the destiny of our Party and nation.

Zhou Yang (1979), a veteran ideologue in the Party, put the debate in the perspective of China's modern intellectual development, arguing that the debate was the third mind-emancipation movement in modern China.[16]

Organizationally, the neo-Maoists were displaced by the supporters of Deng. Chen Yun, Wang Zhen, Deng Yingchao, and Hu Yaobang were elevated to the CCP Politburo. Particularly significant was the appointment of Hu as secretary-general of the CCP Central Committee and concurrently director of the CCP Propaganda Department. As secretary-general, Hu was in charge of the daily operation in the CCP headquarters and supervision of the Party organizations at all levels. Another important move was the appointment of Chen Yun as the head of the Financial and Economic Group that was responsible for the formulation of economic and financial policies. One of the immediate specific tasks of Chen was to launch a three-year economic readjustment program.[17] Thus Hua's power was increasingly diluted. After the Third Plenum, Deng emerged as the most powerful figure in the CCP hierarchy and remained so until 1997 when he died. It was in the midst of this political transition that the CCP Beijing Party Committee passed a resolution to rehabilitate the Tiananmen Square demonstration in April 1976. It cast a shadow over the neo-Maoists who had been consistently opposed to this move.

The CCP convened a Theoretical Work Conference lasting from 18 January 1979 to 3 April 1979 in the aftermath of the Third Plenum but the Conference was suspended for nearly a month between February and March. The initial purpose of the Conference was to deepen the campaign against the "Gang of Four", and to explore theoretical questions arising from the reform policies such as intellectual emancipation and the Party's democratization process.[18] The participants raised sensitive issues such as eliminating the personality cult, abandoning the life tenure of the senior Party/state cadres, and negating Mao's theory of the dictatorship of the proletariat. At the beginning, Deng seemed to be satisfied with the progress of the Conference. He encouraged the attendants to discuss the problems of intra-Party democratization fully on 27 January 1979, before he went to the United States for a state visit. From 29 January to 5 February, Deng was abroad. He launched the so-called self-defence war against Vietnam on 17 February. The war lasted for about a month and the Chinese troops withdrew from the Vietnamese border on 16 March. Unexpectedly, Deng (1984:166-191) delivered the speech on upholding the four cardinal principles in the Conference on 30 March, signalling the limits of CCP political tolerance. To the surprise of everyone, Deng had changed his attitude one hundred eighty degrees in the interlude of the Conference (Ruan Ming 1994:62-63).

There were three factors that caused the dramatic change of Deng's thinking. First, the punitive war against Vietnam did not go as smoothly as the leadership had envisaged. The PLA suffered a great loss, which generated controversies in the leadership about the modernization of the army, for the war exposed the grave weaknesses of the PLA, such as the inefficient transportation system and the backwardness of the equipment. The PLA was ill-prepared for modern warfare. Second, the Xidan Democracy Wall campaign (the Beijing Spring) had gained momentum of its own. The initial criticism of the "whateverists" by the *daizibao* (big character-posters) had the endorsement of Deng and Ye, [19] but the criticism took on its own dynamics. Increasingly, the spate of big-character posters turned on the current Party top leaders and even the CCP political system as a whole. Furthermore, as the mistaken policies of the CR were reversed, those who had been sent to the countryside during the CR now asked to be resettled and given a job in the cities. When they could not get a satisfactory reply from the government, they resorted to street demonstrations. The Party leaders took it as a sign of increasing social chaos. Coercion was contemplated to quell the chaos. Third, the de-deification of Mao, de-ideology of the Party, and the rehabilitation of the purged leaders had confounded the Party die-hards and incited a strong backlash from the Party fundamentalists. The Third Plenum affirmed the historic significance of the debate on the criterion of truth, but it had also sown the seeds of a split among the senior leadership.

Confronted with these challenges, Deng took a step backward and retracted his reformist position after his return from the United States. His notorious speech on the four cardinal principles insisted that the realization of the four modernization was still the primary task of the Party, but the task must be realized on one prerequisite--the upholding of the four cardinal principles. He (1984:180-181) asserted:

> The Central Committee considers that we must now repeatedly emphasize the necessity of upholding these four cardinal principles, because certain people (even if only a handful) are attempting to undermine them. In no way can such attempts be tolerated. No Party member and needless to say, no Party ideological or theoretical worker must ever waver in the slightest on this basic stand. To undermine any of the four cardinal principles is to undermine the whole cause of socialism in China, the whole cause of modernization.

The *People's Daily* spread Deng's message by publishing an editorial on the sanctity of the four cardinal principles. With Deng's back up, the authorities began to arrest the democratic activists. Wei Jingsheng was arrested on 29 March 1979. He was sentenced to fifteen years of prison on 16 October 1979. Throughout 1980, democratic activists were imprisoned, independent publications shut down and spontaneous literary organizations banned. Wang Xizhe was the last activist arrested in May 1981. The "Beijing Spring" came to an abrupt end.[20] This completed the first reform cycle.

> It must be noted that agricultural reform was in full swing at the time of political crackdown on democratic activists. Serious attempts were made to resolve the distribution crisis. The CCP issued the *Decision On Some Questions Concerning the Development of Agriculture (Draft)* and *Regulations of Work for Rural People's Communes (Draft for Trial Implementation)* that officially formalized the production responsibility system on 11 January 1979. The general policies for agricultural modernization were also laid down. The Second Session of the Fifth NPC passed seven important laws including the Law of the People's Republic of China on Joint Ventures with Chinese and Foreign Investment. The CCP and the State Council approved in principle the creation of "special export zones" in Shenzhen, Zhuhai, and Shantou on 15 July 1979. In 1980, the name was changed to "Special Economic Zones", and Xiamen became one of the four SEZs. *Fang* and *shou* occurred simultaneously, but in different realms.[21]

The Second Cycle (1980-81)

Deng continued to consolidate his position within the Party in 1980. The CCP approved of the posthumous rehabilitation of the former vice-chairman of the Party and president of the Republic, Liu Shaoqi, at the Seventh Plenum of the Eleventh CC on 23-29 February 1980. Important personnel changes were effected. The "little Gang of Four": Wang Dongxing, Wu De, Chen Xilian, and Ji Dengkui were removed from the Politburo. Deng's two proteges Hu Yaobang and Zhao Ziyang were elevated to the SC of the Politburo. Hu was elected as the general secretary of the newly reconstituted CS. Hua's political decline was unstoppable.

Exteriorly, Deng was merciless in suppressing the socio-political forces challenging the authority of the CCP, but his determination to reform the Party/state polity remained unchanged. He delivered the seminal speech on the reform of Party and state leadership in August 1980 at an expanded Politburo meeting.[22] As I have argued earlier, the gist of his speech on the political reform was the institutionalization and establishment of socialist legality of the CCP Party/state system. Democratization of the CCP and social life was one of the main goals of his political structural reform package. A former associate of Hu Yaobang and one of the writers of the Third Plenum communique has this observation (Ruan Ming 1994:179):

> When Deng proposed to reform the Party/state system, he was serious. The political reform was one of the key goals of the reform. He has three goals. First, economically, to catch up with Western industrialized countries; second, politically, to create a higher form of democracy that is superior to capitalist democracy; third, organizationally, to groom more talents than the Western counterparts. He dared to change the Stalinist and Maoist highly centralized authoritarian system and attacked bureaucratism, over-centralization of power, patriarchy, and life-tenure system. He held that three kinds of democratization must be institutionalized: the democratization of the Party, of economic management, and of social life.

Deng's sincerity in political structural reform can hardly be questioned as he urged concrete measures to be devised and implemented as quickly as possible. Following the guidelines of Deng's speech, Liao Gailong, a research fellow of the Office of Central Policy Research, gave a speech in the Central Party School on 25 October 1980, in which a radically new political structure was proposed. His proposals, if implemented, would amount to a complete overhaul of the CCP Party/state structure.[23] The following table shows the proposals of Gengshen reform, in contrast to the CCP existing Party/state structure:

Table 4.2
Liao Gailong's Gengshen Reform Package

Existing Structure	Reform Proposal
The Party	
-CC	Renamed as Central Executive Committee
-Politburo (abolished)	A standing committee set up
-CS	Unchanged
-CDIC	Unchanged
-CAC	Unchanged
The State	
-NPC (abolished)	Two chambers: Territorial Chamber and Society Chamber
-About 3000 NPC deputies	Reduced to 1000
-SCNPC (abolished)	Set up an executive committee
-300 SCNPC members	Reduced to 60-70 members
	Set up a monitory body
Society	
-Party-control social groups	Autonomous social groups Independent of Party
-Party-control enterprises	Enterprise heads democratically elected

Source: Liao Gailong 1980:41-46

In congruence with the spirit of Deng's reform program in the late 1970s, Liao emphasized the importance of establishing a democratic political system as the ultimate goal of the reform. For Liao, democracy is not merely instrumental, but has an inherent value in itself. Liao (1980:41) summarized the essence of Deng's seminal talk: the democratization of both the Party and the state. At the end of his speech, Liu asked whether the political structural reform would be aborted. He foresaw that resistance would pop up but that ultimately the reformers would triumph (1980:47). Liao's optimism was perhaps well-grounded as China heralded a new era of four modernizations after the demise of the Maoist model.

Unfortunately, Liao's speech looked like a rainbow. No sooner had the reformist intellectuals hailed the reform package than it was quickly withdrawn and buried. [24] Only the setting up of the two Central Commissions became a reality (the CDIC in 1978 and CAC in 1982), and to some degree, industrial management in the state enterprise was democratized. The slogans to build "a high degree of democracy" and "a high degree of civilization" were incorporated into Hu Yaobang's political report in the Twelfth CCP Congress in 1982. Throughout 1980, the reform initiatives were maintained as the spirited election campaigns at the county levels held across the whole country in the latter half of the year showed. Based on the new Electoral Law passed at the NPC in the previous year, the first direct elections at the county levels exhibited unprecedented openness and liveliness.[25] For instance, the candidates at Hunan Teachers' College in Changsha conducted a heated election campaign, in which the political structural reform was a dominant theme. Twenty seven year-old Liang Heng campaigned on the platform that he opposed the kind of Marxism-Leninism propagandized and taught all over China. Liang alleged that "people have sunk into servitude, no different from slavery....How can we speak of a nation of citizens when both people and officials are like this?" (Nathan 1985:213) At Beida, a total of 29 candidates vied for two vacancies in Haidian District People's Congress in Beijing. Wang Juntao, a 22 year-old physics student, openly questioned whether Mao was a true Marxist. Hu Ping, a philosophy graduate student, declared before the CCP officials that free speech was nonexistent in China (Black and Munro 1993:64-65).[26]

There were two other important political events in 1980. Firstly, Hua's fate was sealed. At the expanded CCP Politburo meeting in November, he was heavily criticized. The meeting agreed to recommend to the Sixth Plenum to remove Hua from the chairmanship of the CCP and CMC. Hu Yaobang was elected as the general secretary of the restored

CS in the Fifth Plenum of the Eleventh CC in February 1980 and would replace Hua as the chairman of the CCP in the Sixth Plenum in June 1981. Deng was elected as the chairman of the CMC at the same Plenum. At this juncture, as soon as the "whateverists" fell off completely and the common ground was lost, the reformists began to disintegrate. A conservative faction within the CCP emerged (Ruan Ming 1994:110). The second event was the trial of the Lin Biao clique and the "Gang of Four" between 20 November to 23 December 1980. The final verdict was that Jiang Qing and Zhang Chunqiao were sentenced to death with two years of reprieve, Wang Hongwen to life sentence, and Yao Wenyuan to sixteen years of imprisonment. The trial was broadcast by television and it was a political stage show. Nevertheless, the first step towards the strengthening of socialist legality was achieved.

However, in the midst of reform euphoria, Chen Yun for the first time raised the slogan *fandui zichanjieji ziyouhua* (oppose bourgeois liberalization) at the Central Work Conference at the end of 1980. Sensing the overheated economy and the burgeoning budget deficit, he called for the tightening of fiscal and financial policies. He proposed an alternative twenty-four-character economic strategy, "suppress demand, stabilize price, abandon development, seek stability, slow down reform, stress readjustment, big concentration, and small devolution" (Ruan Ming 1994:112).

Externally, the crisis in Poland also contributed to the conservative backlash. Politically controlled by the Soviet Union, the Polish Labour (Communist) Party and government had been constantly plagued by economic crises and the rising dissatisfaction with the Party cadres by the Polish people since the 1950s. Every time the workers played the vanguard role in the protest movements and negotiated a settlement with the government. In mid-1980, the economic crisis loomed large and the glaring privileges of the party and government officials again triggered the discontent of the workers who then organized an independent trade union *Solidarity*. Instantly, its leader Lech Walesa became a national hero. The Polish government was increasingly unable to control the independent union and paralysed by the crisis. *Solidarity* claimed a membership of 10 million, and gained the enormous moral support of the Polish Catholic church. Alarmed by the critical situation in Poland, the conservative elements in the CCP took steps to warn the Party. Hu Qiaomu wrote a letter to Hu Yaobang on 24 September 1980, expressing his concern over the Polish crisis-ridden situation. In an internal memorandum discussing the letter of Hu Qiaomu, Wang Renzhong, then the chief of the CCP

Propaganda Department, issued a notice to stop publicizing Deng's speech on Party/state leadership reform delivered in August. Wang pointed out that the Polish crisis was not only an economic problem, "it is a political problem" (Ruan Ming 1994:108).[27]

In responding to these concerns, Deng conceded and made a major policy retrenchment. Deng signalled that the tasks of readjusting the economy and maintaining social stability and the Party's unity had to be the top priorities. He (1984:33) emphasized that

> Without the leadership by the Party a big country like China would be torn by strife and incapable of accomplishing anything.

Chen Yun's recommendation that the need for a high degree of centralization and unification in economic policy making was accepted. Deng (1984:343) also declared no new experiments in the enterprise reform would be implemented in 1981 lest disrupting political stability.

Throughout 1981, the conservative ideological backlash came particularly strong from the PLA. Traditionally, the PLA was a stronghold of Maoist ideology. It was the army that started Mao's cult in the early 1960s when Lin Biao replaced Peng Dehuai as defence minister in 1959. During the CR, the PLA became the only institutional force that could sustain Mao's rule, quelling the chaos and restoring the country to order. Mao was the founder of the PLA and had been the chairman of the CMC since 1935. In the late 1970s, the adulation of Mao was deep-seated and evaluating Mao's ruling record was an extremely sensitive issue in the army, touching the nerves of many generals who had followed Mao all their lives. The resistance of the PLA to the mind-emancipation campaign was so great that Deng had to direct his criticism to the PLA at a speech at the Central Work Conference in the end of 1980, warning them (Baum 1994:122-123)

> Within the army there has existed a problem of not paying sufficient attention to the spirit of the Third Plenum....Many people have not understood the Third Plenum....(It) represented a fundamental change in the Party's political, organizational, and ideological line, namely a change from "leftist" mistakes to a down-to-earth approach....These people had not yet freed themselves from "leftist" shackles.[28]

Wei Guoqing, then director of the PLA General Political Department, was critical of the fashions of "worship of capitalism" and bourgeois liberal tendencies at a conference held in January 1981. In February the PLA launched a campaign to emulate Lei Feng, the martyred soldier canonized by the CCP, who became the role model for the country in the 1960s. In April and May, the PLA generals stepped up the criticism of the "right deviationist" view which held that the four cardinal principles were contrary to the spirit of the Third Plenum of the Eleventh CC (*People's Daily* 24 April 1981).

One of the fiercest verbal assaults was directed to Bai Hua, a veteran army writer. His film script *Kulian* (Unrequited Love) was severely attacked in an ideological campaign that tried to restrain liberal proclivities among the intellectuals. Bai Hua was criticized by a special commentator in a front-page commentary called "Four Cardinal Principles Cannot be Violated" in the *Liberation Army Daily* on 20 April 1981. The screenplay was published in a Shanghai journal in September 1979. It was a story about a young Chinese intellectual who went to the United States in the 1940s to study painting. Fuelled by strong patriotism, he returned to China to help build socialism after 1949. However, after he came back, he was ceaselessly haunted by political campaigns and even became a fugitive himself. At one point, he lamented: "My life has been an affair of unrequited love, of a one-sided affair." The intellectual finally was able to meet his daughter and she told him, "Father, you love your country,...Does your country love you?" (*Cheng Ming* June 1981:96) Bai Hua was criticized for being "negative about patriotism", "violating four cardinal principles" and "making mockery of Mao Zedong Thought". In the course of the criticism campaign, several prominent authors were also involved, including Ye Wenfu, author of the poem "General, You Cannot Do This!", Sha Yexin, co-author of the play "What If I Were Real ?", Wang Ruowang, author of his autobiography *Hunger Triology*, and Liu Binyan, author of "Between Human and Monster".[29] The campaign won the support of Deng, who singled out Bai Hua in particular for criticism in a speech in July. He (1984:369) repeatedly stressed the need to uphold "Party leadership, without Party Leadership, there definitely will be nationwide disorder, and China will fall apart."

Another key event in 1981 was the passing of the *Resolution on Certain Questions in the History of Our Party Since the Founding of the People's Republic of China* in the Sixth Plenum on 27 June 1981. The principal goal of the document was the assessment of Mao in the history of the CCP and PRC.[30] Its completion signalled the CCP temporary consensus on the status of Mao and the extent of de-Maoization. The drafting started in early 1980 and then continued for more than a year. The need for such an evaluation was too evident in view of the reform strategy at the beginning of the 1980s. Having engineered the demise of the "whateverists" faction and secured the victory in the mind-liberation movement, Deng had stamped a personal touch on the new political-ideological line. However, the Maoist shadow still hung heavily over the whole Party. The appraisal of Mao became ever more urgent as Hua descended from the political front stage. The proper or "correct" assessment of Mao would help clarify the confusion of mind produced by the dramatic shift of the general political line. Desperately in need of a reform alliance to press forward with the four modernizations, Deng hoped to secure the support of all the major power-brokers in the CCP and PLA with such a "balanced" appraisal.

Deng was extremely serious about the drafting of the Party document and he had given numerous speeches to the drafting committee, nine of which were published (Deng Xiaoping 1984:276-296). Deng (1984:292) cited that in the drafting there were three central issues:

> First, with regard to Comrade Mao Zedong: Which were primary, his achievements or his mistakes? Second, in the last thirty years and especially the ten years before the Cultural Revolution, were our achievements or mistakes primary?....There is the third question: Should we blame Comrade Mao Zedong alone for all the mistakes of the past, or should others also take some responsibility?

In fact Deng had all the answers before he posed the questions. The final document bore the personal touch of the new helmsman. In Deng's talk with the drafting committee on 18 March 1981, the basic tenets of the *Resolution* had already taken shape (1984:284:5).

> On no account can we discard the banners of Mao Zedong Thought. To do so would, in fact, be to negate the glorious history of our Party. On the whole the Party's history is glorious....We did triumph in the revolution....The appraisal of Comrade Mao Zedong and the exposition of Mao Zedong Thought relate not only to Mao personally but also to the entire history of our Party and our country.

With these remarks by the ascending "paramount leader", it was not surprising that the final document resolved that the chief responsibility of the ultra-leftist policies indeed lay on Mao, but it was the error of "a great proletarian revolutionary" (CCCCP 1981:41), and Mao Zedong Thought "is the valuable spiritual asset of our Party....our guide to action for a long time to come"(CCCCP 1981:72). Clearly, in substance, the *Resolution* was a step backward from Deng's speech on the Party and state leadership reform, but he did not give in to the conservatives for nothing. Firstly, by recognizing Mao's "merits are primary and his errors are secondary" (CCCCP 1981:56), Deng secured his unity by getting the endorsement of the whole Party for his modernization program. From then on, his main attention could be directed solely at economic development for the country. Secondly, Deng was able to dilute the revolutionary substances of Mao Zedong Thought. The theory of the continued revolution under the dictatorship of the proletariat was completely negated. Hua Guofeng's leftist errors were mildly criticised, and the Third Plenum of the Eleventh CC was hailed as the turning point of the CCP history (CCCCP 1981:47). Most important of all, Mao's Thought was interpreted as a body of doctrines collectively contributed by the veteran revolutionaries. The basic tenets were reduced to three: to seek truth from facts, the mass line, and independence. In short, Mao Zedong Thought was "Dengified".[31]

In the second half of 1981, Deng turned to the issue of rejuvenation of the Party leadership. In a speech to the provincial and municipal Party secretaries, he (1984:361) stressed that the problem of political succession had become extremely urgent. If the issue could not be resolved "within three to five years, we shall be faced with catastrophe". In a speech to the CCP Politburo, Deng (1984:374) emphasized that

> All our veteran comrades should understand that the promotion of cadres who are more revolutionary, younger, better educated, and more professionally competent is a strategic need for the revolution and construction.

Besides the promotion of the younger cadres, Deng further called for the mandatory retirement of the old cadres and a complete streamlining of the Party/state bureaucracies and staff (1984:365). Zhao Ziyang, who had replaced Hua as the premier of the State Council a year before, revealed a broad plan in restructuring the inefficient and bloated bureaucracy in his 1981 government *Work Report*.

The Third Cycle (1982-83)

The first half of 1982 was devoted to the preparation of the Twelfth CCP Congress in September. The twin goals of the Congress were the rejuvenation of the Party/state leadership and the institutionalization of the Party/state governing machinery. The Congress passed a new Party Constitution, in which the CCP urged all the Party members to act within the laws of the state. To mollify the veterans, the CAC was set up to allow them to preserve their previous privileges associated with their rankings and positions. With the concentration of so many revolutionary veterans and in view of the patriarchal nature of the CCP political structure, the CAC became a powerful informal decision-making organ within the CCP. The most important achievement of the Congress was the forced retirement of senior cadres at the provincial level. At the top Politburo level the rejuvenation was less marked. The succession problem became more serious. Politburo SC members octogenarians Ye Jianying (86), Chen Yun (77), Li Xianian (73) refused to step down. Ye Jianying bluntly said to the reporters, "I'll perform my duties with all my energy....and stop only when I die" (*People's Daily* 7 September 1982).

On the whole, the Congress was significant. The political report delivered by Hu Yaobang recognized the historic importance of the Third Plenum of the Eleventh CC in 1978. Hu (1982) vowed to create a new phase of socialist modernization and called for the establishment of a "highly democratic socialist society" and he was extremely emphatic about socialist legality:

> Our Party must lead the people to make and perfect provisions, laws, regulations, as to guarantee the strict implementation of laws....Those laws and regulations once passed by the state power organs, the whole Party must obey.

Hu also called for the rapid realization of the four generation rejuvenation criteria in the Party/state machinery, and the trimming of the central and provincial political apparatus. The CCP had come a long way from the Maoist era. Ten years had elapsed since the aftermath of the Lin Biao fiasco in 1971. The CCP metamorphosis was striking and the colossal changes in the ten years could be shown by the following table:

Table 4.3
Evolution of the Chinese Political System, 1972-82

Attribute of the system	1972	1982
Method of change	Revolution	Reform
How leaders view the process of change	Dialectical	Linear
Method of policy implementation	Mobilization class struggle	Rule of bureaucracy
Main task of governance	Elimination of lingering bourgeois influence	Raising economic production and living standard
Mechanisms for integrating policy	Networks of personal relation, coercion	Regularized personnel system, coercion, planned allocation of resources
Extent of institutiona-lization	Low, rule by man	Low, major efforts to rebuildinstitutions

Rule at top	One-man rule	Collective leadership (at least in principle)
Nature of politics at top level	Unbridled factionalism below top leader	Struggle among factions and opinion groups governed by unwritten rules
Popular confidence	Low	Somewhat improved

Source: Oksenberg and Bush 1982:15

The Fifth Session of the Fifth NPC in November 1982 passed a new state Constitution, the fourth since the Republic was founded, in which the formal power of the NPC and SCNPC was greatly expanded.[32] But the four cardinal principles were incorporated into the Preamble. In analyzing the new Constitution, Baum (1993:350-351) argued that

> On the whole, China's new Constitution represented a conceptual attempt to balance the inherently conflicting imperatives of *fang* and *shou*....The document reflected a clean break from the political philosophy of the Cultural Revolution. At the same time, however, it fell short of institutionalizing the pluralistic rule of law, resembling instead a rationalized variant of neoclassical Leninist rule by law.

However, the increasingly liberalizing intellectual and political atmosphere had emboldened the intellectuals to cast a skeptical eye on the "truthfulness" of Marxism. In the early winter of 1982/3, a vigorous debate on the relevance of the Marxist notions to contemporary China broke out. Two important Marxist concepts were involved: the notion of *yihua* (alienation) and *rendao zhuyi* (humanism). It has been estimated that between 1978 and November 1983, more than 600 articles on these themes were published in newspapers and magazines in China (Brugger and Kelly 1990:148).

The concept of alienation is central in Marxist classics. Marx's important early work *Economic and Philosophical Manuscripts* dealing exclusively with this notion was not published until the 1930s. The publication of this treatise marked a new stage of Marxist studies. The central issue is whether there are two Marxs or one Marx, i.e. whether a young and mature Marx should be distinguished with two separate foci to his revolutionary thought, or whether there was one Marx who had continuously developed his ideas over the entire life span without any hiatus (Tucker 1971:165-176). The classification is not merely academic in Chinese reform context, and it has profound political significance. For those who hold the former view can often draw inspiration from the early Marx, who took humanity as the central theme of his doctrine. The profoundly humanist orientation is in stark contrast to the later or mature Marx, who emphasized the iron law of historical inevitability and endless class struggles.[33] The early work of Marx was translated into Chinese in the 1950s, but the works failed to make an impact on the political and intellectual scene. It was almost two decades later that, after the tortuous experience of the CR, the reformist intellectuals found a new meaning in the early works of Marx which stress human dignity and values. Therefore, the notion of alienation was subject to a new interpretation.

At the end of the 1970s and early 1980s, in the aftermath of the great debate on "Practice is the sole criterion of theory", Chinese intellectuals enjoyed the most relaxed period since 1949. The open-door policy was implemented, and increasing contacts with Western countries became possible. Various strands of intellectual currents, such as existentialism, Freudian psychology, structuralism, analytical philosophy, and critical theory of the Frankfurt School, were brought in, and eagerly digested by the intellectuals and university students. For three decades, social sciences other than Marxism-Leninism were not allowed to be disseminated. It was Wang Ruoshui, then a deputy editor-in-chief of the *People's Daily*, who rediscovered the notion of alienation. Wang was asked by the Department of Journalism of the Graduate School of CASS to give a talk on philosophy to students in June 1980. After the talk, he was asked by one of the students to explain the notion of alienation. Off-guard, Wang gave a short explanation. The explanation later exploded into the greatest intellectual debate in the early 1980s. Finding that the response of the audience was hot, Wang elaborated the notion in another talk in the office of the *People's Daily*. The speech was published in an internal publication *xinwen zhanxian* (*News Front*). It turned out that the article was to spark an extremely heated debate (Wang Ruoshui 1986:198).

Developing the Marxian notion of alienation, Wang proposed a theory of "socialist alienation", and applied the notion to the analysis of socialist society in general and, China in particular. Wang argued that, in contrast to the prevalent orthodox view, the concept of alienation was not a bourgeois concept, and thereby could be used by social scientists to account for the dark side of socialist society. Socialism is in serious trouble. Upon its publication, a widespread response was noted. Some praised Wang, while others rebutted him. The debate involved several key issues, such as: What is humanism? Is humanism universal or class-based? Is humanism a world view or a set of ethical codes? Does Marxism contain elements of humanism? Is there any difference between bourgeois humanism and revolutionary humanism? But the most important question for Wang remained: is there alienation in socialist China nowadays? Wang's answer was affirmative. Alienation exists in China, and it is manifested in three forms. He (1986:189) argued that:

> Why does this issue (the problem of alienation) attract so much attention? The problem arises from socialist practice. Now the notion gains new meaning. Does socialism have alienation? Socialist practice has proved that alienation does exist in different spheres. There is not only alienation in ideological sphere, but in political as well as economic spheres.

Wang Ruoshui (1986:191) defined alienation as a process by which an object originally created by human beings becomes externalized and independent of human beings. It becomes a force that oppresses or even controls human beings. Dogmatism and personality cult are concrete cases of ideological alienation. The cult of Mao during the CR was a manifestation of ideological alienation. Political alienation means the abuse of power by the Party/state officials. Power should serve the interests of people, but now in China power is misused and serves the interests of corrupted officials. Thus the public servants of the Republic have been transformed into masters of the people. The Party/state apparatus is beyond the control of the people, and it has become an alienated power over the people. Wang further argued that Marxian exploitation is only one form of economic alienation. There are other forms of alienation. Wang Ruozhui (1986:196-197) alleged that the government's inability to observe the objective law of economic dynamics or development, resulting in a massive waste of natural and human resources, is precisely a manifestation of economic alienation. Moreover, bureaucratism and the problems of *tizhi* (system) are also related to economic alienation.

Wang's article aroused a widespread debate. Sharing the view of Wang that alienation existed in socialist society, one author even argued that it existed in communist society (Brugger and Kelly 1990:146).[34] At the beginning, the Party took no stand, allowing, indeed, "hundreds of schools of thought blooming". Not before long, the new theory received a powerful push from an important Party theoretician and vice-minister of the Propaganda Department, Zhou Yang, who had been the cultural Czar for nearly three decades preceding the CR. In a speech commemorating the hundredth anniversary of the death of Marx in 1983, Zhou (1983) publicly endorsed the new theory. He stressed that "we must comprehend (alienation) before we can overcome". Trying to avoid an open conflict with Party orthodoxy, Zhou, however, still upheld the superiority of the socialist system, and claimed that socialism could eliminate different forms of alienation by itself. Zhou claimed that the origin of alienation did not lie in socialism itself. In fact, the reformist political line since the Third Plenum was intended to overcome socialist alienation. The speech was published in the *People's Daily* on 16 March, making the new theory more respectable and influential.[35]

By the second half of 1983, it was apparent that the Party conservatives saw the need to put a brake on disseminating the notion. They saw the debate beginning to attract an increasing number of intellectuals and young students became new converts in the new theory. As always, academic debates often become political issues in China and the Party intervenes. "Politics take command" is still prevalent but its form is less extreme than during the pre-reform era. Deng Xiaoping, the patriarch, took a stand, and once he took a stand it was final. Delivering a speech on the "Urgent Tasks of the Party on Ideological and Propaganda Fronts" in the Second Plenum of the Twelfth CC, Deng charged (1987:30-32) that

> Some comrades have deviated from the Marxist orientation.
> They have engaged in discussions of the value of the human
> being and alienation....(They) have only been interested in

criticizing socialism, not capitalism....Their position will only
lead people to criticize, doubt and negate socialism.

Once being labelled as "anti-socialists", those who hold unorthodox views
would be considered as "class enemies" and academic discussion would
comes an end.   "Class enemies" are excluded from constitutional
protection. Deng's remark was brief and it was a political declaration. It
was left to other Party ideologues to elaborate his standpoint. Hu Qiaomu,
the Party's putative Marxist spokesman, responded with a long article
entitled "Concerning the Problems of Humanism and Alienation" on 27
January 1984 in the *People's Daily* (RC 1984:1-63). Pinpointing in
particular Wang Ruoshui, Hu summarily attacked the advocates of
"socialist alienation". Following the orthodox interpretation of Marxism,
Hu argued that the notion of alienation was only applicable to capitalism.
In socialism, alienation disappeared. In Hu's view, Marx used the notion
in his early works, but in his mature writings such as *Class Struggles in
France (1850), The Eighteen Brumaire of Louis Bonaparte (1851-2), The
Civil War in France (1871), Critique of Gotha Programme (1875), and
Anti-Duhring (1876-8)*, the notion disappeared. According to Hu (RC
1984:46), the notion was confined to the stage of capitalism and was not
part of "scientific socialism". He accused Wang and Zhou of interpreting
the notion arbitrarily and irresponsibly over-generalizing the concept
socialist societies, consequently confusing the mind of young people.
Skepticism on socialism and CCP leadership had been generated.   The
debate was brought to an abrupt end, with the Party taking a clear stand.

In an interview with the British sinologist Stuart Schram, Deng
Liqun, then the CCP propaganda chief, expressed the view that the Party
was particularly irritated by Wang Ruoshui on two issues: first, Wang's
complete negative attitude towards Mao and Mao Zedong Thought, and
second, Wang's view that China's socialist system was in no way more
democratic than capitalist society (Schram 1984:).[36] Meanwhile, under
the mounting pressure of the conservatives and name-calling criticism by
the liberal Party chief Hu Yaobang in a CAC meeting, Zhou Yang was
forced to submit self-criticism and recant publicly over his "erroneous
view" (*People's Daily* 6 November 1983). He claimed that his usage of
the concept was careless, and he failed to draw a clear line with the
bourgeois interpretation of the concept. Thus, his interpretation might
provide political ammunition for the anti-socialist groups to negate
socialism and the leadership of the CCP. Wang Ruoshui, however,
refused to criticise himself, and he was removed from the deputy

editorship of the *People's Daily*. Hu Jiwei, the editor-in-chief, was transferred to the SC of the NPC.

In retrospect, it is interesting to examine the arguments of both sides purely from an intellectual point of view. Indeed, Hu Qiaomu was not wrong when he argued that Marx's concept of alienation was confined to capitalism. But this is a truism because a socialist system had not been established in Marx's time. The real issue is, of course, whether the notion could be applied to a socialist society. Marx specifically analysed the production and circulation of commodity in capitalism. His "theory of labour" suggests that commodity produced by wage-labourers becomes an instrument by which capitalists exploit workers. From this angle, Wang's definition of alienation is correct. While Marx rooted alienation in the private property system, Wang and Zhou used the notion to cover a variety of negative phenomena under socialism, such as personality cult, official graft, abuse of power, nepotism, patriarchy, economic inefficiency, wastefulness, and environmental degradation, etc. The ambiguous connotation of the term is too evident, and indeed they committed the fallacy of over-generalization. Intellectually, their standpoint cannot be justified.

On the other hand, Hu Qiaomu's downgrading of Marx's alienation in his mature work is misleading. The discussion of alienation in Marx's mature works takes a more subtle form. It can be found in Marx's most influential work *Capital*, in particular the section on "Fetishism of the Commodity and Its Secret" (Tucker 1978:319-29). Tucker (1971:176) argued that the Marxism of the *Communist Manifesto* evolved directly out of the Marxism of the *Manuscripts of 1844*. The notion of alienation still existed in the mature Marx and it remained Marx's central concern throughout his entire life. In China's social context, academic discussion for the sake of seeking truth is luxurious. In fact, both reformist intellectuals and conservatives are not arguing for the sake of theory. They understood perfectly well the political implications or significance of their ideas. Evidently, reformist intellectuals, such as Wang and Zhou, were in search of a theory within Marxist tradition that can provide theoretical justification for the reform policies. Orthodox Marxism had been too closely associated with Mao's calamitous ultra-leftist policies, subsequently losing all intellectual credibility. New elements have to be introduced to socialist thought in order to restore the intellectual vigour of Marxism and legitimacy of the CCP. The reformist intellectuals have found a humanist element in early Marx. But they were rejected by the Party's orthodox fundamentalists, who considered their ideas too subversive. The popular acceptance of the theory must be seen in the context of the CR, in which millions of people were killed and human dignity thrashed. Yet the Party's power-holders failed to see the strong underlying currents of society (Li Zehou 1987:202-203) and the Party refused to be revitalized through an ingenious interpretation of early Marxism.

The Second Plenum of the Twelfth CC in October 1983 decided to launch two rectification movements: the Party rectification to purge "three kinds of people", and against *jingshen wuran* (spiritual pollution). "Three kinds of people" meant the followers of the Lin Biao clique and the "Gang of Four", who might still be in power in spite of the personnel changes of the CCP. The move was to eliminate ultra-leftists within the Party. On the other hand, the anti-spiritual pollution campaign was targeted at liberal intellectuals who went far too right, according to the Party conservatives. The Party rectification movement would last for three years, starting from the second half of 1983. The first stage would last for one year and it would cover the Party committees and PLA offices at the central, provincial, and autonomous areas. The second stage would extend to the county and local levels (CCCCP 1983).

After the Second Plenum, a tidal wave of articles criticizing the theory of "socialist alienation" appeared in the national newspapers and magazines. The accusations were too familiar: violating the four cardinal principles and deviating from the Party's correct political line. In the inaugural speech of the Association of Scientific Socialism in Nanjing on 23 October, Wang Zhen repeatedly called for the toughening of ideological laxity among the cadres, and for the first time he equated the advocates of "socialist alienation" with "anti-Party, anti-socialist crimes" (*Ming Pao* 4 November 1983).

Due to the resistance of the intellectuals and the dissension in the top leadership, the anti-spiritual pollution campaign did not last long. It lasted for only 28 days (Ruan Ming 1994:150). Determined to restrict the campaign to the ideological sphere, Hu and Zhao, astutely, gained the support of Deng Xiaoping, and fought back. At an enlarged Politburo meeting in November 1983, Hu claimed that the campaign had gone too far, disrupting economic reform, rural reform in particular. If the campaign continued, the general line of the Third Plenum would be overhauled (*Cheng Ming* January 1984:12). Hu and Zhao issued a five-point guideline in circumventing the campaign. First, the current political-ideological situation necessitated such a campaign. Second, it should by no means spill over into realms other than the ideological field. Third, the ultra-leftists must not be allowed to make use of this campaign to distort the general line of the Third Plenum. Fourth, the Party must continue the open-door policy and the economic modernization program. Fifth, the main task of the Party was to purge the Party of "three kinds of people" and engage in economic construction. Consequently, the extension of the campaign must be prevented (*Cheng Ming* February 1984:9). Showing their political clout, the Dengist reformists were able to contain the campaign.[37]

The Fourth Cycle(1984-85)

Following Hu and Zhao's counter-offensives, the *People's Daily* published a series of editorials in February and March 1984 critical of the catastrophe created by ultra-leftism in the pre-reform era. The articles stressed that at the present stage the principal ideological enemy of the Party was still leftism. The agricultural reform in the rural areas would not shrink, but further expand. In a move to set the intellectuals' hearts at ease, the editorials emphasized that China's open-door policy was a long-term strategic goal of the country that needed the collective contribution of the intellectuals (*People's Daily* 20 February; 15 March; 1 and 2 April 1984).

In economic policies, 1984 began with a strong push to reform under Deng, who toured Shenzhen, Zhuhai and Xiamen SEZs in late January and early February. During the tour, Deng had completely affirmed the policy of setting up SEZs by saying publicly that "the development and experience in Shenzhen prove that our policy of setting up SEZs has been correct" in Shenzhen and "Zhuhai SEZ is fine" in Zhuhai (*Cheng Ming* March 1984:10).[38] After Deng returned to Beijing, he declared the reform policy should be *fang*, not *shou*, on 24 February. More cities should be opened to foreigners and overseas investors (Ruan Ming 1994:160). Following Deng's declaration, Hu and Zhao announced the opening of 14 cities for foreign investment in a forum jointly organized by the CS and State Council. The cities included Shanghai, Tianjin, Guangzhou, Ningbo, Wenzhou, Fuzhou, Dalian, etc. Additionally, "development zones" would be established in some of the open cities to allow development at a quicker pace.

By now, the political atmosphere had changed significantly. Ultra-leftism became the target of verbal assault. In an important commentary in the *People's Daily* on 1 April, the author charged that the main source of ideological laxity was due to leftism. This represented a significant change of heart on Deng's part, who, only a few months before, had warned of the dangerous tendencies of rightism among the Party's ideological workers. The new ideological proclivities had then become a component of the Party's rectification movement, which had entered the second stage in March. The drive to stamp out the ultra-leftists went into full force. At the end of the campaign, the official sources revealed that 40,000 members were expelled from the Party, among whom about 25 percent belonged to "three kinds of people" (Baum 1994:168).

Another important theme in the first half of the year was the recruitment and promotion of the *disan tidui* (third echelon). In an interview with Louis Cha, publisher of Hong Kong's *Ming Pao*, Hu Yaobang disclosed that "now two-third of the members in the CC are over sixty, This is the real crisis." (Cha 1984). Consequently, breeding younger talents became as urgent as ever. Hu also disclosed that a Party Representatives Conference would be held to speed up the process of "blood rejuvenation" the following year.

The Third Plenum of the Twelfth CC in October 1984 was a landmark in the reform period, for it adopted the long awaited document *Decision on the Reform of the Economic Structure* (CCCCP 1984). The document signified that economic reform in the rural areas since 1978 had been basically completed. The Dengists then brought economic reform to cities. 1984 was the watershed year by which the ten-year span from 1978 to 1989 was classified by two stages (Chen Ziming 1992). The CCP aimed to establish a *shehui zhuyi youjihuade shangpin jingji* (socialist planned commodity economy).[39] The *Decision* argued that "plan" and "market" were not opposite and in fact they constituted a unity. It further argued that:

> the full development of a commodity economy is an indispensable stage in the economic growth of society and a prerequisite of the economic modernization....The extensive growth of the commodity economy may also lead to certain disorder in production, and there must be guidance, regulations, and administrative control through planning.

In a tone to reconcile the conflicting ideological demands, the document argued that the difference between socialism and capitalism was not the market, but the ownership system. The operation of the law of value was free from ideological tint, and it should be observed even in a socialist economy. The document introduced a series of important reform measures. For instance, it urged a further reduction of mandatory planning for the state enterprises and the expansion of individual enterprises. By instituting the withdrawal of the Party committees from enterprises in principle, the autonomy of enterprises was encouraged. The "manager responsibility" system was to be enforced. The irrational price and wage systems were to be gradually reformed. It envisaged a comprehensive marketization reform package involving price, finance, wage, labour, enterprise, and factory management in five years.

The urban reform ushered in a period of unprecedented economic boom for the cities, both for good and bad. The enterprises gained a new degree of autonomy and started to produce more consumer goods using market force as guiding criteria. *Getihu* (individual household enterprises) sprang up everywhere. Between 1983 to 1985, the number of officially registered private businesses and individual households doubled from 5.9 million to 11.7 million. However, with the advent of the commodity economy, a new kind of entrepreneur emerged. They were the *taizidang* (princelings), i.e. the children or blood relatives of the Party senior cadres. Their power and connections in the Party/state bureaucracy give the "princelings" extraordinary convenient networks for reaping huge profits (He Ping and Gao Xin 1995). The hatred towards the "princelings" proved to be one of the most important catalysts for the outbreak of the 1989 pro-democracy movement. The privileges of the CCP senior leaders manifested in a new form. This was perhaps the most important cause for the worsening legitimacy crisis after the mid-1980s.

Meanwhile, the deregulatory measures in the 1984 economic reform document had a profound psychological effect on the masses. Fearful of an inflationary spiral, people rushed to buy essential commodities and withdraw money from banks. With demand up, supply failed to meet the demand. Prices rose. A vicious circle was formed. Inflation was due not only to purely economic factors, but to non-economic factors such as official corruption and profiteering. Evidently, corruption was more rampant in the reformist era than in the Maoist period. Baum (1993:368) explained:

> Although economic crime and corruption were hardly unknown in China during the Maoist era, their severity was limited by the relatively small financial rewards and relatively high social and political cost involved. Now, however, in the more permissive, "to-get-rich-is-glorious" environment of post reform China....there was a manifold increase in both the incentives to engage in corruption (in the form of substantially greater economic payoffs and diminished ethical

> constraints) and the opportunities to do so (presented by the
> rapid proliferation of deregulated, contracted-based
> commercial exchanges). With the stakes thus raised and the
> transaction costs lowered, corruption and economic crime
> began to flourish.[40]

On the political-ideological front, the second half of 1984 was a period in which the reformist intellectuals displayed the most daring spirit in seeking academic freedom and independent viewpoints on Marxism. In the Fourth Congress of the Chinese Writers' Association, Hu Qili, a Politburo member, raised the slogan of "creative freedom" for the first time and asserted that writers and journalists should not be subject to political persecution. Further, in a gesture that would surely be welcomed by the intellectuals, Hu suggested that the Party would give up talking about eliminating spiritual pollution and combating bourgeois liberalization (*Pai Shing* 16 February 1987:4). In early summer, in a move that showed the decline of the conservatives, the stubborn standpatter Deng Liqun was removed from the CCP Propaganda Department, and replaced by liberal Zhu Houze, a staunch supporter of Hu Yaobang.

However, conservative pressures were mounting amidst the reform plethora. In a move to give in to the Party's hardliners, Hu Yaobang (1985) gave a speech concerning the Party's view on the nature of news reporting at a CS meeting on 8 February 1985. He affirmed the importance of the news media adhering to the Party line, serving as the "mouthpiece of the Party". He also reiterated that the Party would never give up the fight of combating anti-spiritual pollution, a view directly contradictory to Hu Qili's statement earlier in the Fourth Congress of the China's Writers' Association. "On the whole, newspapers should devote 80 percent of their coverage to the report of positive side of socialism and 20 percent to the negative side", he said. He rejected the popular demand that there should be unofficial newspapers published by social organizations independent of the Party.

The impact of Hu's speech was immediately felt. In March, *dierzhong zhongcheng* (A Second Kind of Loyalty), an investigative report by the scathing writer Liu Binyan, was banned from publication, even though the first instalment had already been serialized in January 1985 in an inaugural issue of a Shanghai journal. The authorities withdrew the issue and stopped the remaining instalments. Liu was charged with making two political mistakes: first, Liu had made a mockery of the icon soldier Lei Feng, a move that deeply offended the conservatives; second, Liu had touched on issues involving China and foreign countries, mainly the Soviet Union. Later on reflection in his memoir, Liu (1990:272) said that 1985 was the worst year since he was readmitted to the Party in 1978. For the whole year, the censorship was so tight that, being a senior reporter in the *People's Daily*, he could not publish any article in that authoritative newspaper. Liu published three investigative reports in other newspapers and magazines, but the places and persons involved had to be omitted in order not to incur the wrath of the provincial officials. In May, he was prohibited from visiting Germany. The "Second Kind of Loyalty" was widely read by readers both inside and outside China. It gained world-wide fame for Liu. The Party diehards had reasons to ban its publication. Liu strongly condemned the blind obedience to a single leader and the Party. In lieu of subservient attitude towards the authority and the Party leaders, Liu proposed a second kind of loyalty to the Party-the courage to follow one's moral conscience (1990:252-253).[41] Perhaps in a move to minimize the negative impact of his press speech, Hu had a lengthy interview with a Hong Kong journalist Lu Keng (1985), discussing a wide range of domestic and international issues. In the interview, Hu reiterated the irreversibility of the reform policy and the need for constructive criticism of the Party's rectification. More significantly, Hu mentioned that the labels of "anti-Party", "anti-socialism" and even the rightists might well be abandoned in the future (Lu Keng 1985:15).[42]

1985 saw the continued factional power struggles between the reformists and conservatives, with reciprocal gains and losses. Hu's shifting ground between the conservative press speech and revealing interview indicated the degree of political manoeuvre by both sides behind the scenes. Even Deng had to change position over the open-door policy within several months. In March, Deng argued that the open-door policy was needed to overcome China's three hundred years of poverty and isolation from the outside world. But confronted with the mounting economic difficulties and illicit commercial activities, Deng backed away from his earlier support of the SEZs in July. Instead, he mildly claimed that the establishment of the SEZs was merely an experiment, the correctness of which had yet to be demonstrated (1993:130). In August, Deng reverted to his former position, arguing that the establishment of the SEZs was a correct policy (1993:133). The rapid change of the stand over the issues of the open-door policy and SEZs shows that a great debate was going on behind the scene. The policy of setting up the SEZs was controversial from the very beginning within the Party. The conservatives likened the SEZs to the foreign-dominated enclaves in China before 1949, but the Dengist reformers insisted on using the SEZs as a window for foreign investment and technology transfer, with a view to realizing China's four modernizations. By 1985, new concerns over the rising economic crimes and other illicit commercial activities were raised. The conservatives also attacked widespread negative phenomena such as smuggling, gambling, prostitution, and pornography. In a tour to Xiamen SEZ in early 1985, the Party chief ideologue Hu Qiaomu charged that (*Cheng Ming* August 1985:10)

> SEZs are not Special Political Zones. Solely foreign-invested enterprises are in fact concessions. The concessions of old China started from economic activities. The Qing government did not care and the economic enterprise later began to enjoy extra-territorial rights in China.

Making use of two of the most notorious scandals in Fujian Province and Hainan Island, the conservative CDIC was able to get rid of two of the boldest reformist officials, Ren Zhongyi, Guangdong Party secretary, and Xiang Nan, Fujian Party secretary.

The convening of the Party Representative Conference on 18 September 1985 signaled the triumph of the rejuvenation policy in the CCP. [43] The Conference was convened to discuss two major issues: the draft proposals of the Seventh Five-Year Plan to be implemented in 1986 and organizational readjustment. However, it was the leadership reshuffle that required a exceptional Party Conference (Goodman 1986). The Thirteenth CCP Congress was still two years away and Dengist reformists intended to speed up the process. In response to the queries of reporters, Zhu Muzhi, the spokesman of the Conference frankly admitted, "We cannot wait two years. Everyone would have grown older. Some comrade's health may have changed. It is better to change slowly" (*Wen Wei Po* 19 September 1985). The Conference selected 56 new CC members and 35 alternate members. The turnover was the greatest since 1949. The overwhelming majority belonged to the "third echelon". 70 percent were college-educated, and the average age was 50 (*Wen Wei Po* 23 September 1985). The Conference also selected 56 new CAC members and 31 new CDIC members. Particularly noticeable was the decline of the PLA influence. At the Fourth Plenum of the Twelfth CCP Congress, held just before the Party Conference, six senior military leaders including Ye Jianying, Nie Rongzhen, Xu Xiangqian, Wang Zhen,

Song Renqiong, and Li Desheng, resigned. During the Party Conference, nine PLA Politburo members and 26 army officers retired to the CAC. Six new Politburo members were relatively young except Yao Yilin who was 68. The new faces included Tian Jiyun (56), Qiao Shi (61), Wu Xueqian (64), Li Peng (56), and Hu Qili (56). Hu, Qiao, and Tian were also elected as the CS members. The other two new CS members were even younger: Wang Zhaoguo (44) and Hao Jianxiu (50) (*Wen Wei Po* 25 September 1985).

The reform in the PLA was particularly striking in 1985. Aside from the retirement of the senior military marshals in the CCP Politburo and CC levels, 47,000 army officers, about 10 percent of the entire officer corps, were listed for retirement before the end of 1986. While on an official visit to New Zealand in March, Hu Yaobang announced that the PLA would be reduced by one million men in two years; this represented nearly one-quarter of the entire PLA force. In June, Deng, as the chairman of CMC, ordered the reorganization of the regional PLA command structure, reducing the existing 11 army regions to 7. The reorganization was accompanied by streamlining in the PLA general staff headquarters and the General Logistic Department (Li Kwok-shing 1990:489-496).

By 1985, China had undergone marketization and political participation reforms for seven years. Significant repercussions in the economic and political-ideological realms had occurred. The reforms had torn apart the monolithic societal fabric created and sustained by the CCP until the late 1970s. Social liberalization had taken place. The "second liberation" in agriculture had boosted the morale of the peasantry, and permitted the farmers to cultivate their land at their own choice, though legally the land still belonged to the state. The peasantry was free from "slavery" imposed by the commune structure. The urban reform beginning in 1984 allowed the enterprises and production plants to enjoy unprecedented autonomy towards the Party/state. The Party committee began to withdraw from state factories. The head was popularly elected by the floor workers, free from Party intervention. The intellectuals gained more opportunities to go abroad and could access different strands of Western thought. Most significantly, the Party/state reaffirmed the strategic importance of the intellectuals in the modernization drive. In sum, semi-autonomous social-political forces had been unleashed. The crises of participation, distribution, penetration, and legitimacy had been resolved to some extent.

Undeniably, the reform also created social illnesses unheard of in the Maoist era, such as prostitution, rampant inflation, and widespread official graft. The economic reform had also produced extreme inequity between regions and individuals. The CCP's "let-a-part-of-population-to-get-rich-first" policy only benefited a minority, most notably individual enterprises and families of the powerful Party/state officials. Meanwhile, corruption and inflation had infuriated the urbanites. All these combined to create a process of social mobilization, i.e. increased mass social or political activities which may involve political or non-political demands for changes by using newly available means such as demonstration, formation of organized interest groups or petitions (Halpern 1991:39). Signs of mass urban unrest began to show in 1985. The 1986/87 and 1989 student demonstrations were the consequences of social mobilization produced by years of reform beginning in the late 1970s.

A riot occurred in Beijing after a soccer match when the national China team was defeated by the Hong Kong team in May, thereby depriving China of the possibility of participating in the Olympic soccer tournament to be held in 1988 in Seoul. Shortly afterwards a group of 300 former Beijing residents, who had been sent down to the countryside during the CR, demonstrated before the headquarters of the Beijing Municipal Government and demanded the right to return to Beijing. A new round of price decontrol further induced a sense of psychological fear among the residents, propelling them to consume, lest the cash would depreciate.

Amidst the urban decay, it was the university students who spearheaded the protest movement. There were multiple causes for the 1986 student demonstrations, but the main one was economic. The spiralling inflation had corroded people's confidence in the reform. The students had long been dissatisfied with poor dormitory conditions, low government subsidies, rising costs of living and official corruption. Particularly students were extremely discontented with the relationship with Japan. China's markets were flooded with Japanese products, especially automobiles. They were furious particularly over the invitation of 3000 Japanese youth by Hu Yaobang to attend the 35th anniversary of the PRC. On 12 September, Beida students posted *daizibao* inside the campus to protest over the visit of the Japanese prime minister to the Shinto shine in cenxctral Tokyo which honoured the militarists who had launched the war against China. The students further called for the demonstrations to be held in Tiananmen Square to protest against Japanese economic imperialism and the revival of militarism. The top leadership was concerned with the situation, but their efforts to stop the demonstration failed. In the aftermath of the demonstrations, Hu Qili and

Li Peng held a series of forums with Beida students to pacify them. They mildly criticized the radicalism of the students. The successful demonstrations and their safe return to the campus set a precedent for the massive student demonstrations in late 1986.

The Fifth Cycle (1986-87)

By the end of 1985, the tense political atmosphere seemed to be relaxing. One sign of this was that the muckracking author Liu Binyan (1990:274), who had been denied an exit visa abroad, was allowed to visit Germany again in November. To show the substantial progress of socialist legality, the Xinhua News Agency issued a balance account of the work of SCNPC on 14 October 1985. From 1979 to 1985, it said, the SC of the NPC had passed more than 40 sets of laws. The State Council had issued more than 300 by-laws and about 540 sets of provincial administrative laws. Across the country, more than 2700 legal consultation agencies and legal firms had been set up. The government had either established or restored 5 universities of politics and law. Thirty-one universities had department of legal studies and the total student enrolment reached 16,000 (Chen Ruisheng 1992:579).

The "Liu Zaifu incident" shows the reformist triumph in the power struggles. Liu was a writer and literary scholar. After the CASS introduced popular direct election among its various research institutes at the end of 1984, Liu, as an associate research fellow, was elected as the director of the Institute of Literature. He became famous by proposing an alternative literary theory other than "socialist realism". By suggesting human subjectivity as the focus of creative writing, Liu implicitly criticized Mao's instrumental theory of literature, i.e. literature should serve the interests of revolution.   His heterodox view of literature displeased the hard-liners. Lin Mohan, a conservative writer, accused Liu of being a humanist (a charge that could constitute counter-revolutionary crime during the CR) in an article in the *Brightness Daily* on 21 February 1986. While attending the CPPCC at the end of March, Liu proposed to the Conference that the Party's chief focus had shifted to economic modernization, a similar shift should also occur in the cultural-ideological arenas, for cultural and economic development must be in tandem. His view immediately attracted the criticism of Chen Yong, director of the Policy Research Bureau of the CS, in *Red Flag*. Zhu Houze, director of the Party Propaganda Department, apparently was not happy with Chen's criticism of Liu. *People's Daily* published two commentaries on literary writing on 12 and 19 May, urging "people to be cautious in criticizing bourgeois liberalization" and "now it is more important to protect people who dare to explore than criticize." With the stand of the central authority revealed, Liu was left to peace.

Hu Qili made a tour to Shanghai from 17 to 21 April. He held five forums with the natural and social scientists within four days, and delivered many speeches in Shanghai. The thrust of his speeches was that the CCP had made great efforts to create a "harmonious and amiable environment conducive to economic modernization". Hu's tour was in fact the prelude to a major offensive in the reform policy, particularly ideological-political arena.   Expectedly, a group of young scholars in Beijing started a new round of intensive discussion on the political structural reform. The second wave of political structural reform was on the march.   The Chinese Social Scientists organized a forum on the "political reform in the socialist societies" from 28 to 29 April. Echoing the Gengshen reform package in 1980, the forum again reaffirmed that "democratization is the essence of political reform and the ultimate goal" (ZSK 1986:6). The forum listed five areas in the political reform: first, popular participation; second, socialist legality; third, administrative efficiency; fourth, free from corruption; fifth, rational organizational structure (ZSK 1986:7). The second wave of the political structural reform began.

In one of the internal speeches to the senior cadres on the economic situation, Deng (1993:160) evinced that the implementation of political structural reform must not be delayed, and that economic reform cannot be separated from political structural reform. He argued:

> We must push forward political structural reform, lest we will be out of step with the situation....We must streamline the bureaucracies and staff and extend socialist democracy. We must arouse the enthusiasm of the masses and the grass-root organizations. Bureaucracies have increased. There are many new enterprises, but they are registered by the Party cadres. The decentralized power was transferred to them. They get hold of the power and dampen the spirit of the enterprises....In 1980 I proposed the political structural reform but concrete proposals were not made. Now it is high time to put political reform into the agenda. The bloated bureaucracy will stifle economic reform. You devolve the power and they re-concentrate. It is useless.

As I argued in chapter 3, 1986 was the year of the second great political reform tide. Unlike the first tide of political reform when the institutionalization of rule of law was the dominant theme, the second tide was characterized by the economic problems produced during the first half of the 1980s. In the clearest statement ever issued by the CCP authority, Deng (1993:165) argued that

> Political structural reform and economic reform are interdependent and mutually reinforcing. Without political reform, economic reform will not succeed. The essential problem is the personnel. You need people to do things. If you disperse the power, they concentrate it. You can do nothing. From this point of view, the ultimate success of economic reform depends on political structural reform.

The message was clear. Political structural reform was to be the instrument of economic reform. Without political structural reform, economic reform count not go further. The impact was immediately felt. To concretize the proposals of the political reform, a forum was convened in the Central Party School from 10 to 12 July. The participants included Chen Yizi, director of Institute of Economic Reform in the State Council, Gong Xiangrui, professor of legal studies in Beida, Gao Fang, professor of international politics at the Chinese People's University, and more than 130 senior Party/state officials (*Cheng Ming* September 1986:15). Wang Zhaoguo and Zhu Houze were invited to give speeches. Wang declared that political structural reform was in reality the self-perfection of socialism. Zhu was cautious in drawing hasty conclusions and simply stated that political structural reform was not something novel, it had been an on-going process ever since 1979 (*Cheng Ming* September 1986:15).

Among the intellectuals, Yan Jiaqi, director of the Institute of Political Science, and Fang Lizhi, vice president of the University of Science and Technology at Anhui, played the most influential role in the second wave of political reform. Yan and Fang had opposite styles. Being a moderate scholar, Yan always insisted on working within the system, while Fang was openly critical of the CCP leaders and the defects of the system. Yan (1987:65-70) was the first person to suggest ending life tenure for the senior cadres, and the suggestion was accepted by the CCP. Since the Twelfth CCP Congress in 1982, the policy had been strictly enforced. Yan was particularly acute in the analysis of the CCP political system. In an article published in the *Liberation Daily* on 13 August 1986, Yan laid bare the three basic defects of the CCP political structure:

> First, we have not defined the scope of function, powers, and responsibilities of the Party organization as distinct from government organizations....Second, powers are over-centralized and the initiatives of local authorities are hardly brought into full play....Third, we have never defined the scope of functions, powers, and responsibilities of the government organizations as distinct from those of the economic enterprises and social institutions....[44]

Reduced to the bare essence, Yan argued that the principal obstacle to political reform was the problem of over-concentration of the political power. The urgent task was to demarcate definitely the scope and function of the Party/state and society. He proposed four kinds of division of power: first, the horizontal division of power, i.e. the dispersion of power between the CCP, NPC, and local authorities; second, the vertical division of power, i.e. power between hierarchies of Party/state organizations; third, the division of power between the Party/state bureaucracy, and social and economic organizations; fourth, the definition of power between the Party/state and people (1990:3-7). Yan was coopted by Zhao Ziyang to be one of his advisors in the 1986 political structural reform. After the Thirteenth CCP Congress Yan left the official power circle and engaged in academic writing. Though Yan did not participate in any organized opposition activities until the 1989 pro-democracy movement, he was hated by the conservatives.[45]

Compared with Yan, Fang Lizhi was more radical, not in substance but in style. There is, in fact, no difference in their views regarding China's political structural reform, i.e. the sort of political system that is desirable in China. Fang was an astrophysicist, and his knowledge of social science was minimal. What made him a national hero, particularly among university students, was his outspokenness about politically sensitive issues. Even after he was expelled from the Party in early 1987, he did not shy away from sensitive questions posed by reporters. On several occasions, he openly criticized senior Party and government officials. More importantly, he named names. For instance, he (1987:60) chided Zhang Baifa, deputy mayor of Beijing, who knew nothing about physics, for leading a physics delegation to the United States. He (1987:118) ridiculed Hu Qiaomu for not knowing astronomy. He (1987:119) criticized Zhou Gucheng, a historian and vice-chairman of the

SCNPC, for saying that 3000 to 0 was more democratic than that of 51 to 49. At one time, he even (1987:119) pointed out a mistake about astronomy made by Zhao Ziyang during a visit to Italy. Fang's contribution to the democratization of China lies in his forceful elaboration and presentation of intellectuals as an independent force in Chinese society, which is one of the most important prerequisites of four modernizations (1987:222). Fang was praised as "China's Sakharov", and indeed his daring spirit of challenging CCP authority was rarely matched among Chinese intellectuals inside China (Link 1990). It was reported that vice-premier Wan Li once visited Fang on 30 November 1986 at the University of Science and Technology. Wan gave a warning to Fang, reminding him that all university presidents had to follow the Party line. Fang was not convinced. At one point Wan told Fang, "I have already granted you enough freedom and democracy." Fang fought back and retorted, "What do you mean enough democracy? It was the people who made you vice-premier. It is not up to any single leader to hand out democracy and freedom" (Stavis 1988:95).[46]

By mid-1986, the publicity campaign to bolster political structural reform had reached a boiling point. Wan Li delivered his famous speech on the democratization of the Party/state decision-making process on 31 July. Intellectuals were excited by his speech. What they felt most happy about was the message that people were encouraged to participate in discussing politically sensitive issues (Liu Binyan 1990:279-280). From September to November, in a series of meetings with foreign dignitaries, political structural reform was the central issue that Deng raised (1993:176-180).

Prompted by Deng, Zhao Ziyang established a five-person "discussion group" of political structural reform under the SC of the Politburo.[47] The five persons were Zhao, Hu Qili, Tian Jiyun, Bo Yibo, a conservative, and Peng Chong, a vice-chairman of the SCNPC with no clear-cut political proclivity. Under the "discussion group", Zhao set up a bureau that served as a think tank, and co-opted social scientists and Party/state officials in drafting relevant documents. The bureau was headed by Zhao's political secretary Bao Tong, together with He Guanghui, Zhou Jie, and Yan Jiaqi (Yan Jiaqi 1992a:174-175; Wu Guoguang 1997). The flurry of organizational activities and propaganda campaign in the mass media engendered great expectations on the part of intellectuals, students, and people that a comprehensive package on political structural reform would be passed when the Party's Sixth Plenum of the Twelfth CC was convened on 28 September.

But perversely, the Plenum produced nothing other than the Resolution Concerning the Guiding Principle for Building a Society With an Advance Culture and Ideology (CCCCP 1986). The document represented an anti-climax and temporary hiatus of both camps. On the one hand, the *Resolution* affirmed the reform course taken since 1978; on the other, it exhorted the establishment of a socialist civilization founded on "Marxism and four cardinal principles". It pointed out the tragic consequences of extending class struggles, but it warned that the class struggle would continue to exist for a long period of time. It urged people to learn advanced technology and management skills from the West, but it attacked the capitalist "exploitative" system. Ominously, it did not mention the great mind-emancipating debate in 1978. Socialist legality and the institutionalization of legal institutions were urged but all these had be carried out under "Marxism-Leninism-Mao Zedong Thought as guiding principles".[48] It was once again a classic balancing act by Deng trying to steer down the middle of the road. The popular reaction to the *Resolution* was that it was basically a conservative manifesto (*Cheng Ming* November 1986:10). Political reform was shelved and the Party reformists gave in. The disappointment over the pace of political reform became one of the underlying causes that sparked the student demonstrations in late December 1986.

The first student demonstration began on 5 December. About 3000 students, mainly from the University of Science and Technology, but joined by students from other universities in Hefei, demonstrated before the municipal government in protest against the improper procedure of the nomination of candidates in the coming county/district People's Congress elections (Tsang Wai-yin 1989:4). Four days later, several thousand students took to the streets again in commemorating the fifty-first anniversary of the anti-Japanese student movement on 9 December 1935. On the same day, 2500 students from Wuhan University joined the demonstrations. The students cried out, "We want democracy, and long live the Constitution" (Tsang Wai-yin 1989:19). News of demonstrations spread quickly across China as the Voice of America disseminated the news through its broadcasts. Over the next few days, demonstrations broke out in Nanjing, Guangzhou, Shenzhen, Kunming, Shanghai, and Beijing.[49] From early December 1986 to the beginning of January 1987, students from more than 150 universities and colleges in 17 cities participated in the demonstrations. The total number of students involved was estimated to be 75,000. The largest single demonstration was reported to have occurred in Shanghai where 40,000 students assembled (Tsang Wai-yin 1989:118).

The official press did not report the student demonstrations until 21 December and in an indirect manner. Xinhua News Agency accused students of obstructing the traffic and destabilizing social order. It was reported that 31 policemen were injured. The editorial in the *People's Daily* on 23 December exhorted students to "treasure and develop the current unified and stable political situation". In a move to curb students' enthusiasm, the Shanghai municipal government and the SC of the People's Congress of Beijing enounced regulations restricting demonstrations. The *People's Daily* published an editorial on 29 December "Promoting Democracy Cannot Deviate the Four Cardinal Principles". On the same day, several conservative gerontocrats, Wang Zhen, Bo Yibo, Song Renqiong, Deng Liqun, and Hu Qiaomu blasted the demonstrators (Tsang Wai-yin 1989:175-176). Guan Weiyan, the president of the University of Science and Technology, and the vice-president Fang Lizhi were removed from office on 12 January 1987. Fang, Wang Ruowang and Liu Binyan, were expelled from the Party on 14, 19, 23 January respectively.

The student demonstrations had deepened the conflicts within the top CCP leadership. In the power showdown, Deng sided with the conservatives. The liberal general secretary Hu Yaobang was forced to resign in an expanded Politburo meeting on 16 January 1987. By resigning, Hu exposed his political weaknesses. His patron-client relationship with Deng was shattered. His promotion of his former subordinates in the Communist Youth League earned him the charge of factionalism. He incurred the wrath of the octogenarians by, first, making use of the anti-corruption campaign to eliminate conservatives, and, second, promoting younger cadres too zealously, thus becoming a threat to the gerontocrats (Chang Parris 1987:34-5).[50]

Notwithstanding the exhortation to "combat bourgeois liberalization for at least twenty years" by the CCP Politburo Central Document No.1 (*Cheng Ming* February 1987:10), the ensuing rectification campaign seemed mild in comparison with the anti-spiritual pollution campaign in 1983. Besides Hu Yaobang, only two senior Party/State officials were removed from office. The CCP Propaganda Department chief Zhu Houze stepped down because of his tolerant attitude towards intellectuals and students. Public security minister Ruan Chongwu was replaced apparently for his inability to contain student demonstrations. However, many prominent intellectuals were blacklisted. Wang Ruoshui and Zhang Xianyang, a researcher in the CASS, were dismissed from the Party. Wu Zuguang, a veteran playwright, was asked to leave the Party. Su Shaozhi retained his Party membership, but was relieved of his directorship of the Institute of Marxism, Leninism, and Mao Zedong Thought in the CASS. Sun Changjiang, deputy editor-in-chief of the *Technology Daily,* was to be expelled from the Party, but Marshal Nie Rongzhen intervened and he was spared the penalty (Yan Jiaqi 1992a:188-189).[51] Among the liberal editors and journalists suspended from their posts were Liu Zaifu of the *Literary Criticism* and Liu Xinwu of the *People's Literature.* Other prominent liberal intellectuals harassed included Hu Jiwei, Yu Guangyuan, Li Honglin, Wen Yuankai, Xu Liangying, Guo Luoji, and Gao Yang (*The Nineties* April 1987:25-27; May 1987:40-42). Several outspoken newspapers and magazines were suspended or denied registration. These included the *Special Economic Zone Workers' News* and the *Special Economic Zone Literature* (Shenzhen), the *Youth Forum* (Hubei), *the Science, Technology, Information Report* (Anhui), the *Society News* (Shanghai), and the *Modern Man News* (Guangzhou). The more notorious *World Economic Herald* was criticised but not shut down (*Pai Shing* 16 March 1987:21; *Cheng Ming* March 1987:13).

As with the 1983 anti-spiritual pollution campaign, the newly-promoted acting general secretary Zhao Ziyang exercised restraint on the movement right from the beginning. As soon as Hu left office, Zhao began to impose damage-control measures. The editorial "To Combat the Bourgeois Liberalization in a Healthy Manner" in the *People's Daily* on 2 February declared the need to uphold four cardinal principles, but also to limit the extent and scope of rectification. The editorial was based on the Politburo Central Document No. 4 enunciated at the expanded Politburo meeting on 28 January 1987 (*Pai Shing* 16 February 1987:3). The Document urged the cadres to grapple with the "correct" boundary of the campaign, which should not involve rural policies, science-technological fields and literary creation. Furthermore, the targets were not the "democratic parties", and the people's livelihood should not be disrupted. Unity and stability should be held supreme in the campaign. In a move to show the continuity of the reform policy despite the leadership change, Zhao set to guarantee the world in a Chinese Lunar Year speech that "China will not launch a political movement to oppose bourgeois liberalization....It will strictly be limited within the CCP and carried out only in the political and ideological fields" (ZZWY 1987:1208-1209). More significantly, in summarizing the developmental experience since the Third Plenum of the Eleventh CC for the first time, Zhao (ZZWY 1987:1216) raised the formula "one focus, two fundamental points":

> The general line from the Third Plenum is that starting from Chinese reality, establish socialism with Chinese characteristics. There are two fundamental points: one is to uphold the four cardinal principles; another is to uphold reform, open-door policies. These two points are interdependent. Emphasizing only one point is not following the general line of the Third Plenum.

Zhao's political ascent and moderate policy announcements embarrassed the conservatives. He Jingzhi, a conservative vice minister of culture, was reported to have said, "Last time, the anti-spiritual pollution campaign lasted for only 28 days, this time, not even that" (Ruan Ming 1994:208).[52]

Zhao reiterated the need to circumscribe the campaign in another speech on 13 May. After that, the conservative backlash began to recede. Meanwhile, Zhao and his five-person discussion group (and its bureau) of political reform continued to operate (Yan Jiaqi 1992a:185). By then the bureau had expanded to 19 members. Their concern mainly focused on the separation of the Party and the government. The draft on the political reform was passed at the Seventh Plenum of the Twelfth CCP Congress in mid-October, and was rectified by the Thirteenth CC in late October. The opening of the Party Congress signalled a hiatus in the conservative assault on the liberals, and it meant a temporary *modus vivendi* between the conservatives and reformists. The *shou* process came to an end. Once again the reformists were on the offensive.

The Sixth Cycle (1988-89)

The Thirteenth CCP Congress held from 25 October to 1 November 1987 passed the political report of Zhao Ziyang (1987b) that contained a significant section on the political structural reform. Overall, two themes dominated the Congress agenda: political structural reform and leadership succession. In Zhao's political report, a theory of the primary stage of socialism was expounded, in which a theoretical foundation for justifying the launching of reform policies was laid. In polity, seven areas of political structural reform were outlined.[53] Zhou's periodization of the socialist stages was unprecedented since 1949. In his struggles with the GMD and Japanese invasion, Mao (1975 V.2:341-342) had conceptualized his Communist revolution in two stages: new-democratic revolution and socialist revolution. The new democratic revolution was to overthrow the rule of GMD, bureaucratic capitalists and drive out foreign imperialists. After 1949, a political order of new democracy was called for. The socialist revolution began in 1956 after the collectivization of industries and commerce and communization of rural villages. The orthodox view of the Party held that exploitation disappeared after 1956 and that China was in a transition to communism. In legitimizing the reform policies, the reformist intellectuals devised the theory of the primary stage of socialism which divides socialism into several stages. China was in the initial stage of socialist development. Zhao decreed that the initial stage of socialism would take a hundred years to complete (from the mid-1950s to mid 2050s). The chief task of the Party in this stage was to achieve the four modernizations.

In the Congress, significant leadership changes were made at the Politburo level: ten out of 20 members bowed out, including Deng Xiaoping, Chen Yun, Li Xiannian, Peng Zhen, Hu Qiaomu, Wang Zhen, Xu Zhongxun, Yu Qiuli, Yang Dezhi and Fang Yi. Yang Shangkun (80) remained the only veteran in the new Politburo. The SC of the Politburo comprised five persons: Zhao, Hu Qili, Li Peng, Qiao Shi, and Yao Yilin (70) who was the oldest member. The average age of the SC of the Politburo was only 63. Moreover, the inclusion of younger members such as Jiang Zemin (61), Li Ruihuan (53), Li Tieying (51), and others reduced the average age of the Politburo from 70 to 64.[54]

In economic policies, reform in the direction of marketization was not abated despite the ideological-political differences in the top leadership. Under the slogan of "the state regulates the market, the market guides the enterprise", Zhao exhorted more use of market forces in the state sectors. Furthermore, the market would be created in sectors such as labor, information technology and real estate (1987a). He also called for the introduction of price reform if a rising level of income was realized. In an interview on 29 October, Zhao predicted that only 30 percent of China's economy would be subject to central planning within two or three years (Baum 1994:219). Politically, Zhao's ascent was dramatically shown when he ordered the suspension of the *Red Flag*, official organ of the CC since 1956, in May 1988 and the publication of a new journal, *Qiushi* (Seeking Truth).

Entering 1988, the problem of high inflation became the focus of concern for all walks of life (*The Nineties* February 1988:61-63). In the first quarter of 1988, Zhao, as the new general secretary of the country, reiterated several times the resoluteness of the Party to continue the reform, but he also pointed out the necessity to control inflation. As the head of the powerful CCP Finance and Economics Group, Zhao particularly devised a new economic strategy of developing the "coastal areas", a further expansion of the open-door policy. The new strategy would fully make use of the comparative advantages of coastal areas to boost exports. Domestically, the CCP deregulated four kinds of foodstuffs: pork, eggs, vegetables, and sugar, which caused a chain reaction of price hikes of other products. More significantly, spurred by the corruption of "princelings", it produced a psychological fear among the people who rushed out to buy whatever they could find in the market. The price hikes immediately triggered the protests of the students.

The problem of inflation had been almost unheard of in the pre-reform era when the country was under the command economy. The inception of reform policies saw the onset of an inflation curve. In 1979 and 1980 the inflation rates were 2 percent and 6 percent respectively. Between 1978 and 1983, the increase of the consumer price index was 14.5 percent, while the increase in the wage rates was 34.5 percent. The increase in wages was more rapid than that of the consumer prices. After 1985, the situation turned worse and the inflation rate became double-digit. According to a survey by the State Statistics Bureau in 1987, the living standard for 20 percent of urbanites fell, which meant that inflation had outpaced the wage increases (Chen Ziming 1992:191-192). The increase in the consumer price level was 7.3 percent in 1986 (in December it was 9.1 percent in comparison with the same month of the previous year). In 1987, the rate of increase of the consumer price level was 6 percent (SSB 1987 and 1988). However in 1988, the rate of inflation jumped to 18.5 percent; in fact by December it was 26.7 percent (Li Peng 1989). The price increase of some foodstuffs was higher than the national average. Zheng Zhiping, director of the State Consumer Price Bureau, disclosed in the NPC session in March 1988 that the rate of increase of the price of vegetables was 44.6 percent (*The Nineties* May 1988:66).

Furthermore, inflation was not only caused by the shortage of an aggregate supply of goods but also by the hybrid nature of the economic system and the inequality of the power structure. In a one Party dominated state, only the powerful officials have access to production materials. In a partially marketized economy, enterprises were thrown into the highly competitive market. They had to use "back-door" relations in order to get materials for production. The money they spent would be automatically transferred to the price of their products (Lan Yuan 1988). More often, they had to bribe officials who controlled production materials, thereby causing the inflation spiral. However, under this highly volatile social mood, Deng and Zhao were not deterred from pushing forward with the price reform measures. In an expanded Politburo meeting in May, Deng and Zhao insisted that price reform should continue, but, to channel popular discontent over inflation, wage reform should also be linked with price reform (*Cheng Ming* July 1988:7). In a meeting with a North Korean delegation on 19 May, Deng seemed very determined (1993:262-263)

> This move (the price reform) is not easy. It takes great risk, but the masses should understand the central government. We must make this decision....we must overcome the difficulties. There is no perfect policy.

One month later, Deng continued to call for a further expansion of the open-door policy and domestic reform (1993:269-270). From April to August, massive urban unrest took place. There was a signatory movement by Beida students over the rampant inflation. Massive industrial strikes occurred (*Cheng Ming* June 1988:10; July 1988:6-13; August 1988:6-11). To avoid further provoking the masses, the government announced the decontrol of cigarettes and alcoholic beverages in July, but it also announced that new price deregulation would not be carried out in the second half of 1988.

The rising social discontent and urban unrest put the top leadership to a test. Differences of opinion over the price reform could be detected among the leaders. After several months of behind the door maneuver and a potentially explosive social situation, Deng and Zhao, due to mounting intra-Party pressures and increasing social panic, were forced to back down. In the Third Plenum of the Thirteenth CC on 26-30 September, the Party passed in principle the *Tentative Plan Concerning Price and Wage Reform.* It was no more than a face-saving document for Deng and Zhao. The radical price reform package was dropped and put off for an indefinite future. In public meetings, Deng (1993:277) began to change his stance. He approvingly talked about *zhili zhengdun* (managing and restructuring). Zhao engaged in self-criticism on many occasions. Aside from his radical price reform package, Zhao was also criticised for his permission to let Fang Lizhi go abroad to attend academic conferences and let the television documentary series *Heshang* (River Elegy) be broadcast (*Cheng Ming* December 1988:6).

In a committee structure reshuffle in the same Plenum, the powerful Finance and Economics Group with Zhao as its head was disbanded. Subsequently, Zhao lost control over economic policy-making power (Li Kwok-shing 1990:162). The communique of the Third Plenum of the Thirteenth CC emphasized the importance of "managing economic environment, restructuring economic order", a backtracking slogan. The communique also warned of the risk of launching a price reform too hastily. The price reform would be launched slowly and gradually, considering all other factors involved and the Party should monitor the strict control of inflation (*The Nineties* November 1988:21-22). The document in fact declared the death of the price reform.

Political-ideologically, Zhao was also on the defensive. The six-part documentary *Heshang* was broadcast in June, and it was severely criticized by General Wang Zhen. The documentaries explored the transfusion of Western culture to China and how China responded in light of Western cultural infiltration. The authors used the Yellow River (traditionally known as the sorrow of China because of its floods) as the symbol of China's deep-seated conservatism and isolationism. The Ocean symbolized openness, vibrancy, and other cultural traits that are lacking in Chinese feudal tradition. The script writers made no attempt to hide their contempt for China's abject poverty and traditionalism. Wang Zhen, reading beyond the lines, charged the film was reactionary, for it "cursed all Chinese and it wanted to get rid of the CCP and welcome the GMD to return" (*Cheng Ming* December 1988:12). Siding with writers, Zhao Ziyang was against launching a rectification movement to criticize "River Elegy", but to avoid putting himself into a worse position, he gave in to the conservatives. He agreed to ban the series and devise ways to contain "bourgeois liberalization" in the Party (*Cheng Ming* December 1988:9-10).

1989 was the year of the Dragon in Chinese Lunar calendar. The symbol of the dragon in traditional China signified supreme authority and fortune. Therefore, it should have been a year of prosperity and well-being. But the year began with an ominous sign of *shou*, a political sign that the liberal Zhao had lost influence over Party affairs. The year was the tenth anniversary of the opening of the Theoretical Work Conference in 1979. But those who were most active and outspoken in supporting reform and an open-door policy were denied attendance by the CCP Propaganda Department to the Conference. These Party elite included

Wang Ruoshui, Yu Guangyuan, Yu Haocheng, Li Honglin, Yan Jiaqi, Guo Luoji, Wang Yuanhua, all of whom were politically harassed by the conservatives. Su Shaozhi was the only one who attended the commemorative meeting. He gave a speech that stunned everyone (1992:303-311). He accused the senior officials of violating the Party's "double hundred" policy. Lip service was always paid to the policy but the policy was hardly carried out in practice. He was strongly in support of Yu Guanyuan and Wang Ruoshui who were left jobless and did not have opportunities to publish what they thought. Further, Su accused Hu Qiaomu of using his power to suppress dissenting views in the debate on the theory of "socialist alienation". He argued (1992:306):

> Implementing academic freedom is the central concern of the academics. We must summarize the lessons since 1957...."double hundred" policy failed, because the Party does not implement the political freedom provision contained in the state Constitution. The Constitution does not prohibit people from discussing political questions, but in practice, those holding unorthodox views are often punished.

In discussing the development of Marxism in contemporary world, Su admitted that there had indeed been a crisis of Marxism, but the crisis was due to the ossification of the Party Marxist doctrines in state socialist countries. For a long time, Marxism was sanctified by political authorities and did not advance with changing times. He (1992:310) argued that

> Marxism is not a set of dogma. It is a method of research. It is a science that continues to develop, and its "truthfulness" can only be confirmed by practice.... Marxism is a plurality of doctrines. No one can monopolize the explanation of Marxism. No one can decide who are Marxists or who are not.

Su's speech was not published, and he was finally dismissed from the Party by the conservatives. Su was forced to exile after the 1989 Tiananmen massacre.

Three important events concurred in 1989: the seventieth anniversary of the May Fourth Movement, the fortieth anniversary of the founding of the Republic, and the two hundredth anniversary of the French Revolution. The year, however, began with a *shou* in the political-ideological fields. Hu Qili banned the publication of a historical investigative novel about the Peng Dehuai incident in 1959, a work by Su Xiaokang and two other writers. He further instructed that literary works about Party/state leaders must be censored before publication. Production of films relating to the CR was banned. Su Xiaokang, Wang Juntao, and Chen Ziming were blacklisted. Wang in particular was accused of engaging in "counter-revolutionary activities" (*Cheng Ming* January 1989:8-9).

The intellectuals were on the defensive, but they were not cowed into the Party line. After ten years of reform, social liberalization had reached the point of no return. Fang Lizhi, the most outspoken dissident intellectual, again took the lead in counter- attacking. Fang wrote an open letter to Deng Xiaoping on 6 January, asking him to grant an amnesty to Wei Jingsheng and all other political prisoners on the occasion of the three anniversaries. Fang's letter caused a series of reactions. An open letter to the SC of the NPC and the CCP signed by 33 scholars and writers was made on 13 February, repeating the same demand of an amnesty for Wei Jingsheng and political prisoners (*The Nineties* March 1989:18). On 26 February, a group of 42 prominent social and natural scientists wrote an open letter to the Party/state leaders. The letter did not mention the release of the political prisoners. Instead, it urged a genuine implementation of political structural reform and an improvement of living standards for the middle-age and old intellectuals (*The Nineties* April 1989:20). Again, it was followed by another open letter signed by 43 writers and journalists on 14 March, reiterating the demand of Amnesty (*The Nineties* April 1989:25). The wave of petitions was closely watched by Chinese overseas intellectuals in Hong Kong, Taiwan, and North America. Several petitions followed with signatories amounting to thousands. To go one step further, overseas intellectuals set up a "liaison group for promoting democracy in China" with Fang Lizhi as its head. The group published a manifesto, listing five demands. First, people should have the right to publish independent newspapers. Second, the government should protect the right of assembly. Third, the executive head of the government at the county/district levels should be popularly elected. Fourth, all political prisoners should be released. Fifth, the policy of the separation of the Party from the government should be strictly implemented (*The Nineties* March 1989:28-29).

The rising wave of protest by intellectuals both inside and outside China provided ammunition for the conservatives to mount an attack on Zhao Ziyang. Zhao was alleged to have made three policy mistakes: first, the declining agricultural production in 1987/88; second, the overheating of the economy in 1988; third, the so-called bourgeois liberalization of the intellectuals. The conservative general Wang Zhen charged that Zhao had committed rightist errors, and another conservative Bo Yibo saw the waves of petitions as a slanderous attack on the CCP Party/state (*Cheng Ming* April 1989:6-7). Confronted with the conservative attack, Zhao managed to sail through the storm, certainly with the support of Deng. At the same time, he was preparing for the visit of the Soviet leader Mikhail Gorbachev to China in May. Gorbachev was the first Soviet leader to hold a summit with his Chinese counterpart in almost two decades. The summit was expected to normalize Sino Soviet Union Party relationships.

With the announcement of the coming visit by Gorbachev, it was clear that though Zhao's power was eclipsed, he would not be toppled before the summit. At the Second Session of the Seventh NPC from 20 March to 4 April, the drive to political structural reform was curtailed. Under the conservative premier Li Peng (1989), progress in the separation of the Party and government was reported, but no call was offered to deepen the reform. Meanwhile, social tensions were not subsiding. Riots had broken out in Lhasa in December 1988 but were suppressed. More violent clashes occurred on 7 March 1989, resulting in the declaration of martial law on Lhasa, the first time in any Chinese city since 1949. University students became restless again. Nanjing students demonstrated first on 24 December 1988, and demonstrations soon spread to Beijing, Wuhan, and Hangzhou. They cried out for democracy and human rights. The Party apparatus was able to contain the demonstrations. However, it was the death of Hu Yaobang on 15 April 1989 that triggered the largest spontaneous social movement since 1949 and, in fact, in modern Chinese history. As soon as the news of Hu's death was announced, students took to the streets. They proclaimed Hu to be "the soul of China", and laid white funeral wreaths on the Monument of the People's Hero to pay tribute to him.[55]

From 15 April, when Hu died, to the 4 June massacre, China became the center of the world. Coincidentally, the visit of Gorbachev to China on 15 May attracted thousands of foreign journalists from around the world.[56] It was in the limelight of the world's television cameras that the CCP coercive machinery, obviously with the endorsement of Deng, slaughtered its people on 4 June. It is obvious that, from the beginning, the top leadership was divided over the way of handling the student movement. Indeed, the different attitudes at the top prevented the leaders from containing the movement from spreading. Nonetheless, the combined effect of the political and economic reform produced social-political forces that were beginning to be independent of the CCP. The Tiananmen crackdown could be perceived as a confrontation between these social-political forces unleashed in the 1980s and the monolithic Party/structure.[57] With the crackdown, the *fang* cycle definitely came to the end.

On reflection, there were two turning points in the series of events leading to the political meltdown (Yang L.Y. and Ma Yiyang 1991). First, Zhao Ziyang's visit to North Korea from 23 April to 30 April proved to be fatal. In his absence, the *People's Daily* editorialized on 26 April that the student demonstrations were a "planned counter-revolutionary conspiracy". The next day, 400,000 students took out to the streets in protesting against the editorial. Despite his approval of the editorial, Zhao changed his mind after he came back from North Korea.[58]   Zhao's moderation was shown in his speech to the Asian Development Bank on 4 May when Zhao stated that "the reasonable demands of the students must be met through democratic and legal means". The fissure at the top and the differences of approaches were immediately detected by the students (Shen Tong 1990:222).

The second turning point of the movement was 16 May, the date that Zhao, as general secretary of the CCP, met Gorbachev. In the meeting, Zhao revealed the "secret": the First Plenum of the Thirteenth CC had made a resolution that Deng still had the power to make decisions on the most important national and Party issues. The revelation implicated that Deng was the mastermind behind the move that labelled students as counter-revolutionaries. This further provoked the students. Expectedly, the next day, a demonstration of more than a million people was held. The slogans were directed against Deng. The revelation implied the inevitable parting of Zhao and Deng. Zhao was alone now. On the same day, Yan Jiaqi and Bao Zunxin issued an open manifesto, declaring that "the Qing Dynasty has disappeared for 76 years, China still has an emperor, a senile and fatuous dictator. The student movement is not turmoil, but a patriotic pro-democracy movement that buries the last dictatorship" (Cheung Ki-fung 1989:100). The State Council imposed martial law on eight districts of Beijing, including Tiananmen Square on 20 May. Zhao was last seen on the morning of 19 May in Tiananmen Square, bidding farewell tearfully to the students. By then, Zhao's downfall was definite.[59] Despite the support of the whole populace and senior Party/government officials, the movement was mercilessly suppressed. The degree of support of the movement within the Party/state was tremendous, as revealed by Chen Yizi (Ruan Ming 1994:254)

> 80 percent of the senior cadres below the Departmental level supported the pro-democracy movement. 70 percent of the cadres at the ministerial and vice-ministerial level were sympathetic to the movement. The three PLA vice-chairmen of the NPC were the first ones who were against the use of force. Eight hundred retired generals objected to the military crackdown.

The biggest social movement in modern Chinese history was crushed. With Deng's support, the hard-liners triumphed.[60] Zhao Ziyang was stripped of all his Party and state posts in an expanded Politburo meeting from 19 to 21 June but he was able to retain his membership. The decision was rectified by the Fourth Plenum held two days later. Jiang Zemin was elected as the general secretary of the CCP. Hu Qili lost his post in the Politburo. Yan Mingfu and Rui Xingwen were dismissed from the CS. Wang Meng, a liberal writer and Minister of Culture, was forced to resign. Jiang Zemin, Song Ping, and Li Ruihuan became the new members of the SC of the Politburo. A massive clean-up campaign in the Party began and thousands of people were arrested. A *shou* cyclical process set in, and it has not been opened up again in the political-ideological arena.

The reformists were backed up by popular forces but they could not introduce more comprehensive political structural reform to Chinese polity. By 1989, the economic and political reform had been going on for about ten years, but the country was still ruled by the iron-fisted veteran revolutionaries. Military machinery was the most important institutional basis that the CCP could rely on in time of crisis. As chairman of the CMC, Deng could command the brutal force that the CCP needed to repel the challenges from the awakening masses.

The *Fang/Shou* Cycles, the Role of Deng and Chen

As I have shown, the shifting of the *fang/shou* cycles was closely connected with the role of Deng Xiaoping and Chen Yun in Chinese politics. Throughout the 1980s, in clashes between Party reformists and conservatives, Deng's endorsement proved to be decisive in a political system with power concentrated at the top. Without Deng's consent, reform was halted. With his support, the Party reformists advanced reform measures in 1978, 80, 82, 84, 86 and 88. However, as noted at the beginning of this chapter, despite Deng's supreme position in the CCP hierarchy, his power was not unlimited. He was circumscribed by other Party octogenarians. As conservatives counterattacked, Deng had to give in, as evidenced in the years of 1979, 81, 83, 85, and 89. The bottom line was political stability. The 89 social movement was perceived as seriously threatening the foundation of the Party/state rule. In the end he had to sacrifice Hu and Zhao. The key conservative figure was Chen Yun who maintained a large network of *guanxi* (Ruan Ming 1992). It was reported that Chen's endorsement was sought before Deng's decision to suppress the pro-democracy movement (*Cheng Ming* August 1989:9). In fact, not only did they collaborate in the brutal crackdown of the movement, their role had also been both contradictory and complementary throughout the reformist era in the 1980s. They both dominated the zig-zag political development of the PRC in that epoch.

Teiwes (1984:93-99) has characterized the Chinese political system as pervaded by two kinds of rule: normative and prudential rules. The normative rules are the official or formal guidelines on how elitist politics should be conducted, and what kind of activities are tolerated, such as emphasis on the principle of collective leadership, ban on factionalism, civilian control of the military and Party discipline. Prudential rules are the rules or rather understanding that are likely to lead the elite to success in the political struggles. The prudential rules are not explicit rules but involve institutional power bases of the leaders. There are several origins, such as the institutional arrangements of the system, the particular tradition of the dominant elite, revolutionary credentials and the prevailing political culture, including the maintaining of a broad alliance of friends and followers and a network of *guanxi*, development of patron-client ties, and the support of the PLA. Throughout the history of the PRC, being a Leninist revolutionary Party, the CCP has never placed higher value on the formal procedures or routinization of the Party institution mechanism. It is clear that prudential rules are always more important than normative rules, though the two are inextricably linked. The important roles that Deng and Chen played in the 1980s are precisely because they satisfy the prudential rules. They exercised power through informal channels.

Both, in fact, belong to the first generation of revolutionaries who fought to found the PRC, despite Deng's claim that he was the core of the CCP second generation (1993:310). Both have been in the ruling center of the CCP for several decades. Both maintained a massive network of *guanxi*. In terms of Party seniority, Chen was even higher in ranking than Deng, who was one year older than Chen.[61] As early as 1933, Chen was elected a member of the SC of Politburo, and concurrently held the post of director of the CCP Organization Department. He was ranked the sixth leader in the Seventh CCP Congress in 1945. After 1949, Chen was head of the powerful Finance and Economics Group that made fiscal and economic policies in the early 1950s. Deng had been in Paris from 1920 to 1924. He was elected a member of the CC in 1945. Among the military leaders, he was ranked only after Zhu De and Peng Dehuai. He spent nearly 15 years in a military career until early 1950s and was the political commissar of the famous Second Field Army in the civil war. His military contribution to the founding of the Republic was fully recognized when Mao suggested that the title of marshal should be conferred on him, even though Deng rejected it.

Chen had been long engaged in economic policy making. In fact, the Stalinist style of command economy in China was set up by Chen (Ruan Ming 1995b). He introduced mandatory selling and buying of agricultural products by the peasantry. He supervised the elimination of private business in the 1950s. Deng Liqun had praised him as the architect of the objective law of socialist economy (Ruan Ming 1994:111). Throughout his life, Chen Yun's economic strategy had, remarkably, stayed more or less the same. In the Maoist era, he was criticized as far too rightist; for that he had laid dormant for nearly 15 years; while in the reformist era, his economic thinking became anachronistic. He held that in socialist economy, public ownership must be predominant. The function of market force could have a supplementary role in a predominately state-owned economy. He emphasized balanced growth, and administration was necessary to achieve this goal (Lardy and Lieberthal 1983:XIV-XXI). His economic ideas can be summarized in his "bird-cage" theory. In the early 1960s, he came in from the cold to rescue the economy ruined by Mao's GLF. In the late 1970s, when the economy was overheated, he became the head of the Finance and Economics Group and set out retrenchment policies to cool down the economy. But after the urban reform in 1984, he was seen as increasingly irrelevant in the reform tides led by Zhao Ziyang.

Unlike Chen, Deng's career was in the military and Party affairs. In economic policies, he turned to Zhao, and after 1992 to Zhu Rongji, then a vice-premier. Deng had been the chairman of the CMC from 1982 to 1989 in which he passed the torch to Jiang Zemin. Even after his formal retirement, his authority can hardly be replaced in the PLA. In a revolutionary Party which fought fiercely over 28 years to seize political power from the GMD, the importance of the military force could hardly be minimized.[62] Chen Ziming (1992:252-253) argued that in China the rational-legal norms were not sufficiently institutionalized to resolve political crises in a peaceful way. In the past three decades, there were four occasions that PLA intervened to resolve a crisis: first, ousting Liu Shaoqi from the Party; second, the Lin Biao fiasco; third, the arrest of the "Gang of Four", and fourth, the 4 June crackdown. I would argue that the reason that Deng became the "paramount" leader in the reformist period was precisely because of his undisputed position in the army, in spite of the Party seniority of Chen. Deng was almost the lone reformer among the gerontocrats. Chen's networks seemed much wider than Deng's, but Deng's links with the PLA proved decisive. [63]

Notwithstanding the substantial differences with Deng, Chen never openly challenged Deng's marketization policies. As Mao said once, in Party affairs Chen has strong discipline. Once the Party (in the reformist period, very often this means Deng) makes a decision, he complies. Therefore, he could maintain a cordial relationship with Deng despite the vast differences in the economic developmental strategies (Chen Liu 1995). To some extent, Chen's moderation exerted a degree of restraint on Deng who always urged the speed and pace of economic development be quickened. After 1984 when Zhao Ziyang proposed the notion of "planned commodity economy", Chen gradually lost decisive influence over the reform course. His only non-economic contribution to the CCP was his urge to recruit as quickly as possible political successors.[64]

Despite their enormous gap in ideas and working styles, as Party veterans, Deng and Chen shared one most important similarity: determination to maintain the political hegemony of the CCP. Deng was more pragmatic, down-to-earth and nationalistic than Chen (Evans 1995:313). In fact, Deng's lack of interest in ideology gave the conservatives such as Hu Qiaomu and Deng Liqun much room to manoeuvre. This explains the fact that counterattacks always came from cultural-ideological fields. In a way, Deng was more liberal than Chen in introducing reform and open-door policies. Until his death in April 1995, Chen had never been to the SEZs, which certainly show his disapproving attitude on the policy. Obviously, Deng's initial desire to reform the Leninist-Stalinist type of polity was sincere, but he has too many limitations. He was a man of contradictions. He thought China could get the best possible world. He believes that market economy could coexist with monolithic political order; ideological conformity with "dual hundred" policy; and a highly democratic polity with the Party's ruthless maintenance of political and social stability. History seems to repeat itself. As in Mao's later years, it is tragic that the momentum of development in a vast country like China is decided by an old man of failing health again.

Unlike Mao, Deng is strong but not a charismatic leader. He wields enormous power, but he was circumscribed by other veterans. He was only the first among equals. By reversing Mao's policies, Deng hoped to shape a broad alliance within the Party that would accept his politics and economics of modernization. By steering a middle course, Deng was able to sail through the tumultuous path of intra-Party struggles, but with a heavy price. Baum (1993:342) pinpointed the tragedy of Deng:

> As the decade wore on....Deng found it increasingly difficult to steer a middle course of *fang* and *shou*....Unable to create a viable structure of authority that combined both *fang* and *shou*, and unable to locate a successor acceptable to all major factions, he was unable to retire from active leadership....Yet the more he intervened in the decision process *ex cathedra*, the more elusive became his quest for a rationalized political order. Therein, perhaps lay the supreme paradox of Deng's political stewardship: in his quest to lead China out of "feudal autocracy" of the Maoist era toward modernity and rule by law, Deng increasingly resorted to highly personalized instruments of control-instruments that were the very antithesis of the system he sought to create.

Notes

[1] The classic analysis of the cyclical phenomena in modern Chinese politics remains G. William Skinner and Edwin A. Winckler's article (1980).

[2] In a book about contemporary China published in 1999 (MacFaguhr 1999), the concept of policy cycles was not even mentioned once.

[3] Two insiders' account of the intra-Party intrigues was particularly revealing. See Ruan Ming (1994) and Wu Jiang (1995). Wu and Ruan were former subordinates of Hu Yaobang and they both pointed out that there were two reformist and conservative camps in the CCP. Further, in the reformist camp there were substantial political differences between Hu Yaobang and Zhao Ziyang.

[4]Selden (1988) has characterized the Maoist era as a "mobilizational era", in which political campaigns always start from the above. In the Dengist era, the Party/state became more passive and less totalitarian. Mathew McCubbins and Thomas Schwartz (Shirk 1993:57-59) argued that the CCP's control of Chinese society has changed from "police-patrol oversight" to "fire-alarm oversight".
[5] For more details about the notion of civil society, see chapter 7.
[6]Paradoxically, the first detailed outline of the cyclical process in the Dengist era was given by Deng Liqun, one of China's most powerful orthodox Marxists and former propaganda chief of the CCP (Ruan Ming 1994:168-71). When Hu Yaobang was the general secretary of the CCP, Deng was labeled as the "underground general secretary". He remains one of the most fierce critics of Jiang Zemin's political and ideological lines to date (Fewswith, 2001).
[7]In identifying the economic cycles, Chen Ziming (1992:296-297) pointed out that reform years were: 1979, 1980, 1984, 1986 and 1987 and the retrenchment years were: 1981, 1982, 1983, 1985, and 1988.
[8]Wei Jingsheng was released in September 1993, six months earlier than his full term imprisonment, apparently in exchange for the granting of the Most Favoured Nation (MFN) trading status by the United States. After June 4 1994, Wei was arrested by the security police again. After being kept in custody for one and a half years, he was formally charged with "the attempt to overthrow the government" in December 1995. He was sentenced to fourteen years of imprisonment. In 1998, Wei was sent to the USA for treatment. Since then he has been in exile.
[9]They were expelled from the CCP for the second time. They were expelled once in the Anti-Rightists campaign in 1957. Wang died in 2000 and Fan and Liu are now in exile in the United State.
[10]There was a controversy as to who ordered the PLA to open fire on the civilians. Some said that it was Yang Shangkun, the vice-chairman of the CMC, and some said that it was the individual commanders who were empowered to act according to situations. However, as a revolutionary Party which believes that " political power grows from the barrel of a gun", it is unthinkable that Deng would leave the final decision to individual generals. In fact, in an interview with *New York Times* in January 1995, Deng Rong, Deng's youngest daughter, admitted implicitly that her father should be held responsible for the 4 June killings (*Open* February 1995:11).
[11]Due to the limited space in this book, I shall concentrate on the Dengist reform cycles and the treatment of Maoist cycles will be brief. The article of Skinner and Winckler outlined the policy cycles in Mao's era until 1969. Therefore, in light of the disappearance of policy cycles in the 1990s, of the there is much room for future research on the cyclical process in the history of the PRC.
[12] The coalition under Hua could be roughly subdivided as follows: the "whateverist" group led by Hua with the beneficiaries of the CR, such as Wang Dongxing, Wu De, Chen Xilian, Ji Dengkui, Chen Yonggui; the "petroleum"

group led by Li Xianian, with followers such as Yu Qiuli, Kong Shien, and Chen Muhua; the pragmatist group led by Deng Xiaoping, with his proteges Hu Yaobang and Zhao Ziyang, and long time associate Wan Li. The Chen Yun group included Yao Yilin, Bo Yibo, Deng Liqun. There were elder veterans with no clear cut political inclinations, such as Ye Jianying, Xu Xiangqian, Nie Rongzhen, and Deng Yingchao (Chang Parris 1981:6-8).

[13] The article was originally written by Hu Fuming, an associate philosophy professor at Nanjing University. It was a contribution to the "philosophy" page of the newspaper. The editor-in-chief sensed the timely relevance of the article. After nine revisions, the article was finally published and the name of the author was omitted. The final draft was approved by Hu Yaobang (Tao Hai 1989:23-24).

[14] Philosophically, the statement "practice is the sole criterion of testing truth" is untenable. First, in logic and mathematics, we do have "truth" that is not necessarily tested by social practice. Second, the term "practice" is vague. It is methodologically commonsense that "true" theory in natural science or social science must be verified by experience or experiment. Can experiments be called "practice"? Even if they can, the testing of the political line or revolutionary theory is entirely different from the testing of any scientific hypothesis. In retrospect, in the context of China's political evolution in the late 1970s, what is important is the political implication or impact of the debate not the scientific nature of the statement itself.

[15] Again "to seek truth from facts" was philosophically unsound. Pure facts simply do not exist. Facts are chaotic, and they are meaningful only in relation to a theory or a conceptual framework. In fact, it is impossible "to seek truth from facts". Facts can be used to test a theory or a statement, but facts themselves are meaningless. The statement is an expedient political slogan that intends to change the mindset of the people.

[16] The other two mind-emancipation movements were the May-Fourth Movement in 1919 and the Yenan Rectification Movement in 1942. Zhou's interpretation of China's modern intellectual history was prejudiced. None would dispute the emancipatory significance of the Chinese mindset of the May-Fourth Movement, but the Yenan Rectification Movement in the CCP in fact was a movement to establish the supreme position of Mao's thought. It laid the foundation of establishing Mao's thought as the general guideline of the CCP three years later. Instead of a mind-emancipation movement, it was actually a mind-restraining movement. See Li Zehou (1987) on the essential differences between the May-Fourth movement and the Chinese Communist Movement.

[17] In his ambitious ten-year (1975-1985) economic development program pronounced in 1977, Hua called for the construction of 120 major projects, 14 major industrial bases and infrastructure capital investment projects, which were equivalent to all those in the previous 28 years (Liao Gailong 1991:332). After Deng Xiaoping ascended to power, the development program was criticized by

reformists and discarded altogether. Chen Yun's task was to set realistic targets and devised viable development strategy for the post-Hua leadership.

[18]The idea of initiating a Theoretical Work Conference was suggested by Marshal Ye Jianying. In the course of debate on the criterion of truth, Hong Fu, then the editor-in-chief of the *Red Flag* had prepared an article critical of Hu Fumin's article. When the article was submitted to Ye for consideration, he suggested that the Party should convene a conference to discuss a whole range of issues regarding the debate or on issues of theoretical significance (Ruan Ming 1994:59).

[19]In a speech delivered at the Central Work Conference on 13 December 1978, Ye Jianying stated that "the Third Plenum was the prototype of the intra-Party democracy, while the Xidan Democracy Wall was the example of the people's democracy." The sentences were deleted when his speech was issued as a Party formal document (Ruan Ming 1994:50).

[20]For the chronology of the activities of "Beijing Spring", see *The Seventies* (June 1981:15-17) and also chapter 2.

[21]From my analysis of the first reform cycle, the trend of *fang* and *shou* took place not only longitudinally, i.e. in a time sequence, but also horizontally, i.e. cross-sectionally. Throughout the 1980s, the two dimensions of the reform cycle occurred from time to time. Clearly, the economic and political-ideological cycles were not synchronous.

[22]For details of Deng's speech, see chapter 3.

[23]The speech was later known as the Gengshen reform package (Liao Gailong 1980) and it was never officially released. After 1981, the package was simply dropped.

[24]Liao's reform proposal was extremely radical in Chinese context. I suspect it was never intended to be implemented. To be sure, the conservatives inside the CCP would never have accepted it. As a shrewd politician, Deng should have well foreseen the obstacles. The proposal probably served as a litmus test to evaluate the reaction of the conservatives. The fact that such an important speech was delivered by a middle ranking Party research fellow may well support my conjecture, for if the proposals encountered stiff opposition, Liao could be dispensed with easily.

[25]There emerged many implementation problems. See Nathan (1985) chapter 5.

[26]Hu Ping was elected but he was barred from taking his seat in the local People's Congress. Wang was pressured to write self-criticism. Coincidentally, at the nearby CASS, Chen Ziming was similarly barred from taking his seat. Hu emigrated to the United States in 1986. Wang and Chen were arrested in the wake of the 4 June crackdown. Both were imprisoned for thirteen years. Wang was sent to exile in 1994. Chen was once released in 1994 but re-arrested later and re-released again. Now, he is put into house arrest whenever sensitive occasions arise.

[27]The Polish crisis in 1980 created anxiety among the CCP leadership as a whole. In one of the internal documents issued by a provincial Propaganda Department

on 25 November 1980, the Party propagandists surmised that the Polish crisis was rooted in three factors: first, mistaken economic policies; second, the corruption and abuse of power of the senior Party cadres; and third, dependence on the Soviet Union. The Polish authorities adopted some measures to ameliorate the crisis but failed to resolve the crisis. The CCP had adopted some of the measures that were absorbed in the Gengshen reform package (*The Seventies* April 1981:36-40).

[28]Deng's relationship with PLA generals was strained after the reform began. A case reported by the Agence France Press may well be symbolic though it might not be true. Xu Shiyou, one of the senior generals displaced by Deng in the military reshuffle, reported to have clashed with Deng in the Fifth Plenum in early March 1980. Xu was said to have taken a revolver and fired at Deng but missed (Baum 1994:408).

[29]The works of Ye and Sha attacked the special privileges of the PLA generals. Wang's writings documented the grim conditions during the CR. Liu's piece exposed the corruption network in the CCP grass-root bureaucracy. All these infuriated the Party conservatives.

[30] The *Resolution* drafting committee was presided over by Deng and Hu Yaobang. Formally Hu Yaobang was in charge of the whole process, but the actual writing of the document fell on the shoulders of Hu Qiaomu, the Party chief ideologue. According to Ruan Ming (1994) and Wu Jiang (1995), these two Hus had profound differences over the reform course in the 1980s. The cited case over the analysis of the Polish situation in mid-1980s was one of them.

[31]In his sixth talk about the Resolution drafting, Deng (1984:289-290) quoted Chen Yun who argued that two points should be inserted into the draft: first, a section reviewing the entire history of the CCP , and second, a section encouraging people to study some Marxist philosophy, in particular, Mao's work. In comparing his works with Deng's famous "cat" catchphrase, Chen Yun was more orthodox than Deng.

[32]For details on the strengthening of the NPC, see chapter 3.

[33]In the 1950s and 1960s, the political dissidents in the Soviet Union and Eastern Europe deliberately engaged in the debate about young/mature Marx. The purpose was political. In Leninist state socialism, the dissemination of other political thought was prohibited. The study of young Marx at least fell on the boundary sanctioned by the government. Their goal was to "raise the banner of Marxism to undercut Marxism" (Tucker 1978:XXVII). In a similar vein, the debate on alienation by the Chinese intellectuals was not purely academic. They were two decades behind their Eastern European counterparts.

[34]Brugger and Kelly (1990) devote a lengthy section to the discussion of this issue.

[35] There were fierce behind-the-scene struggles on the publication of Zhou's speech. Right after the speech, Hu Qiaomu rang the Central Party School, charging that Zhou had made a grave "political mistake" by supporting the notion

of alienation. He asked for the forum to be extended for three days, so that criticism meetings of Zhou's speech could be organized. He also called on the *People's Daily* to stop publishing Zhou's speech and he suggested that Zhou's speech should be published in an internal journal. Hu Jiwei and Wang Ruoshui, editor-in-chief and deputy editor-in-chief of the *People's Daily*, ignored his warning and published the speech (Ruan Ming 1994:150). Later, they both were penalized for their courageous act.

[36]Wang's evaluation of Mao, Mao Zedong Thought, and the CR can be seen in his speech at the Theoretical Work Conference on 13 February 1979 (1989:213-241) and two other related articles (1989:242-262). Wang was finally dismissed from the CCP in the 1987 anti-bourgeois liberalization campaign. Wang died in 2001 of cancer.

[37]After the Second Plenum, Deng Xiaoping felt that his speech in the Plenum was too "left", and that he was betrayed by Deng Liqun and Hu Qiaomu, who drafted the speech for him. Deng decided to dismiss Deng Liqun from the CCP Propaganda Department. But the news was leaked and the Voice of America broadcast the news. To prove the Voice of America wrong, Deng cancelled the move (Ruan Ming 1994:150).

[38]The issue of the SEZs is one of the central issues that divides the Dengist reformists and conservatives. Chen Yun remained the only elder statesman in the CCP who had never been to the SEZs until he died in April 1995.

[39]The notion of a "planned commodity economy" was first suggested by Xu Muqiao, a noted reformist economist, in 1981. In response, Chen Yun formulated his notion of a "bird-cage" socialist economy (Baum 1994:171).

[40]In analyzing the corruption of the "princelings", Baum (1994:175) has wrongly put the blame on the so-called Hainan scandal in 1984. In fact, the "princelings" played no part in the scandal. Three persons were held responsible for the scandal: the Party secretary of Hainan Island Yao Wenshui, the executive head Lei Yu, and Chen Yuyi, the director of foreign trade (Hu Ping and Zhang Shengyao 1988:407-446).

[41]In the article, Liu, in fact, outlined three kinds of loyalties. Despite its ban from publication, Wan Li, then a Politburo member and vice premier, personally talked to Liu and indeed encouraged people to have the second kind of loyalty (1990:280-281).

[42]Baum wrote that (1994:180-181) Deng Liqun was able to get Hu's speech published without his prior approval when Hu was abroad. Baum's source is based on Lu Keng (1985). I have checked the original Chinese source, and found that this was only a conjecture by Lu Keng, and it was explicitly denied by Hu Yaobang (Lu Keng 1985:13).

[43]The Party Constitution (CCCCP 1982 Article 12) stipulated that the Party committee at the county level or above could, if necessary, convene a Party Representatives Conference to discuss and resolve important and urgent issues. In

the CCP history, only two Party Representatives Conferences were held before 1985. They were held in 1937 and 1955 (*Wen Wei Po* 19 September 1985).

[44] The quotation was cited in Stavis (1988:52).

[45] For Yan's ideas of political structural reform, see also chapter 3 and C.L. Chiou (1986). Yan left China after the crackdown of 1989. He was elected the chairman (1989-90) of the Front for a Democratic China, a pro-democracy organization organized by the democratic activists living in exile, on 24 September 1989 in Paris; Yan still writes regularly for Hong Kong publications.

[46] Apparently Fang was not involved in the 1989 pro-democracy movement (Shen Tong 1990), but his role in triggering the 1986/87 student demonstrations was undeniable. Student demonstrations started at the University of Science and Technology, where Fang served as executive vice-president. Baum (1994:201) observed that when the students began to demonstrate in early December 1986, the arc of political contagion followed rather closely the itinery of Fang's 1985-6 lecturing tours in Central China. After the 4 June suppression, he sought political asylum in the U.S. Embassy in Beijing. After a year of deliberation and negotiation, the CCP allowed him and his wife to go abroad. Fang and his wife now live in the U.S.A.

[47] According to Yan Jiaqi (1992a:174), the Party's general secretary should take charge in implementing political reform. The fact that Deng brushed aside Hu Yaobang and asked Zhao, the premier, to draft the documents means that Hu's influence on Party affairs was on the decline. Wu Guoguang (1997) provides an insider's account of the issues that the group discussed.

[48] There were fierce power and ideological struggles preceding the Plenum. The Plenum was a setback for the reformists. There were four items on the initial agenda: first, preliminary discussion on the political reform; second, succession arrangement in the Thirteenth CCP Congress to be held in 1987; third, assessing the economic situation and open-door policy; fourth, discussion on spiritual civilization. None of the items reached agreement except the fourth (*Cheng Ming* November 1986:6).

[49] The students were deeply dissatisfied with problems largely emerging in the reform period, such as poor living standard, low government subsidies, official corruption, inflation, power inequality, and the privileges of the "princelings", but the immediate causes of the demonstrations varied in the different localities (Tsang Wai-yin 1989). Students from the University of Science and Technology protested against the improper nomination procedure in the coming county election of the local People's Congress. In Shanghai, demonstrations started as one student was beaten up by a security guard at a rock-and-roll music concert. Students in Zhongshan University in Guangzhou demanding the government control inflation, and students in Shenzhen were angry at the new increased university fee. Finally, students from Beijing and Nanjing rose up in support of fellow students in other places. University students were greatly influenced by

Western thought, and they were more outspoken than the older generations (Yang Deguang 1991).

[50]The CCP Central Document No. 3 (1987), catalogued Hu's political misdeeds. First, he had resisted fighting spiritual pollution and bourgeois liberalization in the ideological sphere, culminating in the student turmoil. Second, he promoted the rule of man. Third, Hu twisted the Party's direction of "unifying " thoughts; instead he shifted the focus to economic work. Fourth, he neglected Chinese reality by promoting high consumption. Fifth, in seeing foreign dignitaries, he revealed Party/state "secrets". Sixth, he claimed to represent the CCP, which he was not entitled to (*Pai Shing* 16 February 1987:4-5).

[51]Deng Liqun, in fact, listed altogether 12 prominent intellectuals to be purged in the anti-bourgeois liberalization campaign. He even named Bao Tong and Yan Jiaqi, two important members of Zhao's bureau of political structural reform. He wanted to send his men to take over the *People's Daily* and the Ministry of Culture. All these moves were resisted by Zhao Ziyang (Ruan Ming 1994:209-210).

[52]From the date that Hu Yaobang's resignation was announced (16 January 1987) to the date of the issuing of Central Document No.4 (28 January 1987), was only 12 days.

[53]The initial ideas of the primary stage of socialism were first suggested by Su Shaozhi (1988) in the mid-1980s. Despite the downfall of Zhao Ziyang, the future CCP Congresses have retained the concept. See Jiang Zemin's political report in the Sixteenth CCP Congress (Jiang 2002).

[54]The ultra-leftist Deng Liqun was planned to be included in the new Politburo. But in the Thirteenth CCP Congress, a competitive election was introduced into the election of the CC. Deng was eliminated in the election and failed to qualify for election to the Politburo (Ruan Ming 1994:211-214).

[55]I shall not go into the details of the events leading to the June 4 massacre. Schell (1994) and Yang L.Y. and Ma Yiyang (1991) provide a broad picture of the tragedy. A day-to-day chronology of the events from a participant's point of view is provided by Shen Tong (1990). A chronology of events is also provided in *Cheng Ming* June 1989:56-58.

[56]Gorbachev had become a hero by launching *glasnost* and *perestroika* in the Soviet Union after he ascended to power in 1985. He had become a source of inspiration to the Chinese intellectuals and students alike. In 1989, students hailed Gorbachev as "a true reformer", and "we want Gorbachev" banners were seen. For details about his reform policies, see Lane (1990).

[57] There have been numerous works analyzing the events. Short and concise social-political analyses about the massacre are provided by Anita Chan (1991), Dittmer (1989), Nathan (1989), Stavis (1990), Su Shaozhi (1989), Walder (1989).

[58]According to Chen Yizhi (Yang L.Y. and Ma Yiyang 1991:53), Bao Tong, Zhao's assistant, revealed that the published 26 April editorial was different from

the one that was telexed to Zhao when he was in Pyongyang. If this is true, then most likely Li Peng was planting a conspiracy against Zhao.

[59] There were intriguing struggles among the leadership, including the PLA generals. For details, see *Cheng Ming* May and June 1989; Cheung Ki-fung 1989:173-195; Schell 1994:58-175; Nathan and Link (2001).

[60] In accounting for the violent clashes between the CCP and students, Tsou Tang proposed a "theory of disinformation" (1991). He argued that both sides miscalculated due to the distorted nature of information flow channels on the CCP Party/state structure. The theory assumes that if the leadership had "sufficient" information, the tragedy could have been avoided. But the fact that there were moderate elements in the CCP, and that they tried to resolve the crisis in a peaceful way show that the CCP knew after all what was happening. The important thing in the confrontation is not how much information the leadership received, but how they perceived the events. It is crystal clear from the experience of the 1986/87 student demonstrations that the hardliners inside the Party including Deng would not tolerate any challenge to their authority.

[61] Deng was born in 1904 and Chen in 1905.

[62] Ruan Ming thinks otherwise (1994:227-228). He argued that the major source of power for Deng was in the Party not the PLA. It is true to some extent. The CCP always stresses the civilian control of the army, but the importance of the military can not be denied. At the critical juncture, force becomes the only means to resolve crisis, such as the arrest of the "Gang of Four" in 1976 and the crackdown on the 1989 pro-democracy movement.

[63] Ruan Ming (1992) pointed out the networks maintained by Chen as follows: In the Party hierachy: Song Ping and Liu Feng (CCP Organization Department), Hu Qiaomu and Deng Liqun (ideology watchdogs); Bo Yibo, Wang Zhen, and Song Renqiong (CAC); in the government hierachy: Li Peng and Yao Yilin (State Council), Wang Renzhi and Xu Weicheng (Propaganda Department), Gao Di (*People's Daily*), Yu Wen (CASS), He Jingzhi (Department of Culture), Ai Zhisheng (Department of Television and Broadcasting), He Dongchang (Commission of Education).

[64] Chen may well have been the force contributing to the formation of the "princelings" within the CCP. As early as the 1930s when he was in charge of the CCP Organization Department, he was in favour of breeding the off-spring of revolutionary leaders to become political successors. It seemed that he had not abandoned the idea in the 1980s (Chen Liu 1995).

CHAPTER FIVE

THE POST-TIANANMEN RETRENCHMENT

This chapter deals with the crisis that the CCP faced and the repressive measures adopted by it in the aftermath of the 4 June bloodbath. First, I shall discuss the impact of the pro-democracy movement on the CCP Party/state polity and the retrenchment on all fronts after the brutal crackdown. I shall focus on three dimensions, namely the purges of intellectuals and students, the tightening control of mass media, and the mass clean-up within the CCP and hierarchy. Secondly, there will be an analysis of the reform policies of the political structure in the early 1990s, particularly around the Fourteenth CCP Congress in October 1992. Following the analysis of cyclical flux in chapter 4, I shall be examining whether the seventh cycle of *fang* and *shou* in the ideological-political realm had occurred in the early 1990s.

Mass Purges in the aftermath of the 4 June Crackdown

The factional power intrigues behind the scenes over the mass killings in June 4 were revealing.[1] It was reported that as early as 19 May, after the SC of the CCP Politburo had cast its vote in Deng's home to announce that martial law be imposed on some districts of Beijing, including Tiananmen Square, Zhao Ziyang, sided only by Hu Qili, immediately tendered his resignation but it was rejected by Deng. After 20 May, he was practically put in "house arrest" at his home. He allegedly expressed his opinions regarding the suppression of the student movement,

> I cannot suppress the students and I don't want to commit this crime. Even if I die or lose my position, I will uphold my opinion firmly. I know I should be responsible for the

> economic problems, but the move of a hunger strike by students was beyond my expectation. I don't want the situation to become like this, but I am still against suppressing the students (*The Mirror* June 1989:24).

The mass arrests began on 6 June after the troop reoccupied Tiananmen Square. The clampdown on the liberal intelligentsia and student leaders was the regime's top priority. The CCP government put 21 student leaders on the "most-wanted" list and issued arrest warrants for other prominent intellectuals as well. They included Fang Lizhi and his wife Li Shuxian, Wu'er Kaixi, Wang Dan, Chai Ling, Li Lu, Feng Congde, Shen Tong, Zhang Boli, Han Dongfang, Yu Haocheng, Yan Jianqi and his wife Gao Gao, Wan Runnan, Su Xiaokang, Yuan Zhiming, Zheng Yi, Bao Zunxin, Chen Ziming, and Wang Juntao. Also on the list was the singer Hou Dejian and scholars Liu Xiaobo, Zhou Duo, and Gao Xin.

Fang Lizhi and his wife Li Shuxian successfully sought political asylum in the American Embassy in Beijing and went into hiding in the Embassy until the US government reached an agreement with the Chinese government to let them go abroad for "health reasons" in the mid-1990s.[2] In the weeks following the 4 June bloodbath, many intellectuals and students were able to evade the government's dragnet through the assistance of a network organized by the Hong Kong-based group known as the Alliance in Support of the Patriotic Movement in China (*Pai Shing* 1 July 1991:49-53).[3] They included: Wu'er Kaixi, Chai Ling, Zhang Boli, Yan Jiaqi and his wife, Feng Congde, Chen Yizi, Wan Runnan, Su Xiaokang, Yuan Zhiming, and Zheng Yi. Chen Ziming, Wang Juntao, Wang Dan, and Bao Zunxin were hunted down by the security police. Han Donfang and Yu Haocheng turned themselves in to the authorities after going into hiding for a period. The singer Hou Dejian spent about ten weeks in the Australian Embassy after the crackdown and later gave himself up.

The moderate *Brightness Daily* reporter Dai Qing, despite her princeling background (the adopted daughter of the late Marshal Ye Jianying), was arrested and put into the famous Qincheng Prison for more than a year. By the spring of 1991 the Chinese government had confirmed a total of 2,578 arrests. However, Hong Kong sources put the number at more than 4,000, of whom 1,730 were convicted and sent to prison (*Cheng Ming* December 1991:14). With the initial round of harsh clampdown and arrests and the stabilization of the regime in the second half of 1989, Beijing lifted martial law in January 1990 and released the first batch of 573 political prisoners. In an internal forum with students of higher institutions in January, Chen Xitong, the then Beijing mayor, disclosed that among the 4,000 cases of arrests, 60% of them had been released (*The Mirror* February 1990:36).[4]

In May 1991, the second batch of political prisoners were released, including prominent intellectuals such as Dai Qing, Zhou Duo, and Cao Siyuan of the Stone Corporation. The release was timed to coincide with the US Congressional debate on the granting of the Most-Favoured-Nation (MFN) trading status to China. The invasion of Kuwait by Iraq in August 1990 triggered a new Middle-East crisis and successfully turned the world wide attention away from China. In late 1990 and early 1991, at the height of the Persian Gulf crisis, the CCP brought 31 intellectuals and students to trial and convicted them with various terms of imprisonment. At the same time 45 detainees were released without any charges against them. Chen Ziming and Wang Juntao were given the harshest sentences of all, each receiving 13 years of imprisonment on charges of "counter-revolutionary activities and propaganda".[5]

Literary commentator turned dissident Liu Xiaobo was convicted; he was nonetheless released after showing "sincere repentance" for his behaviour. Wang Dan, who topped the "wanted list" of student leaders, received a relatively light indictment of four years. Ren Wanding, the old pro-democracy fighter of "Beijing Spring" was sentenced to seven years. Hou Dejian, the internationally-known singer, was deported to Taiwan in June 1990. One of the last ones to be tried and convicted was Bao Tong, the former political secretary of Zhao Ziyang and a member of the CC. In July 1992, he was sentenced to nine years of imprisonment for charges of "leaking state secrets and counter-revolutionary propaganda incitement".[6] Bao was an important personage in the reformist era and he had actively participated in the drafting of numerous important CCP Party resolutions, reports, and speeches of the top leaders. Among them were: speeches and documents in the National Natural Science Congress in 1978 (delivered by Deng Xiaoping and Fang Yi), the speech on the educational work in 1979 (delivered by Deng Xiaoping), the speech on the reform of scientific-technology system (delivered by Deng Xiaoping), the CCP Central Document No. 3 in 1987, the speech on separating the Party and government by Zhao Ziyang to the Seventh Plenum of the Twelfth CC, the political report of the Thirteenth CCP Congress and the amendment to the CCP Party Constitution in 1987, reports of the Second Plenum of the Thirteenth CC and the Third Plenum of the Thirteenth CC, and the editorial "Think of the Collective and Preserve Stability" of the *People's Daily* on 29 April 1989.

Higher learning institutions were the battleground over which the hard-line post-Tiananmen CCP leadership attempted to regain control and eradicate the inundation of "bourgeois liberalization". As soon as the "counter-rebellion" was quelled, all presidents of the tertiary institutions were assembled for two weeks in Beijing to be brain-washed with the official version of the 4 June events and to be infused with the "correct" political point of view (*Cheng Ming* October 1989:20). Materials about Western political systems and theories were weeded out and ideological education was strengthened. The Party's control over the higher learning institutes was strengthened when the CCP announced the reform of the higher education system was to be suspended, and reverted back to the pre-reform system of "the president under the leadership of the Party Committee" (*The Mirror* December 1990:36). In a public speech, Li Tieying, a Politburo member and the director of the State Education Committee, said that China must have "socialist universities with Chinese characteristics, and "those teachers who do not want to propagate socialism can quit and those students who do not believe in socialism can leave" (*Ming Pao* 9 July 1991). He indicated that socialist universities cannot be compared with Western bourgeois universities. "No matter how backward they are, our colleges are still colleges with Chinese characteristics".

Military training was introduced to the freshman class of Beida and Tsinghua University in 1989 for one year. In a throwback to the CR, one million college students were asked to go to the countryside in the summer of 1991 to learn from workers and peasants. Furthermore, the State Education Commission claimed they would check the dissertations of the post-graduate students in the past five years for signs of "bourgeois liberalization". The authors of the "poisonous weeds" would be subject to disciplinary action unless they recanted (*Ming Pao* 9 July 1991). The CASS, the breeding ground for leading liberal intellectuals, suffered the most thorough clean-up. The Institutes of Political Science and Marxism-Leninism were singled out for attacks and the conservative ideologues even threatened to close down Marxism-Leninism Institute and replace it with an Institute of Contemporary Marxism. In total, at least 120 staff and researchers were subject to disciplinary action and 6 were imprisoned (*SCMP* 1 March 1991).

The mass media played an important part in the Tiananmen pro-democracy movement and the hardliners considered it a "hotbed" where iron-fist control should be restored.[7] After 4 June, senior cadres working in the press with reformist tendencies and associated closely with Zhao Ziyang were replaced by more conservative cadres. Qian Liyan and Tan Wenrui, the director and the editor-in-chief of the *People's Daily*, were replaced by an army general Shao Huaze, the editor-in-chief of the *Brightness Daily*, was replaced by Zhang Changhai. Du Duocheng, the director of the Department of Publication and Press, was forced to resign and Mu Qing, the director of the Xin Hua News Agency, was suspended from his duties. Across the country, more than twenty editors and reporters were arrested, and among them were Dai Qing, Zhang Weiguo of the *World Economic Herald*, Gao Yu of the *Economic Weekly*, Sun Changjiang of the *Technological Daily*, and Yang Long of the *Chinese Youth*. More than ten editors and reporters in the *People's Daily*, the Xin Hua News Agency, the Central Television, and the Central Radio, were arrested. Moreover, a dozen widely-circulated magazines were banned including the *Thinkers*, the *Economic Weekly* edited by Wang Juntao, the New Observer by Ge Yang, who was in the United States when the magazine was closed down, *The Chinese World*, the *Seiku News Bulletins*, the *New Era* and the *The Hainan Record* in Hainan (*Cheng Ming* October 1989:18-19). The editors-in-chief of two of the most popular literary magazines, *People's Literature* and *Literary Bulletin*, changed guards. Liu Xinwu and Xie Yongwang were replaced by left ideologues.

A mass rectification campaign was conducted in the six months after 4 June within the CCP Party/state, in order to eradicate the influence of Zhao and his associates. The "work teams" and sometimes martial law troops were stationed practically in all the central Party and government units. In the first half of 1990, the Party launched an unprecedented "re-registration" campaign: all the Party members lost their membership automatically until they re-registered and satisfied the ideological requirements of total devotion to Marxism-Leninism and the 'correct' view of the 4 June incident. Moreover, the Party members and sometimes non-Party members and officials had to write a day-to-day account of their activities during the period of student demonstrations so that the Party could know their whereabouts(*The Mirror* October 1989:37).

The top level leadership above the ministerial level underwent a mass reshuffle (Li Kwok-shing 1993). In the Fourth Plenum of the Thirteenth CC held on 23-24 June 1989, attended by 184 old-timers of the CAC, Zhao Ziyang was stripped of all Party posts but retained the CCP membership. Despite his denial of culpability (1994) in handling the 1989 student movement, Zhao was accused of "splitting the Party". The communique of the Fourth Plenum stated that during his leadership grave policy errors had been committed including the laxity in upholding the four cardinal principles and consequently the neglecting of the Party's ideological work and the construction of socialist spiritual civilization (*The Mirror* July 1989:38). In the same plenum, Jiang Zemin was ascended to the post of general secretary. Five days after the Fourth Plenum, the Eighth session of the SC of the Seventh NPC was convened on 29 June to dismiss Zhao from his remaining state post: the vice-chairman of the state CMC.

Hu Qili, another liberal SC member of the Politburo, was stripped of his posts in the Politburo and CS, but retained membership in the CC, and he was spared from further penalty. Yan Mingfu, the United Front minister and member of the CS, and Rui Xingwen, a member of the CS, were dismissed from their posts. At the ministerial level, An Zhiwen, the vice-minister of the State Commission for Economic Structural Reform, and Du Runsheng, the director of the Rural Policy Research Centre, were forced to resign. The Public Security minister Wang Fang was demoted to be one of the vice-directors of the Central Committee on the Comprehensive Management of Social Security established in March 1991. Wen Jiabao, Zhao's protege and director of the General Office of the CCP, was replaced by Zeng Qinghong, Jiang Zemin's closest subordinate from Shanghai. Jiang Zemin, the Shanghai mayor and a Politburo member, was elevated to replace Zhao as the general secretary of the CCP.[8] 72-year-old Song Ping was promoted to the SC of the Politburo and held the concurrent post of the head of the powerful CCP Organization Department. 55-year-old Tianjin mayor Li Ruihuan, who would be in charge of propaganda and ideology, became an SC member of the Politburo and a member of the CS. Ding Guangen, who was said to be one of Deng's closest partners in playing bridge, was promoted to the CS. Xu Jiatun, the then Hong Kong Xin Hua News Agency director, went into exile in April 1990, and he was replaced by Zhou Nan, an assistant minister of foreign affairs. Wang Meng and Ying Ruocheng, the minister and the vice-minister of culture respectively were forced to resign.[9]

Besides the civilian leadership, a mass reshuffle also took place in the PLA. Evidently, the PLA was divided on how to handle the student demonstrations. Deng Xiaoping resigned his post of chairman of the CMC in the Fifth Plenum of the Thirteenth CC in November 1989, and Jiang succeeded him as the chairman. Yang Shangkun replaced Zhao Ziyang as the CMC's first vice-chairman. Liu Huaqing, a 73-year-old former Second Field Army general, was picked by Deng to become the second vice-chairman of the CMC. Yang Shangkun's half brother Yang Baibing, aged 69, became the newly-created secretary general of the PLA. Old general Hong Xuezhi, reportedly having sympathy with the students, was released from his post of the deputy CMC secretary-general and appointed to the far less significant position of the vice chairman of the CPPCC. By April and May, the CCP also completed the reorganization of the seven regional military commands leadership. Except for the regional command structure of Shenyang, all the senior commanders and political commissars were replaced. A rectification drive was also carried out in the 600,000 People's Armed Police. The original commander and political commissar were dismissed. The entire organization was placed under the operational control of the CMC, rather than under the ministry of public security, as before. The reorganization of the PLA took place not because of the deep divisions among the old generals in the light of the 1989 pro-democracy movement, but also in the light of the execution of the Romanian dictator Ceausecu by the army in Eastern Europe. The geriatrics considered that the collapse of the Romanian despotic regime due to the disunity of the army. After learning the lesson, the consolidation of the PLA became the top priority for the CCP in 1990/91.

In the light of the impact of the 1989 pro-democracy movement and *sudongbo* (the waves of the reform of the Soviet Union and Eastern Europe), the repressive measures to stamp out enemies boiled down to one thing: the survival and monopoly of political power of the CCP. The all-round attacks on the elements of "bourgeois liberalization" intended to root out potential or real threats to the CCP. In a commentary in the *People's Daily* (24 April 1991), the conservative author gave an all-embracing definition of "bourgeois liberalization". It meant:

> Negating the socialist system and advocating the capitalist road....Politically, it advocates the Western-style multi-party politics and the parliamentary system, negating the leadership of the Communist party and the dictatorship of the proletariat. Economically, it advocates private enterprise and the market, negating public ownership and the planned economy. Ideologically, it advocates multi-dimensionalism in ideas, negating the leading position of Marxism-Leninism and Mao Zedong Thought.

In a single stroke, the ultra-leftists attempted to eliminate all the reformist intellectuals and senior cadres that emerged under the leaderships of Hu and Zhao. One of the signs of the ideological tightening after 4 June was the restoration of the themes of class struggle in the mass media. In a key article in the Party theoretical journal the *Qiushi* (Seeking Fact) in early 1990, Wang Renzhi, the then propaganda chief, pointed out that "We must use the class viewpoint of Marxism, and the Marxist methodology of class analysis to assess the counter-revolutionary rebellion of 1989. Only then can we see clearly the profundity, seriousness and danger of the struggles between the two roads." In the speech commemorating the Fortieth anniversary of the establishment of the PRC, Jiang Zemin (1989a) described the Tiananmen massacre as a bitter "class struggle" between the four cardinal principles and "bourgeois liberalization", a life and death struggle for the Party/state. In a throwback to the CR, the theme of the "two line struggles" was revived. According to Deng, the struggle against bourgeois liberalization would continue for twenty years (1993:196). Nonetheless, the stand-patters and the gangs of conservative elders pointed a finger at Deng when Yuan Mu, State Council spokesman and Li Peng's right-hand man, made a summation of CCP history since 1949, implicitly criticizing Deng as being responsible for the inundation of bourgeois liberalization in the past ten years (*People's Daily* 10 October 1989).

It was Deng Xiaoping who brought the international element into the context of the 4 June events and gave birth to the theory of "peaceful evolution" when he met the martial law troops three days after the massacre. He pointed out that the "counter-revolutionary rebellion" was the result of a combination of external and internal factors. "The storm will come sooner or later. This is determined by the major international political climate and China's own minor climate"(1993:302). In the light of the international situation such as the Persian Gulf crisis, the fall of the Berlin Wall in 1990, the collapse of the Romanian regime in late 1989, the Soviet coup in August 1991 and its subsequent disbandment, the CCP hardliners had an urgent sense of crisis. Reminiscent of the "two-camp" (socialist camp and capitalist camp) theory in the early 1950s, the conservative ideologues rekindled the theory of international class struggles in 1989/90, hinting that imperialism tried to change China's socialism by 'peaceful evolution' In a speech to the Central Party school, Jiang (1990) pointed out:

> Internationally, the hostile forces continue to carry out peaceful evolution strategy, supporting anti-communist and anti-socialist forces. The situation is clear. This is the

continuation of the struggles between two systems and two
kinds of ideological thinking in the world order.

The USA was branded by the CCP as the arch neo-imperialist, staging a
conspiracy against China, and the 1989 democracy movement was cited
as proof of American infiltration in the PRC. The hardliners traced the
American strategy of peaceful evolution back to the early 1950s and
implicated the importance of Taiwan and Hong Kong in this conspiracy.
In his report to the SCNPC at the end of June, Beijing mayor Chen Xitong
(1989) repeatedly accused American and other foreign conspiracies of
trying to overthrow the CCP political order. He further accused the anti-
communist forces in the USA, Hong Kong and Taiwan of co-opting
bourgeois elite in the mainland and supporting them to fabricate anti-
communist propaganda and subverting the socialist order. Wang Ruihua,
a conservative ideologue of Beijing Normal University, openly enunciated
that the struggle between peaceful evolution and anti-peaceful evolution
was the new form of class struggle under the changed historical
circumstances (*SCMP* 11 September 1990).

One of the most outspoken critics of "Yankee imperialism" was He
Xin, a researcher and literary critic in the CASS, who became the
intellectual paladin of Li Peng. In an internal paper that was widely
circulated within the CCP leadership in early 1991, he charged that the
single goal that the USA had in helping Kuwait maintain its sovereignty
and in destroying the Iraqi war machine was world domination. After the
victory in the Middle East, he alleged that the USA would move to
establish an Asian-Pacific empire and China was the only obstacle to the
American unification of the world in the light of the Soviet collapse
(*SCMP* 27 February 1991). In a more alarming tone, He even predicted
that a third world war would break out in the coming decade in view of
the deepening conflicts between the North and the South, within the
capitalist camp. After some time, he became the leading apologist of the
Li Peng regime. However, He's stardom was short-lived. After Deng's
southern tour in the early 1992, his fame plummeted. He was elected as a
deputy in the CPPCC and his vocal anti-Americanism failed to find a
receptive ear in Jiang Zemin.

Ideologically, the conservatives put the whole reform era into doubt
as they raised the debate on the "surname" of the reform and open-door
policies. In their view, there were two different kinds of reform measures,
and in the process of implementation, one has to ask the nature of the
policies. In an article in the *Brightness Daily* (10 August 1991), the author

argued that in actual life "there were reform concepts and measures surnamed socialist and capitalist". If the Party did not distinguish the "surname" (capitalist or socialist), then reform would become wholesale Westernization.[10] Moreover, the adulation of Mao was revived in an attempt to darken the reformist era. Mao was hailed as the prophet against peaceful evolution (Qi Fang 1990:10-11). Referring to the dramatic changes in Eastern Europe, Wei Wei, a conservative author, wrote an article commemorating the 97th birthday of Mao, saying that "the series of changes in the international arena have proven how correct Mao's judgement was on matters like class struggle, the struggle between the two roads (socialism and capitalism) and the possibility of the revival of capitalism" (*Brightness Daily* 27 December 1990).

In 1990/1991, a Mao *re* (fever) was deliberately whipped up by the Party's propaganda machine. To some degree there was mass support on the Mao phenomenon. For example, in 1991 more than 1 million people visited Mao's native village Shaoshan in Hunan Province. His collected works sold more than 1 million copies and Mao's pictures were used to decorate homes as well as windscreens of taxis, vans and coaches (*Ming Pao* 14 January 1992). The causes of this *re* were multifarious. It was, first of all, deliberately promoted by the leftist ideologues to launch a comprehensive ideological attack on the reformists in the light of the Soviet collapse, the democratization of Eastern Europe, and China's internal democratic forces pressing for changes. Secondly, there arose a sense of nostalgia among the disillusioned people when they looked back on the old Maoist days as relatively pure in the government, a time of secured income, and austere living style, without spiralling inflation. For young intellectuals, with discussions of the Western political theories banned after 4 June, the reversion to Mao's texts seemed to provide a relatively safe way to political theorizing. Economically, as a marketization system had been established in the previous ten-year reform, goods were commercialized and Mao, as a symbol of national disaster or salvation, became a saleable commercial product as well. Selling Mao souvenirs could reap huge profits (Zhang Zhabin and Song Yifu 1991:254-281).

Political Structural Reform in the early 1990s

In terms of the political structural reform, the post-Tiananmen retrenchment heralded a new regressive epoch. For nearly a whole year after the 4 June bloodbath, the term political structural reform disappeared from Chinese mass media. Newspapers, magazines and radio broadcasts were filled with articles of condemning "bourgeois liberalization", emphasizing the themes of class struggles and anti-peaceful evolution. In his three important speeches in 1989/90 (1989a, 1989b, 1990), Jiang Zemin did not mention the term "political structural reform". The *leimotif* of his speeches was the constant emphasis on the presence of long term struggles between peaceful evolution and anti-peaceful evolution, infiltration and anti-infiltration, "bourgeois liberalization" and the four cardinal principles. Neither was it mentioned in the *Decision in Further Structuring, Managing and Deepening the Reform* (CCCCP 1989) passed at the Fifth Plenum of the Thirteenth CC on 9 November 1989. In thearena of economic reform, the *Decision* listed several serious economic problems in the past few years, including the imbalance between the total social aggregate supply and demand, agriculture and industries, infrastructural construction and manufacturing industries, and the decreasing macro-control power by the central government over the regions. The *Decision* intended to spend three years or longer in managing and restructuring the economy and resumed the harmonious comprehensive development of the economy. To beef up the coercive Party/state apparatus and to strengthen ideological education were the central themes in this important CCP document.

It was not until the passing of *Decision Concerning to Strengthen Relationship between the Party and the Masses* (CCCCP 1990) at the Sixth Plenum of the Thirteenth CC on 12 March 1990 that the term "political structural reform" reappeared for the first time since the 4 June massacre. The *Decision* vaguely called for the establishment of socialist democracy at the local and central levels. The Party members in the NPC were encouraged to liaise with the non-Party deputies and to strengthen the supervisory and legislative functions of the SC of the NPC. However, the focus of the Party document was on the strengthening of the Party apparatus. In his *Government Work Report* in March 1990, Li Peng explicitly outlined three themes to be the main substance of future political structural reform: first, to continue to improve the system of the People's Congress; second, to improve the system of multi-party cooperation and consultation under the leadership of the CCP; third, to set up mechanisms and procedures of democratic decision-making and supervision. Simultaneously, Deng had also raised the problems of political structural reform. He claimed that the focus of political structural reform was on the two systems: the system of the People's Congress and multi-party cooperation and consultation under the leadership of the CCP

(*The Mirror* March 1990:33). In his speech commemorating the seventieth anniversary of the establishment of the CCP, Jiang (1991) laid bare the three "musts" and "don'ts" of socialist politics: first, the dictatorship of the people's democracy must be upheld on the basis of the alliance of workers and peasants, the system of the people's democracy should not be negated; the system of the People's Congress must be upheld, the Western parliamentary system should not be introduced; multi-party cooperation and consultation under the leadership of the CCP must be upheld, and Western multi-party politics should not be introduced.

However, in an internal speech reminiscent of the ideas of the political structural reform in the early 1980s, Deng again pointed out that the prevalent political structural reform had three goals: first, consolidating socialist system, second, developing socialist productivity, and third, promoting socialist democracy and boosting the incentive of the masses. The policies to concretize these goals included the rejuvenation of the geriatric cadres, streamlining the bloated Party/state bureaucracy, and overcoming the phenomena of bureaucratism. At the same time, Deng explicitly rejected the introduction of universal franchise for the nation-wide election of the NPC deputies and the Western model of "division of power" among three branches (*The Mirror* March 1991:27). The idea of separating the Party and the government was no longer mentioned.

In his 1992 *Government Work Report*, Li Peng mentioned one pre-4 June political structural reform measure that would be vigorously pursued in the future, i.e. the establishment of a modern civil service system. Li emphasized:

> As economic reform deepens and modernization develops, we should gradually and positively press for governmental institutional reform. Now our bureaucracy is too bloated and inefficient....We must separate the government and enterprise, redefine the functions, streamline the bureaucracy and increase efficiency and set up a system of civil service.

In the political report delivered in the Fourteenth CCP Congress by Jiang Zemin (1992), aside from the above-mentioned political reform measures, another pre-4 June measure was announced, i.e. rendering decision-making procedures more scientific.

The re-commitment to the political structural reform was not totally bogus, but the emphasis this time was wholly different from that under the

Hu-Zhao leadership. The most important item of the previous political structural reform, i.e. the separation of the Party and the government, was scrapped. Furthermore, the regime's emphasis on political stability was almost obsessive. Nearly all the senior Party and state officials stated that political structural reform had to be conducive to the stability of the country. Implicitly, all reform measures were presumed to be potentially disruptive. Even such a liberal Politburo SC member as Li Ruihuan as saying to say that "the construction of Chinese democratic politics must be based upon the premise of unity and stability" (*People's Daily* 21 May 1993).

In a move widely perceived as tightening the grip over the monopoly of political power, the CCP devised a strategy of the so-called "cross leadership" in the Fourteenth CCP Congress in 1992. This refers to the policy that all the key Party/state and legislature posts would be held concurrently by the SC members of the Politburo. Consequently, Jiang Zemin, the anointed successor of Deng, became the head of the Party, state and PLA. Li Ruihuan concurrently held the post of the head of CPPCC and Qiao Shi took up the post of chairman of the NPC. Li Peng was again elected as the premier in the NPC. The practice was soon followed by many provinces, with the Party secretaries adding the heads of the government and legislature, notable examples including Heilongjiang, Hainan, and Hubei provinces.

Now even the policy of blood rejuvenation took a backward turn. Since the early 1980s, four criteria had been instituted to formalize the selection process, and the emphasis on the selection tended to favour professional competence and ability rather than ideological orthodoxy under the Hu-Zhao leadership. Now the tide had turned. Between "expertness" and "redness", the balance tipped to the latter. In particular, after the failed Soviet coup in August 1991, the emphasis on "redness" heightened. Chen Yun was reported to have said that the CCP must ensure that "Yeltsin-like figures" would not emerge in China. He repeated his slogan of selecting young cadres in 1940 when he was the head of the CCP Organization Department in Yan'an period: "cadres should have morality and ability, but morality should be the main consideration" (*SCMP* 4 September 1991).[11] Morality, of course, meant total devotion to the Party prevalent political line and Marxist orthodox. In his political report to the Fourteenth CCP Congress, Jiang Zemin emphasized that the "cross-century leaders" chosen to lead the country to the next century must be "trustworthy" Marxists.

In fact, administrative reform became the key component of the political structural reform under the Jiang-Li (and Zhu Rongji) leadership. In the 1980s, there were two administrative reforms, 1982/83 and 1988. The former produced a dramatic reduction in the total number of ministries and departments, but the efforts were aborted after several years and it failed to produce desirable consequences. The administrative trimming announced in Zhao Ziyang's report to the CCP Congress in late 1987 encountered a similar fate. With the beefing up of the Party/state authorities and re-centralization of power in the wake of the 4 June crackdown, the natural consequence was the expansion of the Party/state bureaucracy and tightening of the power. The fastest growth of personnel was registered in the areas of police and security branches including the staff of courts and procuratorates. By late 1991, the total number of police force in the country had increased to 800,000. In 1990, there were altogether 500,000 staff of Party and government establishments. Every year, the ranks of cadre-level staff swelled by 1.1 million across the country, with only 400,000 departing (*SMCP* 31 January 1991).

With the policy of streamlining the bloated bureaucracy announced in the report of the Fourteenth CCP Congress in 1992, a major administrative trimming exercise was launched in 1993. In his *Governmental Work Report* (1993), Li Peng announced that the number of ministries, departments, and offices would be reduced from 86 to 59 and *ad hoc* units reduced from 85 to 26. The total number of 9.2 million staff of the government departments and offices at various levels across the country would be reduced by 25%. In mid-1993, the State Council issued instructions to the provinces and directly affiliated cities requiring them to limit the number of departments to 55 and 75 respectively, and to shrink their staff establishment by 20% and 15% respectively. Shandong province seemed to have fared the best in the trimming campaign. In 1993, nearly 7,000 units were closed down with 56,000 personnel leaving the government, enabling the province to save 120 million yuan in government salaries (*Wen Wei Po* 21 June 1993).

In an internal talk, Jiang Zemin disclosed the total number of the Party and government staff as about 30 million, and he said that those who were hived off from the government should go into service industries (*Wen Wei Po* 15 March 1993). However, much of the reduction was accomplished by turning the government ministries or departments into "privatized" economic corporations. For instance, the Ministry of Aeronautics and Astronautics became the Aeronautical Industries Corporation; the Ministry of Light Industry changing to General

Association of Chinese Light Industry; and the Ministry of Textile Industry was transformed into the General Association of Chinese Textile Industry, with greatly reduced staff (*Wen Wei Po* 17 April 1993). In 1991, Zhang Zijian, the vice-minister of the Personnel Department, expressed his feeling that the central government would spend five years or longer to establish a civil service system at the central and provincial levels (*Wen Wei Po* 12 October 1991). In August 1993, Beijing announced the temporary regulations for the establishment of the civil service system within three years. Criteria were set for the classification of grades, promotion or demotion, and salary schemes. The ratio between the highest-paid civil servant and the lowest would be 6 to 1, with the salary of the premier at 1,200 yuan a month. The so-called Western-style civil service system remained distinctively Chinese in character (*Ming Pao* 22 March 1993). For instance, the temporary regulations stated that the promotion of cadres was based on the principles of morality and ability. Here, as noted by the senior leadership after 4 June, morality meant "redness" or Marxist orthodox. It is indeed difficult to see how the ideological principles can be reconciled with the modern civil service system, which is supposed to be politically neutral.

Another key piece of the political structural reform after 4 June, as repeated by the CCP leadership in the early 1990s, was multi-party co-operation under the leadership of the CCP. On 7 February 1990, the CCP published the document *On Upholding and Perfecting the System of Multi-party Co-operation and Political Consultation under CCP Leadership*. Deng Xiaoping exhorted that the flower-vase function of the eight democratic parties should be replaced by genuine political participation. The non-CCP politicians would be put in a position of real power. However, by mid-1990, about 800 non-CCP members became state cadres at the county levels across the whole country, and only 14 politicians became cadres at the vice-ministerial and provincial levels (*The Mirror* March 1990:33). By late 1991, the number of non-CCP cadres increased and the State Council disclosed that there were about 1,200 cadres who became leaders at different levels of the Party/state apparatus, including three vice-ministers (IOSC 1991). Furthermore, there was at least a vice-governor or vice-mayor in 11 provinces and directly-administered cities all of whom were non-CCP members (*People's Daily* 2 November 1991). Rong Yiren, the pre-1949 big capitalist, the Chairman of the All-China Federation of Industry and Commerce, was elected as the vice-president of the PRC in the Eighth NPC in 1993, the highest state post occupied by a non-CCP politician.

Commenting on the document, Fei Xiaotong, the famous sociologist and chairman of the Democratic League of China, heaped praise on the multi-party co-operation system, saying that the system "was rooted in Chinese soil and was widely accepted by Chinese people" and the "Western multi-party system was totally unsuitable for China" (*Wen Wei Po* 23 June 1991). In 1993 and 1994, under the leadership of Li Ruihuan, who became the chairman of the CPPCC in 1992, the status of the CPPCC seemed to have risen. Non-CCP politicians were, for the first time in thirty years, allowed to join high-power CCP overseas delegations. In Shanghai and Guangzhou, think tanks were set up and professionals and consultants of the democratic parties were invited to advise the municipal governments on local affairs. By mid-1994, about 16 non-CCP figures served as vice-ministers in ministries and commissions in the State Council, yet none was a full minister.

The NPC under Qiao Shi, chairman and Tian Jiyun, the first vice-chairman, obviously has been strengthened since 1993 when they were elected to these positions. The two leaders reiterated that they would enhance both the legislative and supervisory functions of the NPC. The goal of establishing a socialist market system gave the NPC extra room for exercising political clout. Market economy requires a sound and comprehensive legal code. In 1993, the year after Deng Xiaoping's *nanxun* (southern imperial trip), the NPC enacted a record number of 67 laws and regulations, half of which were concerned with economic development. They included a company law, some statutes on banking and securities, anti-trust laws and regulations against insider-trading (Willy Lam 1995:308-309).

Tian Jiyun, the once protege of Zhao Ziyang, was particularly enthusiastic in boosting the supervisory role of the NPC. In April 1993, he said that "we must further develop democracy and further boost the people's supervision. This is very important for improving governmental work." He even exhorted the mass media to expose the Party/state officials who violated the constitution and laws (*SCMP* 7 April 1993). According to Willy Lam (1995:309-310), Qiao and Tian made two moves that broke the traditional practice of the NPC. First, to deal with the increasingly heavy workload of the legislature and specialization of the legal drafting, they began to assemble a team of professional drafters. Before that, the NPC had never had such a team of specialized drafters. Second, they encouraged the local, municipal or provincial People's Congress to pass legislation ahead of the NPC. In a trip to Guangdong province, Qiao said that "national legislation are not comprehensive and regions could formulate local legislation according to local conditions" (*Ming Pao* 20 April 1993).

Despite all these reforms in streamlining the Party/state apparatus, the strengthening of the CPPCC, the enhancing role of the eight democratic parties, and finally increasing the political clout of the NPC, the most basic tenet of the reforms remained unchanged: the inviolability of the four cardinal principles, particularly the ruling status of the CCP.

The New *Fang* and *Shou* Cycle ?

By mid-1991, two years after the 4 June massacre, it seemed that Deng Xiaoping was contemplating a *fang* cycle, at least in economic policy. The policy of "restructuring and managing economic environment" was initially determined in the Third Plenum of the Thirteenth CC in 1988, with out-of-control inflation, explosive budget deficit, expanding infrastructural constructions, and bottlenecks in transportation (Li Peng 1989). After 4 June, the retrenchment policy continued and pervaded all fronts. Sensing the seriousness of the overheated economy, the CCP decided in the Fifth Plenum of the Thirteenth CC in November 1989 to spend three years or longer to complete the tasks of restructuring and managing the economic environment. *The Decision Concerning Further Restructuring, Managing and Deepening Reform* (CCCCP 1989) was intended to solve the following economic problems: gradually reducing the inflation rate to single digit, restricting the issuing of money, balancing the budget, raising productivity, keeping the average annual growth rates between 5% and 6%, resolving the bottlenecks in energy and transportation, restricting social aggregate demand and credit or loan. The policy of "sustaining stability, and harmonious development" was the key theme when Li Peng (1991) announced the Eighth Five-Year Plan in the Fourth Session of the Seventh NPC in 1991.

Unlike the political structural reform cycle, the economic reform cycle was basically a progressive one, as I argued in chapter 3. Despite the 4 June crackdown and its ensuing "restructuring and managing" macro-economic policy, the overall economic reformist orientation was not abandoned. The radical price reform package dropped dead in mid-1988. Zhao was severely criticized by the octogenarians for his mishandling of economic policy. In the policy announcements by the CCP leadership after 4 June, reform and an open-door policy in economic sphere had never totally been condemned, but there occurred a change of concrete policies. One item on the agenda of the economic retrenchment was the "restructuring" of the individual and private economic sectors. On one occasion, Jiang Zemin had said that the CCP intended to make the private enterprises bankrupt if they conducted illegal business. Furthermore, he emphasized that those who engaged in exploitation could not be admitted into the Party (*The Mirror* November 1989:49). The employees in individual enterprises were reduced, for the first time since the early 1980s, from 6.48 million in 1989 to 6.14 million in 1990 (ZTZ 1995:18). In fifteen years, under Jiang's leadership, the CCP would revolutionize its ideology, rejecting the class-based nature Party, admitting private capitalists into the Party (Jiang 2002).

Chen Yun's famous analogy of a "bird-cage" economy was revived and re-emphasized. In his speech commemorating the fortieth anniversary of the establishment of the PRC, Jiang (1989a) reiterated the strategic importance of public ownership in a socialist economy and insisted that all other forms of ownership, such as individual enterprises, foreign enterprises and Chinese-foreign enterprises were to serve only supplementary functions. On 17 October 1989, in a meeting with the experts of fourteen countries who came to attend an international conference on governmental administration reform, Li Peng emphasized that the most important principle of the reform was that public ownership could not become private ownership, and China would follow the policy of the "synthesis between planning and the market regulation" (*The Mirror* November 1989:52). As we shall see, Jiang and Li were soon to change their stands in the light of Deng's *nanxun* onslaught.

By mid-1991, dissatisfied with the conservative Jiang-Li position, Deng, as a 87 old man, was contemplating his "final offensive" in pressing his reformist efforts forward. Amidst the frontal attacks of the ultra-leftists, Deng astutely prepared the "northern assault" in Shanghai in the spring of 1991. In an internal speech Deng had with Jiang Zemin and Li Peng in October 1990, Deng stressed the importance of continuing reform and opening up policy for the country. The policy was, he claimed, the lessons the Party summarized during the previous thirty years of economic stagnation and social chaos. Though restructuring of the economy and political stability were essential, they could not nonetheless be used to override reform and open-door policies (*The Mirror* November 1990:39). Deng spent the 1991 Chinese New Year in Shanghai, but before he left for Shanghai, he had hinted that nobody listened to what he said in Beijing nowadays and he was forced to publish articles in Shanghai (*The Mirror* May 1991:25). Similar to the reformist era ushered

in by Deng in the late 1970s, the breakthrough first occurred in
ideological-cultural arenas. Deng hinted that China required the second
thought-liberation movement in the 1990s. In a series of articles published
in Shanghai's *Liberation Daily* in March and April, the author Huang
Puping called for emancipation of mind, discarding out-dated thinking
and more daring thinking mode.[12] The themes sound familiar, and, in fact,
this was the echo of Deng's thinking as far back as the end of 1990. On
the eve of the Seventh Plenum of the Thirteenth CC, Deng talked to the
members of the SC of the Politburo. He (*The Mirror* May 1991:30)
emphasized that

> Further reform and opening up require new thinking. We
> have to be faster, better, more bold, and higher. More than
> ten years ago, I suggested the thought-liberation movement,
> to seek truth from facts. Now we are at the beginning of
> another ten years. I still want to raise the problem of thought
> emancipation. Thought emancipation needs to be further
> upgraded. Reform and opening up require new thinking
> mode, and economic construction is now at a new stage. We
> have to prevent our thinking from being stagnant.

Zhu Rongji and Chen Xitong, the two mayors of China's most populous
cities, reiterated the same themes in the first half of 1991. Chen was
particularly articulated in supporting Deng's calling and in an internal
speech in the SC of Beijing Party committee he listed seven aspects as
manifestations of ossified thinking of the cadres: first, to equate socialist
commodity economy with capitalism; second, to counterpose foreign
capital with national independence; third, to counterpose restructuring and
managing with reform and opening up; fourth, some enterprise leaders
were not ambitious enough and were content with running   small
enterprises; fifth, some cadres were not daring enough in trying out new
experiments; sixth, to counterpose the sense of urgency in tackling
problems with over-ambition; finally, in the analysis of the situation,
some cadres could see only negative factors and overlooked positive
elements. Supposedly these criteria could be used to judge whether cadres
were out-dated.

   One of the most important economic reform initiatives after the 4
June suppression was the opening up of the Pudong area in Shanghai. It
was first given the green light by Deng in Lunar New Year 1990. It was a
major reform push in view of the tense political atmosphere and economic
austerity policies in Beijing. At first, Li Peng made sure that the new

development zone would not follow all the SEZs' preferential policies, but the move, he praised, was indeed "another major step China has taken to deepen reform and expand its open-door policy" (*SCMP* 19 April 1990). However, Pudong began to take off only after the second visit by the patriarch in Lunar New Year in 1991. As it turned out, perhaps because of the back-up of Deng and the persistence of Zhu Rongji's lobbying efforts, Pudong was granted more autonomous power than that of the SEZs, such as the power to allow foreign banks to set up branches in Shanghai.

In retrospect, the thought emancipation campaign launched simultaneously with the opening up of the Pudong was not accidental. In the second Lunar New Year visit, Deng exhorted, in an internal speech, that the leading cadres responsible for the development of Pudong should be more daring in devising concrete financial and fiscal policies in deepening the economic reform. In a spirit congruent with the tone of Huang Puping's commentaries, the New Helmsman argued that there was no formula in open-door policies and new situations demanded innovative thinking. He predicted that if the reformist policies were to be pursued, Shanghai would surpass Hong Kong or Singapore in twenty or thirty years (*The Mirror* March 1991:35). He regretted that the CCP had not opened up Shanghai earlier (1993:366)

If Huang Puping's reformist commentaries were the first signals of Deng's counter-offensives against the conservative camp in Beijing, then obviously the diehards in Beijing had not received the message. Unaware of Deng's secretive moves, in a visit to Shanghai in November 1991, Li Peng criticized Huang Puping and said that the influence of the commentaries was "extremely bad" (*The Mirror* January 1992:32). The conservative ideologues like Deng Liqun, Gao Di, Xu Weicheng, and Wang Renzhi dominated the propaganda machinery of the central government and Li Ruihuan, the SC member of the Politburo in charge of propaganda was often sidestepped. The mass media in Beijing were disseminating the strategic importance of anti-peaceful evolution on a daily basis, in particular in the light of the failed Soviet coup in August 1991. The patriarch realized that if stronger signals were not emitted, then his reformist theory of "one centre and two fundamental points" would be buried forever.

The Eighth Plenum of the Thirteenth CC concluded with little controversy with the passing of one central document relating to rural reform. While advising the senior leaders to minimize debates and quarrels, Deng was making preparation to embark on his final offensive. In January and February 1992, Deng, accompanied by Yang Shangkun and his family, toured Shenzhen, Zhuhai, and Wuhan, and then spent his third consecutive Lunar New Year in Shanghai. This was his second visit to Shenzhen and Zhuhai. Similar to the first one, his visits showed strong support for the SEZs, thus implicitly the open-door policy. During the tour, Deng conducted wide-ranging talks on nearly all the controversial issues facing the CCP. The key points included: first, at present, that the principal danger confronting the Party was leftism. Second, the theory of "one centre and two fundamental points" could not be changed and there could not be another centre of focus for the CCP other than the economic development. Third, the fundamental line of the Third Plenum of the Eleventh CC must continue for a hundred years. Fourth, market was not the monopoly of capitalism, and market and planning were the only methods of allocation of resources. Fifth, China must seize the opportunity to develop in the context of favourable international environment. The speed of development could be faster. Sixth, formalism must be reduced, and the Party should have done concrete things for the people and should not engage in empty talk (Deng Xiaoping 1993:370-83).[13]

The impact of the *nanxun* talks on CCP proved that Deng, despite his role as an ordinary member, was still the final arbiter of all the important CCP policies. His words instantly became policies. In the light of his talks, the CCP Politburo convened a meeting in February and issued Central Document No. 2, endorsing Deng's call for a new wave of market reform in broad terms. Central Documents No.4 and No.5, which were issued in mid-1992 outlined the concrete details as to how this could be achieved. For the first time since 1978, foreign and Hong Kong businesses were allowed to invest in areas other than tourism, industry and some sectors of infrastructure, such as banking, insurance, real estate, and department stores. By the end of 1992, semi-private law firms, clinics, real estate agents, and stock brokers were set up. Following the trip to the Southern provinces, Deng made an inspection trip to the Capital Steel Company in May 1992, and gave a talk lasting more than three hours. The themes of his talk in May were similar to the *nanxun* talks (*The Mirror* July 1992:31-35). By choosing the largest state enterprise as the point of inspection, Deng seemed to hope that future economic reform would be focused on state enterprises.

Under the impact of Deng's reformist counter-offensives, Li Peng's 1992 *Government Work Report* in the Fifth Session of the Seventh NPC had to undergo more than 140 revisions before it was passed by the deputies. He was forced to add in the *Report* that the main task for the

CCP was to prevent leftism and uphold Deng's theory of "one centre, two fundamental points" for "a hundred years" (*Ming Pao* 2 April 1992). In the Fourteenth CCP Congress held in October 1992, the important themes of the *nanxun* talks were fully reflected in the political report delivered by Jiang Zemin (1992). In responding to Deng's criticism of formalism and engaging in formal and empty talks, the report was only 20,000 Chinese characters, one of the shortest Party Congress reports. Following Deng's talks in the southern provinces, Jiang identified leftism as the main danger and vowed to uproot the ultra-leftist tendencies within the Party. He further called for the establishment of a socialist market economy and further opening up to foreign capital and making use of Western advanced management skills and technologies. In terms of political structural reform policies, the focus was, as noted earlier, on improving the NPC and the system of multi-party co-operation. The separation of the government and enterprises was stressed and streamlining the bloated government bureaucracy was considered an important task, coupled with the establishment of a modern state civil service system.

Emboldened by Deng's call for emancipating the mind, the liberal intellectuals galvanized their forces, for the first time since the 4 June crackdown, to launch an anti-leftist crusade in the ideological-cultural realm. Their aim was, in fact, simple: to render moral support to Deng's call for market reform. On 14 June 1992, about one hundred intellectuals gathered at the Olympic Hotel in Beijing to hold an academic forum on reform and open-door policy. The forum was organized by Yuan Hongbing, a young Beida law lecturer under *neikong* (internal control) of the public security branches.[14] The participants included Wang Ruishui, Li Rui, Sun Changjiang, Wu Zuguang, Lin Jingyao, Zheng Zhongping, and Qian Chuan. Wang Ruoshui, the former deputy editor-in-chief of the *People's Daily*, reiterated the theme of corruption of absolute power, and called for renewed political structural reform to eradicate official graft (*The Mirror* July 1992:44-47). Zheng Zhongping, the former deputy editor-in-chief of the *New Observer*, elaborated Deng's theory of anti-leftism (*The Mirror* July 1992:51-52). Lin Jingyao, a prominent social scientist, urged to overhaul the monopoly of the theoretical interpretation by the Marxist orthodox ideologues over the general political line of the CCP (*The Mirror* July 1992:48-50).

The meeting was followed by another conclave on 27 October, whose goal was to disseminate the reformist ideas of the Fourteenth CCP Congress. About fifty liberal authors including Wang Meng, the former minister of culture, participated in the meeting. Two anti-leftism books

The Tides of History and *Memorandum on Anti-Leftism* were published in 1992. The contributors included prominent liberal authors such as Ba Jin, Li Zehou, Li Rui, Xia Yan, and Liu Xinwu. One of the fiercest attacks on the leftist ideologues was fired by Hu Jiwei, the former chief editor of the *People's Daily*. He traced leftism to the 1950s, and asserted that since 1978 the struggle between fighting rightism and leftism had been fierce. He accused the conservatives of setting hurdles in propagating Deng's reformist thought in the central mass media, such as *People's Daily, Brightness Daily*, and *Seeking Truth* (*Cheng Ming* July 1992:34).

In spite of the anti-leftist salvo by Qiao Shi and Tian Jiyun in the aftermath of Deng's *nanxun*,[15] Deng was not prepared to let loose in the ideological-cultural arena. For one thing, these two books, despite their pro-reform proclivities, were banned. In one of the meetings of the CAC before the Fourteenth CCP Congress, Yuan Baohua, one of the SC members of the CAC, criticised *The Tides of History* as " raising the reformist banner but trying to reverse the verdict of 4 June", and Deng Liqun named Hu Jiwei, whose article, Deng said, "was wrong in every word" (*The Mirror* December 1992:29). Despite the ouster of the conservatives in the Fourteenth CCP Congress, the Party's control over the mass media was as tight as ever. Shao Huaze, who replaced Gao Di as the director of the *People's Daily*, was as leftist as the latter. By early 1993, the anti-leftist crusade was losing its momentum, and the intellectuals realized that Deng was not wholeheartedly devoted to comprehensive reform. He would not forsake his so-called "double iron-fisted" policy. What Deng had in his mind was a reformist model of "hard politics and soft economics": preserving the status quo in politics and establishing a market system in economy. After 4 June, Deng's skepticism over liberal intellectuals lingered on. The CCP treated the natural scientists and social scientists differently. In 1991, the top leadership, who saw the immediate contribution by the scientific and technological personnel, began to woo the scientific intellectuals, giving them special subsidies and awards (*Ta Kung Pao* 9 December 1991). But the social sciences liberal intellectuals were denied such treatment, especially those who were active before 4 June crackdown and were blacklisted by the CCP Central Propaganda Department.

In economic policy, there was definitely a new round of *fang* and *shou* cycle after the 4 June bloodbath, but not in the ideological-political sphere. The *nanxun* talks started the *fang* cycle and by 1994/95, a *shou* cycle seemed on the way when Zhu Rongji exercised the macro economic control due to the overheating of the economy. The strict ideological-political control remained unchanged. Judging from the organizational and personnel structure of the CCP leadership in the Fourteenth CCP Congress, four kinds of political forces were excluded: first, the reformist cadres under Zhao's leadership. Tian Jiyun was transferred to the NPC. Second, the ultra-conservatives, such as Deng Liqun, Gao Di, Song Ping, and Yao Yilin all stepped down. Third, gerontocrats such as Chen Yun, Yang Shangkun, Bo Yibo, Wang Zhen and all members of the CAC lost their formal positions. Fourth, general Yang Baibing lost his influential position of the secretary-general in the CMC.

It is easy to see what kind of men Deng wanted in the ruling body of the CCP. First of all, he wanted cadres who vigorously pursued economic reform. The dramatic elevation of Zhu Rongji to the SC of the Politburo was a sign.[16] Secondly, he wanted the conservatives to hold fort politically, and the 4 June verdict to remain unchanged. Consequently, the Jiang Zemin-Li Peng system remained unchanged. Thirdly, to consolidate Jiang as the core of the third generation of the CCP, he had to remove any force that was perceived as a potential threat to the status of Jiang. General Yang was removed precisely as he was accused of factionalism and contempt for Jiang.

Notes

[1] *The Tiananmen Papers* gives a full picture of how the mass crackdown decision was arrived. In fact, the pro-communist monthly *The Mirror* in Hong Kong had published graphic details on the rows between two lines in the early 1990s. One piece of information that had not been revealed before was that Li Ruihuan was originally picked up by Deng to succeed Zhao Ziyang.

[2] In fact, according to James Lilley, the then American Ambassador in Beijing (*Open* September 1995:70-1), Fang and his wife went to the US Embassy twice. The first time, they were turned away and it was the second time that they were accepted by the Embassy.

[3] Through the clandestine operation "Yellow Bird", at least one-third of the student leaders on the "wanted list" were able to escape from the CCP mass round-up in China mainland. The Alliance was formed in the aftermath of the June 4 and it still exists today, with Hong Kong veteran democratic activist Szeto Wah as its chairman.

[4] The heaviest punishment was reserved for workers and what the authorities called *liumang* or *baotu* (ruffians or thugs). The first batch of people to be

executed by the CCP in the wake of 4 June were three young workers who set fire to the train in Shanghai on 6 June. In the last two weeks of June, about 35 people, mostly unemployed youth, were executed. Apparently, no student or intellectual was executed for taking part in the pro-democracy movement.

[5]Wang Juntao was released on parole for "health reasons" and he was sent into exile in April 1994. Chen was also released on parole at the end of 1994, but after 4 June 1995, he was re-arrested and put back into prison and later released again.

[6]According to Chen Yizi and Wu Guoguang (*Ming Pao* 21 August 1992), the only "state secret" that Bao Tong leaked was the news of the resignation of Zhao Ziyang on 17 May 1989. But in fact the news was widespread among senior cadres. The charge of "counter-revolutionary propaganda incitement" was even more absurd. Chen show the *Six Statements Concerning the Present Situation* of three Institutes and one Association (Han Minzhu 1992:250-251) to Bao. What Bao said was that you can express your opinion if you do it within the law. Later they both expressed dissatisfaction over the hard-line attitude of Li Peng. Chen Yizi concluded that Bao in fact became the scapegoat of Zhao Ziyang. See also Bao Tong (2001).

[7]The first and the last impartial reports on the student demonstrations appeared in 27 April *People's Daily.*

[8]Apparently Jiang was chosen for his non-involvement in the 4 June suppression. However, Chinese sources said that in late May 1989 Jiang was called by Deng to handle the crisis in Beijing. He became the head of a secret committee called the Emergency Committee to Handle the Tiananmen Square Turmoil (Willy Lam 1995:392). According to the *Tiananmen Papers*, Deng had originally designated Li Ruihuan to be the successor of Zhao, but it was opposed by other veterans.

[9]Wang was the only cabinet minister who did not go to compliment the martial law troops after 4 June. Ying openly expressed sympathy with Zhao Ziyang in the Third Session of the Seventh NPC and said that "Unlike the 'Gang of Four', Zhao Ziyang would not be indicted. They killed people. Zhao's case belongs to ideological realm" (*Wen Wei Po* 23 March 1990).

[10]The idea of surnaming reform and open-door policies was in fact first proposed by Jiang Zemin, who, after being vehemently criticised by Deng Xiaoping, changed sides and dropped the idea after Deng's tour to the southern coastal provinces in early 1992.

[11]In recruiting and promoting young cadres, Deng and Chen Yun had profound differences. As early as the 1940s, Chen thought that nothing was wrong with passing the buck to the off-spring of the revolutionary leaders. In his view, at least they were more reliable. It seems that, after 50 years, Chen had changed little. In the light of Ceausescu's execution and the Soviet failed coup, he had reportedly said that recruiting the off-spring of the leaders at least had one advantage: they would not dig the graves of their parents (*The Mirror* November 1991:25). The formation of the CCP princelings was mainly due to the influence of Chen Yun (Chen Liu 1995).

[12]Huang Puping was the pseudonym used by the Propaganda Department of Shanghai municipal CCP Party committee and the series of commentaries was masterminded by Zhu Rongji, who was the Party secretary and mayor of Shanghai (*The Mirror* November 1991:24-25). Soon after, Zhu was elevated to the post of vice-premier and finally elected one of the SC members of CCP Politburo in the Fourteenth CCP Congress in 1992.

[13]The official version and the private-circulated version of Deng's *nanxun* talks were different. For example, in the private version, Deng highly praised the work of Zhao Ziyang and the contribution he made to economic reform. Moreover, he pointedly named Deng Liqun, Song Ping and Li Ximin as ultra-leftists. Most important of all, he implicitly criticized Chen Yun for his stubbornness in refusing to visit SEZs (*The Mirror* April 1992:33-36). In the official version, all these remarks disappear.

[14]In the Chinese system, a person who is under *neikong* will have trouble going abroad, publishing articles or books, and even contacting people. He/she may be under surveillance by the public security branches for 24 hours a day.

[15]Tian, being the former protege of Zhao Ziyang, was manifestly at odds with the Jiang-Li nucleus. On two occasions he showed his contempt for the leftists. First, he launched one of the most eloquent attacks on leftist ideologues. He claimed that if the Marxist fundamentalists would like to practise orthodox socialism, let them have a piece of land where contact with the outside world was cut off, food was rationed, commodity exchange forbidden, and jobs assigned (*Pai Shing* 1 June 1992:4-5). Second, in the Third Session of the Eighth NPC, when he held a discussion with the Guangdong delegation, he vociferously attacked the "one vacancy, one candidate" method of election (*Cheng Ming* April 1995:6-9).

[16]Zhu was riding a "helicopter" in his political career. He was only an alternate CC member in the Thirteenth CCP Congress in 1987. He surpassed the CC, and Politburo membership and was elected directly to the SC of the Politburo.

CHAPTER SIX

STABILITY AND REFORM: POLITICS IN THE 1990s

The 1980s began with the most comprehensive political reform packages ever devised by the CCP announced by Deng Xiaoping in August 1980 in the expanded meeting of the CCP Politburo but ended with the massive purges of the liberal intellectuals and reformist leadership. The 1990s started with political stagnation in the aftermath of the June 4 bloodbath but ended, ideologically, with the exposition of a new theory for the CCP, the so-called 'Theory of Three Represents' in 2000 by Jiang Zemin. It looks as if the cycle of reform had emerged again. In fact, it is not. The pendulum shift of policies from one extreme to another largely disappeared in the 1990s.[1] Instead, moves towards economic reform speed up, culminated in the accession to the WTO. On the contrary, moves of political structural reform lagged behind. In the beginning of the 21st century, the political monopoly by the CCP remained unchanged.

Deng died in February 1997, five months before the historic handover of Hong Kong to China by the British government. Due to his failing health, Deng had gradually lost political influence since the 14th CCP Congress in 1992. The 1990s, especially the latter part, were dominated mostly by the personality of Jiang Zemin (Willy Lam 1999:13-18). At the 16th CCP Congress, his 'Theory of Three Represents' was inserted into the CCP Constitution and recognized by the whole party to be a further development of Deng Xiaoping Theory. In the aftermath of the 4 June crackdown, Deng Xiaoping had said the newly selected leaders of third generation, "About the political structural reform, the greatest goal is to achieve a stable environment. I talk with the Americans, the highest interest for China is stability." (Deng 1993:313). On 28 September 1995, Jiang Zemin delivered one of the most important speeches in his tenure as the General Secretary of the CCP in the Fifth Plenum of 14th CCP Congress, which is entitled "To Handle Correctly Certain Relationships in the Process of Socialist

Modernization Construction". At the top of the agenda was the relationships between reform, development and stability. According to the top leadership, reform, in particular economic reform, must be pursued; development is the enhancing of national strength and stability is the pre-condition of development. Indeed, it is the search for equilibrium in these three sets of relationships that shaped the major forces and dynamics of Chinese politics in the 1990s. Against this background, this chapter attempts to capture the pattern of political development in the 1990s in general and the political structural reform in particular.

Tightening Ideological Control

In the aftermath of the 4 June massacre, when Deng Xiaoping (1993:287,290,306) said that the greatest failure in the reform era was in education , he did not mean education in the traditional sense, such as knowledge acquisition, skill dissemination and moral imbuing process. What he meant was, in fact, the failure in the CCP' ideological indoctrination in the education sectors, particularly among the university students. For, after all it was the university students who initiated the 4 June pro-democracy movement after the death of Hu Yaobang. In his view, the lack of ideological control had led to the spread of the so-called bourgeois liberalization and indirectly to the split of top CCP leadership and the ensuing chaos following the death of Hu Yaobang on 15 April 1989. The top leadership has learnt two important lessons from the 4 June bloodshed. First, knowing the full impact of powerful modern mass media, the conservative leadership realized that strict ideological censorship must be exercised upon the reformist intellectuals, and second, a leadership split at the top must be avoided at all costs for the split would endanger societal stability and threaten the CCP directly. These are the lessons that the CCP leadership is still taking in the 21st century.

Jiang Zemin ascended to power in the midst of 4 June mass purges, and he was involved in the decision- making process even before the curfew was imposed on 20 May 1989 (Nathan and Link 2001). His crackdown on Shanghai's *World Economic Herald* pleased the hard-line leadership. In essence, Jiang was a conservative man (Willy Lam 1999:12-18). Having become the general secretary of the CCP, he shifted economic policies to the left. On one occasion, he asserted that the CCP would make individual enterprises bankrupt if necessary. His speeches were full of leftist rhetoric (1989a; 1989b; 1990). Afterwards, the term 'political structural reform' virtually became a taboo and it was banned in the mass media for almost half a year. Starting in late 1989, however, the term began to reappear in the newspapers and gradually in Party documents and policy announcements. However, the term was used with a different connotation. With the crumbling of the communist regimes in the Soviet Union and Eastern European countries, the CCP was determined to strengthen the Party authority and fostered government administrative and extractive capacities. In the mean time, premier Li Peng stated that political structural reform had never stopped (1991). A condition had been attached to the political structural reform,that is societal stability. The CCP leadership tried now to refocus the contents of the political structural reform by using the term 'political reform with Chinese characteristics'. Li Peng (1991) stressed that "political restructuring should be conducive to the stability and prosperity of the country rather causing social disturbance." Jiang Zemin considered that the political structural reform should perfect socialist democracy and legal system. He emphasized that Western ideas of democracy and freedom were not compatible with China's 'national conditions'. He added that "The (political structural reform) must be commensurate with the country's tradition, history, culture, and the development levels of education and the economy." (in Willy Lam, 1995: 242) Furthermore, in the commemorative speech on the seventieth anniversary of the CCP, in outlining the 'socialist politics with Chinese characteristics', Jiang Zemin (1991) declared that there must be a 'three insistence and three nos' policy',

> We must insist on the people's democracy dictatorship, led by the working class and based on the alliance of workers and peasants; we must not weaken and abandon the people's democracy dictatorship. We must insist and try to perfect the NPC system and must not set up a system similar to Western parliament. We must insist and perfect the multi party cooperative system led by the CCP; we must not weaken or negate the leadership of the CCP and adopt a Western type multi party system (*Wen Wei Po,* 2 July 1991).

In early 1995, Jiang pronounced that a faithful CCP member had to distinguish the seven differentials between Marxism and adulterated Marxism or bourgeois liberalization (*Mirror* June 1996:22). The seven contrasting pair of concepts are as follows: First, the true Marxism must not be confused with anti-Marxism or pseudo-Marxism; second, the socialist economy versus private ownership; third, socialist democracy versus Western parliamentary democracy; fourth, dialectical materialism versus subjective metaphysics; fifth, socialism versus feudalism; sixth, learning advanced things from the West versus blind worship of he West; finally, civilized and healthy style of lifestyle versus a negative, decadent lifestyle.

In the wake of the 1989 crackdown, to protect himself from the ultra-leftist attacks, Jiang had put forward a theory of Surnames: the nature of reform should be defined as either socialist or capitalist. Reform capped with capitalist would be purged. With this move, the conservative leadership would characterize all the reforms during Hu-Zhao era as 'capitalist' and China's reform and the open era would end. However, doctrinal purity was rejected by Deng Xiaoping, who, on the contrary, formulated a theory of 'three favourables': raising productivity, boosting the people's standard of living, and elevating the comprehensive strength of the nation (*Mirror* April 1992:24-25). Any policy or measure that would be favourable to the three tasks would be considered 'socialist'. This was the further development of his thesis of black cats and white cats. Having lost two of his most intimate proteges in two years and surrounded by bundles of conservatives, Deng began to be impatient about the pace of economic reform (*Mirror* January 1991: 30-31; February 1991:26-27).   He planned to restart the reform engine. However, throughout the 1990s, the strategy that economic reform preceded political structural reform remained the cardinal principle. After the suppression of the pro-democracy movement, the CCP obviously encountered another major legitimacy crisis which, to Deng Xiaoping's mind, could only be saved by more radical economic reform (Deng 1993:307).

Despite the political setbacks, Deng's determination to pursue economic reform remained unshaken. In the second half of 1990, he allied with Shanghai Party secretary Zhu Rongji, to publish a serious of commentaries (pen name Wang Puping), criticizing the conservative backlash and insisting on the importance of the reform policies. At the same time, Deng formulated 'no controversies' to advance economic reform (*Mirror* April 1991:28-29). The series of tactical moves culminated in the trip to the Southern provinces (*Nanxun*), which successfully turned Jiang into a reformist, at least in economic arena. The victories of the Southern trip by Deng was manifested in the 14th CCP Congress Political Report made by Jiang (1992). Ideologically, the

Party should put its focus on anti-leftism and economically, the establishment of a socialist market economy was called for.

Riding with the wind of changes, the non-establishment intellectuals headed by Yuan Hongbing, a Beida lecturer, published an edited anti-leftism volume titled *Lishi de Chaoliu* (Currents of History). Hu Jiwei, former editor-in-chief of *People's Daily*, was one of the writers. As soon as it was published, it was banned by the Propaganda Department of the CCP. The book was charged with three crimes. First, the essays were edited and written by activists in the 4 June events; second, this was a counter-attack by the bourgeois rightists using Deng's southern trip as an excuse; third, the book revealed the problems between two views of reform (*Mirror* June 1992:37-38). Not content with the ban, Yuan Hongbing organized an academic forum titled "Reform and Open Door Policy, Strengthening the Country, Enriching the People" at which more than a hundred of intellectuals including some writers of the volume and other reformist intellectuals such as Wang Ruoshui participated. In a speech, Wang said that, in the reign of Maoist rule, leftism was the main current of thoughts, and this had destroyed China's development for almost twenty years. Deng had reversed the leftist trend by emphasizing reform but the habitual influence would not eradicated so easily (*Mirror* July 1992:44-47). In the three years since 4 June crackdown, this was the first time since 4 June crackdown that a spontaneous gathering organized by non-establishment intellectuals. The conservative force strongly condemned the forum and Deng Liqun personally attacked Yuan Hongbing for committing bourgeois liberalization, a great crime after 4 June (*Mirror* July 1992:30). On the eve of 14th CCP Congress, a group of respectable writers including Ba Jin, Wang Meng, Hu Jiwei, Yu Guangyuan and Sha Yiexin, etc. published a volume entitled *Fang Zuo Beiwanglu* (Memorandum on Preventing Leftism) and the literary monthly *Chinese Writers* organized a forum in June and published the speeches in the magazine. The focus was on "eliminating the leftist obstacles, literary writings can flourish" (*Nineties* January 1993:47-48). It was banned soon and the forum was attacked.

In the aftermath of 14th CCP Congress, the top leadership reached three points of consensus: first, quickening the process of reform; second, shelving political reform measures and third, tightening ideological control. In maintaining political stability, the Propaganda Department established an ideological monitoring unit consisting of fifty personnel to examine materials in the mass media at the central level (*Mirror* June 1993:28-29).

Clearly the new CCP leadership was wary of spontaneous moves that were not controlled by the Party, even though they were critical of conservative forces. Despite the harsh measures, the non-official intellectuals tried to push political reform by petitions to the top leadership. One of the earliest attempts was organized by Chen Ziming who allied with eleven famous intellectuals, including Liu Xiaobo, the literary critic and Chen Xiaoping, a legal expert. On 25 February 1995, the group sent the petition, together with twelve signatures, to the NPC. The gist of their petition was to demand that the CCP to curtail the rampant corruption. By writing on a topic that was the concern of the nation, they hoped that their petition would not be perceived as a threat to the leadership. Following the first petition, it was followed by two other petitions. On 28 February 1995, the student leader Wang Dan took the lead of organizing a petition, signed by 22 people, demanding the CCP abolish the labor camp system. On 2 March, Chen Zimin group also sent their second petition to the Party, demanding the Party to "preserve personal freedom of citizens and abolish security detention" (*Nineties* April 1995:29-31).

The second wave of petitions was sparked by the external events. 1995 was the year designated by the United Nations to be the Year of Tolerance. Echoing the appeal, on 15 May 1995, Xu Liangying, a veteran scientist in the Academy of Science, organized a petition signed by 45 intellectuals. The petition raised three demands: first, stop suppressing so-called ideological enemies, observing strictly the freedom of thought and religious beliefs; second, launch a re-evaluation of the 4 June events and release all prisoners arising from 4 June events; third, release all prisoners and detainees because of their thought or writings. Most surprisingly, the petition was headed by Wang Ganchang, one of the foremost nuclear physicists in China. In the eve of the six anniversary of 4 June crackdown, Wang Zhihong, wife of Chen Ziming, and 52 others wrote an appeal letter titled "To learn lessons of blood and pushing forward democratic and legal processes". The letter demanded the CCP should enact a series of legal codes to ensure the protection of human rights for the citizens, which included Law of the Press, Law of Assembly, Law of Constitutional Court and finally publish a declaration of human rights and human freedom (*Nineties* June 1995:76-79).

Again, on the eve of ten anniversaries of the 4 June events, 105 victims' families, notably among them was former professor of the People's University Ding Zilin, launched prosecution charges against premier Li Peng who violated the principles of protecting human life and freedom inherent in the Chinese constitution, United Nations Charter and the International Covenant of Civil and Political Rights which China had signed in the previous year (*Open* July 1999:8-9). All these petitions and letters certainly fell on deaf ears. Not only the CCP did not accept their moderate demands, but they were instead harassed (Chen Ziming), exiled (Wang Dan), kept under surveillance (Ding Zilin), and made to recant (Wang Ganchang).

Apart petitions from societal sectors (from the so-called right), there were petitions or appeals from the 'left', coming notably from Deng Liqun, once the underground general secretary in the mid-1980s. In late 1995, the neo-Maoists circulated a 'Ten-thousand Character' petition which is titled "Certain Factors that Affect out National Security" among senior cadres, attacking marketization as if would undercut the basis of socialism and would lead to the demise of the CCP. It raised the specter of "the substitution of the dictatorship of the proletariat with the open and direct dictatorship of the capitalists." (Willy Lam 1999:364). In early 1996, the neo-Maoists circulated another petition, warning of the emergence of a 'Gorbachev-type' of leadership within the Party. It further warned that 'peaceful evolution' was highly possible in China and the West was looking for its representatives in China and neo-capitalists were becoming a class (*Open* May 1996:18-19). In March 1997, Deng Liqun and his associates circulated the third petition titled "Certain Theoretical and Policy Problems Concerning Insisting the Status of Public Ownership", in an attempt to influence the agenda of the CCP Congress held later in 1997. As the title suggested, the focus of the petition was on exclusively the importance of public ownership. It asserted that "without the guiding status of the public ownership and national economy, there would not be socialism with Chinese characteristics" and it further argued that " if the guiding status of the public ownership was lost, then the economic basis of the ruling CCP would be gone and classes would be polarized. The state would become the appendage of the international capitalism." (*Open* March 1997:54-61).

These orthodox Marxist treatises had little influence even in the Party. More influential was the rise of neo-conservatives. The origin of neo-conservatism can be dated back to the neo-authoritarianism in the 1980s (Kalpana Misra 1998: 208-209). Joseph Fewsmith has captured the spirit of the neo-conservatism by defining it as follows: "(It) indicated a desire to find a middle path between the traditional conservatism of the Old Left (as examplified ideologically by more orthodox Marxist-Leninists such as Chen Yun) and 'radical reformers' (as epitomized culturally by the film *River Elegy* and economically by advocates of privatization). In general, neo-conservatism accepted market economics, albeit with some caveats, but desired a greater role for the state."(Fewsmith 2001:80). Fewsmith was right when he pointed the middle ground position of the ideological orientation of the neo-conservatism but he was wrong when he said the position "must be understood as a loose term, indicating a set of concerns and a broad intellectual orientation rather than a well developed and consistent body of thought" (Fewsmith 2001: 80). By the beginning of the 21st century, neo-conservatism or the new Left, together with liberalism, had developed into the two main coherent and consistent bodies of thought covering analyses on aspects such as the nature of Chinese society, the nature of Chinese state, the notion of social justice, the views on international situation, whether freedom or democracy was the developmental goal for China,   the nature of civil society, the role of efficiency or equality, the notion of revolution or reform or tradition, the nature of modernity, etc (*Ming Pao Monthly* May 2002: 33-40; *Open* June 1995: 48-52; *Open* December 1999:51-53).

The ideas of neo-conservatism were first systemically expounded by a group of young intellectuals associated with *China Youth Daily* in the aftermath of the failed Soviet coup in August 1991(Fewsmith 2001: 98-100). They circulated a paper entitled "Realistic Responses and Strategic Options for China after the Soviet Upheaval". The monograph was associated with some princelings such as Chen Yuan, son of Chen Yun, and Pan Yue, the son-in-law of Liu Huaqing. The gist of the tract was to attack both ideological extreme, the so-called 'utopian socialism' and 'utopian capitalism', and strive for a middle ground. The central concern was to how the CCP had changed from a revolutionary party to a ruling party. They were certainly for the continuous governance of the CCP but they were concerned about how politically stability could be maintained. The theses were repeated when Pan Yue submitted a paper on the changing status of the CCP in late 1990s (*Open* July 2001:28-38). In retrospect, the paper was ignored by the the Jiang-Zhu leadership.

Sha Yiexin, a veteran drama script writer, pointed out that the propaganda machine of the CCP had four features. First, the Party is supreme. According to the "Theory of Three Represents", the Party represents the whole nation and therefore could not be criticized. Second, the uniformity of public opinion, so it allows no dissenting voice. Third, all mass media are the mouthpiece of the Party/state. Fourth, no law would be passed to govern mass media. The late Chen

Yun had told the following to the party members: "In KMT period, they had passed a press law. We studied it and made use of its loopholes. Now we don't have to pass the law. We could do whatever we like" (*Open* September 2003:89-91).

China claims that there is no press censorship but, in fact, the censorship is most rigorous. All the propaganda departments of the Party Committees at the various levels exercise censorship. Furthermore, the Party Committees in the mass media also exercise censorship and more sensitive materials would be submitted to the Propaganda Ministry of the CCP for decision. After reform policies were launched, control began to loosen. Since the Fourteenth CCP Congress, the Propaganda Ministry set up a "Press News Reading and Assessment Coordinating Unit" to exercise control. After the Fifteenth CCP Congress, the Ministry instructed different provinces and cities to set up "Reading and Assessment Teams" to serve as censorship units. The result was a long list of banned books, journals and magazines. Numerous editors and publishers were warned, penalized and driven out from the professions (*Open* August 2003:83-89).[2]

Suppressing Organized Opposition

The CCP is a highly unified Party/state/military structure. Despite the incessant ideological and political conflicts within the Party, it has never allowed external political societal forces to grow unhindered even in the reform era. Along with the marketization of the economy, the coercion over the society has shrunken considerably but the CCP has never tolerated organized opposition or even potential organized forces. The 4 June events certainly taught the Party a good lesson. "Nipping the disturbances in the bud" as the former Beijing mayor Chen Xitong said. In fact, this has been guiding principle in tackling the non- CCP forces in the past two decades. Even in economic corporations, the Party very often occupies the dominant position. More recently, the Party called for the revival of the Party cells in all economic enterprises, even under the relative relaxed climate of Hu Jintao-Wen Jiabao new leadership (*Ming Pao* 20 August 2003).[3]

The harsh crackdown in the aftermath of the 4 June killings silenced all political dissent within the Party as well as outside. Ideologically, the elites became more conservative and calling for stability became the focus of the regime efforts. In early 1992, 4 June student leaders Wang Dan and Guo Haifeng were given medical parole. As the final International Olympic committee vote approached in

September veteran activists Wei Jingsheng, Xu Wenli and Wang Juntao were free in a move to impress upon the Olympic committee members Beijing's good will in observing human rights records. But the activists had not organized together then and they were marginally connected with each other (Teresa Wright 2002: 907-908). After the failure of the bid to host the year 2000 Olympic, the political climate became tense again and the activities of the dissenters became more intense, so the oppression came and Wei and Wang were arrested again.

In the late 1990s, the external environment provided a fertile soil again for the development of the dissent. In 1997, China signed the International Covenant on Economic, Social, and Cultural Rights. The US president Clinton was planning a visit to China in June 1998 and UN High Commissioner for Human Rights Mary Robinson was expected in September 1998. In October, China signed the International Covenant on Civil and Political Rights. In the meantime, internally, the 'counter-revolutionary' clause was repealed by the NPC in March and substituted with the clause of 'national security', a move showing the continuing de-ideologization of the CCP. In September the same year, the Fifteen CCP Congress called for the need to rule by law   and made references, for the first time, to human rights. Under the relaxed climate, Wang Youcai, one of the 1989 student leaders, had the idea forming an opposition party; he was perhaps influenced by Wang Bingzhang who was the founder of *China Spring* and had earlier slipped into China to contact dissidents in early 1998. He was found and expelled. Wang and his friends in Hangzhou decided to announce the news on the eve of Clinton's visit, hoping that the timing would preclude official suppression. On 25 June, the group presented an "Open Declaration of the Establishment of the China Democracy Party (CDP) Zhejiang Preparatory Committee" and a draft constitution. The aim of CDP was to "establish a constitutional democratic political system" and peaceful means must be used in processes. The group "opposes terrorist activities" (Teresa Wright 2002:910). Subsequently, preparatory committees began to form in twenty-four provinces and cities.

The UN Covenant on Civil and Political Rights guarantees the right to form political parties but no legal procedures had been developed in China to establish the status. The preparatory committee of the CDP tried to test the official limit by applying for a legal status at the Zhejiang provincial civil affairs bureau. Surprisingly, the bureau accepted the application. But later Wang was detained and interrogated. He was told his application was rejected. In the following months, five provincial preparatory committees had tried to register in different civil affairs bureaux but some were refused and some received no response. Evidently, the leadership in Beijing was contemplating how to response to these application. In early November, the CDP members, among them the veteran activist Xu Wenli, declared the establishment of the "First CDP National Congress Preparatory Work Group". Shortly after, they also set out to form a "CDP Beijing-Tianjin Regional Party Branch", the first time a national opposition party was founded after 1949.

However, the repression was swift. With the departure of Clinton and Mary Robinson, the favorable external factors were gone. Most of the chief organizers were arrested. In July and October 1999, there were more detentions and imprisonment of the dissidents. Some managed to escape and some went into hiding. Beginning in December, almost all CDP leaders were rounded up and imprisoned. By the end of 1999, the CDP had ceased to exist. Despite its moderate demands and peaceful action, the CDP was still repressed. However far the reform stride may be, the official tolerance of opposition was extremely limited under the Jiang Zemin reign. However, there was a new characteristic which was the wide use of internet in disseminating news and information (Teresa Wright 2002:919-921).[4]

Similarly, the *Falun Gong* sect saga provides another example of using internet to make liaison among the followers and eventually to be perceived as posing a threat to the CCP leadership. The most publicized event of *Falun Gong* was the encirclement of Zhongnanhai, the nerve center of the CCP political establishment, by over 10,000 members from six provinces and municipalities on 25 April 1999 (*Open* May 1999:17-19). According to Xinhua reports, before the 25 April incident, the *Falun Gong* followers had organized 18 encirclements, demonstrations, and attacks on media, TV stations, and even encircled municipal government buildings in different provinces. Between 19 and 23 April 1999, Professor He Zouxiu, a member of Academy of Science at Tianjin, wrote an article arguing against the youth practising *qigong* and he also criticized *Falun Gong* as unscientific. Subsequently, *Falun Gong* members assembled about 1,600 members to protest against the article before the Tianjin municipal government. Several days later, the followers targeted at Zhongnanhai.

Falun Gong was a religious and quasi-religious group without any hierarchy and organizational structure, according to its adherents. But the authorities claimed otherwise and charged that it had strict hierarchical order and structure and had Li Hongzhi as its head (James

Tong 2002: 637-638). The society was founded in 1992 by Li Hongzhi. In the beginning, he gave *qigong* seminars and training sessions and soon gained enormous influence in various provinces. In October 1996 he went to the USA with a tourist visa and since then he was able to have a green card and stayed in the US. By the time the Falun Gong movement was banned in July 1999, the regime claimed that it had 39 main stations, 1,900 guidance stations, 28,263 practice sites across the country and 2.1 million practitioners inside China (*Brightness Daily* 15 August 1999). Some estimates were even larger. According to a Guangdong source *Nanfang Ribao* (*Southern Daily* 27 July 1999), it had a following of 130 million.

The sect has traditional Buddhist and Daoist elements. Essentially, it is not different from traditional religions (Kang Xiaoguang 2000:160-164). The reasons that in a span of several years the *Falun Gong* could appeal to millions of followers inside China as well as overseas must be sought in the context of the marketization reform since the late 1970s. All religions are sets of belief systems. The collapse of Marxist-Leninist ideologies and the cult of Mao after the reform had a profound impact on the psychology of ordinary citizens. The revival of traditional religions in the reform era was a substitute for the ideological void in a rapidly changing Party/state context. The spread of Christianity and Catholicism was heavily constrained by the CCP leadership and was forced to go underground in developing followers. *Falun Gong* emerged and spread its influence by disguising itself as one of the health-strengthening traditional *qigong* practicing groups.

According to Kang Xioaguang, a member of the Academy of Sciences, four factors contributed to the appeal of the *Falun Gong* (2000:169:178). First, the rise of *Falun Gong* was a spiritual response to the crisis in faith on the part of population in the context of valuational confusion created by the demise of communist ideology and Mao's cult. Second, as a millennial movement, the notion of equality and justice was important in the doctrine. The market reforms had created an extreme poverty gap and the concentration of political power enabled the CCP Party/state to exercise unrelenting coercion to stifle general discontent. *Falun Gong* at least, in the pursuit of justice in the future, satisfied the partial psychological and spiritual needs of the population. Third, as a health-strengthening organization, the sect's *qigong* and various training exercises were body strengthening moves. Moreover, the market reform in the public sector in general and the hospital sector in particular had made medical costs very expensive.

Without a credible social insurance system, it is imperative to keep one's body healthy. The sect fulfilled the psychological need for security. Fourth, as a social organization, mankind is constantly in search of group identity. In the actual organizations or work units, one is confronted with interest pursuits and power intriguing struggles and only in this spiritual organization, one's equality was totally achieved and one need not worry about the greed, thirst for power, corruption and hypocrisy.

However, similar to the Christian church and the Catholic church, what the CCP feared most was not the religious beliefs but rather the organizational power that *Falun Gong* manifested during the 25 April 1999 incident. Most alarmingly, other religious groups were in its control yet before the incident the CCP knew nothing about the group (*Open* June 1999:11-13). As Kang Xiaoguang rightly pointed out (2000:2), "The conflicts between the CCP and *Falun Gong* was not in the belief or whether it was an evil cult or not, but in the organization, in the number of followers. It has too many followers which is beyond official tolerance. A deeper issue is the question who has the power to organize groups? Could people organize groups in pursuit of common interest? Or whether the power is in the hand of government or people?"

Strengthening the NPC or Three-Cornered Power Game?

In the 1980s, the NPC was revived and transformed and its powers were greatly expanded under the new constitution of 1982. As outlined in the chapter 3, the institution had made substantial progress in the liberalization orientation. According to official source, the total number of laws enacted by the NPC and the SCNPC from 1979 to 1998 amounted to 332, which covered administrative, economic, criminal and civil areas (*People's Daily* 23 March 1998). The NPC deputies had flashed their muscles on the voting of state presidents, premiers and chairmen of the NPC, mostly by negative votes or abstention votes.

The process of shaking off the rubber-stamp image of the NPC was accelerated in the early 1990s under the chairmanship and vice-chairmanship of Qiao Shi and Tian Jiyun, two noted reformists who had been appointed at the Eighth NPC held in March 1993. First of all, Qiao began to recruit foreign legal experts to reorganize the NPC's Legislative Commission which drafted the country's economics legislation and laws, as economic reform went into full swing after Deng's southern trip. Second, Qiao followed the late NPC chairman

Peng Zhen's policies of legal reform in the 1980s, making full use of its SC as the operative mechanism. In fact, the SCNPC gained expanded power bestowed by the new constitution in 1982. The NPC has developed several other functions besides law-making. The function of supervising judicial and administrative apparatus was strengthened and it has also established administrative penalties for misconduct on the part of officials in administrative and judicial organizations. It has exercised investigation power in law enforcement more often. From 1994 to 1996, the SCNPC had organized forty-six inspection groups for the purpose of monitoring the enforcement of the laws at the sub-national levels and reports were sent to the SCNPC after inspection. The SCNPC would discuss these reports and referred to relevant authorities for the solution (Wang J. 1999:91). The legislators were pushing for a Law of Supervision that would enable to the deputies to call from State Council senior officials and judicial units to explain their policies or to impeach them if they failed to justify their policies by 1997 or 1998. It was resisted by the officials (*Ming Pao* 20 November 1996).

Since the late 1980s, the NPC had tried to assert its role independent of the Party and government. The 1995 statute of the declaration of the Martial Law was an example. Knowing the coerciveness of the martial law troops during June 1989, the law tried to restrain the troops by introducing stipulations such as that " Martial law personnel should as far as possible avoid using weapons." In the Third Plenary Session of the Eighth NPC held in April 1995, the NPC demonstrated its institutional assertiveness in three occasions. Firstly, Wu Bangguo and Jiang Chunyun, two close followers of Jiang Zemin, nominated to be vice-premiers, were was elected with more than one-third of negative votes from the deputies, to the astonishment of the Politburo. Secondly, the Education and Banking laws were rejected by one-fourth of the delegates. Third, in the Fourth Plenary Session of the Eighth Congress held in March 1996, over a quarter of the delegates refused to grant approval to the work reports of both the Supreme People's Court and Supreme People's Procuratorate. Furthermore, the amendments to the Criminal Procedure Code were another piece evidence on the NPC's assertion of independent power. The amendments were drafted by the SCNPC and passed in 1996 Plenary Session. The amendments greatly liberalized criminal procedures in the PRC. However, it was met with strong opposition from the Ministry of Public Security (MPS) and the Supreme People's Procuratorate because the amendments included some lenient provisions such as the abolition of administrative detention. In China, it is still a widely practiced procedure that allowed the security organs to incarcerate suspected persons indefinitely without trial or gaining access to a lawyer.

There were other acts of rebellion by the NPC and sub-national people's congresses. In January 1993, the provincial people's congress of Zhejiang was supposed to elect a new governor. The Party committee, through the presidium, nominated the incumbent governor Ge Hongsheng, a new rising star, who had been recently elected as one of the CC members. The deputies ignored the signals from the above and nominated two more candidates for competition. One withdrew and the other contestant Wan Xueyuan, one of vice governors, was elected. In the competitive elections for the vice governors, six of the nine candidates nominated by the deputies were elected (*Cheng Ming* April 1994:9-11). In May 1989, the Hunan provincial people's congress moved to impeach the vice governor Yang Huiquan whose inability and corruption angered the deputies. The deputies were successful in dismissing him (Ming Xia 2000:168). In Minqing county of Fujian province in March 1994, the county people's congress vetoed a government decision about the price of tap water. However, the government did not accept this and proceeded with the decision. The congress openly condemned the move and forced it to cancel the decision (An Chen 1999: 201). The provincial people's congress of Guangdong declined to confirm the appointment of the two department heads in February 2000. Shenyang municipal people's congress of Liaoning did not pass the work report of the municipal court in February 2001. The municipal people's congress of Hechi of Guangxi rejected the government work report on the management of the internet bars. In January 2003, the municipal people's congress of Yueyang of Hunan failed to elect the mayor nominated by Party committee in the first round and he was finally elected in the second round but the election process was strongly condemned by the deputies (*Apple* 5 January 2003). In May 2003, in Shenzhen Futian district, a Party-nominated candidate was defeated in the election of the deputies and Wang Liang, a US educated master-degree holder, won the election as an independent (*Apple* 22 May 2003).

As the marketization of the economy proceeds and China's merging with the world capitalist economy accelerates after the accession to the WTO, the NPC and the sub-national people's congresses have been gaining enormous powers and authority, which were manifested in the following aspects. First, legislative effectiveness: notwithstanding the national legislature, which has made more 300 laws since the late 1970s, more than 5,300 local laws were passed by the sub-national people's congresses. Second, economic decision-making: As China's economy becomes more internationalized, the burden to legislate lies with the NPC. In fact, most of the legislation was concerned about economics. Third, expanding power in the periphery: The NPC had given generous support to the legislative processes in the sub-national level, such as the support given to the Hunan provincial people's congress in ousting the vice governor. Fourth, judicial review: the power to interpret the laws and determine the constitutionality of local laws and administrative decrees lies in the NPC. Fifth, informational power: the NPC has become a cohesive institution in the whole political system. Sixth, veto power: the NPC and sub-national people's congresses certainly have the veto power vis-as-vis the personnel appointment. The potential restraint imposed by this power served to remind the CCP of its limitation, (Ming Xia 2000: 127-128).

However its secondary role in the Chinese polity has remained unchanged. During the 4 June crisis, despite the calling of urgent meeting and potential impeachment of Li Peng by more than fifty SC members of the NPC, they were not able to convene a plenary meeting to investigate the Tiananmen chaos. The incidents show the feebleness of the NPC. The CCP leadership believed that the role of the NPC in the 1990s should not be changed. A few days after the crackdown, Deng addressed the officers of troops of the curfew, stating the inviolability of the existing political structure. He said "In the reform of the political structure, one thing is certain: we must adhere to the system of the people's congress instead of practicing the separation of the judicial, executive and legislative powers upon the American pattern. As a matter of fact, not all the Western countries follow the pattern of separation of powers" (Deng 1994:299).

Despite the negative votes, the refusal to pass the Party-nominated candidates for official positions, and other supervisory mechanisms exercised by the NPC or local people's congresses in the 1990s, there have been control mechanisms by the CCP over the legislative bodies that would make the collective rebellion of the members almost impossible. First, most if not all the NPC deputies were CCP members. Approximately, two-third of the deputies from 1988 to 1998 were CCP members. In particular for the SC members of the NPC, it was estimated that since 1983 the percentage of CCP members in SCNPC was not below 75 (An Chen 1999: 163). With the dominant influence by the Party members in the NPC and SCNPC, it was guaranteed that the legislative intent would not deviate from the Party line. Second, furthermore, there existed the Party committee within the SCNPC, which could command the loyalty of the Party members. The Party committee could at the same time serve as a bridge between the Party and state. Despite the lack of detailed analyses of the internal channels of communications within the Party/state, it is widely known that every piece of important legislation must be examined and approved by the CCP Politburo. In a move to control the provincial people's congresses, starting with the 14th CCP congress, the Party's first secretary should at the same time hold the chairmanship of SC of the people's congresses and during the 1990s this practice was widely adopted.

After two decades of reform and the strengthening of the NPC, has the political system become a three-cornered power game or are the three corners of equal angles (An Chen 1999: 166-171)? Or has the system become a 'semi-anticipatory democracy' ?(Ming Xia 2000: 128) The answer is, in fact, far from definite. In spite of greater tolerance towards intra-party/state dissent, it is clear that the CCP has always remained the power arbitrator.

Administrative Reform

Comparing with the strengthening of the NPC, which serves as a relatively minor check and balance on the State Council, the administrative reform or streamlining of the bureaucracy was the most important reform measure in the 1990s from the top leadership. Similar to the 1980s, there were two waves of administrative reform in the 1990s. The first one started in 1993 and the second one in 1998. The background to the administrative reform or organizational restructuring was, on the one hand, China's inexorable march towards a marketized economy and, on the other hand, the re-emergence of bureaucratism in the early 1990s. At the Fourteenth CCP Congress held in October 1992, the leadership called for the establishment of a socialist market economy. In 1993, the CCP even desired to achieve a socialist market system before the end of the twentieth century. Jiang Zemin's Political Report (1992) stated the importance of administrative reform in the process of rapid modernization. He stated that " If we are to reform the political structure, deepen the economic reform, establish a market economy and accelerate the modernization drive, we must make it our urgent task to streamline the organizational structure and to simplify administrative layers." He condemned the phenomena of bureaucratism, such as "bloated bureaucracy, over-staffing, merging of government and enterprises which directly hinder the deepening economic reform and influence the relationships between the Party and people."

The budget of the Party/government personnel had almost become unbearable. In 1979, the number of Party/state cadres was 2.79 million. Ten years later, it had shot up almost double to 5.43 million and in 1998 there were 30 million cadres. In twenty years, the number of government personnel increased more than ten times. The population increase certainly was less than ten times in twenty years (Liu Zhifeng 1998: 63). In the first half of 1990s, the changes of the government function which means the separation of the government and enterprises became the focal point of the political structural reform, along with the administration in the state machinery (Chan and Drewry 2001).   The separation of government from the enterprises was seen as the beginning of the switch of government function. In addition, the ultimate goal of the administrative reform was to establish a socialist market economy, which would pave the way for the accession to the WTO.   After the Sixteenth CCP Congress, the reform focus shifted to instituting so-called grass-root democracy in the countryside or villages. In engineering the 1993 State Council reform, Li Peng basically summarized the administrative reform in the 1980s as a failure. He criticized the bureaucracy's failure to meet the challenges of modernization or economic development.   The problems nowadays in the state apparatuses were "merging of the state and enterprises, the relationships not well defined, bloated staffing and low efficiency" (1993).

In the early 1990s, the organizational units including ministries, commissions, affiliated and working organizations had increased from 80 in 1988 to 86 in 1993. The total Party/state cadres at the end of 1991 was 9.2 million and fiscal expenditure was 140 billion yuan, accounting 37% of the GDP. The reform proposal attempted to reduce the total amount of staff from 36,700 to 29,200 in the central administration, a 20% reduction, cutting 86 working units to 59 (Liu Zhifeng 1998:306-307). The reform concentrated on changing of the pattern of the economic ministries. The sectoral reform or streamlining took place in three ways. First, some government ministries were changed to *jingji shiti* (economic entities) with no administrative functions. The administration and running of these entities were left to market forces, such as the abolition of the Ministry of Aeronautical Industry and setting up of the Aeronautical Industrial Company, etc. Second, some departments became *hangye zonghui* (professional associations), which would be subordinated directly to the State Council, and they were established to replace some ministries such as the Ministries of Light Industries and Textile. The goal of these professional associations was to co-ordinate policies and exercise macro-supervision over the professions and facilitate services for the professionals. Finally, the carryover or newly-created administrative ministries were given streamlined administrative structures, which would engage in planning, coordination, servicing and supervision of the industries concerned. The retained Ministries included Railway, Transport, Forestry, and Agriculture, etc. The newly set up Ministries included Ministries of Mechanical Industry, Electronic Industry, etc. To improve the efficiency of the State Council, reshuffling also took place within the State Council's affiliated organizations and it took three forms, first, retaining the important working units, such as Hong Kong and Macau Affairs Office; second, merging with the original ministries and becoming a sub-unit or *ju* (bureau), such as National Earthquake Bureau and National Property Management Bureau; third, merging with the Ministries and becoming a *zhineng ju* (functional bureau) such as the National Herbal Medicine Management Bureau. With these measures, the number of affiliated and working units was reduced from 44 to 18 (GOSC 1995:8-10).[5]

Luo Gan, then secretary-general of the State Council, decreed that the government departments had to change functions, simplify administrative structure and decentralize decision-making power, in line with marketization reform. The government bureaucracy must be simplified and the enterprises have to enhance the competitive edge by entering the market. In the reform process, twenty-seven ministries and departments were eliminated, including seven specialized economic departments. The number of cadres was reduced by 20 percent, from 36,700 to 29,200 (GOSC 1995: 10).

The 1990s was a rapidly developing era for China. Economic growth was in double-digit figures and incorporation into the world capitalist economy quickened. The negotiations with the USA over the accession to the WTO had been going on since the mid-1980s. However, by mid-1990s, the administrative reform seemed to be failing in the midst of the marketization of the economy. As Li Peng stated in his Government Work Report (1998) "Despite achievement had been made in the previous reform attempts, because of the objective constraints, a lot of problems remained unresolved. The contradictions between the organizational apparatus and socialist development had become increasing apparent, such as over-staff bureaucracy, inseparation of the government and enterprises, the growth of bureaucratism and corruption and fiscal burden." In 1998, China had 33 million Party/state cadres whose salaries were paid by the state. Among them 25 million personnel belonged to various kinds of public institutions and 8 million were cadres at all levels of the administration (Chan and Drewry 2001:557). The financial budget of these staff accounted for almost 40% of the total budget of the state (Liu Zhifeng 1998:24-25).

The 1998 administrative reform was the most drastic and comprehensive organizational streamlining in the history of PRC. 40 ministries and commissions in the State Council were slashed to 29, a reduction of 27%. More than 200 bureaus, about 25% of the total, were also abolished. Furthermore, the reform aimed to reduce the State Council employees to 16,700, a reduction of 47.5% (GOSC 1998:39). In 1997, Jiang Zemin had already laid bare the rationale and principles of this administrative reform. In his Report to the Sixth Plenum of the 15th CCP Congress, he said,

> In accordance with the requirement of a socialist market economy we need to alter the functions of the government and separate them from those of enterprises so that enterprises will be truly given the power with regard to production, operation and management. Following the principle of simplification, uniformity and efficiency in reform, we shall establish a highly efficient, well-coordinated and standard administrative system, with a view to improving its service to the people. The departments in charge of comprehensive economic management should shift their functions to macroeconomic control, and specialized economic departments should be reorganized or reduced. We shall improve the works of departments supervising law enforcement and cultivate and expand social intermediary organizations. We shall deepen the reform of the administrative system, statutorily delimiting the structures, functions sizes and working procedures of the state organs and ensuring that their sizes are kept within authorized limits and their redundant personnel are reduced.

There are three measures suggested in the Report, namely changing some ministries into enterprises or corporations set up under the State Council, streamlining or the outright abolition of some government

ministries or commissions, and the downsizing of staff. The direction of
the reform was similar to the 1993 reform and the overall goal of the
reform was to create a 'small government, big society' environment
which could facilitate economic reform. After the ninth NPC in March
1998, the administrative reform began to take full force. First, 15 out of
40 ministries and commissions of the State Council were eliminated,
such as   the Ministries of Electrical Industries, Mechanical Industries,
Internal Trade and Labor, etc. Second, half of the 32,000 personnel
within the State Council would be transferred or discharged. The
guiding principle in the reform regarding personnel was that no one
was to be unemployed. The personnel had to be either re-deployed or
retrained. In three years, one million central and local government
cadres positions were cut. Third, in the planned economy era, the
ministries and commission were designed to micro-manage the
economy and state enterprises. Some economic management units were
downgraded from commission and ministry status to departmental
status. Their powers and functions were limited to three major tasks:
macro management, guidance in structuring industry and facilitation of
fair competition among business sectors. The direct management of
enterprises was prohibited. The State Planning Commission would be
redesigned as the State Development Planning Commission.   The
State Planning Commission had been directing the economy since the
1950s but the new renamed Commission would take charge of macro
management of regulation, long term development planning and
maintenance of general economic equilibrium. Market force would be
the chief determinant of the economy. In addition, the Organization
Laws of the State Council would be revised to provide more flexibility
in regulation. Fourth, four ministries and commissions were newly
created to meet the challenges imposed by the advent of globalization
such as Ministries of Information Industry, Labor and Social Security,
etc. There were 22 carry-over ministries and commissions. At the local
level, the Organization Laws of Localities would give more autonomy
to the local governments in implementing central government policies.
Finally, local governments would have to follow the reform measures
but local variations would be allowed and also the extent of
marketization in the Western regions was different from the coastal
developed areas.

     Chinese   social   scientists   have   labeled   the   cycles   of
streamlining-swelling-re-streamlining re-swelling as 'historic vicious
cycles' (Liu Zhifeng 1998:317). Previous attempts at re-organization
had failed. Xie Qingkui, a political scientist at Beida, analyzed the

'vicious circles' or lack of success in organizational reform as being due to five factors. First, the CCP as a ruling party had designated Marxism and Leninism's democratic centralism as theoretical guiding line for the Party as well as whole country. Centralization was the key feature of the system. Second, the systemic features of the former Soviet Union had a shaping influence on the formation of the existing PRC socio-political-economic system. The influence was difficult to erase. Third, under the reign of Mao, efficiency was not an important factor worth mentioning. The PRC always emphasized the importance of quantity rather quality. Therefore, streamlining was not considered necessary in eradicating bureaucratism. Fourth, perhaps influenced by traditional dynastic conventions, the Party/state cadres had the psychological factor that they could not demoted or downgraded. This allowed for the expansion of bureaucracy. Fifth, the Perhaps the most important factor was institutional.   For a long time, there has not been any institutional check or curbing on the centralization of power of the CCP (Liu Zhifeng 1998: 323-324). Despite the fact that the marketization reform was in full force in China, it is difficult to believe that the organizational reform measures would succeed given the past experiences.[6]

Instituting Grass-roots Elections

Besides the organizational streamlining which focused on the separation of the government and enterprises and efficiency enhancement within the bureaucracy, the CCP leadership seemed to play up the grass-roots or self rule elections since the mid-1990s. Grass-roots elections or democracy was another big piece of political structural reform in the second half 1990s. After 1949, there were three stages of development in the organization of grass-root structure in the rural areas. First, from 1949 to 1957, was a stage which the *xiang* (town) administrative structure co-existed with agricultural co-operatives. Second, from 1958 to 1982, People's Communes were established and that dissolved. Large and small production teams also existed. Finally, after 1982, the new state constitution was passed and decreed the establishment of village committees in the rural areas. There were three phases in the development of the village self rule. First, from 1982 to 1987, this phase began with the 1982 state constitution which requires the establishment of the resident committees and village committees in the rural and urban areas as mass self rule organizations. Second, from 1987 to 1990, the *Provisional*

Organic Law of the Village Committee of the People's Republic of China was promulgated by the Thirteenth SC Meeting of the Sixth NPC in 1987, stating that the law came to effect on 1 June 1988. Third, after 1990, the self rule governance was accepted by the top CCP leadership and extend to the whole country (Bai Yihua, Yang Kaiwang and Chih-yu Shih 1998: 255-257). The origin of the village committees emerged in two Guangxi counties (Yishan and Luocheng) in late 1980. The first Villagers Representative Assembly was set up in nanlou village (Hebei). The village committees were formed by local villagers and cadres to manage village affairs in the midst of the breakup of the People's Commune and production teams. They reported to the higher authorities and finally Beijing accepted the form and legitimized the formal structure in the 1982 state constitution (O'Brien and Lianjiang Li 2000:465).

Officially, the 930,000 villages across the country were required to hold elections on village heads and committee members after 1988. Between 1988 and 1990, about 1,093 villages were selected by the Ministry of Civil Affairs (MCA) to be trial cases. The MAC set up special training workshops to recruit cadres to conduct the village committee elections. In the early 1990s, the MAC selected the "demonstration villages" by applying the official guidelines which were adopted and made public in April 1994. The guidelines decreed that direct and competitive elections must be held at the village level. Second, the "village representative assemblies" should be established and oversee the elected village committees. Lastly, village charters and codes of conduct for cadres and villagers by the representative village assemblies were issued.

The direct democracy at the village level was backed up by the CCP leadership as a whole. Li Peng said that "In our country democracy starts with the grass-roots, because for an ordinary villager the person who is of direct concern is not the governor or the county magistrate....but he chairman of the village committee."(*SCMP* 1 December 1998). Zhu Rongji (1999) emphasized that "To develop democracy and perfect the mechanisms that reflect the public opinion so that public opinion could be absorbed into the government's decision making process. We must further strengthen the system of democratic decisions and cautiously and consistently develop the function of the village committees." In the Fifteenth CCP Congress in 1997, Jiang Zemin (1997) pointed out that "To extend grass-root democracy, guarantee the direct exercise of democratic rights, manage their own affairs and create a happy life, are the widest practice of socialist democracy." Evidently, from the official perspective, village elections both have the form and substance of democracy. According to the official documents, they fulfilled five purposes. First, the villagers have the power to manage their own affairs and be the masters of their future. Second, the elections show that the villagers have the ability to exercise democratic rights. Third, the elections improve the relationships between the villagers and Party/state cadres and eased tensions on both sides. Fourth, the elections improve the relationships and communications between the Party as a whole and the peasantry. Fifth, the elections generate incentives for the peasantry in managing their own affairs (Bai Yihua, Yang Kaiwang and Chih-yu Shih 1998:260-261).

Since the concept of self rule for the mass organization was first conceived in the 1980s and elections of the village committee heads started in 1988, why did the CCP leadership blow up the issue into one of the major pieces of political structural reform in the mid-1990s ? During Clinton's 1998 visit to China, he was invited to discuss village elections with the peasants in Xia He village near Xi'an (*Ming Pao* 27 June 1998). There were four reasons. First, the most thorny issues in the Sino-US relationship were first the Taiwan problem and second the human rights issue. In the aftermath of the 4 June crackdown, human rights became the issue that the US government must handle with China. China's human rights record was so poor that it was practically defenseless in the face of the US accusations. Every year since the early 1990s the issue of human rights would heat up as the Congress renewed the Most Favored Nation trade status of the PRC.

China began to use two tactics to counter attack the USA. First, publishing a human rights report on the USA and charging the USA with adopting double standard or selective standards in assessing the human rights record of other countries. Second, trying to play up the self rule village committees elections and claiming that China, in fact, has more basic democratic rights for the people than the USA. Second, village elections could serve as delaying tactics by the hard-liners to the reformists within the Party who were asking more radical reform pace. Third, since the reform started in the late 1970s, the Party's totalistic power over society in general and in rural areas in particular, had shrunken considerably. The stability in the rural areas indeed worried the leadership. By allowing the elections to take place, at least the elected heads would have legitimacy and would perform as best as they could to win the next elections and thereby stabilize the situation in the rural areas. According to an internal document, the Party structure has collapsed in up to 30% of China's village.[7] Fourth, the village committees are mass organizations of self rule and they are not even part of the formal executive structure of the political system. They are extremely remote from the power core in Beijing and therefore certainly would not threaten the power base of the CCP.

Are the village elections truly democratic? In an empirical study, Robert A. Pastor and Qingshan Tan (2000) have observed many such elections and discussed with many MCA officials. They have come to the following conclusion. First, there was not a complete set of data on the entire country. In response to the question posed to the MCA officials about how many village elections were conducted according to the election laws, the officials answered "Perhaps 50%, frankly we do not know." Party village secretaries usually served on the village election committee that supervised village elections and therefore could wield enormous influence in election outcomes. According to their estimate, probably less than half of the village heads ran competitively. There has been widespread use of proxy votes and secret balloting was not always used. There were also different voting procedures even though the MCA had been trying hard to standardize them. One thing the authors were sure was that "There is no evidence that national leaders are trying to control villages. This may be because the Communist Party is not threatened by village elections....The Party's interest in free elections, however, might not be so impartial if the elections move up the ladder of the government" (Robert Pastor and Qingshan Tan 2000:508-509).

In another study identifying the locus of decision- making power in the Chinese village, Jean Oi and Scott Rozelle (2000) suggested that the broadly inclusive village assemblies and partially- elected village committees meet only infrequently. Moreover, there appeared to be wide variations in the actual power for the smaller village committees (5 to 7 persons). For some, the elected committee is the seat of power decision, for some the Party secretary decides every thing. The variations seems to tie in with the nature of village economy and the changing bases of power in China's countryside after the de-collectivization in the early 1980s. However, they found out that the percentage of Party members in the village committees (64% and 65% in two cases) were more than the MCA officials claimed (25 to 35% generally) (2000:521).

According to a Chinese social scientist, unlawful activities were widespread and they could be manifested in the following five ways

(Bai Gan 2001)[8]. First, bribery to gain the necessary votes to be elected. One vote normally cost from 20 yuan to 30 yuan. However, a Party secretary of a village in Yangjiang City, Guangdong Province spent totally 300,000 yuan on votes and also manipulated the ballot to be elected as the director of the village committee. Second, appointed or assigned elections, this means that instead of allowing the villagers to vote, the township government directly appointed or assigned the director or committee members. Third, the election organizations broke the laws in different forms, such as not allowing competitive elections to be held; not providing secret ballots; not selecting formal candidates in the villager representative meeting; sometimes electing the director or members of the village committees by the village representatives only, etc. Fourth, illegal procedures, sometimes the electoral committees were selected by the township government; sometimes votes by proxy were not strictly carried out by relevant laws; ballots were not counted; sometimes voter participation failed to be reported, etc. Fifth, there were various ways to sabotage the elections by unlawful means. Sometimes the old members refused to transfer power to the newly-elected members and sometimes the town government dismissed the elected director or members without going through a village meeting (Bai Gang 2001: 17-21).

The revised Organic Law of the Village Committees was passed by the 5th SC of the NPC in November 1998. With that, the village elections or self government shed their trial status and elections procedures have been standardized. According to the Law, the elections must be competitive and the voting must be secret (article 14), and "the members of the village committees are to be elected directly by villager; they may not be designated, appointed or replaced by any organization or individual" (Article 11), etc. However, in a move to guarantee the dominance of the Party, the new Law stipulates that the Party branch is the village's "leadership core " (*lingdao hexin*) (article 3). Therefore, ultimately, "Elections are designed to increase mass support for the Party, and grass-root democracy is understood to be fully compatible with strong state control" (O'Brien and Lianjiang Li 2000:488-489).

Jiang Zemin at one time called for the expansion of direct elections from the village to the township level. The population of a township constituted about 100,000 people. According to Jiang, the local elected organs of power and self-governing mass organizations in both urban and rural areas shall establish a sound system of democratic elections. Indeed, there was breakthrough in the electoral system in the 1990s. In November 1998, a small township called Buyun in Sichuan province held a direct election for the township magistrate (*Ming Pao* 11, 12, 13, February 1999). The election was competitive. In the end the Party representative won by a majority of 12 votes and the election was declared valid by the Party.[9] It was a big step forward in the personnel reform. According to the PRC constitution, the township level has direct elections in the deputies to the local people's congresses. The election was a breakthrough because people were electing an executive head not the legislators to the local people's congress.

Unlike the Buyun election in Sichuan which gained widespread publicity, there was another form of election of the township government head in the late 1990s, which received much less attention. Arguably the question of constitutionality regarding the Buyun election was debatable but the election in Dapeng town, Longgang District, Shenzhen was perfectly constitutional when the CCP launched the so-called "two ticket" election in electing a township head. The electorate could forward their candidates and five were confirmed as candidates and they were voted (first round) on by the electorate of the whole town. The one with the highest votes was recommended to be the only candidate to be voted in the second round of election by deputies of the local people's congress which was in congruence with the state constitution (Wang Weiping 2000: 17-22). However, the Buyun and Dapeng experiences seemed to have confined to Sichuan Province and Shenzhen. In November 2001, a circular issued by the central authorities demanded that the upcoming elections in township and village be conducted strictly according to law which had the effect of banning elections at the township levels (*SCMP* 22 November 2001). Since the Sixteenth CCP Congress in November 2002, the CCP top leadership has decided that to develop intra-party democracy is more appropriate than developing grass-root democracy (*Ming Pao* 10 October 2003; *Ta Kung Pao* 11 October 2003).

Fighting Against Corruption as a Reform Strategy

Corruption could be defined as the use of public power in pursuit of private benefits (Wang Hunin 1990: 145; Hu Angang 2001: 2-4). In the Chinese context, the immoral conduct is manifested in many aspects: misappropriation of public or government funds, receiving or offering bribes, involvement in smuggling activities, collecting taxes illegally, receiving kickbacks and exchanging benefits, etc. It must be admitted that in the 1950s and 1960s, there were relatively fewer corruption cases in the PRC. The most serious case was the case in 1952 of the district Party secretary of Tianjin called Liu Jianshan who was involved to an amount one hundred seventeen thousand renminbi. At the same time there were repeated political campaigns such as Three Antis and Five Antis campaigns to stamp out corrupt elements of bourgeois or anti-revolutionaries. Anti-corruption then was taken as a form of class struggle. The mass purges in the political campaigns prevented people committing corruption because people were afraid of being perceived as class enemies by the new regime(Wang Hunin 1990:33-45). The political and ideological campaigns eliminated the chances of corruption.

The situation changed completely after the reform and open door policies were launched in late 1970s. The focus of the Party's work had shifted from ideological struggles to economic construction and mass political campaigns basically stopped. Huntington (1968: 59-63)argued that in the modernization process, corruption tends to increase tremendously because of three reasons: Firstly, the drastic social changes cause traditional values to change.   Behavior that was accepted by traditional norms would not tolerable by modernized values, such as equality, freedom, openness and transparency, etc. Secondly, the process of modernization has created new venues of prosperity and wealth. New social groups of wealth were also created and this might cause the traditional power elite to exchange political power for financial benefits and social groups want to gain political access to the ruling elite through wealth. Thirdly, the process of modernization produces a demand to enhance the control of governance on the part of the central government and this creates the chances of corruption in the centralization process.

Evidently, the CCP leadership was aware the seriousness of the rampant corruption and its impact on the legitimacy of the CCP. In November 1979, Deng Xiaoping made a speech (1983: 187-202) against special privileges be given to he senior cadres because these would make the senior officials detached from the common people. In August 1981, the Central Discipline Committee sent a decree to the provincial and local Discipline Committee, demanding strict discipline be applied to all Party members. In November 1983, the Second Plenum of the Twelfth CCP passed the *Decision to Rectify the Party*. In December 1985, the State Council and the CCP General Office decreed that all phenomena of corruption including fund embezzlement, briberies, and privileges of cadres be ceased. Important provisions and regulations were pronounced to guide the behavior of the Party members. For example, *Certain Provisions about the Political Life in the Party* in 1980, the *Decision to Fight the Serious Criminal Activities in the Economic Arena* in April 1982, the *Provisions of Prohibiting the Party/state Apparatus Setting Enterprises and Involving in Commercial Activities* in February 1986, the *Temporary Provisions about the Penalties of the State/government Personnel Committing Corruption* in September 1988, etc.

In the 1990s, nearly every year Jiang delivered a speech to the Central Discipline Inspection Committee, emphasizing the importance of a clean government and the style of work of the Party. He even raised the campaigns against corruption to the level of life and death for the CCP (Jiang 2001b:475). Since the mid-1990s, unlike before, instead of emphasizing the Party's examplary functions and the role model emulation effect or the supervisory functions of the Party, the top leadership had been stressing the importance of *zhidu* (institutions). Jiang (2001b:477-478) said that "We must rely on institutional innovation to root out corruption. This is one of the important lessons we learn from the past. Good institutions can prevent effectively the spread of corruption and, on the contrary, bad institutions can spread corruption." Therefore, graft-fighting units were set up across the country. By mid-1996, more than 1700 Anti-corruption Bureaus had been erected in 29 provincial, 289 district and municipal levels and 1,400 grassroots Procuratorate. Mechanisms of public participation in fighting corruption were also established. There were 2929 centers or hotlines where citizens could file reports and complaints (*Ming Pao* October 9 1995).

Despite of all these rhetoric and measures, corruption was sprouting across the country. There were tremendous increase from the 1980s. The number of corruption cases can be seen from the following tables for the 1980s:

Table 6.1

Number and Amount of Corruption and Bribery Cases in the 1980s

Amount	Corruption/bribery
Over 10 thousand	1908/368
Over 100 thousand	100/22
Over 200 thousand	30/6
Over500 thousand	18/4

Source: Wang Hunin 1990: 66-68

In the 1980s, corruption and bribery cases involving amount more than 500 thousand renminbi were relatively few.[10] In 1980, when the minister of trade Wang Lei refused to pay in a Beijing restaurant and caused a public outcry, he was publicly criticized by the CDIC. This was the first senior official at the provincial level who was exposed and condemned. However, the first senior provincial level official who was charged with a criminal offence and subsequently imprisoned did not occur until 1987. By the late 1990s, the number of middle-ranking and senior officials who committed corruption had shot up sharply. In 1999, according to the annual report of the CDIC, the number of officials who were prosecuted was as follows: 4092 at county/department level, 327 at district/bureaus level, 17 at provincial/ministerial level. In 2000, 4146 county/department level, 331 at district/bureaus level, and 21 at provincial/ministerial level (*The Mirror* February 2000:31). Moreover, the amount involved was shockingly large. For example in 1996, there were 397 cases of corruption that involved amounts from one million to ten million yuan, and 59 cases amount of more than ten million yuan (*The Mirror* November 2000:35). The highest official who was executed over criminal charges of corruption had accepted bribes up to 40 million yuan in 2000. In 1999, the Party secretary of Ningpo misappropriated public funds amounting to 1.2 billion yuan and the vice-mayor of Shenyang had lost 36 million yuan in gambling in Macau. In a district in Guangdong, an official who was in charge of a financial department appropriated public funds up to 150 million yuan (*The Mirror* April 2000:21).[11]   By the end of last century, even the CCP leaders admitted that five important features had characterized this rampant corruption: first, most cases involved a great amount of money; second, senior officials were involved; third, organized/gang corruption occurred;

fourth, officials joined criminal gangs; fifth, power greedy officials were making quick profit out of he post (*The Mirror* March 2000:26).

Without doubt, corruption caused great losses to the Chinese government. Many customs officials in Fujian, Guangdong and Guangxi provinces were involved in smuggling activities and the financial loss for the state levies could be seen from the following tables:

Table 6.2
Statistics on Exposed Smuggling Activities (in yuan)

Year	No. of cases caught	Value (100million)	Value of each case (100 million)
1979	0.07	0.07	0.05
1980	0.51	0.51	0.14
1981	1.06	1.06	0.30
1982	1.02	1.02	0.31
1983	0.59	0.59	0.17
1984	1.36	1.36	0.50
1985	7.09	7.09	3.0
1986	6.11	6.11	3.31
1987	1.67	1.67	1.28
1988	2.34	2.34	2.29
1989	5.58	5.58	4.67
1990	6.01	6.01	5.15
1991	7.13	7.13	5.35
1992	13.18	13.18	13.24
1993	23.00	23.00	33.96
1994	22.88	22.88	34.59
1995	44.30	44.30	75.96
1996	92.89	92.89	151.53
1997	67.35	67.35	92.70
1998	83.81	154.00	183.57

Source: *Economic Journal* 26 January 1999 (Quoted from Hu Angang 2001:52)

Although the number of smuggling cases caught was relatively fewer in the 1990s than the 1980s, the amount uncovered was much larger. This trend had been increasing since the late 1980s. In 1998, the amount was 15.4 billion yuan, a great loss to the state revenue. Moreover, according to Hu Angang (2001:34), the financial loss caused by different types of corruption amounted to 13.2% to 16.8% of China's GDP by the second half of the 1990s. As he said, " Corruption has become the greatest social pollution in China" (2001:62). Furthermore, according to Vito Tanzi, an IMF analyst, corruption would bring consequences other than just financial loss to the government. First, corruption would paralyze the governmental ability to exercise effective supervision over public sectors. Second, corruption would distort the incentive mechanisms as people would indulge in non-productive activities. Third, corruption would add to the extra cost of production and services. Fourth, corruption would distort the government ability to enforce agreements and property protection. Fifth, corruption would decrease the legitimacy of the market economy and sometimes even democratic politics. Sixth, corruption would deprive the poor of the opportunities of earning potentialities.[12] Hu Angang explicitly pointed out (2001: 22) that "The main source of corruption comes from the Party/state in which extremely complicated and possessing various degrees of influences of interest groups have been formed. A significant part of these groups have evolved into what the former Soviet Union bureaucratic privileged strata. They try to maximize their interest and at the same time they become the greatest obstacle to reform anti-corruption drive. This is an essential feature of social change since the reform and open policies were launched." The root of the rampant corruption lies in the unchecked power of the CCP. The CCP has more than sixty million members and the Party members hold thousands of position ranging from village head to the state president. Moreover, the Party holds that the Party should dominate in every field. In the reform era, despite the shrinking power in the Party/state over society, the tremendous national resources are at the hands of the Party apparachik. Mass media have been under strict control from the Central Propaganda Department. In the name of political stability, many serious cases of corruption were forbidden to be reported.[13]   The problem is that basically nobody watches the watchdog?

Limitations of the Reform

Since the reform started in the Third Plenum of the Eleventh CCP
Congress, Deng Xiaoping was the key figure in the whole reform era
until he died in 1997. He claimed himself to be the core of the second
generation of the CCP leadership since 1949. His anointed successor
Jiang Zemin was the core of the third generation. In the twenty years of
the reform process under them China's economic structure and, to some
extent, its political structure changed significantly. First, the
replacement of public ownership by a mixed mode of ownership
including private ownership. Now, individuals can own private
properties and set up private business, and through the shareholding
system the state sectors were transformed into non-state sectors.
Second, China's GDP growth rate between 1980-1990 averaged 9.5%.
In politics, the Marxist orthodox line was abandoned and class
struggles as the key link discarded. Then, four modernizations became
the primary task of the CCP. In the past twenty years the NPC, CPPCC
and State Council underwent different degrees of reform. In addition,
there were elections at the village and township levels. However, the
limitations of these reforms were evident. The nature of these reforms
in Deng and Jiang's eras were different. The turning point was the
Tiananmen pro-democracy movement in 1989. Before the crackdown,
Deng's political structural reform was hindered by internal "two front"
struggles, i.e. ultra-leftist tendencies and bourgeois liberalization. In the
1990s, to enhance the legitimacy of the CCP in the wake of oppression,
the consolidation of political power was the primary goal of the
political line, to prevent "peaceful evolution" by the Western capitalist
countries. The implementation of the political reform became a means
to maintain the incumbent political system and its main goals were to
facilitate economic marketization and maintain societal stability.

In the 1990s, the dilemma of the political reform was less
complicated than that of the 1980s but the pace of the reform slowed
down. The term political reform disappeared in the mass media for a
while and it re-emerged only at the end of 1989. The goal and contents
of the political reform had changed. The "separation" concept of the
Party and government disappeared and the strengthening of the Party
leadership became the main threat in the new stage of political reform.
Deng began to talk about the fine-tuning and perfecting "democratic
centralism" within the Party, which means overt dissension from the
Party would not be allowed. To avoid the repetition of the June 4 events,
the center of the Party could not be split. There was no mention of the

separation of the Party and government after the Political Report in the Fourteenth CCP in late 1992. The slogan had changed to the "perfection of socialist democracy" and the primary concern was with stability as the slogan went "stability must overwhelm everything." The Fourteenth CCP Congress, the scope of political structural reform was narrowed to streamlining the Party and state administration, to carrying out a new civil service system, and to promoting multi-party cooperation under CCP and spiritual civilization.

In the 1980s, the main concern of Deng Xiaoping's notion of political structural reform was the separation of the Party and government, but the main focus in the 1990s, was on the efficiency, or effectiveness of the NPC and administrative body. Moreover, the CCP leadership emphasized the separation of the government from the enterprises, which means the administrative units should cease the intervention with the state enterprises (Willy Lam 1995:247). The move to separate the Party and government took a backward step comparing with separation of the Party with government.. Political power was more overtly concentrated. All the Standing Politburo Committee members filled the key Party/state posts. Jiang Zemin alone occupied the posts of the state presidency, the Party general-secretary and chairman of the CMC. Li Peng was the premier and Li Ruihuan became the chairman of the CPPCC and Qiao Shi the chairman of the NPC. The fusion of power or the concentrated power pattern had a beautiful name "cross leadership". The tradition stayed until today. Furthermore, Deng Xiaoping's speech on the reform of cadre and leadership system remained the most comprehensive political reform blueprint to date.

Notes

[1] See chapter 4 for details on the cycles of reform   policies. Since the early 1990s, students of Chinese politics have lost interests in the concept of cycles and the academic discussions have been on the notion of corporatism and civil society. See chapter 5.

[2] Censorship was even applied to the foreign dignitaries. Hillary Clinton's autobiography *Living History* was translated into Chinese and published in the PRC. However, references to Harry Wu's imprisonment in China, 4 June events and human rights in China were deleted from the book (*Apple* 26 September 2003). Most interestingly, the Party newspaper *People's Daily* was censored by local authorities. On 28 August 2003, the edition of People's Daily carried an

article titled "Who tore down the building, but for whose profit?", criticizing the officials of Jiangxi province. The edition did not appear until two days later and four pages were removed.

[3]I and my colleague have done some empirical studies on the role of the Party secretary and the director in the state enterprises. See Wong Yiu-chung and Chan Che-po (2002).

[4]The use of electronic media had been instrumental in the demise of the former Soviet Union. The spread of internet in China had caused some observers to make a similar prediction (Gordon Chang 2001). Would the Soviet experience be repeated in China? For detailed analysis, see chapter 8.

[5]For details in the number of staff in each ministry, commission and bureau, consult GOSC (1995). However, the number of personnel in the Ministries of Defense, National Security, Public Security, Supervision and the Commission of National Science and Technology, Office of Taiwan Affairs and Office of the Press, was not released. Some statistics are very interesting. For example the Ministry of Foreign Affairs had the largest established staff (2000), followed by the Ministry of Finance (950) and Ministry of Agriculture (925). However, a bureau dealing with patents has a staff of 1260.

[6]The 10th NPC in March 2003, at which Wen Jiabao was elected to be the premier, did not introduce any reform program in the State Council make up. Only two ministries were cancelled.

[7]Mark O'Neill (1997). A vote for the village. *South China Morning Post*, 12 April.

[8]According to Bai (2001), his report was based on on-site observations and investigations and letters of appeal or disclosure to the departments of civil affairs. I doubt very much that the Western observers of the village elections could ever gain access to these letters.

[9]There was a debate as to whether the election of the township government head was constitutional or not, because according to the Chinese constitution, the township head should be elected by the corresponding level of people's congress not directly by the people.

[10]However, in the 1990s even in one province Huibei officials committing corruption amounted to 2244 officials. 718 cases involved amount more than 100 thousand yuan, 59 cases between 500 thousand yuan and one million, 8 cases dealing more than 10 million (*The Mirror* March 2001:32).

[11]In the 1990s, the two highest Party/state leaders who were convicted of corruption were CCP Politburo member the former Beijing mayor Chen Xitong and vice chairman of the SCNPC Cheng Kejie. The highest senior official who was executed for the crime was vice governor of Jiangxi province Hu Changqing in 1999. Chen's case, in fact, was more political nature than financial. The amount was more than a million yuan so the case was not so serious as compared with other corrupt officials. Most believed that his power struggles with Jiang Zemin caused his downfall. While Cheng's case involved more than 40 million yuan.

[12]Quoted from Hu Angang (2001), pp.228-231.

[13]One of the recent examples was the Shanghai billionaire Zhou Zhengyi. It was reported that he had conspired with the Shanghai officials in the 1990s to get hundred of hectares of urban land without spending too much. He was able to borrow billions of dollars from the banks through personal connections (*Open* July 2003:23-27).

CHAPTER SEVEN

MARKETIZATION, LIBERALIZATION AND DEMOCRATIZATION

After reviewing the political structural reform in the reformist era, I would now like to discuss some theoretical issues dealing with the problems of relationships between the three variables, namely economic marketization, social liberalization, and political democratization. A theoretical exploration of their relationships will be attempted. As noted earlier, I shall take these three variables as equivalent to the terminology of the "crisis and sequence" approach introduced in the first chapter: distribution, penetration, and participation. Preceding the discussion of the relationships between these three variables, the combined effects of the reformist policies on the socio-political arenas will be analyzed. In fact, the previous chapters have outlined a preliminary sketch of the socio-political repercussions of the reformist policies. More empirical data are used in this chapter to illustrate concretely the consequent impact on the socio-political realms in China in the 1980s and 1990s.

Next, one of the key concepts that has emerged in the discussion about the policy impact in China reform period among students of Chinese politics since the late 1980s is the notion of civil society. Some postulated the notion as a descriptive term that depicted the Party/state relationships while others posited it as a democratization strategy within China (for details see the analysis in this chapter). I shall critically examine the usage or misusage of this concept, and clarify some related issues such as the theoretical import of this notion, its meaning, and its applicability in China's political evolution in the aftermath of the 4 June massacre (Wong Yiu-chung and Chan Che-po, 2002).

Finally, I shall explore the relationships between marketization, liberalization, and democratization, which have become a hotly debated subject in social sciences circles in recent years (Gourevitch 1993; Harrison and Huntington 2000; Hawthorn 1993; Merquier, 1993; O'Donnell 1993; Streeten 1993; Whitehead 1993), particularly, in the aftermath of the disintegration of the former Soviet Union and Eastern European communist regimes in 1990/91. Gorbachev's *Glasnost* and *Perestroika* and Dengist reform in China were often seen as two models of reform in the state socialist countries. The two countries have taken two drastically different paths, and with diametrically opposite consequences: the dissolution of the Soviet Union on the one hand and the brutal crackdown on the Tiananmen pro-democracy movement and subsequent astounding economic growth on the other. In relation to the three hypotheses formulated in Chapter 1, I shall probe into the inter-relatedness of these variables and put them in the Chinese perspective.

Socio-political Consequences of the Economic Reform

As noted in chapter 4, the economic and institutional reforms had, in the aftermath of the thought emancipation movement in 1977/1978, initiated a process of social mobilization which began in the late 1970s (Halpern 1991). Having 80% of the population living in the countryside,[1] China's reformist policies began in the rural sectors. The contract responsibility agricultural system based on the production team was first introduced in late 1977 in Anhui Province by Wan Li, the then first Party secretary. Wan Li formulated the first major CCP rural reform policy document *Some Rules Concerning the Problems of the Present Agricultural Policy* in early 1978 (Lin Yan 1993:72-74). Deng Xiaoping, who had just been rehabilitated in the Third Plenum of the Tenth CC in July 1977, immediately detected the significance of the policy document. In early 1978, when he was passing through Sichuan Province, en route to Pakistan for a state visit, he recommended the new policies to Zhao Ziyang, the then first Party secretary, who endorsed the policies enthusiastically. The new policies included: first, to enhance the autonomy of the production teams. They were allowed to divide the production tasks among some smaller teams or large households in the form of production contracts. Second, the size of the private farm plot of the household was increased. Third, sideline production activities were encouraged and rural markets were reopened for the sale of the agricultural products that exceeded the production contracts according to demand and supply. With remnant orthodox Maoists still in power in

Beijing, the path-breaking new rural policies propelled the PRC into a new era.

With the Third Plenum of the Eleventh CC affirming the importance of four modernization and changing of gears towards economic development as the key tasks, the CCP published the document *On Some Questions of Accelerating Agricultural Development (Draft Resolution)*, in which the rights of ownership and self-management of the people's communes, production brigades, and production teams were ensured. Household plots, complementary family occupations, and village market trades were considered to be necessary components of socialist economy, and not "tails of capitalism" which had to be cut off as soon as possible. In September 1979, the Fourth Plenum of the Eleventh CC approved the document *Resolution on Some Questions of Accelerating Agricultural Development*, in which the most important issues in rural policies were outlined. In December 1980, the CCP Agricultural Work Conference formally endorsed the household responsibility system as a long-term strategic goal in rural areas (Liao Gailong 1991:346).

The household responsibility system was formally introduced in early 1981, and soon afterwards, the people's communes were abolished. From 1979 to 1983, 98.3% of the production teams across China had adopted the household responsibility system (ZDJ 1990:188). By 1984, the agricultural reform was said to be basically completed. The reformists secured a major political victory in agricultural reform. From 1979 to 1983, the annual growth rates in agricultural output value was 7.9% (ZTN 1984:16). The per capita income for the peasantry had increased from 134 yuan in 1978 to 310 yuan in 1983 (ZTN 1984:13). In the first half of the 1980s, the improvement in the peasants' living standard was striking. The number of bicycles and sewing machines per 100 households more than doubled in seven years, and radios more than tripled. The number of watches increased by five times. Furthermore, television sets, refrigerators, and videocassettes began to appear in the countryside. Undeniably, the production responsibility system had contributed to the tremendous development of agricultural productivity in the rural areas.

Meanwhile, a debate regarding the new economic strategy was going on within the Party. Hu Qiaomu (1978), the Party's putative chief ideologue and then president of the CASS, took the first shot by publishing an important article in 1978. He called for, first, the development of productive forces based on objective economic leverages rather than administrative intervention; second, advanced capitalist economic management should be studied by state socialist countries;

third, the role of legal codes in economic management should be strengthened; fourth, the importance of the autonomy of the production teams was affirmed; and the popularization of economics knowledge in order to solve economic problems in the course of modernization was urged.[2] The article was path-breaking in the aftermath of the death of Mao. A new modernization strategy was widely perceived to be in the making.

Meanwhile, the Maoist economic strategy was severely criticized for having the following weaknesses. First, the policy of class struggle had led the living standard of the people to stagnate for two decades, and stifled the production incentive of peasants as well as workers. Second, too much emphasis was put on heavy industries, resulting in the neglect of light industries and a consequent scarcity of consumer goods. Third, production was disguised by false statistics, and the centrally controlled bureaucratic management of the economic system had resulted in massive wastefulness. Fourth, the policy of autarky had insulated China from the outside world, resulting in the lack of advanced management skills and technological know-how. Fifth, too much emphasis was put on the quantity of the products rather than the quality. Furthermore, the policy of promoting capital accumulation left the people with nothing to spend. Of course, even though they had cash, there was hardly anything to buy (Chang David 1989:87-91).

With the publication of *Decision on the Reform of the Economic Structure* (CCCCP 1984),[3] the CCP decided to reform the urban industrial system and commercial sectors, with the strategic goal of establishing a "planned commodity economy based on predominantly public ownership". However, the subsequent urban reform engendered intractable social and economic problems. Despite the crisis-ridden situation, the marketization orientation of the economic reform was unequivocably pursued by Deng Xiaoping. In the second half of the 1980s, the urban reform focused on the following four aspects, with an emphasis on changing the structure of public ownership (CCCCP 1984; Zhao Ziyang 1987b, 1988).

First, the autonomy of the enterprises and factories was enlarged by regulating the distributional relations between the enterprises, factories and the central government, separating management and the Party/state administrative units, and reforming the wage and labor system. Second, the circulation system of the commodities was reformed by setting up a three-tier price system, namely mandatory price (decided by the state's administrative orders), guidance price (encouraged by the state through various kinds of economic levers), market price (decided by supply and demand); and by reducing the governmental scope of control in the product selling and buying systems.

Third, reform of the macro economic and fiscal system was introduced through the restructuring of the financial sectors, taxation and foreign trade systems. Fourth, the structure of ownership had to be changed to accommodate the market mechanism in the economy. In Maoist times, there were two kinds of ownership: ownership by the whole people (state) and ownership by the collective. Since 1978, and in particular after the urban reform in 1984, with the shrinking of the state enterprises in the economy and the implementation of the open-door policy, the pattern of ownership has begun to diversify. Besides ownership by the state and collective, *getihu*, private enterprises, joint ventures, cooperation between Chinese and foreign companies, wholly-foreign-owned enterprises, and joint stock companies, began to proliferate.

By the end of the 1980s, a hybrid economic structure emerged. The internal components of the economy had changed significantly. The change in the ownership pattern was tremendous. The percentage of the state enterprises had decreased from 78.8% in 1980 to 59.7% in 1987, in terms of industrial output value. In 1980, individual enterprises were almost negligible, but by 1987 they had contributed 3.6% to the total national industrial output value. Even more striking was the change in the retail trade. The percentage of the state enterprises had drastically decreased from 84.2% in 1980 to 38.6% in 1987(ZTN 1988:24). The individual enterprises and other non-collective types of enterprise contributed more than one-quarter to the entire retail trade of the country in 1987. The individual and other types of enterprise had begun to play an increasingly significant role in the consumption pattern of the people's daily livelihood.

In terms of employees, the absolute number of different types of enterprise increased steadily. The following table shows the working population in different types of ownership at the end of 1980s:

Table 7.1
Working Population in Different Types of Ownership

Year	State	Collective	Joint	Individual Venture
1978	7,451	2,048		15
1980	8,019	2,425		81
1981	8,371	2,568		113
1982	8,630	2,651		147
1983	8,771	2,744		231
1984	8,637	3,216	37	339
1985	8,990	3,324	38	450
1986	9,333	3,421	43	483
1987	9,654	3,488	50	569
1988	9,984	3,527	63	659
1989	10,108	3,502	82	648
1990	10,345	3,549	96	614

Unit: ten thousand   Source: ZTZ 1995:18

The table shows that, from 1978 until 1988, the employees in individual enterprises had increased steadily, from a mere 15,000 in 1978 to 6.59 million in 1988. The reduction in 1989 and 1990 was obviously due to the retrenchment policy after the 4 June crackdown. But, in 1991, the figure jumped to 6.92 million and by 1994, it was 12.25 million (ZTZ 1995:18). Similarly, the employees in joint ventures had increased from 370,000 in 1984 to 960,000 in 1990, more than double in six years. Obviously, because of population increase, the number of labourers working in the state enterprises was still predominant and its absolute number of employees increased every year. But the relative contribution to the economic activity of the entire country seemed to be declining. Incidentally, the CCP also gave on the green light to private enterprises in 1990. In several years, the number of employees in private enterprises increased from 570,000 in 1990 to 3.32 million in 1994 (ZTZ 1995:18).

However, the social chaos and economic confusion created by the quickened 'price reform' in 1987/1988, implemented by Zhao Ziyang and supported by Deng Xiaoping, played a contributing role to the outbreak of the 4 June social movement. In the two years after the

Tiananmen crackdown, economic reform was stalled and the term political structural reform disappeared in the mass media. Radical price reform was replaced by the dominant theme of 'planned economy combined with market regulation' which had been championed by Chen Yun. Jiang Zemin, the new general secretary, was a conservative. It was he who said that, "We have to make all individual enterprises bankrupt" in the aftermath of 4 June (The Mirror 1991). He also initiated the so-called 'surname' debate on socialism – the debate whether reform should be capped by the adjectives 'capitalist' or 'socialist'. It was stopped by Deng Xiaoping who called on the non-debating attitude on all major issues so that the Party's focus could be devoted to economic construction.

The southern trip by Deng in the spring of 1992 broke the stalemate of economic reform. Under the influence of Deng, the 14th CCP Congress in October 1992 called for the establishment of a socialist market system in China which heralded a breakthrough in the CCP reform strategy (Jiang Zemin 1992). The document engendered another wave of reform euphoria among the regional and city authorities and boosted reform enthusiasm to an unprecedented stage. The provincial authorities thereafter made heavy investment in real estate and established many 'development zones' in a bid to attract foreign capital. Issuance, financial service, accounting services and retail services were open to foreign investment. The 'bubble economy' was formed. Understanding the overheated economy, in November 1993, the top leaders proposed to set up a socialist market system at the end of 20th century and the establishment of a modern enterprise system in China in the Third Central Plenum of the 14th CCP Congress (CCCCP 1993). [4] The policy of 'macro-adjustment-control' was launched and given over to vice premier Zhu Rongji, who was transferred from Shanghai to be one of the vice premiers in charge of economic production in 1991 in the State Council.

Very soon, Zhu became the first vice-premier and was in charge of the PRC's overall economic policies. From then to the 10th NPC in 2003, the year he stepped down as premier, he was labelled as the 'economic tzar' of China. With him in charge, China was able to steer clear of financial confusion and overheated economy and finally achieved a 'soft landing' in 1996. [5] A shareholding system was introduced in large scale starting in the mid-1990s and reform of the state enterprises became one of the focuses of economic reform when Zhu became premier in 1998. Along with that negotiation with the USA on the accession to the WTO had been going on for many years and final agreement was achieved in 1999 (Willy Lam 1997:363-368).

The economic reform was undertaken for more than two decades, and culminated with the accession to WTO in 2001. It is commonly accepted by economists that the PRC has achieved phenomenal economic growth, maintaining average growth rates of 7% to 8% in the 1990s. The following table shows the per capita GDP among Chinese in the reform era.

Table 7.2
Per capita GDP (yuan/person)

Year	Per capita GDP
1980	460
1981	489
1982	526
1983	582
1984	695
1985	855
1986	956
1987	1,103
1988	1,355
1989	1,512
1990	1,634
1991	1,879
1992	2,287
1993	2,939
1994	3,923
1995	4,854
1996	5,576
1997	6,054
1998	6,307
1999	6,547
2000	7,084
2001	7,543

Unit: one hundred million   Source: ZTN 2002: 3-1

From the official figures, it shows that in two decades China per capita GPA increased more than fifteen times. In the first half of the 1980s, the growth rates were relatively slow and later the growth accelerated. The phenomenal growth occurred in 1993/94 and 1994/95. The per capita GDP increase was almost a thousand yuan in 1993/94, and more than nine hundred yuan in 1994/95.

The per capita annual income (both net and disposable) of the urban and rural households can be shown by the following table:

Table 7.3
Per capita annual income

Year	Per capita net income of rural household		Per capita disposable income of urban household	
	Absolute value (yuan)	Index (1978=100)	Absolute value (yuan)	Index (1978=100)
1978	133.6	100.00	343.4	100.00
1980	191.3	138.99	477.6	127.02
1985	397.6	268.94	739.1	160.39
1990	686.3	311.20	1510.2	198.10
1991	708.6	317.43	1700.6	212.37
1992	784	336.15	2026.6	232.91
1993	921.6	346.91	2577.4	255.13
1994	1221.0	364.36	3496.2	276.83
1995	1577.7	383.67	4283.0	290.34
1996	1926.1	418.20	4838.9	301.56
1997	2090.1	437.44	5160.3	311.85
1998	2162.0	456.21	5425.1	329.94
1999	2210.3	473.54	5854.0	360.62
2000	2253.4	483.48	6280.0	383.69
2001	2366.4	503.79	6859.6	416.30

Source: ZTZ 2002: 95

Additionally, the following table shows the major durable consumer goods for 100 urban households:

Table 7.4
Number of major durable consumer goods per 100 urban households at the year-end

Item	1985	1990	1995	1999	2000	2001
Woolen Coat (unit)	116.2	169.98	204.15	195.23	169.63	172.67
Woolen Blanket (unit)	86.79	123.82	139.75	145.72	143.27	146.17
Wardrobe (unit)	102.08	99.85	88.3	85.06	83.45	84.68
Sofa (unit)	131.49	157.3	210.12	210.11	198.82	204.93
Writing Desk(unit)	80.06	87.23	88.14	86.63	83.44	84.79
Composite Furniture (set)	4.29	19.29	46.23	57.36	57.82	64.14
Sofa Bed (unit)	5.53	16.45	36.46	47.91	52.22	64.14
Bicycle (unit)	152.27	188.59	194.26	183.03	162.72	165.42
Sewing Machine (unit)	70.82	70.14	63.67	55.43	51.46	50.64
Electric Fan (unit)	73.91	135.5	167.35	171.73	167.91	170.74
Washing Machine (unit)	48.29	78.41	88.97	91.44	90.52	92.22
Refrigerator (unit)	6.58	42.33	66.22	77.74	80.13	81.87
Colour TV set (unit)	17.21	59.04	89.79	111.57	116.56	120.52
Video Disk Player (unit)				24.71	37.53	42.62
Tape Recorder (unit)	41.16	69.75	72.83	57.18	47.93	48.90
Camera (set)	8.52	19.22	30.56	38.11	38.44	39.79

Source: ZTN 2002:328

The table shows that the Chinese urban household has achieved relative modernized prosperity in the reform era. The possession of the symbols of traditional living standard has declined, such as bicycles, sewing machines, wardrobes. Instead modern items of good living increased tremendously such as sofas composite furniture, refrigerators, color TV sets and electric fan. More importantly, video disk players began to appear in homes. In 2001, more than 40% of the families possessed the item.

The ownership structure has also changed considerably in the 1990s as shown by the following table in the employment of staff and workers in the PRC:

Table 7.5
Employment of staff and workers in China by ownership

Year	Total Number of Employed Persons	State-owned Units	Urban Collective Owned Units	Other Ownership Units
1991	64,799	10,664	3,682	216
1992	65,554	10,889	3,621	282
1993	66,373	10,920	3,393	536
1994	67,199	10,890	3,211	748
1995	67,947	10,955	3,076	877
1996	68,850	10,949	2,954	942
1997	69,600	10,766	2,817	1,085
1998	69,957	8,809	1,900	1,628
1999	70,586	8,572	1,772	1,846
2000	71,150	8,102	1,499	2,011
2001	73,025	7,640	1,291	2,235

Sources: ZTZ 2000,2001,2002 and National Bureau of Statistics (1999): Comprehensive Statistical Data and Materials in 50 Years of New China

The table shows the continuing increasing trend for the total number of employed persons due to, evidently, population increase and at the same time, the decreasing trend of employed persons in the state-owned and collective sectors due to the marketization reform. The employed persons in other ownership units has incessantly increased.

Despite the twists and turns of political-ideological reform, the economic reform, launched in the late 1970s, has not been slackened and it has been relentlessly pursued. By the end of year 2002,according to the statistics of the China Industry-commerce Bureau, the individual/private enterprises have reached 2.2152 million households which employed 29.306 million workers and staff. The private/ individual sectors now provided 20.46% of the entire GDP and they accounted for 9.3% of total revenue collected by the PRC government (*Ta Kung Pao* 18 March 2003). Their role in the national economy has become so important that the CCP leadership decided that in the 16th CCP Congress entrepreneurs *minban qiyejia* should be absorbed into the Party's power core (Jiang Zemin 2002).

It has been demonstrated by the social sciences students that economic development is highly positively correlated with political democracy. However, as I have pointed out, logically it is not a *necessary* relationship. Although democracy and freedom are two distinctive concepts, the two concepts are almost non distinguishable. Moreover, as argued by Milton Friedman (1982), the market is intricably linked with freedom. Therefore, marketized reform within a planned economy certainly promotes individual freedom, at least in the economic sphere.

Because of the economic reform, the withdrawal of governmental control in the past two decades from the rural economy, enterprises, and factories significantly reduced the totalistic power of the CCP Party/state over Chinese society as a whole. Tsou Tang (1986:151) observed the reformist politics from a modern Chinese historical perspective:

> The true, historic significance of the revaluation and resulting changes (initiated by Deng) lies in the reversal of the profound trend that began after the May-4th period and was characterized by increasing penetration of politics into all spheres of social life. This reversal signifies the retreat of politics from the control of society. In other words, the relationship between political power and society in China is beginning to undergo a change in direction.

Indeed, according to Tsou (2002) the self-limitation imposed by the CCP over Chinese society represented the first retreat of the all-embracing political power since the May-4th Movement in 1919. The concentration of power reached an unprecedented stage with Mao's personality cult alone during the CR. After the demise of Mao's cult, political life began to assume normalcy. In the reform era, notwithstanding the upholding of the four cardinal principles, social life could not possibly be unaffected by the combined economic and political structural reforms. Naturally, other dynamic factors were working as well. The Dengist pragmatic reinterpretation of Mao Zedong thought has de-ideologized the role of Mao and subsequently brought about de-politicized social life in China. The focus of the Party's task became economics-oriented. Intellectuals, in spite of their meagre income and grim living conditions in general, became articulated, and their intellectual horizons broadened as a result of increasing contacts with the outside world and liberalized environment within the country.

Indeed, the profound socio-political changes in the 1980s and 1990s in China can be summarized by the title of one of Schell's most eloquent essays: "The Re-emergence of the Realm of the Private in China" (1990). One of the most horrendous features of totalitarianism is the abrogation of the demarcation of the private and public (Party/state). The Party/state is capable of interfering with every aspect personal life. Milan Kundera, a famous Czech writer, called it "the rape of privacy" (Schell 1990:425):

> Totalitarian society, especially in its more extreme versions, tends to abolish the boundary between public and private; power, as it grows ever more opaque, requires the lives of citizens to be entirely transparent. The ideal of life without secrets corresponds to the ideal of examplary family: A citizen does not have the right to hide anything at all from the Party and state, just as a child has no right to keep any secret from his father or mother.

This is, in fact, a true depiction of social and individual life in the zenith of Maoist ideocracy. The awakening of the self or ego and the retreat of Party/state power from private life of the people have profoundly changed the Chinese psychology. Released from the Party/state shadow, the people, in particular the intellectuals, began to assert their individuality, thus changing the very chemistry of interpersonal relations. To a large extent, the popular support for the student demonstrators in 1989 was a manifestation of this psychological and relational liberation.

In a book that detailed the profound changes in the socio-political life until the mid-1980s, one author listed five areas that had undergone significant changes (Xu Yong 1987). The changes are tabulated as follows:

Table 7.6

The Changes of Social Life During the 1980s

Social life	Pre-reform era	Reform era
Occupation	-Party/state assigned -support life	-more choices -to develop self potentialities
Consumption pattern	-emphasis on quantity -emphasis on physical necessity -aesthetics were neglected	-emphasis on quality -emphasis on enjoyment -appeal to aesthetics
Political life	-monistic channel -emphasis on form	-pluralistic channels -emphasis on substances
Spiritual life	-passive and pessimistic -single ideal-communism	-aggressive and optimistic -pluralistic ideals
Family life	-traditional emphasis on reproduction	-more divorcess emphasis on personal development

Source: Xu Yong 1987:225-235

Looking at the table, one can see the profound changes taking place in the reformist era. More than a decade has passed since the table has been published, the trend over individualist development, practical consideration and good prospect has become ever pronounced as the tables would show. In the book, Xu Yong postulated two kinds of eras: the pre-reform and reform eras. He seems to hold to the fundamental assumption of modernization theory: the dichotomy of traditional and modern society. As modernization forces set in through the economic reform, social life was being transformed. In the realms of occupation and consumption, Party/state control subsided and individualities of the people began to assert themselves. In spiritual life, the ideology of socialism gave way to pluralistic trends. The traditional family structure was being changed as feudalistic clan ties broke down. The area that received least impact was the arena of political life. The fundamental political hegemony of the CCP was not challenged. Despite the introduction of direct election of local People's Congresses and the increasing negative votes in the indirect elections of the various senior Party/state posts, the pluralistic channels of political participation by the people remained questionable.

In the 1990s, the profound psychological and value changes continued, particularly among the youth. In a nation-wide survey in 1996, 52.38% of the youth being interviewed answered 'realize self potentialities and recognized by society' as most meaningful, which shows that the selfless communist ideology had been discarded to a great extent. The importance of the self was shown by another survey which asked the question 'What is the most important thing in your life?' 41.8% answered with 'knowledge and ability', 9.5% answered with 'money' and 4.5% with 'power' (Su Songxing and Hu Zhengping 2000:7-9).

The individualistic tendencies of the youth were confirmed by the following three tables which show:

Table 7.7
The main considerations by the youth when choosing a job (Beijing, Shanghai and Guangzhou)

	Guangzhou	Shanghai	Beijing
High income	24.7%	25.9%	23.4%
Good prospect	30.0%	28.6%	19.1%
Self-interest	13.8%	10.4%	18.5%
Stability	5.6%	9.5%	11.6%
Can practice what has been learn	11.8%	6.2%	8.0%
Self-fulfilling	7.8%	7.7%	8.0%
Working place is near home	1.4%	1.6%	2.5%
Following the wills of others	0.3%	0.7%	0.0%
Intimate relationship with others	2.1%	2.6%	2.9%
High social status	1.4%	1.6%	1.1%

Source: Su 2000: 86

Invariably, the combined percentage of 'high income', 'good prospect' and 'self-interest' in Guangzhou, Shanghai and Beijing accounted for 69.5%, 64.9% and 61% respectively, certainly a clear indication of the wills of the young people.

Table 7.8
The goal of life and work motives

Item (goal of life)	%	Item (work motives)	%
Serving the community without self interest	10.7	Earning some money	29.3
Achieving self value	77.5	Serving the country and the community	14.3
Becoming wealthy	9.4	Achieving self-value	50.3
Pursuit of power	2.5		

Source: Su 2000:140

The individualist tendencies were again shown by table 7.8. The table shows that achieving self-value and earning money are the two most powerful goals for work and life, while the goal of serving the country was almost negligible.

Table 7.9

Why do you think your classmates apply for the CCP membership? ·

	1995 (N=430)	1996 (N=823)
Their beliefs in communism	18% (79)	17% (140)
To pursue a virtuous personality	5.7% (25)	17% (140)
For practical interest consideration	54.9% (241)	27.5% (226)
To create a good condition for one 's study and career		27% (222)
Pressure from surrounding environment	3.6% (16)	2.9% (24)
Others	14.8% (65)	8% (71)

Source: *Qingnian Tansuo* (Youth Exploration), May 1996,P.33 (Quoted from Chan Che-po 1999:399) This is not a direct survey on the interviewed but rather on what they think about their classmates' application for the CCP's membership. Indirectly, the answers reflected their value orientation.

Besides the changes in social consciousness and values, it was detected that according to an empirical study, political diversity at the level of public consciousness had already existed by the end of the 1980s (Zhu Jianhua, Zhao Xinshu, and Li Hairong1990). The diversity of the public consciousness signaled monumental change in China's contemporary political culture.[6] In one of the largest surveys conducted by a non-governmental research institute in the 1980s, the Beijing Social and Economic Sciences Research Institute examined, for the first time since the CCP regime was established in 1949, China's civic culture.[7] These surveys on the political psychology of Chinese citizens were conducted in July 1987. 5,000 questionnaires in total were issued and 3,221 were collected. The researchers obtained 1.5 million pieces of data regarding the mental state of the Chinese on political objects (Min Qi 1989:240-41), which became an important source of information on the public perception of the CCP regime. The following tables (7.10 and 7.11) show the cognitive, affective, and evaluative dimensions of the ordinary Chinese in the CCP Party/state. First, the public image of the CCP:

Table 7.10
The Public's Image of the Chinese Communist Party

Occupation	Good (%)	Not Good (%)	Sample size
Workers	41.67	50.38	263
Individual labourers	37.09	51.62	125
Intellectuals	22.68	69.85	371
Cadres	28.48	68.81	305
Peasants	29.13	58.90	324
Totals*	30.26	61.88	1,419

Source: Min Qi 1989:98
* The total percentage does not add up to 100, because the option "have never thought about it" was excluded.

Evidently, the public image of the CCP in general was poor, as shown in table 7.10. Among all the occupations, only 30.26% have a good image of the CCP, while 61.88% have a poor image of the CCP. Among the occupations, the intellectuals seem to have the poorest perception of the Party image. The "not good" rate comes to 69.85% and the "good" one is only 22.68%. The Party's image fares the best among the workers. 41.67% of the workers consider that the Party's image is good, and 50.38% think otherwise. Most damaging of all, second only to the intellectuals, the Party/state cadres themselves give low marks to the Party image. The "good" ratio comes to only 28.48% and "not good" ratio 68.81%. In China, most cadres are Party members and the data reflect the poor self-image of the Party/state cadres. The following table shows more precisely the Party members' self-image:

Table 7.11
Are You Proud to be a Party Member?

Occupation	Yes (%)	No (%)	Sample size
Workers	54.35	42.80	46
Individual labourers	52.17	45.65	33
Intellectuals	51.04	48.96	175
Cadres	61.50	38.50	226
Peasants	55.56	44.44	81
Totals*	57.02	42.80	472

Source: Min Qi 1989:98
*The "yes" option combines two answers: "once was" and "never felt".

Notwithstanding the majority for the positive option, the number of negative answers is still appalling, over two-fifths. Again, the intellectuals are the group which divide the positive and negative answers equally into half. This shows the seriousness of the crisis of faith in the Party. The "yes" percentage of the cadres is the highest, 61.50%. The peasants give the second highest percentage of positive answers.[8]

In an extensive survey of students at 18 Shanghai universities, only 4% of the respondents felt their friends had joined the CCP to realize communism. 10% thought that the Party was good. 59% replied that their friends had joined the Party because "in reality they want a 'Party card' which they can use as capital to receive future benefits" (Rosen 1990:65-6). An internal report from the Ministry of Education found that most of the children had the idea of getting admitted to the Party for the following reason: once you become a Party member, people will respect you. More importantly, some fourth and fifth graders said:

We all want to join the Party. This is because you can get promotions when you are a Party member. You can have more power when you are promoted. And with power you can become rich. None of the Party members in our village are now poor (Rosen 1990:66-67).

With this image of the Party in the minds of the young pupils, it is not surprising that not even the party members were honoured to be Party members. This is an image consistent with table 7.9.

However, in a sample of 1,230 among non-Party members, in answering the question "do you want to join the CCP?" 56.8% of the respondents did not want to join the Party compared with 43.2% who did (Min Qi 1989:99). When asked whether they were satisfied with the work style of the government officials, the answers were overwhelmingly negative, as can be seen from the following table:

Table 7.12
The Evaluation of the Work Style of the Government Officials

Occupation	Satisfactory	Unsatisfactory	Sample size
Workers	20.63	65.87	255
Individual labourers	20.49	62.29	124
Intellectuals	13.48	76.09	374
Cadres	21.34	68.66	311
Peasants	19.74	68.94	324
Totals*	28.44	69.84	1,418

Unit: percentage
Source: Min Qi 1989:74
* The total percentage does not add up to 100, beacause two options
"don't care" and "never thought about it" have been eliminated.

Again, the intellectuals gave the poorest marks to the government officials, with "unsatisfactory" percentage as high as 76.09% and "satisfactory" rate as low as 13.48%, the lowest among the occupations. The fact that among all the occupations the average "unsatisfactory" rate came to nearly 70% testified to the bureaucratism of the Party/state apparachiks.

Two of the more significant questions were related to the progress of the political structural reform in the 1980s. The first question was "Do you agree that problems in the political system have retarded the development of the country?" and the second question was "At present do you think China needs political structural reform?". The answers are shown in the following two tables:

Table 7.13
The Evaluation of the Political System

Occupation	Yes (%)	No (%)	Sample size
Workers	72.39	27.61	244
Individual labourers	68.29	31.71	123
Intellectuals	72.48	27.54	358
Cadres	74.15	25.85	302
Peasants	71.14	28.85	313
Totals*	72.25	27.75	1,369

Source: Min Qi: 1989:81

Table 7.14
The Attitude towards the Political Structural Reform

Occupation	Yes (%)	No (%)	Sample size
Workers	57.39	23.21	235
Individual labourers	44.82	28.45	115
Intellectuals	78.89	12.66	360
Cadres	80.41	13.28	297
Peasants	53.17	23.94	300
Totals*	66.74	18.69	1,337

Source: Min Qi 1989:83
*The total percentage does not add up to 100, because two options "not clear" and "others" have been eliminated.

The overwhelming majority of the respondents were not satisfied with the existing state of the political system (72.25%) and favoured reform of the political structure (66.74%). The political context in which the surveys were conducted should be borne in mind. Hu Yaobang resigned in early 1987; after a short interlude, Zhao Ziyang took charge and rekindled the *fang* policies. However, widespread official graft and *guandao*, coupled with spiralling inflation, had incited popular wrath among the masses. The demand for political structural reform was urgent. To a large extent, the political structural reform proposals in the political report in the Thirteenth CCP Congress in October 1987 reflected the popular sentiments at that time. It was widely believed that, at that time, economic development would lead to political democracy. The belief was reinforced by the democratizing experiences in Taiwan and South Korea in the mid and late 1980s.

The reform had made the establishment of non-governmental research institutes and large scale research activities possible. [9] Paradoxically, the surveys revealed a grave authority and legitimacy crisis of the Party and dissatisfaction toward the existing political system and the CCP's method of governance. The Maoist regime was characterized by periodic outbursts of popular convulsions, such as the 1956 intellectuals' revolt, the Red Guard mass movement, and the Tiananmen incident in 1976. Political development in China in the 1980s witnessed a change in the rules of the game. The initial economic reform was followed by the reform in the political structure, though very often it was confined to administrative and personnel levels of the CCP-dominated polity. Given these circumscribed political changes, the repercussions on Chinese society were profound. The survey data shows a more open climate had developed since the reform started in the late 1970s and these data of social discontent served to illustrate the undercurrents that contributed to the outbreak of 4 June incidents. As shown earlier, these reforms bred quasi-autonomous socio-political forces within Chinese society. The phenomenon has led academics to debate whether a civil society had emerged or re-emerged in China in the reform era (He Baogang 1997; Wong Yiu-chung and Chan Che-po 2002).

The Re-emergence of Civil Society?

After the 4 June brutal suppression of the prodemocracy movement, a spate of literature exploring the notion of civil society emerged (Chamberlain 1993; Gold 1990a; Huang 1993; David Kelly and He 1992;He Baogang 1997; Lieberthal 1995; Ma Shu-yun 1994; Madsen 1993; McCormick, Su Shaozhi, and Xiao Xiaoming 1992; Miller 1992; Rankin 1993; Rowe 1990, 1993; Schmitter 1995; Solinger 1991; Strand 1990; Sullivan 1990; Wakeman 1993; Walder 1989; Wang Shaoguang 1991; White 1993b; Whyte 1992a). The concept of civil society has certainly had a long history in Western political thought, for it can be traced back to the mid-eighteenth century in the writings of Adam Ferguson, a political theorist of the Scottish Enlightenment. The concept had a place in the treatises of such intellectual giants as Hegel, Marx, Locke, and Rousseau, but they all had different emphases. The revival of this concept in the late 1970s was due to the writings of Antonio Gramsci. It was first used by the dissident movement in the Eastern European Communist regimes. The Eastern European dissidents envisaged a cultural or social private realm that is independent of the all-embracing totalitarian control of the state (Miller 1992:3-5).

In Western scholarship, it seems to me that the first social scientist to use the concept of civil society in the intellectual discourse about the post-Mao era was Tsou Tang's (1986:220) analysis of Chinese political structural reform in 1981, but then the notion was simply assumed and not critically discussed.[10] The initial discussion of this concept centred round the profound changes taking place in the 1980s. Social scientists argued that the amount of social support received by the demonstrating students in Tiananmen Square through non-government sectors, such as the Stone Corporation and the Flying Tiger Squad which were doing liaison work for the students during the 1989 prodemocracy movement, and the "private" research institute founded by Chen Zimin and Wang Juntao (Gold 1990a; McCormick, Su Shaozhi, Xiao Xiaoming 1992; Strand 1990; Sullivan 1990; Whyte 1992a) signalled the birth or rebirth of civil society and "public sphere" in China.

The discourse then moved to the issue "Did China ever possess a civil society?" (Huang 1993; Rankin 1993; Rowe 1990,1993; Wakeman 1993) and its development in late Qing and Republican periods. The question of whether the notion of civil society, that was widely used in East European countries in the 1980s, can be applied to the analysis of contemporary China, is also an important issue in the discourse. Most of the social scientists accepted that a civil society existed in late Qing dynasty and GMD-ruled era. But controversies arose as to the nature and extent of this civil society.[11] They all agreed that civil society was eliminated when the CCP remolded Chinese society according to Marxism and Leninism, and after 1978, it re-emerged in the post-Mao reform epoch (Gold 1990a, Lieberthal 1995, McCormick, Su Shaozhi, and Xiao Xiaoming 1992, Strand 1990, Sullivan 1990, Gordon White 1993b, Whyte 1992a).

Several issues need clarification: first, the meaning of civil society and public sphere. Most of the discussants adopt what I call an "anti-statist" definition of civil society, i.e. civil society was defined by the "distance" of the social organization from the state (Gold 1990a; Strand 1990; White Gordon 1993b; Whyte 1992a). Alternatively, the "anti-statist" definition in particular emphasized the autonomy of social groups. The definition no doubt contains an important component of civil society. The definition can be traced to the Gramscian version of civil society when he defined it as follows (Miller 1992:6):

> The ensemble of organisms commonly called 'private'.....that is to say the sum of social activities and institutions which are not directly part of the government, the judiciary or the repressive bodies (police, armed forces). Trade unions and other voluntary associations as well as church, organizations, and political parties, when the latter do not form part of the government, are all part of civil society. Civic society is the sphere in which a dominant social group organizes consent and hegemony, as opposed to political society where it rules by coercion and direct domination. It is also a sphere where the dominated social groups may organize their opposition and where an alternative hegemony may be construed.

The "anti-statist" definition was particularly prevalent among the exiled Chinese dissidents, who were on the most-wanted list of the powerful CCP Party/state (Ma Shu-yun 1994). As we shall see, this definition was one-sided. There are less controversies on the notion of public sphere which was defined as follows by Habermas:

> A domain of our social life in which such a thing as public opinion can be formed. Access to the public sphere is open in principle to all citizens....Citizens act as a public when they

> deal with matters of general interest without being subject to
> coercion; thus with the guarantee that they may assemble and
> unite freely, and express and publicize their opinions freely
> (Wakeman 1993:111).

The Gramscian version of civil society emphasizes the institutional dimension of society: the degree of institutional autonomy enjoyed by social groups vis-a-vis the state. On the other hand, Habermas' notion of public sphere stresses the consequences that is produced by the institutional autonomy of social groups. One of the social consequences is that social groups can organize hegemony which means that state can no longer monopolize political power.

On the debates of the emergence or re-emergence of civil society in the PRC, there has, however, been a curious lack of discussion on whether a public sphere existed in China (traditional, Republican, or contemporary China). Presumably, the authors implicitly identified this notion with the notion of civil society. One can see clearly that Habermas' definition hardly distinguished these two notions. In fact, as Chamberlain (1993:207-209) and Schmitter (1995) argued, a well-functioning civil society could not be totally autonomous from the state. To say the least, civil society has to operate within the framework of laws set by the state. In the 1989 prodemocracy movement, even the most cited case of the "private" organization, Stone Corporation, with Wan Runnan as the executive president, was not as independent as one might think. [12] Moreover, all organizations have to register with the government. In an in-depth case study of the 99 new social organizations established in a Chinese city in the post-reform era, White (1993b:77) classified them into three categories: official, semi-official, and popular. His findings are shown in the following table:

Table 7.15
Types of New Social Organizations

Nature	Official	Semi-official	Popular	Total
Political	6	2		8
Economic		20		20
Science, technology		42		42
Culture, education			9	9
Sports			9	9
Health			2	2
Social Welfare		1		1
Religious			2	2
Friendly		1	2	3
Public Affairs		3		3
Total	6	69	24	99

Source: Gordon White: 1993b:77

The table shows that in the 99 new social organizations, 62 organizations were concerned with economics and science/technology. More importantly, none of the political and public affairs organizations were "popular", i.e. all were controlled or partly-controlled by the Party/state. 18 out of 99 were about sports, education, and culture. After a detailed examination, White (1993b: 85-87) concluded with the following observations. First, though enjoying a limited degree of autonomy, these organizations could be described as "independent". Second, these organizations did not reflect a clear distinction between "public" and "private", in which the "public", i.e. the state, dominated. Third, these organizations could not be described as "pressure groups", because the pressure was very often mainly one-way. Fourth, very often the membership of these organizations could not be said to be "voluntary". In this perspective, the autonomy of the new social organizations was relative. Compared with the pre-reform era, new social organizations indeed found room for manoeuvre.

The "anti-statist" definition suffers another methodological weakness. Firstly, it is tautological. It can be seen from Gramsci's definition of civil society. In fact, the Gramscian definition already implies the establishment of a full-blown democracy. Surely, a democratic polity entails a mature civil society. Secondly, by defining civil society in terms of the distance the social groups enjoy from the state, any anti-state activities would be considered the birth of civil society. That is why the large-scale anti-Party/state prodemocracy activities in China became a focus in rekindling the discussion about civil society. Nonetheless, distancing from the state was only one aspect of the meaning of civil society. As Shils defines the meaning of the term, three aspects should be included: first, independence from the state; second, effective ties with the state; third, the presence of civility (Ma Shu-yun 1994:185-187). Schmitter (1995) argued that the existence of civil society is premised on four conditions or norms: first, dual autonomy, autonomy both from the state and private units of production or reproduction; second, collective action; third, non-usurpation, i.e. the non-replacement of state power; fourth, civility. Emphasis on only one aspect of the notion is inadequate.

Perhaps overwhelmed by their personal experience in the aftermath of the 4 June massacre, the overseas exiled Chinese dissidents have largely misunderstood the proper part played by the state in a sufficiently well-functioning civil society. Su Xiaokang, one of the script-writers of the widely-known television series *River Elegy*, even included triad societies as one part of civil society. This misleading argument is naturally the logical consequence of the anti-statist definition. In probing into the relationship between *mangliu* (floating population) and the state, though avoiding the defect of the anti-statist definition, Solinger (1991) took China's "floating population" as a part of civil society. She thus overlooked the element in Shils and Schmitter's formulation, i.e. civic consciousness.

Notwithstanding the denotation of the term, its usage caused much confusion. In arguing for the re-emergence of civil society in China, Mayfair Yang (Strand 1990:12) argued that civil society could be distinguished in the economic and political senses. The economic one was a realm of "non-governmental private economic activities and sectional economic interest" and the political sense was a realm of "public and voluntary associations such as religious and cultural organizations, independent newspapers, occupational and professional societies, and local self-government". Kelley and He (1992:38) distinguished between civil society A and civil society B. The former denotes the autonomous organizations and spaces; while the latter implies civil society A plus the self-conscious attitudes towards common political objectives. Alternatively speaking, using more philosophical terminology, civil society A is civil society-in-itself; while civil society B is civil society-for-itself.

Rankin (1993:159), however, adopted the broadest interpretation of all in explicating the term. She in fact equated civil society with a full-blown democracy. In her view, civil society has the following traits: social organizations not dominated by the state and capable of affecting official policies, property rights, means and places of communication for forming and freely expressing public opinion; institutions and processes for individual and group political participation; legal guarantees of all these rights, institutions, and activities; and constitutional limits on state power. However, Wang Shaoquang (1990:112) rejected this view and argued that the existence of civil society was at most a *sine qua non* for the development of liberal democracy.

To clarify the meaning of the notion, first of all, I would argue that it is conceptually superfluous to classify civil society into A or B, and economic or political dimensions, particularly in the context of Chinese politics. As long as the CCP totalistic grip on political power remains intact, the economic "independence" enjoyed by the economic entities will not be guaranteed. There is, to be sure, a matter of degree. As demonstrated vividly by the study of White (1993b), the CCP was forced by the sheer logic of marketization reform to allow the growth of quasi-independent or "independent" social organizations. But since the economic or social organizations cannot cut the ties of the state, it is difficult to say civil society A, let alone type B, existed. Despite the introduction of the share-holding system since the mid-1990s, the Party/state power has never completely disappeared from the state enterprises, as shown empirically by Wong Yiu-chung and Chan Che-po(2002 245-246).

A more theoretically fruitful categorization would be the distinction of a nascent or embryonic civil society and a well-functioning or full-fledged civil society. In the former, the Party/state loosened its grip on society, as in the case of China, and totalistic control over all aspects of life gave way to a method of governance in which political-ideological control was still held supreme, but economic organizations gained certain degrees of market freedom. In the latter, indeed, it can be taken as an equivalent to a Western democratic polity. As Chamberlain (1993) argued forcefully, the existence of a civil society, nascent or full-fledged, could not be separated from the state. Furthermore, various types of social organizations that constitute civil society need regulations set by the state to mediate conflicting sectoral or sectional interests. Therefore, a well-functioning civil society requires that the state abide by the laws set by itself, and legal guarantees and constitutional protection of the individuals and interest groups prevail, which in turn necessitates, to some degree, the democratization of an authoritarian or totalitarian regime. Seen in this perspective, the relationship between a mature civil society and political democracy is only too evident. By equating civil society with a full-fledged democracy, Rankin largely ignored the dynamic process in which a civil society is born. In her conceptualization, it is a zero-sum game: either there is one or there is none. Her argument is untenable.

In October 1993, the China Daily estimated that there were some 1,500 autonomous organizations at the national level and 180,000 local level. By the end of 1996, the statistics of the Ministry of Civil Affairs showed that 186,666 social organizations were registered nationwide and 1,845 were national organizations. Shanghai alone boasted of 7000 organizations. (Saich 2000).

I argue that the concept of a nascent or mature civil society can best explain the social changes in the post-reform China. [13]   As White (1993b:86) concludes in his empirical study:

> One can detect only embryonic elements of anything that could be described as 'civil society'....This relative weakness of 'civil society' must be situated in the context of a semi-reformed command economy in which the state retains its dominant position in the economy. Its weakness must also be perceived within the context of the dynamics of reform, in which this dominance is gradually being undermined as the number of participants in the non-state sectors increases. One can hypothesize, therefore, that to the extent that economic reforms continue and economic development proceeds apace, these socio-economic forces will grow in strength and a powerful 'civil society' will emerge.

Evidence abounds that a nascent civil society is emerging or re-emerging in China. In 1992, China had 14.27 million getihu which provided employment for nearly 23 million workers. There were 120.000 private companies which had more than two million employees. In fact, in Guangdong the private sector had displaced the public sector as the mainstay of commercial and industrial activities by 1994 (Willy Lam 1995:371-373). Even the central government was aware of this growing clout of private enterprise. A commentary in the *People's Daily* (20 June 1994) pointed out:

> Since 1980s, a new class has been formed and is outside the direct control of the government work units, the beginning of a civil society.

However, given the iron grip on political dissent by the CCP Party/state, it is difficult to envisage the full development of a civil society which is the same, as I have shown earlier, as a democratic polity. In a nascent or embryo civil society, "public sphere" does not exist. There could not be any genuine debates on the national issues that involve the people. It is therefore entirely possible that it remains at an embryo stage as long as the institutional tolerance of political dissent is limited. [14] As Saich (2000: 128) pointed out the CCP faced a fundamental dilemma: Continued rapid economic growth is deemed vital to Party survival but this will entail further lay-offs, down-sizing of government bureaucracy and the shedding of more organization functions. This creates the need to expand the social organization sector to take on these functions on behalf of society. At the same time, however, the party's Leninist pre-disposition makes it wary, at best, and hostile, at worst, to any organization that functions outside its direct or indirect control.

Distribution, Penetration, and Participation

Having analysed the origins (Chapter 2), the policies (Chapters 3 and 6), the cyclical process and the predominant roles of Deng Xiaoping and Chen Yun (Chapter 4), Post Tiananmen Retrenchment (Chapter 5) and finally the socio-political consequences (this chapter) of the political structural reform, we can now come back to the theoretical framework set up in the first chapter and examine the hypotheses outlined at the end of chapter 1.

The relationships between distribution (economic reform or development), penetration (the overall ability of the CCP Party/state to exercise control over the populace, in particular university students and intellectuals), and participation (political structural reform) become inextricably complicated in a span of roughly twenty years that is covered by this book. The PRC is a relatively new republic, but the CCP, founded in 1921, is a revolutionary vanguard political party deeply embedded in modern Chinese history. As argued in first chapter, China has a feudal history of nearly three thousand years, cultural identity has been forged over the years and, therefore, national identity crisis is not an issue in China, except in areas such as Tibet and Sinkiang.[15] Therefore, the "sequential order" of the crises can hardly be applied to the Chinese case. Nonetheless, after 1949, the first hypothesis that the government's performance in national identity would trigger demands for political participation on the part of the population would have been true in the early history of the republic, if not for the endless political campaigns initiated by Mao to consolidate the CCP power base since the early 1950s, consequently stifling the political participatory enthusiasm of the public in general and intellectuals in particular.

Distribution and participation are two more important issues in post-Mao reform. The third and fourth hypotheses state the relationship between distribution (economic reform) and participation (political structural reform). They, in fact, outline their reciprocal relationship. They can be stated in hypothetical form as follows: if the participation performance is upgraded, then the demand for distribution will be enhanced, and if the distribution is enhanced, then the demand for participation will be triggered. Alternatively speaking, economic reform will trigger demand for political structural reform and vice versa. As noted in Chapter 1, the modernization theorists argued that, in the long run, a balanced growth in the five crises or problem-areas need to be reached. It follows that economic and political reforms should be in tandem. Whether this is, in fact, true will be discussed in Chapter 8.

There are three views as regards the relative pace of economic and political structural reforms in the Dengist and Jiang Zemin eras. First, China has attempted only economic reform, but no genuine political reform (Overholt 1993; Saich 1991; Shirk 1993), a view that I have criticised as untenable in Chapter 3, because this view considers a multi-party politics as the goal of the political structural reform. Second, the conventional view is that, in contrast to the Gorbachavian model of reform, China put the top priority on economic reform and secondarily political reform. Third, a minority view argues that Deng, in reality, initiated economic and political structural reforms simultaneously (Pu Zingsu 2003; Ruan Ming 1994).

In classifying the stages of Deng's reformist thoughts, Ruan Ming even argued that China's reform started in the political-ideological arena first, at least in the initial period in the late 1970s. He argued (1995a:78-79):

> Between 1978 and 1980, China's economic reform and political reform proceeded at the same pace, with political reform as the engine of the reform. Economic reform was implemented in a relatively relaxed political atmosphere. The two important meetings that Deng Xiaoping chaired were all concerned with political structural reform. The main themes in the Third Plenum of the Eleventh CC were liberation of thoughts, termination of the two 'whatever' instructions, rehabilitation of the wrong and falsified cases committed in the Cultural Revolution, and institutionalization of the legal codes. The meeting in August 1980 was about the reform of the cadre and leadership system.

Ruan Ming took the debate on the sole criterion of testing truth in May 1978 as a component of political structural reform. This, I argue, stretches the connotation of the term too far. Political structural reform is foremost the reform of the *political structure or system*. The debate on the criterion of testing truth was intended to eliminate Maoist fundamentalism. The emancipatory function is well-taken. But structural changes occurred only after the Third Plenum at the end of 1978 and in particular Deng's seminal speech on leadership and cadre systems reform in 1980. In this perspective, the argument that political structural reform preceded economic reform cannot be sustained. At most, he could only argue for the simultaneity of economic and political structural reforms.

In retrospect, I would argue that in the late 1970s and early 1980s, economic and political structural reforms took place more or less at the same pace. They were intended to solve problems at different levels: political structural reform resolving the participation crisis, and economic reform distribution crisis. The linkages between economic reform and political structural reform was not well thought out by the early reformist leaders including Deng Xiaoping. By the mid-1980s, the pace of economic reform became faster, while political reform began to lag behind due to the changing attitude of Deng and the mounting pressures of conservatives. At the end of the 1980s, political structural reform had produced the unintended consequences that the hardliners did not want to see, namely social-political forces that were outside the CCP Party/state and political instability. The conservative ideologues, with Deng's backing, won the battle in the bloody confrontation with the pro-democracy forces in 1989. After 1989, political structural reform halted completely. It was not until two years later that some minor political reform measures were revived. By then, especially after Deng's southern trip in early 1992, the marketization reform had entered a new stage.

The introduction of market as the core of the economic reform has tremendous political implication. A theoretical exploration on the relationships between market and democracy is attempted here (1976:269). While market is a place where a seller and a buyer meet, democracy is defined by Schumpeter as "institutional arrangement for arriving at political decisions in which individuals acquire the power to decide by means of a competitive struggle for the people's vote."

According to Gourevitch (1993:1272-1273), theoretically, there are four types of logical relationship between marketization (distribution or economic reform) and democratization (participation or political reform):

Theory (T1): Markets require democracy.
Theory (T2): Markets require authoritarianism.
Theory (T3): Democracy requires markets.
Theory (T4): Democracy requires centralized planning and public ownership

If the logical possibilities were used against empirical world, the following conclusion can be drawn. The strong version of T1 has certainly been disconfirmed. Many dynamic markets are run by authoritarian governments. For instance, China started marketization reform under an extreme centralized Party/state structure. Under the authoritarianism of Chiang Ching-kuo regime in Taiwan, South Korea in the era of Park Chung-Kee, and even Singapore nowadays, dynamic market mechanisms were operating quite smoothly. Naturally, some loosening of central control is needed for the establishment of the markets, but the relaxation of the central authority does not mean the setting up of a constitutional democracy. In fact, the hyper-growth economies in East Asia and South East Asia in 1970s, 1980s and 1990s until the Asian Financial Crisis have confirmed that political suppression and dynamic markets can co-exist at the same time.

T2 has been falsified by numerous examples around the world, especially in the Western democracies. Moreover, there are cases of political authoritarianism running a devastated market economy, such as Marcos in the Philippines in the early 1980s, Peru in the 1970s and 1980s, and Amin in Uganda in the 1970s, Chile and Zimbabwe nowadays. T4 was disconfirmed in the 1980s. In fact, Gorbachev's reform in the former

Soviet Union and the Dengist reform in the PRC have completely disproved the thesis. There was once a strong current of belief in the West in the 1950s and 1960s that genuine democracy could not be achieved in a free market society and it must be combined with an element of socialism which means public ownership. Socialist democracy contained the component of economic equality. Democracy must be based on public ownership. Democratic socialism was the genuine democracy and liberal democracy was criticised as formalism. This is the ideological foundation of the nationalization policies under British Labour government in the 1960s and 1970s and French Mitterand's socialist government in the early 1980s. This ideology collapsed completely with the demise of the Soviet Union in 1991.

If markets do not need democracy, does democracy require markets (T3)? This is the most interesting question, a question directly linked to our analysis of contemporary China. As I have argued, markets can operate in an authoritarian government, but under a totalitarian government, markets are impossible to develop. The existence of markets depends first of all on the dispersion of power (at least of the power in making economic policies) of the centralized Party/state apparatus. It seems logical to conclude that there are a kind of "elective affinities" (Gourevitch 1993:1271) between democracy and markets. Is the existence of the markets a *sine qua non* for political democracy? In their famous treatises *Capitalism and Freedom* and *The Road to Serfdom*, Milton Friedman and Frederick Hayek advanced exactly the same thesis. Friedman argued that without markets or economic freedom, democracy simply cannot emerge. In a similar vein, Hayek argued that once markets are destroyed, the central command economy will necessarily brings about a totalitarian political system. In essence, they argued that markets are necessary condition of political democracy. Notwithstanding the separateness the of marketization reform and democratization, Whitehead (1993:1372), however, argued that "the issue can hardly rest there":

Most existing theory suggests that economic liberalization and democratization are two separate processes, each subject to its own internal regularities and internal logic. Available evidence from our wide range of examples seems to indicate the same....There are at least as many examples of failure to achieve both together as of success. Nevertheless, the issue can hardly rest there. For one thing all the 'successful developed' countries combine a fair degree of democracy and economic liberalism in an apparently well-mixed proportion, and it is this composite model that others apparently aspire to imitate....A vocal   (and recently growing) current of liberal thought makes ambitious claims of necessary linkage between the two. Other less committed perspectives at least imply a *probabilistic* association (emphasis mine). Two versions have emerged regarding the relationships between markets and democracy. A strong version argues the markets are necessary condition of democracy while the weak version concedes that market and democracy are positively correlated.

Indeed in the context of the political evolution of the PRC in the 1980s and 1990s, the political structural reform, i.e. the CCP's draconian attempt to solve the participation crisis, triggered demands for economic reform, and the economic reform, i.e. the CCP's endeavour to solve the distribution crisis, triggered demands for participation. These two variables had reciprocal effects on each other. Despite the general political line of "one focus, two fundamental points", Hu-Zhao allowed a more tolerant interpretation of this political line, believing that the two dimensions could complement each other. However, this was no longer true after the 4 June massacre. In the 1990s, limited political structural reform was carried out, consisting of streamlining state bureaucracy, grassroots election and anti-corruption measures.

Coming back to the second hypothesis of whether the enhancing of governmental performance in penetration will cause the demand for distribution formulated in Chapter 1, it seems that, looking back at the twenty years of reform, the popularity of Deng reached its zenith in 1985 when the masses raised the banner *Xiaoping ninhao* (Xiaoping, we are well) in the Tiananmen parade in the thirty-fifth anniversary of the PRC. There was such a stark contrast that four years later students raised the banner *Xiaoping ninhaohutu* (Xiaoping, you are so muddle-headed) in the demonstrations. Enhancing the distribution crisis resolving ability no doubt facilitated resolving the penetration crisis, i.e. enhancing the government penetration ability, which in turn enhanced the legitimacy of the Party/state and vice versa, as manifested in the pre-1985 economic reform. There were two periods that the CCP Party/state had resolved the crisis of legitimacy. One was in the late 1970s when the "Gang of Four" was arrested and Deng was rehabilitated. The second period was in 1992 when Deng unleashed the signal of reform in his southern trip to Guandong. The legitimacy the Party enjoyed obviously helped the Party reformists to envisage new reform measures. With high expectation, masses were enthusiastic to the new programmes.

From the Third Plenum of the Eleventh CC in 1978 to the "anti-spiritual pollution" campaign in 1983/84, the three variables, namely distribution, penetration, and participation, seemed to interact quite smoothly. Distribution (economic reform) and participation (political reform) proceeded more or less at the same pace, thus gaining penetration ability among the populace for the Party/state. The legitimacy of the CCP was tremendously boosted through the reformist policies. It reached the peak in 1985. The downfall of Hu Yaobang in early 1987 signalled a landmark for Deng's reformist policies. It showed that the New Helmsman was committed to limiting the political liberalization he heralded in the late 1970s even at the sacrifice of his right-hand man. After the 4 June bloodbath, political reform regressed and the policy of separating the Party and the government was rescinded.

From the mid-1980s, the leitmotif of Deng's reform policies was to cut off the mutual dependence of the distribution and participation problem-areas. Deng obviously had the Singaporean model in his mind (Willy Lam 1995, 1999). Deng might have succeeded in this "separatist" strategy.

Notes

[1]The total Chinese population was 96,259 million in 1978. The urban population was 17,245 million, while the rural one was 79,014 million (ZTN 1984:81). The total population reached 119,850 million in 1994. The urban population was 34,301 million, while the rural one was 85,549 million. In 1978, the urban population accounted for only 17.9% of the entire population. In 2001, because of the industrialization process, the proportion of the rural population had increased to 62.34% (ZTZ 2002:34).

[2]Hu's article was published on the eve of the historic Third Plenum of the Eleventh CC, and was considered to be the most important article in 20 years. It reflected a new economic strategy of the post-Mao leadership (*Wen Wei Po* 13 October 1978).

[3]The details of this document have been discussed in Chapter 4.

[4] For a more detailed discussion on this period, consult Cheung Ka-man (1999), *China: 1949-1997*, Chapter 9, pp.918-1008.

[5] Ibid, Chapter 64, pp.1152-1160.

[6]Political culture can be defined as "a set of attitudes, beliefs, and feelings about politics current in a nation at a given time" (Almond and Powell 1978:25). There are three components in the individual's attitude toward political objects:

cognitive, affective, and evaluative (Almond and Powell 1978:26). This definition, however, ignores the differences of political cultural values between the elite and ordinary people.

[7]The Beijing Social and Economic Sciences Research Institute was founded by Chen Zimin in 1986. At the peak of its activities, the institute had 49 administrative personnel and full-time researchers, and more than 100 part-time researchers. It had academic divisions such as politics, sociology, psychology, and economics (Chen Zimin 1992:516). Naturally, the research institute was disbanded after the 4 June crackdown in 1989.

[8]Tables 7.10 and 7.11 also appeared in Rosen (1990:81). In the column of "occupation", Rosen translated individual labourers as "private economy". This is a wrong translation of Chinese *geti laodongzhe* (individual labourers). The statistical surveys of China reserve distinctive categories for individual and private economy (ZTZ 1995:18).

[9]In the Maoist era, certainly it could not be said that surveys and field work were non-existent, but they were mainly to serve the Party's policies. It was not until the reformist era that more independent and objective research by non-governmental institutions began to emerge (Rosen 1990).

[10]Ma Shu-yun (1994:187) pointed out that Chen Kuide was the first exiled Chinese dissident who employed the concept of civil society in intellectual discourse when he published an article entitled "On New Authoritarianism Again" in *Zhongguo zhichun* (China Spring), March 1990. Ma implied that Chen was the first Chinese intellectual using this concept to explain social and political changes in contemporary China. In fact, in June 1989, before the crackdown, I published an article entitled "From Student Movement to Popular Mass Movement", in which I first used the concept. The article was published in the *Economic Journal Monthly* in June 1989 in Hong Kong. I believe that this was the first time the notion was employed in the Chinese intellectual discourse outside China.

[11]Due to the limited space in this book, I shall not discuss the wide range of complex issues involved in the whole discussion, which, I believe, is a topic for future research. For a more comprehensive discussion see He Baogang (1997).

[12]According to Wan Runnan, Stone Corporation was a private company, but this company could not import anything under Chinese law and therefore, it could not conduct normal international trading business. In order to do business, the Corporation would liaise with a state-run enterprise which could get an import permit. The enterprise would sell Stone Corporation what it wanted and thereby made a profit. At the same time Stone could get what it wanted and prospered. This exchange system was uniquely Chinese, but it also shows the severe limitations on the so-called private company (Wakeman 1993:135). After all, the company was not too "private".

[13]In tracing the roots of the re-emergence of civil society in contemporary China, Whyte (1992a:85-87) was bold enough to hold that the CR had sown the "most

important seeds of this new trend". His reasons: first, the anti-bureaucratic thrust of the CR and the mass criticism of the abuses of authority, elitism, and corruption among officials had a dramatic impact on the population as a whole. Second, the immobilization of the Party/state apparatus (except the PLA) released individuals from day-to-day bureaucratic control of their supervisors and allowed them to think more autonomously. Third, the traumatic experience of many people caused them to abandon their trust in the CCP system. Unlike many proponents who argued the economic reform was the root cause of civil society, Whyte argued it was the CR that contributed most to the re-emergence of civil society. Whyte's argument, however, was one-sided. What he emphasized was the "subjective consciousness" of the participants in the CR, however, as we have seen, the growth of semi or "independent" social organizations is an important component of civil society, which emerged only in the reformist era. It is, therefore, difficult to take *the* CR as the most important factor.

[14]   One of recent examples of the institutional intolerance of the Party/state is shown by the following incident. During the 10th NPC from 5 March to 18 March 2003, several newspapers affiliated with the Propaganda Department of the Guangdong Province were either criticized or banned by Beijing. *21st Global Report*, one of the newspapers, was banned because it had published articles critical of Deng Xiaoping and had interviewed an old veteran Li Yui, who had pushed hard for political reform within the Party (*Ming Pao* 15 March 2003).

[15]In fact, I would argue that it was the strong presence of national identity that gave rise to the Chinese Communist movement in China in the 1920s and Mao was able to galvanize this force into the CCP victory in 1949 (Li Zehou 1987). Nowadays, with the decline of socialist ideology, patriotism has been used by the CCP leaders as the most important ideology to achieve national cohesiveness (Fewsmith 2001).

CHAPTER EIGHT

DEMOCRACY AND DEMOCRATIZATION

This chapter will review the democratic prospects in China, now headed by the fourth generation of leaders with Hu Jintao as its General Secretary. I shall discuss in detail two essays that were representative of the Western students of Chinese politics in the study of the facilitators and barriers of Chinese democratization. Secondly, I shall pinpoint the most important single element in the hurdles for Chinese democratization by using the cultural paradigm expounded recently in the developmental studies. Finally, I shall discuss the prospect of political democratization under the Hu Jintao-Wen Jiaboa new leadership.

Entering the twenty-first century, after a decade of double-digit economic growth, the PRC has become one of the global economic powerhouses. With its 1.3 billion population, one-fifth of world's population, China's prospect of democratization indeed has global influence (Nathan 1998). With the advent of post-Jiang era and the installment of the Hu-Wen leadership, it is now fashionable to ask the perennial questions: What is the prospect of China's political structural reform? What is the democratic prospect of China's political development? (Nathan 1998; Zhao Suisheng 2000; Nathan and Gilley 2002). As noted in the previous chapter, I argued that there is no *necessary* relationship between economic reform (marketization) and political democracy (democratization), though economic reform is definitely conducive to political democracy. Performance in resolving the distribution crisis indeed triggered demand for participation. Alternatively, economic reform liberalizes social life, but it is a long way from the social liberalization to the establishment of a constitutional democracy. At most, it can be said that there is a *probable* relationship between the two, but the materialization of this probability depends on other unique or specific factors, in particular, political-cultural factors.

Ideally, democracy is desirable, but the realization of it must ultimately come down to an analysis of social-political forces supporting democracy and those that are obstacles. First of all, a definition of democracy is required before we move to the next stage. The most authoritative definition of democracy as a procedure or institution is given by Schumpeter (1976). In his path-breaking study *Capitalism, Socialism, and Democracy*, Schumpeter criticized the inadequacy of "classical theory of democracy" which defined democracy in terms of "the will of the people" or "the common good" (1976:250).[1] He advanced what he called "the democratic method": "that institutional arrangement for arriving at political decisions in which individuals acquire the power to decide by means of a competitive struggle for the people's vote" (1976:269). The procedural definition denotes that a political system is democratic if the powerful decision makers are elected through open, fair, and periodic elections, in which candidates compete for votes and the adults are eligible to vote. It goes without saying that the concept also implies the existence of those civil and political freedoms such as freedom to speak, publish, assemble, and organize to conduct electoral campaigns. Most important of all, the concept entails a multi-party polity.

Using this procedural definition of democracy, by all accounts, China is definitely not a democratic polity. The political monopoly is enshrined in the PRC Constitution, and, therefore, no organized opposition was tolerated. The NPC, with two-thirds of its deputies CCP members, is basically a 'flower-vase' with no real power supervising or monitoring the government ministers and policies. Grassroots elections are held in the village level but they are not power organs. Direct elections have been introduced at the county levels regarding the election of the people's congress, but even at that level, the elections are not free from Party/state cadres interference. The challengers of the CCP are harrassed and persecuted by the authorities. Mass media are Party/state-controlled. Freedom of expression is an empty provision in the state Constitution. China has been transformed from a "feudal-totalitarianism" or new-traditional polity into an authoritarian polity.

Nowadays, there is a strong current of liberal thinking in Western scholarship that the Chinese economic reform (distribution) would open a crack on the ossified Leninist system and ultimately lead to a democratic polity (participation). In fact, the modernizationist theses implicitly entail the optimistic linear progression. One of the liberal theorists on Chinese politics outlined the relationship between economic and political reforms in the following way:

> First, by diversifying the economy, it will increase the number
> of social and institutional interests in society and thereby
> make the political process more complex and difficult to

> manage; second, the decentralization and dispersion of economic power deriving from the reforms will reduce the power and authority of existing Leninist political institutions and provide potential resources to this wide array of interests, such that the political system will become more pluralistic and less hierarchical; third, as a consequence of both of the above, there will be increasing tension between the emerging new political process and the old political institutions and rules of the game which will lead to demand to change the latter (Gordon White 1993a:20).

This liberal development hypothesis, i.e. higher socio-economic development leads to higher political participation, may or may not be true, as Huntington and Nelson have argued. Yes, it is true that "other things being equal, economic development tends to enhance political participation. But other things are rarely equal" (Huntington and Nelson 1976:45). In the process of modernization, the authority of the existing social structures was being eroded and the associational linkages were shattered, and new organizational forms were being sought. It is very likely that a civil society would be born in the process. The process of social mobilization set two contradictory tendencies in motion simultaneously: aggravating social turmoil or increasing political participation (Huntington 1968:37-38). Unlike the liberal theorists, in analyzing the relationship between economic development and political democracy, Huntington (1991:72) pointed out the complicated and intriguing relationships:

> Very rapid economic growth inevitably produced challenges for authoritarian leaders. It did not *necessarily* (emphasis mine) lead them to introduce democracy. Between 1960 and 1975 Brazil's GNP grew at an average annual rate of 8 percent. During the same years, Iran's GNP grew at a rate of 10 percent. Between 1980 and 1987, China's GNP also grew at an annual rate of 10 percent. These rates of growth generated highly destabilizing stresses and strains in these authoritarian systems, intensified inequities and frustrations, stimulated social groups to make demands on their government. The leaders of the three countries responded in three different ways. Geisel opened up; Deng cracked down; the Shah shilly-shallied. Democracy, repression, and revolution were the respective results of their choices.

In Huntington and Nelson's view (1976:43-52), two contradictory forces are released in the process of social-economic development and they work in opposite directions. There are several factors as to why higher socio-economic development tends to promote political participation. First, higher social status and income tend to co-vary with higher political participation. As economic development expands the high status social role and increases the wealth, society will become more participant. Second, socio-economic development creates tensions. New groups will emerge and old organizations will be uprooted. The tensions and conflicts will heighten individual and group political consciousness, and ultimately lead to increasing political participation. Third, the growing economy creates multifarious organizations such as trade unions, business chambers, and peasant associations, and a larger number of people will be involved in such organizations. Usually, greater organizational involvement enhances political participation.

Fourth, the complexities of the growing economy necessitate the expansion of the government apparatus, and the role of the government will be increasingly perceived by diverse social groups as relevant to their own interests. Thus, the more they perceive the relevance of the role of the government, the more likely they will take action to influence the government decisions, which means increasing political participation. Fifth, since the emergence of the nation-states in the eighteenth century in Europe, the modernization process has taken place in the context of nation-states. The notion of citizenship has been part of the political culture in national development. All the citizens are equal before the law and the citizens are always vested with supreme constitutional power, at least on paper, both in capitalist and state socialist countries. Therefore, national political culture, to a certain extent, legitimizes or facilitates political participation of the people and subsequently democratization.

However, the countervailing forces are equally strong. First, indeed, economic development does create wealth opportunities and channels of upward mobility. Nonetheless, for many people political participation is a means to other goals. If the goals can be achieved by other means, they would withhold political participation. Consequently, economic development actually decreases the proclivities for political participation. Second, many factors that are correlated with socio-economic development have causes independent of socio-economic development. The awakening of group and individual consciousness, the aggrandizement of the government role, and the expanding organizational involvement may have causes such as foreign aggression, civil war, religious conflicts, and ideological cleavages. These factors are difficult to determine. Third, the expanding scope of the governmental activities may not be a blessing to political participation. In the process of modernization, the bulk of government decisions tend to shift from particularistic concerns to collective or universalistic concerns. This actually decreases the contact between the rural population and the government, causing political alienation. Fourth, the functional specificity of modern society has paradoxically created a professionally political class which, by segregating other social relationships, tends to have a negative impact on political participation.   All these discussions attempt to argue one point: there is no *necessary* link between economic marketization and political democratization. There is probably a probable relationship between these two variables. The realization of political democracy depends on some specific or unique factors in the countries concerned. Most important of all, the goals of the ruling elite is also one of the most important factors in determining national development. If political democracy is not the policy priorities in the national agenda, then the ruling clique would crash the political dissent at whatever cost. Subsequently, political democracy would be difficult to achieve. The ranking of national priorities is, to a very extent, influenced by cultural heritage that is accumulated over hundred of years as in the Chinese case.

In the Chinese context, Huntington's theoretical explanations among economic marketization, social liberalization and political democratization are more relevant than ever, even two decades after the reform and open door policies were launched. Evidently, there are negative and positive forces working simultaneously for political democratization. Undoubtedly, there are cultural factors to be considered in the discussion.

Notwithstanding both sides of the argument, could it be argued that the market economy leads more easily to a democratic polity than a centralized command economy? The answer is yes. Because, as noted earlier, the establishment of markets at least allows the creation of some "private sphere" with which the government would not easily interfere. Market transactions also necessitate the availability of comprehensive legal codes, which hopefully would lead to the rule of law. Market is, as I argued in chapter 7, at best the necessary condition of political democracy and it certainly is not the sufficient condition. What makes democracy sufficient depends on other conditions, especially traditional political culture. To the students of Chinese politics, the statement that a marketized China is comparatively easier to democratize than a Maoist China seems inadequate. No one can offer a specific time table on the pretext that one holds a crystal ball. Because the relationships between economic reform and political democracy are not a necessity, it would be impossible to know the sufficient conditions of China's democracy (just look at Nathan's analysis of China's conditions of lack of democracy). One could only project scenarios. One of the likely scenarios may be that China's democracy may lie in the indefinite future. Looking at China's political development since the 1980s by the "crisis-sequence" approach, one cannot help being amazed at the overwhelming evidence that confirms the three hypotheses formulated in chapter 1. The government's ability in resolving penetration crisis triggered the demand for distribution, as in the case of post-Mao China especially after the third comeback of Deng Xiaoping in 1977. The interaction between participation and distribution became more significant. Resolving participation crisis triggered demand for distribution and vice versa. However, as I have argued, the participation (political reform) demand triggered by distribution (economic reform) can be suppressed. Economic reform and its combined social-political consequences would not inevitably lead to a democratic polity, at least not in the near future. Since China's modernization process continues, there is no reason to believe that the four crises, namely distribution, penetration, participation, and legitimacy crises, would not recur.

The Universalists versus the Particularists

Viewing the policies and measures of the CCP, the political structural reform process is, however, by itself, a process of political democratization though people would question how far the reform would go. Logically, the process would *eventually* lead to the establishment of a democratic polity. But for how long, nobody can answer. As for the CCP Party/state, it is difficult to predict. By sheer dialectics, the CCP tries to combine two seemingly contradictory elements: political monolithic control and market reform. The liberal social scientists argue that, in the long run, these two elements cannot hold together and market reform will ultimately lead to a democratic polity. The problem is, however, how long can the CCP hold? The answer is- it depends. True, the political structural reform by the CCP has limits. So far it has resisted further democratization. Furthermore, the CCP has reiterated that the political structural reform must lead to the further strengthening of CCP rule not vice versa. Theoretically, the CCP hardliners do not reject democracy as such outright. They have a theory of democracy and human rights. What they insist is that democracy must be implemented with the so-called "Chinese characteristics". Here the "universalists" position and "particularists" position emerged. The following table shows the difference between the "universalists" and "particularists":

Table 8.1
Democracy: the Universalists and Particularists

The Universalists	The Particularists
-Democracy is an universal value	-Democracy is a means
-As an ideal and institution, democracy should be and can be applied to all nations	-Democracy is an instrumental value -Democracy is culturally bounded
-Democratic institutions should be built as speedily as possible	-Democratic institutions should be built gradually, depending on education level and political consciousness of the masses, etc.
-The protection of human rights is universal regardless of societal development	-The protection of human rights depends on cultural and societal development

Constructed by the author

The universalists accused the particularists of preserving the status quo and defending vested interests. The particularists accused the universalists of being blind to reality. The Chinese democrats both inside and outside China belong to the "universalists", while the hardliners belong to the "particularists". For the time being, the particularists appear to be hardline authoritarians.

In a study on the third wave of democratization in the late twentieth century, Huntington (1991:109-163) outlined three kinds of political transitional process in which authoritarian (or totalitarian) regimes became democratised: first, transformations; second, replacements; third, transplacements. In transformations the ruling elite takes the lead and initiates the democratization process. In replacements the reformists within the governing hierarchy are weak or nonexistent. The conservatives in the government are resistant to changes. In this context, democratization results when the governing elite totally breaks down or collapses. Transplacements are the process in which democratization is produced by the combined forces within the government and the outside pro-democracy forces. However, Huntington admitted that the demarcation between transformations and transplacements are vague, and many cases could be classified in either category(1991:124).

Notwithstanding the ultimate outcome of China's reform projects, the CCP's political structural reform can, in fact, be considered as a kind of regime transformation: the CCP ruling elite takes the initiative of effecting wide-ranging reform from top to bottom amidst severe legitimacy crisis. When Deng Xiaoping began the reform in the late 1970s, societal oppositional forces were practically non-existent. Even now, more than two decades after the reform policies started, the CCP still does not tolerate organized opposition.   As liberal theorists of political development argued, social-economic development and its consequences such as a rising literacy rate, a marketized economy, a strong middle-class or bourgeois, i.e. social occupational differentiation, all play a contributory role to the democratization experience in the three waves of democratization in the past two hundred years, as Huntington alleged (1991:37). In fact, the explanatory variables for democratization are so many that Huntington (1991:38) arrives at the following general propositions. First, no single variable is adequate to explain the emergence of democracy in all countries or in a single country. Second, no single variable is *necessary* to the development of democracy. Third, the establishment of democracy in any one country is the result of a variety of internal and external causes. Fourth, the combination of causes engendering democracy varies from country to country. Indeed it amounts to specific analysis of the forces operating on the country concerned to reveal the democratic potentials in one country, which I shall presently take up.

Moreover, in explaining the third wave of global democratization process since 1974, Huntington (1991:45-46) identified the following immediate factors that **caused** the third democratization wave in the 1970s and 1980s. First, the deepening performance-legitimacy problems of authoritarian regimes because of economic failures, military defeats, and external influences. Second, enormous economic growth during 1960s, making the improvement of the living standard and the emergence of a strong middle-class possible. Third, the progressive role of the Catholic Church. Fourth, the changing policies of major powerful countries such as the United States, the European Community, and Gorbachev's *glasnost* and *perestroika*. Fifth, the demonstration effect of the first democratized authoritarian regime in stimulating the transitions in other regimes.

It is interesting to see that except the third factor, all the factors were available in the Chinese case, but in reality the 1989 student movement failed to trigger the democratization. Instead, it was brutally suppressed. The **causers** of China's democratization obviously lie not in the general theories, but in some specific or unique social-political-cultural factors. It is fruitless to discuss the theoretical possibility of a one-Party democracy, as Womack did in his article (1989), though he pointed out correctly that democracy has been one of the most persistent aspirations of Chinese political elites since the late Qing dynasty (1991). In analysing the political transition in the Communist regimes in general, and China in particular from a totalitarian country to a democratic polity, Gordon White (1993a:248) devised a dual-step approach: first, the transition from totalitarianism to authoritarianism, and second, from authoritarianism to constitutional democracy. In fact the first political transition has been realized, and to effect the second transition, in his view, two prerequisites must be met: first, the change of the CCP itself, and second, a "grand accommodation" between the overseas opposition forces and the CCP must be achieved (1993a:251-252). The central problem for White's vision is how to effect the change of the CCP itself. Moreover, compromise and accommodation have never been the rules of the game in China's political jiggling in the past two thousand years. As Tsou Tang (1991) pointed out Chinese polity was characterized by 'winner takes all' game rules. The rules have been relaxed to some extent since the demise of Mao' reign but, looking at the fate of Zhao Ziyang, the rules certainly have not been entirely scrapped.   It is difficult to see the Chinese political culture could be changed overnight.

Facilitators and Barriers of Democratization

In an exhaustive study of China's democratization prospects, Whyte (1992b) outlined the factors both favorable to the pro-democratic forces and barriers to democratization. The barriers of democratization include the following variables. First, an historical-cultural argument. China's feudal history and tradition had been a long history of despotism and centralized bureaucracy, ruling a vast empire with extremely harsh repressive force. The feudal dynastic cycle was only overhauled in 1911. Second, a sociological argument argues that China lacks some sociological prerequisites of democracy, such as a legal tradition based on the rule of law, a highly commercialized society that enjoyed relative autonomy vis-a-vis the state, and a large growing bourgeois that constituted a countervailing force to the state. Third, the CCP factor. The societal transformation under the leadership of the CCP since 1949 is, in fact, another barrier to democratization in China. The totalistic control over Chinese society successfully eliminated all the semi- and quasi-autonomous social-political forces after 1949. Fourth, China's huge poverty-stricken and predominantly peasant population, with low education level. Fifth, the "no Gorbachev" argument. It suggested that China failed to produce a top political leader like Gorbachev who could launch sweeping reform amidst conservative surroundings. Finally, the economic argument. The gist of this economic argument is that China's economic reform does not go far enough and its economic difficulties were caused by inadequate marketization reform. This economic argument might have been outdated by the events after the CCP Congress in 1992, which claimed to achieve a socialist market economy. The argument implicitly denoted that market is correlative with political democratization.

However, in Whyte's view (1992b:62-69) on the other hand, there are operative forces working for democratization. First, the problem of history and tradition. According to Whyte, Chinese tradition is not as negative as many think. There are proto-democratic elements such as (i) the rulers and officials were obligated to promote the well-being of the people, (ii) the remonstration tradition by intellectuals, (iii) the abiding faith in the power of education and man's perfectibility, (iv) de facto autonomy enjoyed by local communities and villages, (v) the changes taken place since late Qing until 1949 and it is possible that a kind of "civil society" emerged before 1949. Second, the problem of the components of China's population, such as (i) China's homogeneous population might work for the democratization; (ii) less income gap between the poor and the rich;[2] (iii) increasing urban population. Third, the legacies of Mao and the CR, in particular the anti-bureaucracy mass movement of the red guards. This led to the shattering of faith on the part of many Chinese. Fourth, the problem of mortality. The gang of elderlies are dying. It seems that younger leaders will incline towards democratization. Fifth, the link between economic reform and political trends. Sixth, the influences of external events, such as the collapse of the Soviet Union, the democratization of Eastern Europe and Taiwan.[3]

Seventh, The Tiananmen massacre turned many people into enemies of the CCP regime. These people may try to bring democracy to China.

Nonetheless, after the exhaustive review of the pro- and counter-democratization elements in China, Whyte admitted that it is difficult to judge the likely prospects of democratization in China. "How are we to judge between these contending arguments? I have no ready answer to this question. My main purpose in this exercise has been to persuade readers that the absence of meaningful democratization in China is not inevitable and eternal" (1992b:69). Let me take up where Whyte left off and proceed to a critical analysis of Whyte's arguments and present my views about the democratic prospects in China.

Let me begin with the pro-democratization variables first. First, about the problem of history and tradition. I tend to see Chinese tradition and history more as liabilities and not as assets. The traditional practices and ideals, such as the rulers' obligations to improve the standard of living of the people, the remonstration by intellectuals, the self-rule of local bodies, and belief in education, show precisely the lack of democratic experiences in traditional China. They may be proto-democratic elements, but they have never been 'actualized' and produced a democratic polity in China. Without the modernization process, it is doubtful whether these elements would turn into genuine democratic variables. Until Western penetration, Chinese traditional intellectuals did not even know what a constitutional democracy was. [4] Other "contingent" factors such as homogeneous population, legacies of Mao, and mortality are largely irrelevant to the birth of democratic institutions in China. Moreover, I fail to see the linkages between a homogenous population and democracy. The United States of America has a heterogeneous population and the United Kingdom is homogenous, but both are democratic polities. Mao's legacies were largely negative. He left China with a severe legitimacy crisis. Furthermore, the CCP young cadres might not have more democratic temperament than the gang of elderlies. Judging from the role of Li Peng in the 4 June atrocity, it is doubtful that younger CCP bureaucrats would be ready to imitate Western democracy more than the old geroncrats. The fourth generation of the Chinese leaders, Hu Jintao as its general secretary, are mostly 'technocrats'. [5] Their commitment to the political reform is yet to be seen.

The demonstration effect so important in the collapse of the Eastern Communist regimes failed to produce the same result in China. In fact, the dismemberment of the Soviet Union, the disintegration of Eastern European countries (the separation of Czechoslovakia into two republics, the civil wars in former Yugoslavia and finally the disbanding of

Yugoslavia) produced the unintended effect of consolidating the iron grip of the CCP over Chinese society in the name of maintaining social order and political stability. I would argue that the elitist support in the aftermath of the total breakdown of the Soviet Union and Eastern Europe for the CCP was one of the main reasons that CCP recovered speedily from the shock of the 4 June bloodbath and made the stabilization of the regime possible.[6]

In my view, the only genuine element working for democratization orientation is the element of the linkage between economic reform and political democratization, which I have discussed previously. Economic-social development and its ensuing consequences, such as heightened social consciousness, increasing education level, and heightened civil awareness, definitely have a contributory role in the democratization process. But they do not, as I argued earlier, *necessarily* lead to the establishment of a constitutional democracy.

Two of the pro-democratization factors that were widely discussed by students of Chinese political development in recent years were not mentioned by Whyte. They are: the growing economic-political clout of the regional economies, especially the Southern provinces of China (what someone call the "Gold Coast"), and the system of checks and balances within the CCP Party/state since the Party's Fourteenth Congress in 1992 (Chang Hsia 1992; Chen An 1999; Fewsmith 2001; Friedman 1995; Lam Willy 1999; Ruan Ming 1995a; Su Shaozhi 1995; Xia Ming 2000). At one time, the conflicts between the "regional warlords" and the central government were so intense that a new paradigm of studies for Chinese political development was urged, as argued by Elizabeth Perry (1994). The growing schisms between the *zhongyang* (the central) and *difang* (regions) were real, in terms of the repatriation of financial revenues and political influence. The growing political clout can be detected from the fact that Xie Fei, Party secretary of Guangdong Province, Wu Bangguo, Party Secretary of Shanghai, Tan Shaowen, Party secretary of Tienjin, all became members of the Politburo in the Fourteenth CCP Congress.[7] However, on hindsight, the growing economic-political strength of the regions became a contributory force in democratize China was illusory. In the light of Chinese historical experience, that would not happen. In fact, the central government in Beijing holds three trump cards: first, the control over the PLA, the most important pillar of the CCP power; second, control over the personnel changes; third, control over finance. The third one is a compromise due to the growing regional economies, but the first and second ones are still powerful enough to force the regional "warlords" to back down (Zhu Rongji 1995).

In recent years, the Chinese overseas dissidents (such as Su Shaoshi 1995) have been talking about *liangfang sanquan* (two forces, three powers). *Liangfang* means *difang* (region) and *junfang* (the PLA). *Sanquan* means *dangquan* (the power of the Party), *zhengquan* (the power of state), and *minquan* (the power of people). According to them, these three branches could become a balance-and-check system (Chen An 1999). Qiao Shi and Tian Jiyun have strengthened the role of the NPC in the early 1990s. Indeed, in their tenures they had called for the further enhancement of socialist democracy and to stamp out official corruption through legal means. Despite his negative image abroad, Li Peng continued the role. There were also reports that emphasized the growing influence of the PLA over the major CCP policies.[8] All these might be true to some extent, but whether the intra-Party democracy or power struggles would lead to a democratic polity is highly questionable. Qiao and Li were members of the SC of the Politburo and Tian was a member of the Politburo. Evidently, they could not deviate from any Party policy. Their emphasis on the enhanced role of the NPC was, to a large extent, due to the inevitable drive of economic reform in which a stable set of legal framework is required by foreign investors, especially after the accession to the WTO. Regarding the role of the PLA, the CCP has always stressed *dang zhihui qian* (the Party directing the gun). Traditionally, the Party top leader always holds concurrently the chairmanship of the CMC.[9]   It is highly unlikely that this tradition could be reversed, despite the increasing influence of the retired generals on the CCP decision-making process. In fact, the system of so called 'cross-holding' of office has been implemented since the 14th CCP Congress which means the key state posts must be held by SC members of the CCP Politburo. After the 16th CCP Congress, in the provincial level or below, the trend that the Party secretary would be concurrently holding the chairmanship of the people's congress has been practiced.

Nathan's Nine Cause Framework

In another study on the barriers of democratization in China, Nathan (2000) proposed a nine set cause framework for the failure, namely ideology, national security problems, militarism, political culture, underdevelopment, peasants, flaws in the constitutions/institutions, moral failures of the democrats, and elite transaction theory. Indeed, Nathan's nine causes were so general that it would be difficult to falsify them. However, it would be worthwhile to study them one by one so as to pinpoint precisely what Nathan meant.

First, the problem of ideology. In fact, liberal or democratic ideology was not lacking in China in the twentieth century. Yan Fu, who studied in United Kingdom in 1860s, introduced constitutionalism and Westminster democracy to China. Hu Shih, one of the leading intellectuals in the May-fourth movement, was a disciple of Dewey's pragmatism and liberal democracy. He was professor in Beida and later became the president of the University and attracted a large group of young intellectuals before the founding of the PRC. During Mao's Marxist fundamentalist reign, Hu Shih thought became targets of mass purges in the early 1950s. Dissident thoughts were repeatedly rooted out by political campaigns. However, in the two decades of the open door policies were launched, liberalism again found a large group of followers in China (Fu Guoyon and Fan Baihua 2000; Liu Junning 2000).

Second, the problems of national security. This argument suggests that China's effort for democracy building were constantly frustrated by the external wars waged by the imperialist powers. Alternatively, the argument states that without a stable environment, democracy cannot be built. However, it does not mean that a stable environment would necessarily produce democratic institutions. The history of the PRC would be a good example to show otherwise. The PRC has been at peace for more than five decades but democratic institutions have yet to be built. Since 1949, the PRC has fought four wars but all either outside its borders or along the borders: the Korean war in the early 1950s, the war with India in 1963, the border clashes with the Former Soviet Union in 1969 and the conflict with Vietnam in 1979.

Third, the problem of militarism. Admittedly, the PRC is a quasi-military regime. As the dictum of Mao goes " power grows out of gun barrel'. The nature of the PLA is closely related to the Leninist nature of the CCP. To argue that militarism is an obstacle in China's democratization is tantamount to saying that the CCP is a problem. It is true, but it does not say very much unless the PLA becomes a state army and becomes de-ideologized. This begs the question of reforming the Party/state itself.

Fourth, the problem of political culture. Political culture is one of the most slippery concepts in politics. Values and beliefs can hardly exist by themselves. They can not be measured quantitatively because they are in human beings. It is almost a tautology to say that democratic values produce democratic institutions or authoritarian values produce authoritarian systems. Recent studies on development have placed increasing emphasis on cultural values. It almost becomes a new paradigm (Harrison and Huntington 2000: XXI) in developmental studies. A cultural-centered framework of democracy is being explored.

Fifth, the problem of underdevelopment. The modernization theory argues that the more developed the countries, the more likelier the countries could produce democracy. It entails the linkages between economic development and political democracy. The argument seems to entail that underdeveloped countries could not become democratic countries. In fact, the ruling elite of the PRC is using the exact argument to avoid the political reform. They claim that China is a populous country and its people are poorly educated, and it is underdeveloped, etc. The general truth of the thesis that more advanced countries could lead to democratic countries are probably correct. However, it does not mean that developmentally backward countries could not produce democracy. China is very often compared to India and India is certainly a democracy. Chinese leadership is making use of the argument to delay democratizing the country.

Sixth, the problem of peasant mass. The argument is a variant of the problem of underdevelopment, which seems to imply that the mass peasant, if given free will to vote, would vote for authoritarianism. The argument is without foundation. India, a country with a majority of peasants like China, offers a convincing example to the contrary. Since the 15th CCP Congress, the CCP has implemented village elections across China and the measures have been hailed a tremendous success by the ruling elite. If the CCP really believes in this argument village elections should never have been introduced at all. Despite the pitfalls in the elections, there is no reason to believe that the peasant could not vote in a responsible or meaningful way.

Seventh, flaws in the Constitutions/institutions. This argument could mean either constitutionalism has never been put into practiced in China or there were flaws in designing the constitutions. In general, all the constitutions in the course of hundred years, 1923, 1946, 1954, 1982 have been good ones with the exceptions of 1975 and 1977 constitutions which were made during the CR with exclusive emphasis on the dictatorship of the proletariat. Over the twentieth century, parliamentary democracy were implemented in the aftermath of the 1911 revolution for a brief period and also in the era after the defeat of the Japanese invasion (1940s). The early democratic attempts failed miserably and resulted in warlordism. A few years later after Yuan Shikai's attempt, the restored dynastic rule failed in 1915. The KMT's attempt to practice constitutionalism amidst the civil war with the CCP after 1945 also failed and resulted in the seizing of political power by the CCP. Since 1949, the CCP has never been serious in making the legislature a power center vis-à-vis the CCP.

As Nathan (2000:30) pointed out "Constitutionalism of any sort has not yet really been tried".

Eighth, the problem of the moral failures of the democrats. This argument is similar to the argument of political culture. No matter what the Chinese democrats were at odds with the ruling elite, their personality seems to have inherited values there were directly contrast to democratic polity. Nathan seems to be pinpointing the overseas Chinese dissidents who might have performed a heroic role of resisting tyrannical power of the CCP inside China, but once abroad, they displayed the anti-democratic values such as ignoring proper procedures, being intolerant of deviant opinions, greedy power- seeking, being obsessive with pecuniary rewards, forming cliques, etc (*Open* or *SCMP*). It must be admitted that the overseas dissidents play a relatively minor role in effecting the democratic changes in China, partly because of their personality and organizational weaknesses and partly due to the effective blockade of their influences on the Chinese in China by the CCP.

Ninth, the elite transactions theory. This argument argues that the success or failure of the institutions would come about through the interactions of political elites, operating in pursuit of what they perceive as their best political interests. Yuan Shikai, Chiang Kai-shek and Mao Zedong initially embraced democracy but all gave up. The establishment of democratic institutions did not serve their interests. The message of this theory implies that a set of institutions could only be set up if they serve the interests of the most powerful societal and political forces. By corollary, in Chinese political context, the CCP would introduce democracy if and only if the CCP is facing severe crisis, for democratic reform would certainly affect the vested interests of the Party bureaucrats.

After analyzing the nine set causes, he pronounced that "our investigation has proven inconclusive; democracy has not so far, but it is hard to disentangle specific specific reasons for its failure.....The nature of history is so complex that it does not permit us to identify a single or a small number of key causes of democracy's failure" (2000: 31).

The failure of democracy in China involves a broad spectrum of factors. The nine sets of problems are extremely eclectic; some are internal (militarism); some external (national security); some subjective (moral failure); some are objective (flaws in constitutions); some inter-subjective (elite transaction); some value-related (political culture, moral failures), some institution-related (militarism, constitutions); some about development as a whole; some are about ideology. Methodologically speaking, factors as diverse as these are hard to falsify and amount to offer no explanation at all on China's democracy.

Comparing the two analyses by Whyte and Nathan on China's democratization, Whyte's piece is more specific and relevant to the present context. The obstacles to democratisation in China discussed by him are real, especially the historical and sociological factors such as the lack of a strong bourgeois, poverty-stricken peasantry, low education level of the populace, and low civic consciousness. These are all barriers to democracy, but, theoretically, these barriers will gradually fade as the economy grows. Nonetheless, the historical legacy that shaped the political culture of the geriatric revolutionary generation and the population at large is difficult to shake off, even in the modernization process. It took seven hundred years for the constitutional monarchy in the United Kingdom to evolve. America needed two hundred years to establish a truly checks and balances political system. Herein lies the unique cultural factors that the general liberal theory of development cannot explain. Political cultural elements such as the lack of accommodative politics, the authoritarian personality, the lack of political dissent, the lack of rule of law, and the extremely repressive nature of centralized bureaucracy, and the revolutionary tradition shaped by constant struggles for survival, and patriarchalism cannot be erased easily. As I argued in chapter 1, the neo-traditional politics of Maoist China combines two elements: Stalinist totalitarianism and feudalism. In the process of modernization process initiated by the CCP political elite, the Stalinist state has given way to an authoritarian system (Brugger and Kelly 1990; Harding 1987; Lieberthal 1995; O'Brien 1990; White Gordon 1993a; Yan Jiaqi 1992b), but how much feudalistic elements have been eradicated, it is hard to tell.

It is true that economic development is positively correlated with democratization. Economic development tends to transform social structure, bringing urbanization, a higher level of education, and increasing occupational differentiation that could mobilize mass participation in politics. Secondly, it can engender values such as interpersonal trust, a sense of optimism, that could breed or sustain emerging democratic institutions. The general theory cannot tell people the specific time frame that a country could become democratized. It may take several years or several decades. In Taiwan, more than four decades elapsed before the president was universally elected. Similarly, in South Korea, presidential direct elections were held in the 1980s. Despite the economic prosperity, Singapore has never become a truly democratic polity.

Given continuing economic development, I believe, cultural values are the most important single element that could explain the time frame that is required to achieve democracy. Economic development and institutional factors are universal elements; the cultural values are unique elements in studying democratisation. The cultural values of the ruling elites are particularly crucial in prioritizing the developmental goals (Huntington and Nelson 1976). In a study on culture, Harrison and Huntington (2000) suggested the study of cultural values to be the core element in developmental studies in general and democracy in particular.

In a study of contemporary Chinese political culture, Min Qi (1989:177-178) argued that the element of authoritarian personality structure must be taken seriously in discussing the barriers to democracy in China. The authoritarian personality structure is manifested in four ways: first, the lack of consciousness about procedures, and dislike of pluralism; second, the lack of participatory enthusiasm in organizations and neglect of institutions; third, the lack of knowledge about rule of law and personal obligations and duties; fourth, compliance to leaders and the lack of consciousness of monitoring leaders. These are the cultural values prevalent in Chinese society, in particular among the ruling elites. All in all, I would argue that the unfavourable elements are much more powerful than the pro-democracy elements. I do not see the realization of democracy in the near future, i.e. ten to fifteen years, in China, particularly in light of the strong repressive measures against organized dissenting voices, shown clearly by the forced imprisonment of the leaders of the Democratic Party and the exiling of political dissidents such as Wei Jingsheng, Wang Dan and Xu Wenli.

Post-Jiang Zemin Era

With the stepping down of Jiang Zemin as Party's general secretary in the 16th CCP Congress in November 2002 and the State President in the 10th NPC in March 2003, no doubt, Jiang's power was greatly eclipsed. However, if history is a guide to posterity, Jiang has learnt a lesson from the 4 June events. With Hu Jintao at the helm, Jiang's heart was not at ease. Similar to Deng Xiaoping, Jiang has been presiding over the CMC as an ordinary CCP member. The gun is directing the Party. It is not known how long Jiang will stay as Chairman of the CMC. Despite his precarious position, would Hu dare to push for political reform? I shall offer my analysis on the future of the political structural reform in the light of China's recent political development.

China's political structural reform was started by twin causes: devastating loss of legitimacy and social and economic stagnation during the Cultural Revolution in the initial stage and economic reform in the second stage. While the first cause has lost the impetus after two decades the economic reform is still going on. It is my belief that the political structural reform measures will go on in so far as they are related to the marketization reform, such as quickened legislations, streamlining Party/state bureaucracy, the establishment of a modern civil service and anti-corruption measures.   On the one hand, the CCP will rely increasingly on economic performance to regain legitimacy among the people, as the de-ideology process continues. Nationalism will be increasingly used as the ideological cohesive force (CCCCP 1994; Zhao Suisheng 2000). Despite enormous economic problems, the CCP has been able to succeed to obtain double-digit economic growth in the past decades. With accession to the WTO, China's economic reform would be strengthened. On the other hand, extremely coercive methods are adopted to quell the dissidents' voice, particularly in controlling the mass media. In a move to tighten control over mass media, the Propaganda Department of the CCP has strictly enforced the system of chief editors (for newspapers and magazines) or directors (for radio stations and television stations) under the leadership of the Party Committee. All the important posts such as senior editors and reporters, special commentators and news presenters must be Party members. The democratic parties could recruit members from mass media but they have been prohibited to set up any organization in mass media (*Ming Pao* 11 January 1996). The CCP will continue to beef up its coercive and ideological apparatus. It is difficult to see the CCP introducing any major piece of political structural reform in the near future, in the light of the overwhelming concern with political stability.

I can list six cases in which the CCP's repressive measures were most apparent and the CCP intends to quell the chaos in the "bud".

Case No. 1. On the eve of the Fourteenth CCP Congress, Ms Leung Wai-man, a Hong Kong reporter based in Beijing, obtained a copy of Jiang Zemin's political report to be delivered in the Congress. The *Express Daily* in Hong Kong published the whole report just seven days before Jiang's delivery. It was found that a Chinese journalist named Tian Yie was involved. Leung was immediately expelled from China, while Tian in Beijing was sentenced to life imprisonment for "leaking state secrets" (*The Nineties* December 1992:22).

Case No. 2. Gao Yu, a young and brilliant Chinese journalist and former deputy editor-in-chief of the banned *Economic Weekly*, was arrested in the airport when she tried to board an aeroplane for the United States for further studies in August 1993. Later she was sentenced to six years of imprisonment for, again, "leaking state secrets". In fact Gao Yu had been writing a column on Chinese politics in *The Mirror* Monthly in

Hong Kong. Her articles were disliked by the CCP who tried to keep her mouth shut by putting her in prison. This was her second arrest. She was arrested on 3 June 1989 by the martial law troops and detained for fifteen months without trial (*The Mirror* May 1995:28-9). Later the publisher Xu Simin, veteran CPPCC member tried to distance himself from Gao.

Case No. 3. Xi Yang, a Hong Kong *Ming Pao* reporter based in Beijing, published   a report on the change of interest rate by the People's Bank just a few days before the official announcement. He was persecuted for "leaking state secrets" which, the officials claimed, cost "enormous damage to the state". Despite the strong protest by the Hong Kong mass media, Xi was given a twelve-year sentence (*Ming Pao* 5 April 1994). Xi Yang was given an early parole and he emigrated to Canada.

Case No. 4. On 16 December 1994, a group of fifteen people were sentenced to lengthy prison terms from eleven years to twenty years for "organizing counter-revolutionary activities". They were charged with organizing a political party called "China's free democratic Party". Before they were given the verdict that date, they were held up for two and a half years by the security branches. In October1998, China became a signatory of the United Nations' International Covenant of Civil and Political Rights. To test the sincerity of the PRC, some dissidents started to form an opposition political party in late 1998. Three founding members Xu Wenli, Wang Youcai and   Qin Yunmin were arrested immediately and sentenced to eleven years , twelve years and thirteen years respectively.(*Cheng Ming* Janauary1999:7-8). What is barbaric about the CCP's political persecution was that it does not even respect the laws that PRC legislature passed. Chinese criminal laws allows for five months of custody for investigations. The 15- men group was held for more than two years before the verdict.

Case No. 5. China was entrusted by the United Nations to host the Fourth   World Woman Forum in Beijing in September 1995. Before the Forum was held, the municipal government drove away all the potential "trouble-makers", including Wang Dan, the prominent 4 June student leader, who still has not been released (as of July 1996).[10] To avoid conflicts with the authorities, Ding Zilin and Zhiang Peiquan, professors of the China People's University who have been tirelessly searching for the   identities of the 4 June victims and casualties, moved to Wuxi, their native city in central China, days before the Forum was held. But still they were seen as trouble-makers even when they were thousands of miles from the site where the Forum was held. Upon arrival at Wuxi, they were kept in custody by the security force for their "financial problems". They were finally released after two months of investigation (*The Nineties* December 1995:16).

Case No.6. In the past several years, China has stepped up monitoring mechanisms over internet users. In learning a lesson from the Soviet demise, China has tried to prevent the internet from jeopardising national security or spreading ideas or articles that are subversive of the government. In a meeting about internet monitoring and national security, Jia Chunwan, former public security minister, warned that the job of internet security is very complicated and "we must strengthen the struggles in the internet and enhance the abilities to discover, control, prevent, investigate and strike" (*Ming Pao* 13 April 2002). There were 'four prevents': to prevent the spreading of harmful messages, of viruses, hackers, and leaks of state secrets. At least there were two cases that were connected with the internet police. First, a twenty-two year old student Liu Di, studying in the Bejing Normal University, was arrested for her critical essays of the PRC in the internet (*Ming Pao* 12 December 2002). Another case is that four Beijing young intellectuals aged about thirty were charged with subverting the government and establishing a 'New Youth association' because they published articles criticizing the Party/state on the internet (*Ming Pao* 30 May 2003). Moreover, the Chinese government has ordered, according to one source, all internet bars to install a special software package that could allow the police management centers to supervise the internet users and internet bars. The software has the following functions: first, blacklisting 500,000 overseas websites; second, the blacklisted websites were to be classified into five categories, with the first to be most subversive of the state such as Falun Gong; and those who visit the blacklisted websites too often would be monitored; third, the internet would send a daily report to the centers of management in the public security bureau including the names and addresses of the internet users; fourth, the security officials would record the ID number of the users who visit the blacklisted websites and installed in the computer. The signal would be relayed to the management centers whenever the users gain access to the computer, whether on normal websites or on illegal ones. With this means, the security officials would track down in the computer all the activities of the suspected 'enemies'. (*Ming Pao* 29 June 2002).

It is commonly argued that the Singaporean developmental model is the one that the CCP intends to emulate. This model combines repressive politics and free market economy (Lam Willy 1995).[11] China has become a developmental state (Ming Xia 2000; Gordon White 1993a:4). The political elite is now committed to economic development and they are equally determined to stamp out political dissent. Due to the particularistic cultural elements, there is a strong likelihood that the CCP's 'hard politics and soft economics' may succeed. Seen in this context there is doubt as to whether a *fang* cycle in ideological-political arena will ever emerge. At present, the overriding concern is political stability.[12] The ends justify the means. Any methods can be used to repress dissidents and maintain stability are justified. It seems that China is no nearer the complete resolution of the four major crises: namely distribution, participation, penetration, and legitimacy, now than when the CCP began the reformist programme and ushered in the modernization drive in 1978. Profound changes have taken place but the crises are still present. In distribution, the central command economy was completely abandoned, but the pursuit of a market economy encounters and produces new problems, such as inflation and regional gaps and corruption. In participation, major structural reform stopped after the events of 1989. With the political monopoly of the CCP unchallenged, the political structural reform has limited, though significant, effect. In penetration, though economic reform provides an extra-political channel for the people, official corruption alienates a large section of the population, yet corruption is almost inherent in a Party/state system where mass media are controlled by the Party/state. Political participation is kept to a minimum, and global information flow is kept under strict surveillance by the security branches even on the internets.

I believe that the CCP is now encountering its most severe legitimacy crisis since the mid-1980s. As I analysed earlier, distribution will trigger demand for participation, but whether the demand can be formalized and institutionalized is unknown. In sum, Chinese society will continue to modernize and the economy will develop. In other words, the positive elements produced by the social-economic development for democratization will accumulate. Only when the positive factors ultimately outweigh the negative elements, will democracy arrive. As to when the day will arrive, I think nobody can offer an answer. In the early 21st century Chinese politics will be essentially similar to what they were in the 1980s, as aptly observed by Overholt (1993:248)

> In human rights, China's new prosperity and diminution of totalitarianism constitute one of the most positive contributions to human dignity that has occurred in the twentieth century, but China remains a harshly authoritarian country with the whole gamut of political prisons, arbitrary rule, restrictions on freedom, and undemocratic politics.

The first major crisis that the Hu-Wen new leadership encountered was the SARS (severe acute respiratory syndrome) outbreak that first started in Guangdong in November 2002. Within months, the disease was to spread to a dozen countries around the world and caused the death of hundreds of people. The health minister Zhang Wenkang and Beijing's mayor Meng Xuenong were fired for mishandling the crisis. The swift act has sparked speculation whether the SARS crisis would become China's Chernobyl, a political catalyst for the former Soviet Union in 1986, ushering in a new era of change under Hu-Wen leadership (Baum 2003; Brahm 2003;Link 2003) . It must be pointed out that Chernobyl itself was not landmark as it appears to be. What is important is the ascendance of the reformist and strong leader- Gorbachev who began to implement *Glasnost* and *Perestroka* policies when he became the general secretary of the USSR in 1985.

While the handling of the SARS outbreak was hailed by Western leaders, there is no sign to indicate that the SARS outbreak would contribute to China's drastic political liberalization. As Perry Link(2003) remarked that the current fourth leadership was educated in the 1950s and 1960s " having traveled abroad less than even previous generations (they)are inured to the system in which they rose. It is the only system they truly understand, and control of information is its lifeblood. They are still unlikely to relinquish that control willingly."

Notes

[1] Schumpeter's definition of eighteenth century democracy is as follows: institutional arrangement for arriving at political decisions which realize the common good by making the people itself decide issues through the election of individuals who are to assemble in order to carry out its will (1976:250). The definition is deficient in that simply it presupposes "the existence of a uniquely determined common good discernible to all" which is non-existent (1976:252).

[2] This argument is less true now than before. The new wealth amassed by the political families of the gerontocrats was stunning and it was one of the main targets of the 1989 student demonstrators. According to a report in Hong Kong, Deng Xiaoping's family has accumulated about US$500 million (*Open* July 1995:17). In the era of Jiang Zemin, his son has become one of tycoons in China's telecommunications.

[3] Whyte (1992:68) admitted that, in the short run, these events, in fact, work

against democratization. But in the long run, they will become positive forces.

[4]Yan Fu was the first Chinese intellectual who introduced to China the Western system of constitutional democracy after his return from the United Kingdom in the 1870s. His translation of Darwinism exerted tremendous intellectual power upon Chinese intellectuals in the late Qing.

[5]It is amazing that the nine members of the CCP Politburo SC members elected in the 16th CCP Congress in November 2002, are all engineers. None have studied humanities or social sciences. Among them, Hu Jintao, Wu Bangguo, Huang Ju and Wu Guanzheng graduated from Tsinghua University.

[6]Though no systematic survey was conducted on this issue and I doubt whether it was possible to conduct such a survey in China nowadays, I had chances to talk to the various Chinese scholars from Beijing, Shanghai, and Guangzhou in 1992/93. They almost all expressed unanimously the fear that China would face a similar fate as the Soviet Union. They, in fact, implicitly supported the CCP's ruthless repression of the 1989 prodemocracy movement. The deep-seated fear of *dongluan* (chaos) is embedded in the Chinese personality structure, as Pye keenly observed (1992:198-9). The cultural values were rooted in the top leadership who make key decisions.

[7]Tan died in 1993 and Wu was transferred to the centre and became vice-premier in 1995. The CCP did not fill up the vacancy left by Tan.

[8]It was reported that some retired generals such as Zhang Aiping were worried that Jiang would not be able to lead the PLA after Deng's death and they suggested establishing a "military Advisory Committee" to advise Jiang on military affairs (*Cheng Ming* September 1995:25-26). The proposal was certainly not accepted by Jiang. General Zhang died in July 2003.

[9]From 1936 to 1945, Mao was the de facto Party and military chief and from 1945 to 1976; he was Chairman of both the CCP and the CMC. Deng became the Chairman of the CMC in 1982 and resigned in 1989. Hu Yaobang and Zhao Ziyang were general secretaries in these years.   Jiang Zemin was the general secretary of the Party from 1989 to 2002 and he is still the Chairman of the CMC now. Hu Jintao became the general secretary in November 2002. It is not known how long Jiang will keep the CMC chairmanship. However, most speculated that Jiang would complete one term of service.

[10] Wang Dan is now studying in Harvard, pursuing a Ph.D. in history. He writes regularly for Hong Kong newspapers and magazines.

[11]I doubt whether the CCP can completely imitate the Singaporean model. For all its coercision, there are three things that the CCP cannot possibly copy. First, the People's Action Party in Singapore is subject to periodic national elections. Second, the Singaporean government is an extremely efficient government, a government almost free from corruption. Third, repressive as its laws may be, the rule of law is strictly enforced.

[12]It was reported that China sent a delegation to Indonesia to learn lessons from

Suharto concerning his ruthless repression of the Indonesian Communists in 1966, thus getting thirty years of political stability (*Open* November 1995:32).

CONCLUSION

This book begins with the introduction of a theoretical approach developed by the SSRC in the late 1960s and early 1970s. The "crisis-sequence" approach is a sub-theory of modernization theory and can be most fruitfully applied to the study of developing polity as in the case of China. The approach sees China as engaging in a process of political modernization. The political structural reform is perceived to be initiated consciously by the CCP leadership to modernize its outdated polity. It then goes on to provide a background knowledge of the rise and fall, and rejuvenation, of modernization theory. This book argues that there are few attempts by social scientists to make use of the existing social science theory and apply the theory to the study of contemporary China. This thesis attempts to do so, and hopefully, my endeavor is a successful one. Despite its theoretical fruitfulness, the modernizationist framework is criticized as being too general and lack of specific time frame in studying China's democratization process.

Three important hypotheses are derived from the "crisis and sequence" approach to examine the macro-political development in contemporary China, in particular the political structural reform in the PRC in the 1980s and 1990s. First, performance in *penetration* would trigger a demand in *distribution*. Second, performance in *participation* would trigger a demand in *distribution*. Third, performance in *distribution* would trigger a demand in *participation*. The collapse of the radical clique in the late 1970s gained a new legitimacy for the reformist leadership headed by Deng Xiaoping. My analysis of political development in the PRC in general and political reform in particular, tends to confirm these hypotheses to different degrees. The CCP's reformist ability to gain penetration into the minds of the people triggered the demand for the launching of economic reform. The downfall of the "Gang of Four" in 1976 had cleared the way for a far-reaching reform. The relationship between the second and third hypotheses is particularly close. It is, in fact, the relationship between economic and political structural reforms. Should they proceed in tandem? To the Hu Yaobang-Zhao Ziyang leadership, indeed, they have mutual supportive relationships. In the 1980s, the reform pendulum swings from one end to another. The reform cycles went in see-saw direction. In the 1990s, the policy shifts were less drastic, with the political reform lagging behind.

My study shows that before the mid-1980s the CCP top leadership saw the relationship between distribution and participation, i.e. economic reform and political structural reform, as mutually supportive. Moreover, democracy which political structural reform aimed to achieve was regarded as a goal in itself. After the mid-1980s, political structural reform was still perceived as necessary for successful economic reform, but its importance was downplayed by the CCP leadership. After 4 June 1989, the separation of economic and political structural reforms was envisaged and the notion of political structural reform went through a conservative twist. As I argue in the book, in the past two decades, the top CCP leadership has launched three waves of political structural reform. The first one was at the end of the 1970s. The first wave of the political structural reform took the institionalization of the CCP Party/state political processes and institutions as its goal. Having experienced the lawlessness of the CR, the reformist leadership, headed by Deng Xiaoping, strove to institutionalize the CCP Party/state polity. This period saw, a certain degree of democratization in the CCP Party/state political procedures and processes in China. In fact, most of the political structural programmes were initiated and implemented in this period, i.e. the early 1980s.

After the mid-1980s, the CCP attempted the second wave of the political structural reform but its significance had undergone a subtle change in the minds of the CCP leadership. Now it was considered to be instrumental rather than an inherent goal. Deng had abandoned the programmes to institutionalize the CCP Party/state polity. The economic reform had loosened the social fabric that the CCP set up since the founding of the PRC. The political structural reform was conceived to be a necessary component of reform purely for instrumental purposes: without it, probably economic reform could not succeed. Thus, the substance of political structural reform underwent a drastic change. In the first wave of political structural reform, the notion of democratization was held as a crucial element in the political reform package; while in the second, streamlining the Party/state bureaucracy was conceived to be the major component, without which, Deng had claimed several times that economic reform could not succeed.

After the 4 June tragedy, even the modified notion of political structural reform was suspended for more than a year. Separating the functions of the Party and the government was a key political reform measure in the first and second wave of the political structural reform, but the political structural reform in the early 1990s was scrapped. The notion of the political reform programmes was subject to a new interpretation by the ascending CCP leadership represented by Jiang Zemin. The early 1990s saw the reversing of the political structural reform measures introduced in the early 1980s. The regression was certainly approved by the New Helmsman. Deng, the architect of reform, was politically more reactionary at the end of the 1980s than the late 1970s when he began his great crusade of modernization.

Since the beginning of the 1990s, there has been an increased tightening of control over political dissidents. Economic reform has undergone another round of cycle of *fang* and *shou* since Deng made a trip to the southern coastal provinces. Nonetheless, the CCP leadership never slackened its grip in the political-ideological arena. The cyclical process can be applied to economic reform in the 1990s but none in the ideological-political sphere. As Jiang fiercely consolidated his power, the crackdown over dissidents became more severe. Political structural reform was increasingly perceived to be politically disruptive and conducive to political turmoil. In this perspective, the abandoning of the major political reform measures was not surprising. The third wave of political structural reform occurred in the mid-1990s. In the 15th CCP Congress, the CCP leadership introduced grass-root elections in the village committees, which I have analysed in chapter 6. The new Hu-Wen leadership gives up expanding democracy to a higher level, instead they turn into developing the so-called intra-Party democracy.

It is often said that the reform process cannot be reversed and the CCP has embarked on a modernization process of no return. This I cannot agree with. In China, there is always a possibility of going back to autarky due to the unique political-cultural characteristics. In fact, the 4 June bloodbath is a case in point. By using extreme brutal force, the CCP conservatives were able to turn back the clock. If not for Deng, China's reform era would have been halted after the massacre. In the past three thousand years, China had always been a country in isolation until the invasion of Western powers in the nineteenth century. It was forced open by foreign powers. The Maoist autarky was rooted in China's traditional polity.

In my exhaustive examination of positive and negative factors for the realization of democracy in China in chapter 8, distribution (economic reform) can indeed generate a demand for participation (political structural reform), but whether the demand generated can lead to the establishment of a democratic polity remains questionable, as I argued in chapter 8. To be sure, there is a *probable* relationship between these two variables, but there is no *necessary* relationship. Economic reform alone and its social-cultural consequences cannot ensure the setting up of a pluralistic politics. There are other unique elements. The modernizationist hypotheses that the governmental performance in *participation* would trigger a demand for *distribution,* and vice-versa may be true, but to establish a political democracy belongs to another plane of issues. In sum, marketization, liberalization, and democratization belong to three different orders of concepts, though undoubtedly they are closely related. The "crisis-sequence" approach is useful in that it provides an operating and guiding framework in my analysis of political development of the PRC in post-Mao era. However, the realization of a democratic polity in China requires an analysis of elements that the approach cannot provide.

REFERENCES

Almond, Gabriel A. (1987). The development of political development. In Myron Weiner and Samuel Huntington (Eds.), *Understanding political development* (pp.437-490). Boston: Little Brown & Co.

Almond, Gabriel A. and G. Bingham Powell, Jr. (1966). *Comparative politics: A developmental approach.* Boston: Little, Brown & Co.

Almond, Gabriel A. and G. Bingham Powell, Jr. (1978). *Comparative politics: system, process, and policy.* Boston: Little, Brown & Co.

Almond, Gabriel A. and G. Bingham Powell, Jr. (Eds.) (1992). *Comparative politics today: A world view.* Fifth edition. New York: Harper Collins Publishers.

Amatya, Sen. (1999). Democracy as a universal value. *Journal of Democracy*, July, 10 (3), 3-17.

Bai, Gang. (2001). Village committee elections: Process and challenge. Working paper, Centre for Comparative Public Management and Social Policy, City University of Hong Kong.

Bai, Yihua, Yang Kaiwang and Chih-yu Shih. (1998). Zhongguo dalu jiceng de minzhu gaige: Zhidu pian (The Democratic Reform at the Grass-root Level in Mainland China: Institutional Aspects. Taipei: The Laureate Publishers.

Baker &Mckenzie. (2001). *China and internet: Essential legislation.* Hong Kong: Asia Information Association Ltd.

Bao, Tong. (2001). Zhong guo de yousi (China's Melancholy). Hong Kong: Pacific Century.

Baum, Richard.(Ed.) (1991). *Reform and reaction in post-Mao China.* New York: Routledge.

Baum, Richard. (Ed.) (1993). The road to Tiananmen: Chinese politics in the 1980s. In Roderick MacFarquhar (Ed.) (1993a), *The politics of China* (pp.340-471). Cambridge: Cambridge University Press..

Baum, Richard. (Ed.) (1994). *Burying Mao: Chinese politics in the age of Deng Xiaoping.* Princeton: Princeton University Press.

Baum, Richard. (Ed.) (2003). Is China ready listen to its people? *South China Morning Post*, 8th June.

Beijing Review, China, various issues.

Becker, J.(2000).*The Chinese*. London: John Murray (Publishers) Ltd.

Berger, Peter L. and Hsiao, Michael Hsin-Huang.(Eds.) (1988). *In search of an East Asian development model*. New Brunswick: Transaction, Inc.

Benwick, R. and Wingrove, P.(Eds.)(1999). *China in the 1990s*. London: Macmillan.

Binder, Leonard. (1971). The crises of political development. In Leonard Binder et al.(Eds.), *Crises and sequences in political development* (pp.3-72). Princeton: Princeton University Press.

Binder, Leonard et al.(Eds.) (1971). *Crises and sequences in political development*. Princeton, N.J.: Princeton University Press.

Black, George and Robin Munro. (1993). *Black hands of Beijing - Lives of defiance in China's democracy movement*. New York: John Wiley & Sons, Inc.

Brugger, Bill and David Kelly. (1990). *Chinese Marxism in the post-Mao era*. Stanford: Stanford University Press.

Brahm, Lawrence. (2003). China heads into a new cycle of reform. *South China Morning Post*, 8th June.

Bunce, Valerie and John Echols III. (1986). From Soviet Studies to comparative politics: the unfinished revolution. In Stephen White and Daniel Nelson(Eds.), *Communist politics - A Reader* (pp.317-325). London: Macmillan.

Burns, John P. (1987). China's nomenklatura system. *Problems of Communism*, September/October, 36 (5),36-51.

Burns, John P. (1989a). China's governance: Political reform in a turbulent environment. *China Quarterly*, (119),481-518.

Burns, John P. (1989b). Civil service reform in post-Mao China. In Y.S. Cheng(Ed.)(1989), *China: Modernization in the 1980s* (pp.95-129). Hong Kong: Chinese University Press.

Burns, John P. (1989c). *The Chinese Communist Party's nomenklatura system*. New York: M.E. Sharpe.

Burns, John P. (1999). The People's Republic Of China at 50: National political reform. *Chinese Quarterly,* (159),580-594.

Butterfield, Fox. (1982). *China - Alive in the bitter sea*. New York: Bantam Books.

Cardoso, Fernando and Enzo Falletto. (1979). *Dependency and development in Latin America*. Berkeley: University of California Press.

Central Committee of the Chinese Communist Party (CCCCP). (1977). Zhongguo gongchandang di shiyijie quanguo daibiao dahui wenjian huibian (Documents of the Eleventh CCP Congress). Beijing: Renmin Chubanshe.

Central Committee of the Chinese Communist Party (CCCCP). (1981). *Resolution on the CCP history*. Beijing: Foreign Languages Press.

Central Committee of the Chinese Communist Party (CCCCP). (1982). Zhongguo gongchandang zhangcheng (The Party Constitution of the CCP). Hong Kong: *Wen Wei Po*, 9th September.

Central Committee of the Chinese Communist Party (CCCCP). (1983). Zhonggong zhongyang guanyu zhengdang de jueding (Decision Concerning Rectifying the Party). Hong Kong: *Wen Wei Pao*, 13th October.

Central Committee of the Chinese Communist Party (CCCCP). (1984). *Decision of the Central Committee of the Communist Party of China on reform of the economic structure*. Hong Kong: Joint Publishing Co.

Central Committee of the Chinese Communist Party (CCCCP). (1985). Zhonggong zhongyang guanyu jiaoyu tizhi gaige de jueding (Decision Concerning the Reform of Education System). *Renmin Ribao*, 29th May.

Central Committee of the Chinese Communist Party (CCCCP). (1986). Zhonggong zhongyang guanyu shehui zhuyi jingshen wenming jianshe zhidao fangzhen de jueyi (Resolution Concerning the Guiding Principle for Building a Socialist Society With an Advanced Culture and Ideology). Hong Kong: *Wen Wei Po*, 29th September.

Central Committee of the Chinese Communist Party (CCCCP). (1989). Zhonggong zhongyang guangyu jinyibu zhili zhengdun he shenhua gaige de jueding (Decison Concerning Further Restructuring, Managing and Deepening Reform). Hong Kong: *Wen Wei Po*, 18th January 1990.

Central Committee of the Chinese Communist Party (CCCCP). (1990). Zhonggong zhongyang guanyu jiaqiang dang tong renmin qunzhong lianxi de jueding (Decision Concerning To Strengthen the Relationship between the Party and Masses). Hong Kong: *Wen Wei Po*, 21st April.

Central Committee of the Chinese Communist Party (CCCCP). (1992). Zhongguo gongchandang dishisici quanguo daibiao dahui wenjian huibian (Documents of the Fourteenth CCP Congress). Beijing: Renmin Chubanshe.

Central Committee of the Chinese Communist Party (CCCCP). (1993). *Decision on Some Issues Concerning the Establishment of a Socialist Market Economic Structure.* In *Beijing Review,* 36(47),12-31.

Central Committee of the Chinese Communist Party (CCCCP). (1994). Aiguozhuyi jiaoyu shishi gangyao (The Implementation Outline of Patriotism Education). *Renmin Ribao,* 6th September.

Central Committee of the Chinese Communist Party (CCCCP). (1995). Zhongyang weiyuanhui diwuci quanti huiyi wenjian (Documents of the Fifth Plenum of the Fourteenth CC). Beijing: Renmin Chubanshe.

Cha, Louis. (1984). An Interview with Hu Yaobang. *Ming Pao,* 5th –9th December.

Chamberlain, Heath. (1993). On the Search for Civil Society in China. *Modern China,* 19 (2),199-215.

Chan, Anita. (1991). The social origins and consequences of the Tiananmen crisis. In David Goodman and Gerald Segal(Eds.), *China in the nineties - crisis management and beyond* (pp. 105-130). Oxford: Clarendon..

Chan, Anita, Stanley Rosen and Jonathan Unger. (Eds.) (1985). *On socialist democracy and the Chinese legal system: the Li Yizhe debates.* Armonk: M.E. Sharpe.

Chan, Che-po. (1999). The political pragmatism of Chinese university students: 10 years after the 1989 movement, *Journal of Contemporary China,* (22), 381-403.

Chan, Che-po and Gavin Drewy (2001). The 1998 State Council organizational streamlining: Personnel reduction and change of government function. *Journal of Contemporary China,* (29),553-572.

Chang, Gordon G.(2001). *The coming collapse of China.* New York: Random House.

Chang, Hsia Mary. (1992). China's future: Regionalism, federation or disintegration? *Studies in Comparative Communism,* 25(3),211-227.

Chang, Parris. (1981). Chinese politics: Deng's turbulent quest. *Problems of Communism,* January/February, 30(1),1-27.

Chang, Parris. (1987). China after Deng: Toward the 13th CCP Congress. *Problems of Communism,* May/June, 36(3),30-42.

Chang, David Wen-Wei. (1989). *China under Deng Xiaoping: Political and economic reform.* Basingstoke: Macmillan Press.

Chen, An (1999). *Restructuring political power in China-alliances and opposition (1978-1998).* London: Lynne Kienne Publishers, Inc.

Chen, Hefu. (1980). Zhongguo xianfa huibian (The Constitutions of China). Beijing: Zhongguo Shehui Kexue Chubanshe.

Chen, Liu. (1995). Chen Yun he Deng Xiaoping guanxi de zhenxiang (The True Relationship between Chen Yun and Deng Xiaoping). *The Mirror,* May, (214),22-25.

Chen, Ruisheng et al.(Eds.) (1992). Zhongguo gaige quanshu - zhengzhi tizhi gaige juan (A Comprehensive Book on China's Reform - Political Reform). Dalian: Dalian Chubanshe.

Chen, Xitong. (1989). Guanyu zhizhi dongluan he pingxi fangemin baoluan de qingkuang baogao (Situation Report Concerning Preventing the Turmoil and Quelling the Anti-revolutionary Rebellion). Hong Kong: *Wen Wei Po,* 7th –8th , July.

Chen, Yizhi. (1990). *China: Ten-year reform and the 1989 pro-democracy movement.* Taipei: Joint Publishing Co.

Chen, Ziming, (1992). Fansi shinian gaige (Reflection on Ten Years of Reform). Hong Kong: Contemporary Monthly.

Cheng Ming Monthly (Contending), Hong Kong, various issues.

Cheng, Nien. (1986). *Life and death in Shanghai.* London: Grafton Books.

Cheng, Joseph Y.S.(Ed.) (1989). *China: Modernization in the 1980s.* Hong Kong: Chinese University Press.

Cheung, Ka-man. (1999). *China: 1949-1997, two volumes.* Hong Kong: Hong Kong Policy Research Ltd.

Cheung, Kit-fung et al. (1989). *The Flower of Democracy bathed in blood — Student movement, democracy movement and the fate of the country.* Hong Kong: Pai Shing Cultural Enterprise Ltd.

Chin, Steve S.K. (1976). *The Thought of Mao Zedong: Form and content.* Hong Kong: Center of Asian Studies, University of Hong Kong.

Chiou, C.L. (1986). A discussion on China's political system and political reform with Yan Jiaqi", *The Nineties,* December, (203),40-47.

Chiou,C.L.(1995). *Democratizing oriental despotism.* London: Macmillan.

Coleman, James S. (1971). The development syndrome: Differentiation-equality-capacity. In Leonard Binder et al.(eds.), *Crises and sequences in political development* (pp.73-100). Princeton: Princeton University Press..

Dassu, Monta and Tony Saich. (Eds.) (1992). *The reform decade in China.* New York: Kegan Paul International.

Davis, Winston. (1987). Religion and development: Weber and East Asian experience. In Myron Weiner and Samuel Huntington(Eds.), *Understanding political development* (pp. 221-280). Boston: Little Brown & Co.

Deng, Xiaoping. (1983). Deng Xiaoping Wenxuan, 1975-1982 (Selected Works of Deng Xiaoping). Beijing: Remin Chubabshe.

Deng, Xiaoping. (1984).   *Selected Works.*_Beijing: Foreign Languages Press.

Deng, Xiaoping. (1987). *Fundamental Issues in Present China.* Beijing: Foreign Languages Press.

Deng, Xiaoping. (1993). Deng Xiaoping Wenxuan, V. 3 (Selected Works of Deng Xiaoping, V.3). Beijing: Renmin Chubanshe.

Deyo, Frederic(Ed.) (1987). *The political economy of the new Asian industrialism.* Ithaca: Cornell University Press.

Ding, Xueliang. (1991). The Influence of Neo-Marxism on China. *Democratic China,* February, (6),38-49.

Ding, Xueliang. (1994). *The decline of communism in China-Legitimacy crisis, 1977-1989.* Cambridge: Cambridge University Press.

Ding, Zilin. (1994a). *The factual account of a search for the June 4 victims.* Hong Kong: The Nineties.

Ding, Zilin. (1994b). *The Name List of the June 4 Victims.* Hong Kong: The Nineties.

Dittmer, Lowell. (1978). Bases of power in Chinese politics: A theory and an analysis of the fall of the 'Gang of Four'. *World Politics,* 31 (1),26-60.

Dittmer, Lowell. (1987). *China's continuous revolution.* Berkeley: University of California Press.

Dittmer, Lowell. (1989). Tiananmen Massacre. *Problems of Communism,* September/October, 37(5),2-15.

Dittmer, Lowell. (1990a). Patterns of elite strife and succession in Chinese politics", *China Quarterly,* September, (123),405-430.

Dittmer, Lowell. (1990b). China in 1989: The crisis of incomplete reform. *Asian Survey,* 30(1),25-41.

Dittmer, Lowell. (2001). The new shape of elite politics. *China journal,* (45),83-94.

Dittmer, Lowell and Samuel Kim(Eds.) (1993). *China's quest for national identity.* Ithaca: Cornell University Press.

Etzioni, Amitai(Ed.) (1980). *A sociological reader, second edition.* New York: Holt, Rinehart and Winston.

Evans, Peter. (1979). *Dependent development: The alliance of multinational, state, and local capital in Brazil.* Princeton: Princeton University Press.

Evans, Peter. (1987). Class, state, and dependence in East Asia: Lessons for Latin Americanists. In Frederic Deyo (Ed.) *The Political Economy of the New Asian Industrialism* (pp.203-227). Ithaca: Cornell University Press.

Evans, Peter and John D. Stephens. (1988). Development and the World Economy. In Neil J. Smelser, (Ed.), *Handbook of Sociology* (pp.739-73). New York: Sage Publications.

Evans, Richard. (1995). *Deng Xiaoping and the making of modern China.* London: Penguin.

Fairbank, John King. (1983). *The United States and China, Fourth Edition.* Cambridge: Harvard University Press.

Fang, Lizhi. (1987). Minzhu bushi ciyude — Fang, Lizhi zhengzhi yanlunji (Democracy Is Not Granted — A Collection of Political Essays). Hong Kong: The Earth Publishing Co.

Feldman, Harvey et al. (1989). *Taiwan in a time of transition.* New York: Paragon House.

Feng Jian and Zeng Jianhuai. (1983). Zhongnanhai de chuntian (The Spring in Zhongnanhai). Beijing: Xinhua Chubanshe.

Fewsmith, Joseph. (2001). *China since Tiananmen-the politics of transition.* New York: Cambridge University Press.

Fraser, John. (1980). *The Chinese — Portrait of a people.* Glasgow:Fontana.

Field, Mark. (1967). Soviet society and Communist Party control: A Case of 'Constricted Development'", in Donald Treadgold (ed.), *Soviet and Chinese Communism: Similarities and Differences* (pp.185-211). Seattle: University of Washington Press.

Frank, Gunder. A. (1979). *Dependent development and underdevelopment.* New York: Monthly Review Press.

Friedman, Edward. (1995). *National identity and democratic prospects in socialist China.* New York: M.E. Sharpe.

Friedman, Edward, Paul G. Pickowicz, and Mark Selden. (1991). *Chinese village, socialist state.* New Haven: Yale University Press.

Friedman, Milton. (1982). *Capitalism and freedom.* Chicago: University of Chicago Press.

Fu, Guoyong and Fan Baihua. (2000). Jiliang—Zhongguo sandai ziyou zhishifenzi pingzhuan (Backbones- the Biographies of the Three Generations of Chinese Liberal Intellectuals). Hong Kong: Open Magazine.

Gao, Fang. (1988). Tan zhengzhi gaige (On Political Reform), *The Nineties*, December, (227), 58-64.

Gao, Fang. (1993). Zai tan zhengzhi gaige (On Political Reform Again), *The Nineties*, October, (285), pp.56-60.

General Office of the State Council (GOSC). (Ed.) (1995, 1998). Zhongyang zhengfu zuzhi jigou (The Organizations and Apparatus of the Central Government). Beijing: Gaige Chubanshe.

Gold, Thomas. (1986). *State and society in the Taiwan miracle.* New York: M.E. Sharpe.

Gold, Thomas. (1990a). Party-State versus society in China. In Joyce Kallgren(Ed.)(1990), *Building a nation-state: China after forty years* (pp.125-52). Berkeley: Institute of Asian Studies.

Gold, Thomas. (1990b). Autonomy versus authoritarianism. In George Hicks(Ed.)(1990), *The broken mirror: China After Tiananmen* (pp. 196-211). Chicago: St. James Press.

Goldman, Merle, Perry Link, and Su Wei. (1993). China's intellectuals in the Deng era: Loss of identity with the state. In Lowell Dittmer and Samuel Kim(Eds.), *China's quest for national identity* (pp.125-53). Ithaca: Cornell University Press.

Goldman. Merle & Roderick MaCFarquhr. (Eds.) (1999). *The paradox of China's post-Mao reform.* Cambridge, Massachusetts: Harvard University Press.

Goodman, David. (1986).The national CCP conference of September 1985 and China's leadership changes. *China Quarterly*, March, (105),123-130.

Goodman, David and Beverley Hooper. (Eds.) (1994). *China's quiet revolution.* New York: Longman Cheshire.

Goodman, David and Gerald Segal. (Eds.) (1991). *China in the nineties - crisis management and beyond.* Oxford: Clarendon Press.

Goodman, David and Gerald Segal. (Eds.) (1995). *China without Deng.* Sydney: Imprint Book.

Gourevitch, P.A. (1993). Democracy and economic policy: Elective affinities and circumstantial conjunctures. *World Development*, August, 21(8),1271-1280.

Grew, Raymond.(Ed.) (1978). *Crises of political development in Europe and United States.* Princeton, N.J.: Princeton University Press.

Guangming Ribao (Brightness Daily), China, various issues.

Guangming Ribao Special Commentator(GRSC). (1978). Shijian shi jianyan zhengli de weiyi biaozhun (Practice is the Sole Criterion of Testing Truth). *Guanming Ribao*, 11th May.

Gurley, John. (1976). *China's economy and the Maoist strategy*. New York: Monthly Review Press.

Halpern, Nina. (1991). Economic reform, social mobilization, and democratization in post-Mao China", in Richard Baum(Ed.), *Reform and reaction in post-Mao China* (pp.38-59). New York: Routledge.

Halpern, Nina. (1993). Studies of Chinese politics. In Shambaugh(Ed.)(1993b), *American studies of contemporary China* (pp.120-137). New York: M.E.Sharpe.

Han Minzhu. (Ed.) (1990). *Cries for democracies: writings and speeches from the 1989 Chinese democracy movement*. Princeton: Princeton University Press.

Harding, Harry E. (1984). The study of Chinese politics: Toward a third generation of scholarship. *World Politics*, 36 (2),284-307.

Harding, Harry E. (1987). *China's second revolution: Reform after Mao*. Washington: Brookings Institute.

Harding, Harry E. (1993). The evolution of American scholarship in contemporary China. In David Shambaugh(Ed.) (1993b), *American studies of contemporary China* (pp.14-40). New York: M.E. Sharpe.

Harrison, E. Lawrence and Samuel Huntington. (Eds.) (2000). *Culture matters-How values shape human progress*. New York: Basic Books.

Hawthorn, G. (1993). Liberalization and 'modern liberty': Four Southern States. *World Development,* August, 21(8),1299-1312.

Hayek, Frederick. (1985). *The road to serfdom*. Sydney: Dymock's Book Arcade.

He, Baogang. (1996). *The democratization of China*. New York: Routledge.

He, Baogang. (1997). *The democratic implication of civil society in China*. New York: St.Martin, Inc.

He, Buochuan. (1988). Shanaoshang de zhongguo (China in crisis). Guiyang: Guizhou Renmin Chubanshe.

He Ping. (Ed.) (1994). *The post-Deng China-the analyses of the 43 scholars and experts*. Ontario: Mirror Books.

He Ping and Gao Xin. (1993). *The CCP new power-holders*. Hong Kong: Contemporary Monthly Publishing Ltd.

He Ping and Gao Xin. (1995). *The CCP princelings.* Taipei: China Times Cultural Enterprises Ltd.

Hicks, George. (Ed.) (1990). *The broken mirror: China after Tiananmen.* Chicago: St. James Press.

Hinton, William. (1972). *Turning point in China — An essay on the Cultural Revolution.* New York: Monthly Review Press.

Hong Kong Journalists (HKJ). (Eds.) (1989). *People will not forget — the truth of the 1989 democracy movement.* Hong Kong: Hong Kong Journalist Association.

Hu, Angang. (1999). Zhizai cujin jingjigaige de zhongguo zhengzhi gaige. In Gaige (Reform), (3), 23-26.

Hu, Angang. (Ed.) (2001). Zhongguo: tiaozhan fubai (China: Challenging Corruption). Hangzhou: Zhejiang Remin Chubanshe.

Hu, Ping and Zhang Shengyou. (1988). Zhongguo chao (China Tides). Beijing: Zhuanli Wenxian Chubanshe.

Hu, Qiaomu. (1978). Anzhao jingji guilu banshi jiakuai shixian sige xiandaihua (Follow the Laws of Economics, Speed Up the Realization of the Four Modernization), Hong Kong: *Wen Wei Po,* 13th October.

Hu, Qiaomu. (1984). Guanyu rendaozhuyi he yihua wenti (Concerning Humanism and the Problem of Alienation) In Renmin Chubanshe(Ed.) Guanyu rendaozhuyi he yihua wenti lunwenji (pp.1-63). Beijing: Renmin Chubanshe.

Hu, Qiaomu. (1991). Zhongguogongchandang zenyang fazhan makesizhuyi (The Development of Marxism by the CCP). *Renmin Ribao,* 1st July.

Hu, Sheng. (1987). Wei shenme zhongguo buneng zou ziben zhuyi daolu (Why China cannot follow the Capitalist Road). *Renmin Ribao,* 5th March.

Hu, Yaobang. (1981). Zai qingzhu zhonggong chengli liushi zhounian dahui shang de jianghua (Speech Commemorating the Sixtieth Anniversary of the Establishment of the CCP), Hong Kong: *Ta Kung Pao,* 2nd July.

Hu, Yaobang. (1982). Quanmian kaichuang shehui zhuyi xiandaihua de xinjumian (To Create a New Phase of the Socialist Modernization Comprehensively), Report delivered at the Twelveth CCP Congress. Hong Kong: *Wen Wei Po,* 8th September.

Hu, Yaobang. (1983). Makesi zhuyi weida zhenli de guangmang zhaoyao women qianjin (The Great Truth of Marxism leads us Forward), Hong Kong: *Wen Wei Po*, 14th March.

Hu, Yaobang. (1985). Guanyu dangde xinwen gongzuo (Concerning the Press Work of the Party), Hong Kong: *Wen Wei Po*, 15th April.

Hua, Guofeng. (1979). *Government Work Report*. Hong Kong: *Wen Wei Po*, 26th June.

Hua, Guofeng. (1980). *Government Work Report*. Renmin Ribao, 15th September.

Huang, Philip. (1993). Public sphere/civil society in China? the third realm between state and society. *Modern China*, April, 19(2),216-40.

Huntington, Samuel P. (1968). *Political order in changing societies*. New Haven: Yale University Press.

Huntington, Samuel P. (1991). *The third wave — democratization in the late twentieth century*. Norman: University of Oklahoma Press.

Huntington, Samuel P. and Joan M. Nelson. (1976). *No easy choice — political participation in developing countries*. Cambridge: Harvard University Press.

Information Office of State Council (IOSC). (1991). Zhongguo de renquan zhuangkuang (Human Rights Conditions in China). Beijing: Zhongyan Wenxian Chubanshe.

Jiang, Zemin. (1989a). Zai qingzhu zhonghua renmin gongheguo chengli sishi zhounian dahuishang de jianghua" (Speech Commemorating the Fortieth Anniversary of the Establishment of the PRC) *Renmin Ribao*, 30th September.

Jiang, Zemin. (1989b). Zai dangde shisanjie wuzhong quanhuishang de jianghua (Speech on the Fifth Plenum of the Thirteenth CCP Congress). Hong Kong: *Wen Wei Po*, 22nd November.

Jiang, Zemin. (1990). Weiba dang jianshe cheng gengjia jian qiang de gongren jieji xianfengdui er douzheng (To Struggle and Make the Party Become a Stronger Pioneer of the Proletariat). *Renmin Ribao*, 1st July.

Jiang, Zemin. (1991). Zai qingzhu zhonggong chengli qishi zhounian dahui shang de jianghua (Speech Commemorating the Seventieth Anniversary of the Establishment of the CCP). Hong Kong: *Wen Wei Po*, 2nd July.

Jiang, Zemin. (1992). Jiakuai gaige kaifang he xiandaihua jianshe bufa, duo qu you zhongguo tese shehui zhuyi shiye de geng da shengli. (Speeding Up Reform, Open Door Policy and the Pace of Modernization, Seizing More Victories in Building Socialism with Chinese Characteristics). Political Report delivered in the Fourteenth Party Congress of the CCP on 25th Nov. Hong Kong: *Wen Wei Po* 13th October.

Jiang, Zemin. (1994). Zhonggong zhongyang guanyu jiaqiang dangde jianshe ji gezhong dawenti de jueding (The Decision about Certain Problems on Party Construction). *Renmin Ribao*, 30th September.

Jiang, Zemin. (1997). Gaoju Deng Xiaoping lilun (Holding High the Flag of Deng Xiaoping Theory, Pushing Forward the Construction of Socialism with Chinese Characteristics into the 21st Century). Political Report delivered in the 15th CCP Congree. *Wen Wei Po*, 13th September.

Jiang, Zemin. (2001a). Lun 'sange daibiao' (On the 'theory of three representatives'). Beijing: Central Documents Chubanshe.

Jiang, Zemin. (2001b).Lun Dangde Jianshe (On the Construction of the Party). Beijing: Central Documents Chubanshe.

Jiang, Zemin. (2002). Quan mian jian she xiao kang she hui kai chuang zhong guo te se de she hui zhu yi shi ye xin ju mian (To Construct the Society with Relatively Prosperity Comprehensively, and to Create a New Era in the Construction of the Socialism with Chinese Characteristics). Political Report delivered in the 16th CCP Congress, *Wen Wei Po*, 9th November.

Jin Guantao and Liu Qingfeng. (1990). *The dialogue concerning cultural reconstruction and the future of China.* Hong Kong: Cosmos Books Ltd.

Johnson, Chalmers.(Ed.) (1973). *Ideology and politics in contemporary China.* Seattle: University of Washington Press.

Jowitt, Kenneth. (1978). *The Leninist response to national dependency.* Berkeley: Institute of International Studies, University of California.

Jowitt, Kenneth. (1983). Soviet Neo-Traditionalism: The political corruption of a Leninist regime. *Soviet Studies*, 35(3),275-297.

Kalathil, Shanthi and Taylor Boas. (2003). The net will follow, not lead, China's reforms. *South China Morning Post*, 25th January.

Kallgren, Joyce, (Ed.) (1990). *Building a nation-state: China after forty years.* Berkeley: Institute of East Asia Studies.

Kelly, David and He Baogang. (1992). Emergent Civil Society and the Intellectuals in China. In Robert Miller(Ed.), *The development of civil society in Communist systems* (pp.196-211). Sydney: Allen and Unwin Pty Ltd.

King, Y.C. Ambrose. (1992). *Chinese Society and Culture.* Hong Kong: Oxford University Press.

Kristof, Nicholas D. and Sheryl Wudunn. (1994). *China wakes — the struggle for the soul of a rising power.* London: Nicolas Brealey Publishing Limited.

Kuhn, Thomas. (1970). *The structure of scientific revolution.* Enlarged edition, Chicago: University of Chicago Press.

Lam, Willy Wo-lap. (1995). *China after Deng - the power struggle in Beijing since Tiananmen.* Hong Kong: P.A. Professional Consultants.

Lam, Willy Wo-lap. (1999). *The era of Jiang Zemin.* Singapore: Simon &Schuster (Asia) Pte Ltd.

Lampton, David M.(Ed.) (1987). *Policy implementation in post-Mao China.* Berkeley: University of California Press.

Lan, Yuan. (1988). Gaige de tequan yu guanxi (Privileges and Connections in the Reform), *The Nineties*, June, (221),43-45.

Lane, David. (1990). *Soviet society under Perestroika.* Oxford: Basil Blackwell Ltd.

LaPalombara, Joseph. (1971a). Penetration: A Crisis of Governmental Capacity. In Leonard Binder et al. (Eds.)(1971), *Crises and sequences in political development* (pp.205-232). Princeton: Princeton University Press.

LaPalombara, Joseph. (1971b). Distribution: A crisis of resource management. In Leonard Binder et al. (Eds.)(1971), *Crises and sequences in political development* (pp.233-82). Princeton: Princeton University Press.

Lardy, Nicholas and Kenneth Lieberthal. (1983). *Chen Yun's strategy for China's development: a non-Maoist alternative.* Armonk: M.E. Sharpe.

Lee, Hong Yung. (1991). *From revolutionary cadres to technocrats in socialist China.* Berkeley: University of California Press.

Leys, Simon. (1978). *Chinese shadows.* Victoria: Penguin Books.

Li, Cheng and Lynn White. (1988). The Thirteenth Central Committee of the Chinese Communist Party-from mobilizers to managers. *Asian Survey*, 28(4),371-399.

Li, Honglin. (1986). *Xiandaihua he minzhu* (Modernization and Democracy). *Cheng Ming,* July, (105),11-14.

Li, Kwok-shing. (1990). *The structure of the CCP, government and military apparatus.* Hong Kong: Ming Pao Publishing Co.

Li, Kwok-shing. (1992). *The CCP ruling hierarchy.* Hong Kong: Ming Pao Publishing Co.

Li, Kwok-shing. (1993). The impact of 4 June incident on the high-level personnel change of the CCP. *Asian Studies,* 1(5),48-91.

Li, Oufan. (1989). Cong xueyun kan zhongguo minzu zhilu (The Path Ahead for Chinese Democracy in Light of the Student Movement). *The Nineties,* August, (235),64-67.

Li, Peng. (1989). *Government Work Report.* Hong Kong: *Ta Kung Pao* 31st March.

Li, Peng. (1990). *Government Work Report.* Hong Kong: *Wen Wei Po,* 31st March

Li, Peng. (1991). *Report on Ten-Year Plan and Eighth Five-Year Plan.* Wen Wei Po, 26th March.

Li, Peng. (1992). *Government Work Report.* Hong Kong: *Wen Wei Po,* 21st March.

Li, Peng. (1993). *Government Work Report.* Hong Kong: *Wen Wei Po* 16th March.

Li, Peng. (1994). *Government Work Report.* Hong Kong: *Wen Wei Po,* 11th March.

Li, Peng. (1995). *Government Work Report.* Hong Kong: *Wen Wei Po,* 6th March

Li, Shengping et al. (Eds.) (1989). Zhengzhi tizhi gaige de lilun yu shijian (The Theory and Practice of Political Reform). Beijing: Guangming Chubanshe.

Li, Yongchun and Luo Jian, (Eds.) (1987). Shiyijie sanzhong quanhui yilai zhengzhi tizhi gaige de lilun yu shijian (The Theory and Practice of Political Reform since the Third Plenum of the Eleventh CC). Beijing: Chunqiu Chubanshe.

Li, Yongchun, Si, Yuanqin, and Guo, Xiuzhi, (Eds.) (1987). Shiyijie sanzhong quanhui yilai zhengzhi tizhi gaige dashiji (The Chronology of the Political Reform since the Third Plenum of the Eleventh CC). Beijing: Chunqiu Chubanshe.

Li, Zehou. (1987). Zhongguo xiandai sixiang shilun (Modern Chinese Intellectual History). Beijing: Dongfang Chubanshe.

Li, Zhisui. (1994). *The private life of Chairman Mao.* London: Chatto & Windus Ltd.

Liao, Gailong. (1980). Lishi de jingyan he women de fazhan daolu (Historical Experience and Our Developmental Path). *The Seventies*, March, (134),38-48.

Liao, Gailong. (1991). Zhongguo gongchandang de guanghui qishinian (The Glorious Seventy Years of the CCP). Beijing: Xinhua Chubanshe.

Lieberthal, Kenneth. (1995). *Governing China - from revolution to reform*. New York: W.W. Norton and Company.

Lieberthal, Kenneth and M. Oksenberg. (1988). *Policy making in China: leaders, structures and processes*. Princeton: Princeton University Press.

Lieberthal, Kenneth G. and David M. Lampton, (Eds.) (1992). *Bureaucracy, politics, and decision making in post-Mao China*. Berkeley: University of California Press.

Lifton, Robert J. (1961). *Thought reform and the psychology of totalism*. New York: W.W. Norton and Company.

Lin, Yan. (Ed.) (1993). Zhongguo gaige chao de shilu (The True Record of China's Reform Tides). Hong Kong: Cosmos Books Ltd.

Link, Perry. (1990).The thought and spirit of Fang Lizhi. In George Hicks(Ed.) *The broken mirror: China after Tiananmen* (pp.100-114). Chicago: St. James Press.

Link, Perry. (2003). Will SARS transform China's chiefs? *Time*, 2nd May.

Liu, Binyan. (1990). *The autobiography of Liu Binyan*. Hong Kong: New Light Publishing Co.

Liu, Xiaobo. (1992). *The monologue of the last survivor: 4 June and I*. Taipei: China Times Cultural Enterprises Ltd.

Liu, Junning. (2000). Classical liberalism catches on in China. *Journal of Democracy*, 11(3), 48-57.

Lu, Keng. (1985). An Interview with Hu Yaobang. *Pai Shing*, 1 June, (97),3-16.

Ma, Min. (1993). China's political reform needs to take three big steps. *The Mirror*, (196),57-59; (197),50-55.

Ma Shu-yun. (1994). The Chinese Discourse on Civil Society. *China Quarterly*, March, (137),180-193.

MacFarquhar, Roderick. (Ed.)(1993a). *The politics of China*. Cambridge: Cambridge University Press.

MacFarquhar, Roderick. (Ed.) (1993b). The Succession to Mao and the End of Maoism 1969-82. In Roderick MacFarquhar (Ed.)(1993a), *The politics of China*(pp248-339).Cambridge: Cambridge University Press..

Madsen, Richard. (1993). The civil society and public sphere debate. *Modern China*, 19 (2),108-138.

Mao, Zedong. (1975). *Selected works*. 4 volumes. Beijing: Foreign Languages Press.

Mao, Zedong. (1977). Xuanji (Selected Works). V.5. Beijing: Renmin Chubanshe.

McCormick, Barrett L. (1990). *Political reform in post-Mao China.* Berkeley: University of California Press.

McCormick, Barrett L., Su Shaozhi, and Xiao Xiaoming. (1992). The 1989 democracy movement: A review of the prospects for civil society in China. *Pacific Affairs* , 65(2),182-202.

Merquior, J.G. (1993). A panoramic view of the rebirth of liberalism. *World Development*, August, 21(8),1263-1270.

Miller, Robert (Ed.) (1992). *The development of civil society in Communist systems.* Sydney: Allen and Unwin Pty Ltd.

Mills, William DeB. (1983). Generational Change in China. *Problems of Communism,* November/December, 32(6),16-35.

Min Qi. (1989). Zhongguo zhengzhi wenhua (China's Political Culture). Kuming: Yunnan Renmin Chubanshe.

Ming Pao Daily, Hong Kong, various issues.

Mirsky, Jonathan. (1995). Party chides China's ghastly secrets. *The Australian,* 30 March

Nathan, Andrew. (1985). *Chinese democracy.* New York: Alfred A. Knopf.

Nathan, Andrew. (1989). Chinese democracy in 1989: continuity and change. *Problems of Communism,* September/October, 33(5),16-29.

Nathan, Andrew. (1990). *China's crisis — dilemma of reform and prospect for democracy.* New York: Columbia University Press.

Nathan, Andrew. (2000). Chinese democracy: The lessons of failure. In Zhao Suisheng (Ed.), *China and democracy —reconsidering for a democratic China* (pp.21-32). New York: Routledge.

Nathan, Andrew. (2001). The Tiananmen Papers: An editor's reflection. *China Quarterly,* (167),724-737.

Nathan, A. and Bruce Gilley. (2002). *China's New Rulers.* London: Grata Books.

Nathan, A. and Perry Link. (Eds.)(2001). *The Tiananmen Papers.* New York: Public Affairs.

Ng Hon-man. (1990). *A memoir on the National People's Congress.* Hong Kong: Ming Pao Publishing Company.

Ng, Yu-shan. (1993). Nationalism, Democratization, and Economic Reform: Political Transition in the Soviet Union, Hungary, and Taiwan. Paper presented at the American Political Science Association Annual Meeting, 1-5 September, Washington D.C., U.S.A.

O'Brien, Kevin J. (1990). *Reform without Liberalization: China's National People's Congress and the politics of institutional change.* New York: Cambridge University Press.

O'Brien, Kevin J. and Liangiang Li. (2000). Accommodating 'democracy' in a one –Party state: Introducing village elections in China. *China Quarterly,* (162),465-489.

Oksenberg, Michel. (2001). China's political system: Challenges of the twenty-first century. *China Journal,* (41),21-36.

Oksenberg, Michel and Richard Bush. (1982). China's Political Evolution: 1972-82. *Problems of Communism,* September/October, 26(5),1-19.

O'Donnell, Guillermo. (1993). On the state, democratization and some conceptual problems: A Latin American view with glances at some post-communist countries. *World Development,* 21(8),1355-1369.

Ogden, Suzanne, K. Hartford, L. Sullivan and David Zweig. (Eds.) (1992). *The student and mass movement of 1989.* New York: M.E. Sharpe.

Open Magazine (Monthly), Hong Kong, various issues.

Overholt, William H. (1993). *China: The next economic superpower.* London: Weidenfeld & Nicolson.

Pai Shing Semi-Monthly, Hong Kong, various issues.

Palma. Gabriel. (1978). Dependency: A formal theory of the underdevelopment or a methodology for the analysis of concrete situations of underdevelopment? *World Development,* 6(7),881-924.

Pastor, A. Robert and Tan, Qingshan.(2000). The meaning of China's village elections. *China Quarterly,* (162),490-512.

Peng, Zhen. (1982). Guanyu zhonghuarenmingongheguo xianfa xiugai de shuoming (An Explanatory Note Concerning the Constitution of the People's Republic of China). *Renmin Ribao,* 29th April.

People's Republic of China (PRC). *The Constitution.* 1954, 1975, 1978, 1982 and various amendments.

Perry, Elizabeth J. (1989). State and society in contemporary China. *World Politics,* (41),579-591.

Perry, Elizabeth J. (1994). Trends in the Studies of Chinese Politics: State-Society Relations. *China Quarterly*, September, (139),701-713.

Perry, Elizabeth J. and Jeffrey N. Wasserstrom.(Eds.) (1992). *Popular protest and political culture in modern China.* Boulder: Westview Press.

Plattner, Marc and Larry Diamond.(Eds.) (1998). Will China democratize? *Journal of Democracy*, 9(1), 4-61.

Pu, xingzu. (Ed.) (1999). Dangdai zhongguo zhengzhi (Contemporary Chinese political system). Shanghai: Shanghai Renmin Chubashe.

Pye, Lucian W. (1971a). Identity and the Political Culture. In Leonard Binder et al.(Eds.) (1971), *Crises and sequences in political development* (pp.101-134). Princeton: Princeton University Press.

Pye, Lucian W. (1971b). The Legitimacy Crisis. In Leonard Binder et al.(Eds.)(1971). *Crises and sequences in political development* (pp.135-158). Princeton: Princeton University Press.

Pye, Lucian W. (1986). Reassessing the Cultural Revolution. *China Quarterly*, December, (108),597-612.

Pye, Lucian W. (1992). *The spirit of Chinese politics.* new edition. Cambridge: Harvard University Press.

Pye, Lucian W. (1993). Deng Xiaoping and China's political culture. *China Quarterly,* (135),412-443.

Pye, Lucian W. (1999). An overview of 50 years of the People's Republic of China: Some progress, but big problems remain. *China Quarterly,* (159),569-579.

Pye, Lucian W. (2001). Jiang Zemin style of rule: go for stability, monopolize power and settle for limited effectiveness. *China Journal,* (45),45-52.

Qi Fang.(Ed.) (1990). Heping yanbian zhanlue de chansheng ji qi fazhan (The Emergence of the Strategy of Peaceful Evolution and its Development). Beijing: Dongfang Chubanshe.

Rankin, Mary Backus. (1993). Some observations on a Chinese public sphere. *Modern China,* 19 (2),108-138.

Renmin Chubanshe (RC). (Ed.) (1984). Guanyu rendaozhuyi he yihua wenti lunwenji (Essays on the Problems of Humanism and Alienation). Beijing: Renmin Chubanshe.

Remin Ribao (People's Daily), China, various issues.

Riskin, Carl. (1987). *China's political economy: the quest for development since 1949.* Oxford: Oxford University Press.

Rosen, Stanley. (1990). The Chinese Communist Party and Chinese society: popular attitudes toward Party membership and the Party's image. *The Australian Journal of Chinese Affairs,* July, (24),51-92.

Rosenbaum, Arthur Lewis.(Ed.) (1992). *State and society in China - The consequences of reform.* Boulder: Westview Press.

Rowe, William T. (1990). The public sphere in Modern China: A review article. *Modern China,* July,16(3),309-329.

Rowe, William T. (1993). The problem of 'civil society' in late imperial China. *Modern China,* 19(2),139-157.

Ruan, Ming. (1992). Can Deng Xiaoping fly out of Chen Yun's Cage-Peaceful evolution and anti-peaceful evolution struggles in China", *Pai Shing,* 16 September, (272),6-9.

Ruan, Ming. (1994). Deng Xiaoping empire. Taipei: China Times Cultural Enterprise Ltd.

Ruan, Ming. (1995a). On establishing central authority. *Cheng Ming,* February, (208),70-81.

Ruan, Ming. (1995b).Chen Yun: One of the founders of the Maoist empire. *Open ,* May, (101),20-21.

Saich, Tony. (Ed.) (1990). *The Chinese people's movement: Perspectives in Spring 1989.* London: M.E. Sharpe.

Saich, Tony. (1991). Much ado about nothing: Party reform in the 1980s. In Gordon White(Ed.), *The Chinese state in the era of economic reform: the road to crisis* (pp.149-174). New York: M.E.Sharpe.

Saich, Tony. (2000). Negotiating the state: The development of social organizations in China. *China Quarterly,* (161),124-170.

Salisbury, Harrison E. (1992). *The new emperors — China in the era of Mao and Deng.* Boston: Little, Brown & Co.

Schell, Orville. (1990). The Re-emergence of the Realm of the Private in China. In George Hicks(Ed.), *The broken mirror: China after Tiananmen* (pp.419-427). Chicago: St. James Press.

Schell, Orville. (1994). *Mandate of heaven.* New York: Simon & Schuster.

Schmitter, Philippe.(1995) On civil society and the consolidation of democracy. Ten general propositions and nine speculations about their relations in Asian society. Paper presented at the international conference on "Consolidating the Third Wave Democracies: Trends and Challenges", 27-30 August, 1995, Taipei, Taiwan (ROC).

Schram, Stuart R. (1984). *Ideology and policy in China since Third Plenum, 1978-1984.* London: University of London.

Schumpeter, J. (1976). *Capitalism. socialism and democracy.* London: George Allen & Unwin.

Schurman, Franz. (1968). *Ideology and organization in Communist China.* Berkeley: University of California Press.

Selden, Mark.(Ed.) (1979).   *The People's Republic of China: a documentary history of revolutionary China.* New York: Monthly Review Press.

Selden, Mark.(Ed.) (1988).   *The political economy of Chinese socialism.* New York: M.E. Sharpe.

Shambaugh, David. (1993a).   Deng Xiaoping: The politician. *China Quarterly,* (135),457-490.

Shambaugh, David. (Ed.) (1993b). *American studies of contemporary China.* New York: M.E. Sharpe.

Shen, Tong. (1990). *Almost a revolution.* Boston: Houghton Mifflin Company.

Shirk, Susan. (1993). *The political logic of economic reform in China.* Berkeley: University of California Press.

Shue, Vivenne. (1988).   *The reach of the state.* Stanford: Stanford University Press.

Skinner, G. William and Edwin A. Winckler. (1980). Compliance succession in rural Communist China: A Cyclical Theory. In Amitai Etzioni(Ed.), *A sociological reader* (pp.401-23)*, second edition.* New York: Holt, Rinehart and Winston.

Smelser, Neil.(Ed.) (1988). *Handbook of sociology.* New York: Sage Publications.

So, Alvin Y. C. (1990). *Social change and development: Modernization, dependency, and world-systems theories.* Newbury: Sage Publications.

Solinger, D. (1991). *China's transients and the state: A form of civil society?* Hong Kong: Institute of Asia-Pacific Studies, Chinese University of Hong Kong.

Southerland, Daniel. (1994). Mass Death in Mao's China. *Washington Post,* 17-18 July.

South China Morning Post (SCMP), Daily, Hong Kong, various issues.

State Statistic Bureau (SSB). (1987). Guanyu 1986 nian guomin jingji he shehui fazhan de tongji gongbao (Concerning the 1986 Statistical Report of the National Economy and Social Development), Hong Kong: *Wen Wei Po,* 23rd February.

State Statistic Bureau (SSB). (1988). Guanyu 1987 nian guomin jingji he shehui fazhan de tongji gongbao(Concerning the 1987 Statistical Report of the National Economy and Social Development), *Renmin Ribao* (overseas edition), 25th February.

Stavis, Benedict. (1988). *China's political reforms.* New York: Praeger.

Stavis, Benedict. (1990). Contradictions in Communist reform: China before 4 June 1989", *Political Science Quarterly,* 105(1), 31-52.

Strand, David. (1990). 'Civil Society' and 'Public Sphere' in modern China: A perspective on popular movements in Beijing 1919/1989. *Problems of Communism,* May/June, 39(5):1-19.

Streeten, P. (1993). Markets and states: Against minimalism. *World Development,* August, 21(8),1281-1298.

Student Union of the Chinese University of Hong Kong (SUCU).(Ed.) (1982). *Democratic China — Collected essays of the Chinese dissidents in China.* Hong Kong: Far East Affairs Commentary Association.

Su, Shaozhi. (1982). Jingji fazhan he minzhuhua (Economic Development and Democratization). Beijing: Zhongguo Sheshui Kexueyuan Chubanshe.

Su, Shaozhi. (1988). A symposium on Marxism in China today: an interview with Su, Shaozhi, with comments by various American scholars. *Bulletin for Concerned Asian Scholars.* 24 (1),11-35.

Su, Shaozhi. (1989).1989 minyun de genyuan yu yingxiang (The Origins and Impact of the 1989 Pro-democracy Movement). *Ming Pao,* 4-5, September.

Su, Shaozhi. (1990). Zhongguo zhengzhi tizhi gaige de hongguan yanjiu (A Macro Study on China's Political Reform). *Cheng Ming,* June, (152),56-63.

Su, Shaozhi. (1992). Makesi Zhuyi xinlun (A New Interpretation of Marxism). Taipei: China Times Cultural Enterprise Ltd.

Su, Shaozhi. (1995). Cuozong fuza de dalu zhengju (On China's Political Development), *Cheng Ming,* May, (211),40-6; *Cheng Ming,* September, (215),52-57.

Su, Songxing and Hu Zhengping. (2000). Fenhua yu zhenghe: dangdai zhongguo qingnian jiazhiguan (Fragmentation and integration: Value system of the youth in the contemporary China). Shanghai: Shanghai Social Science Chubanshe.

Sullivan, L. (1990). The emergence of civil society in China, Spring 1989. In Tony Saich (Ed.), *The Chinese People's Movement: Perspectives in Spring 1989* (pp.126-144). London: M.E.Sharpe.

Sun, Longqi. (1990). Zhongguo wenhua de shenceng jiegou (The Deep Structure of Chinese Culture). Taipei: Tang Shan Publishing Company.

Sweezy, Paul. (1975).China: Contrasts with Capitalism. *Monthly Review*, 27 (3),1-11.

Sweezy, Paul. (1980). *Post-revolutionary society*. New York: Monthly Review Press.

Ta Kung Pao, Daily, Hong Kong, various issues.

Taber, George. (1992). Fruits of Prosperity. *Time*, 14 September, pp.20-24.

Tao, Dongmin and Chen Minmin. (1998). Dangdai zhongguo zhengzhi canyu (Political participation in contemporary China). Hangzhou: Zhejiangrenmin Chubanshe.

Tao Hai, Zhang Yide and Dai Qing. (Eds.) (1989). Zouchu xiandai mixin — guanyu zhengli biaozhun wenti de dabianlun (Marching out Modern Superstition — Concerning the Debates on the Problem of Criteria of Truth). Hong Kong: Joint Publishing Co.

Teiwes, Frederick C. (1984). *Leadership, legitimacy, and conflict in China*. New York: M.E.Sharpe.

The Mirror Monthly, Hong Kong, various issues.

The Nineties Monthly (before May 1984 as *The Seventies*), Hong Kong, various issues.

The Seventies Monthly (after May 1984 renamed as *The Nineties*), Hong Kong, various issues.

Tien, Hung-mao. (1989). Social Change and Political Development in Taiwan. In Harvey Feldman et al.(Eds.) *Taiwan in a time of transition* (pp. 3-18). New York: Paragon House.

Time. (1993). China: The next superpower (Special Report). 10 May, pp.12-45.

Tong, Huaizhou. (1978). Tiananmen shichao (Selected Poems of Tiananmen). Beijing: Renmin Wenxue Chubanshe.

Townsend, James R. and Brantly Womack. (1986). *Politics in China*. Boston: Little, Brown & Co.

Treadgold, Donald W., ed. (1967). *Soviet and Chinese communism: Similarities and differences.* Seattle: University of Washington Press.

Tsang, Wai-yin. (1989). Zhongguo xuesheng yundong zhenxiang (The Truth of China's Student Movement). Hong Kong: News Daily Publishing Ltd.

Tsou, Tang. (1986). *The Cultural Revolution and post-Mao reform*. Chicago: University of Chicago Press.

Tsou, Tang. (1991).The Tiananmen tragedy: The state-society relationship, choices, and mechanisms in historical perspectives. In Brantly Womack(Ed.)(1991a), *Contemporary Chinese politics in historical perspective* (pp.265-327). Cambridge: Cambridge University Press.

Tsou, Tang. (2002). *Interpreting the revolution in China.* Hong Kong: Oxford University Press.

Tucker, Robert. (1971). *Philosophy and myth in Karl Marx.* Chicago: University of Chicago Press.

Tucker, Robert. (Ed.) (1975). *The Lenin anthology.* New York: W.W. Norton and Company.

Tucker, Robert. (Ed.) (1978). *The Marx-Engels reader.* New York: W.W. Norton and Company.

Unger, Jonathan. (Ed.) (1991). *The pro-democracy protests in China.* New York: M.E. Sharpe.

Verba, Sidney. (1971). Sequences and Development. In Leonard Binder et al. (Eds.), *Crises and sequences in political development* (pp.283-316).Princeton: Princeton University Press.

Vogel, Ezra. (1967). Voluntarism and Social Control. In Donald Treadgold (Ed.), *Soviet and Chinese communism: Similarities and differences*(pp.168-84). Seattle: University of Washington Press.

Wade, Robert. (1990). *Governing the market — economic theory and the role of government in East Asian development.* Princeton: Princeton University Press.

Wakeman, Frederic, Jr. (1993). The civil society and public sphere debate. *Modern China,* 19 (2),108-138.

Walder, Andrew. (1986). *Communist neo-traditionalism.* Berkeley: University of California Press.

Walder, Andrew. (1987). Actually Existing Maoism. *The Australian Journal of Chinese Affairs,* July, (18),155-166.

Walder, Andrew. (1989). The political sociology of the Beijing upheaval of 1989. *Problems of Communism,* September/October, 38(5),30-40.

Walder, Andrew. (1992). *Popular protest in the 1989 democracy movement — the pattern of grass-roots organization.* Hong Kong: Chinese University of Hong Kong.

Wan, Li. (1986). Juece minzhuhua he kexuehua shi zhengzhi tizhi gaige de yige zhongyao keti (To Make Decision-Making Scientific and Democratic is an Important Part of the Political Reform). *Renmin Ribao,* 15 August.

Wang, C.F. James. (1995). *Contemporary Chinese politic — An Introduction, fifth edition.* New Jersey: Prenctice-Hall, Inc.

Wang, Huning. (1990). Fanfubai — Zhongguo de shiyan (Anti-corruption -- the Chinese experience). Haikou: Sanwan Chubanshe.

Wang, Juntao and Hou Yiaotian. (1992). Wang Juntao qiren qiyan qizui (Wang Juntao: His Personality, Speech and "Crime"). Hong Kong: Comtemporary Monthly Publishing Ltd.

Wang, Ruoshui. (1986). Wei rendaozhuyi bianhu (For Humanism). Beijing: Joint Publishing Co..

Wang, Ruoshui. (1989). Zhihui de tongku (The Pain of Wisdom). Hong Kong: Joint Publishing Co.

Wang, Ruowang. (1988). Tan zhengzhi gaige(On Political Reform). *The Nineties*, December, (227),65-75.

Wang, Shaoguang. (1991). Reflections on the notion of civil society. *Twenty-first Century*, Hong Kong, December, (8),102-114.

Wang, Weiping.(2000).Zhongguo jiceng minzhu fazhan de tupo(The New Breakthrough in China's Grass-root Democracy). Beijing: Shehui Kexiewenxian Chubabshe.

Wang, Xizhe. (1981). Mao Zedong yu wenhua dageming (Mao Zedong and Cultural Revolution) *The Seventies*, February, (133), 26-49.

Warren, Bill. (1973). Imperialism and Capitalist Industrialization. *New Left Review*, September/October, (80),3-43.

Weber, Max. (1985). *The Protestant ethic and the rise of capitalism.* London: Unwin Books.

Weiner, Myron. (1971). Political participation: Crisis of the political process. In Leonard Binder et al. (Eds.) *Crises and Sequences in Political Development* (pp.159-204). Princeton: Princeton University Press.

Weiner, Myron and Samuel P. Huntington.(Eds.) (1987). *Understanding political development.* Boston: Little Brown & Co.

Wen Wei Po Daily, Hong Kong, various issues.

Weng, Byron.(Ed.) (1984). *Essays on the constitution of the People's Republic of China.* Hong Kong: Chinese University Press.

Weng, Byron. (Ed.) (1987). *Essays on the constitution of the People's Republic of China, V. 2.* Hong Kong: Chinese University Press.

Wheelwright, Edward L. and Bruce McFarlane. (1970). *The Chinese road to socialism: Economics of the Cultural Revolution.* New York: Monthly Review Press.

White, Gordon.(Ed.) (1991). *The Chinese state in the era of economic reform: The road to crisis.* New York: M.E. Sharpe.

White, Gordon.(Ed.) (1993a). *Riding the tiger: The politics of economic reform in post-Mao China.* London: MacMillan.

White, Gordon.(Ed.) (1993b). Prospects for civil society in China: A case study of Xiaoshan city", *The Australian Journal of Chinese Affairs,* (29),63-87.

White, Lynn and Li Cheng. (1993). China Coast Identities: Regional, National, and Global. In Lowell Dittmer and Samuel Kim (Eds.) *China's quest for national identity* (pp. 154-93). Ithaca: Cornell University Press.

White, Stephen and Daniel Nelson.(Eds.) (1986). *Communist politics — A reader.* London: MacMillan.

Whitehead, Laurence. (1993). On 'reform of the state' and 'regulation of the market. *World Development,* August, 21(8),1371-1393.

Whyte, Martin King. (1992a). Urban China: A civil society in the making? In Arthur Rosenbaum(Ed.), *State and society in China — the consequences of reform*(pp.77-101). Boulder: Westview Press.

Whyte, Martin King. (1992b). Prospects for Democratization in China. *Problems of Communism,* May/June, 36(3),58-70.

Womack, Brantly. (1982). The 1980 county-level elections in China: Experiment in democratic modernization. *Asian Survey,* 22(3),261-277.

Womack, Brantly. (1984). Modernization and political reform in China. *Journal of Asian Studies,* May, 63(3),417-439.

Womack, Brantly. (1989). Party-State democracy: A theoretical exploration. *Issues and Studies,* March, (3),37-57.

Womack, Brantly. (Ed.) (1991a). *Contemporary Chinese politics in historical perspective.* Cambridge: Cambridge University Press.

Womack, Brantly. (1991b) In search of democracy: public authority and popular power in China. In Brantly Womack (Ed.) (1991a.), *Contemporary Chinese politics in historical perspective* (pp 53-89). Cambridge: Cambridge University Press.

Womack, Brantly and James R. Townsend. (1992). Politics in China. In Gabriel Almond and G. Bingham Powell, Jr. (Eds.) *Comparative politics to-day: A world view* (pp.409-461). New York: Harpers Collins Publishers.

Wong, Siu-lun. (1988). The applicability of Asian family values to other socio-cultural settings. In Peter Berger and Hsiao, Michael Hsin-Huang(Eds.), *In search of an East Asian model development model* (pp.134-54). New Brunswick: Transaction, Inc.

Wong, Yiu-chung. (1979). *China: Thirty years in review*. Hong Kong: Acta Ltd.

Wong, Yiu-chung. (1981). An Interview with Wang Xizhe. *New Left Review*.

Wong, Yiu-chung and Kwok Siu-tong.(Eds.) (1990). *China: Forty years in review*. Hong Kong: Pai Shing Cultural Enterprise Ltd.

Wong, Yiu-chung. (1990). China's democracy movement since 1949. In Wong Yiu-chung and Kwok Siu-tong(Eds.), *China: Forty Years in Review* (pp.29-68). Hong Kong: Pai Shing Cultural Enterprises Ltd.

Wong, Yiu-chung.(Ed.)(2000a). *China: Fifty years in review*. Hong Kong: Oxford University Press.

Wong Yiu-chung. (2000b). From political reform to administrative reform. In Wong Yiu-chung (Ed), *China: Fifty Years in review* (pp.43-61). Hong Kong: Oxford University Press.

Wong Yiu-chung and Chan Che-po.(2002). Corporatism, civil society and democratization in the People's Republic of China. *China Report*, 38(2),233-257.

Wu Guoguang. (1997). *Political Reform under Zhao Ziyang*. Hong Kong: The Pacific Century Institute.

Wu Guoguang and Wang Zhaojun. (1995). Deng Xiaoping zhihou de zhongguo (China After Deng: the Analyses of the Ten Most Urgent Problems). Taipei: World Publishing Compang.

Wu, Harry and Carolyn Wakeman. (1994) *Bitter winds − A memoir of my years in China's Gulag*. New York: John Wiley and Sons Inc.

Wu, Jiang. (1995). Shinian de lu − yu Hu Yaobang xiangchu de rizi (Ten Years with Hu Yaobang). *The Mirror* Publishing Company.

Xia, Ming. (2000). *The dual developmental state-Developmental strategy and institutional arrangements for China's transition*. Aldershot: Ashgate.

Xu, Yong. (1987). Zouxiang xiandai wenming − da biangezhong de zhongguo shenghuo fangshi (Marching Towards Modern Civilization − the Chinese Social Life in the Process of Rapid Change). Beijing: Huaxia Chubanshe.

Yan, Jiaqi. (1987). Quanli yu zhenli (Power and Truth). Beijing: Guangming Ribao Chubanshe.

Yan, Jiaqi. (1988). Wode sixiang zizhuan (My Intellectual Autobiography). Hong Kong: Joint Publishing Co.

Yan, Jiaqi. (1990). Maixiang minzhu zhengzhi (Marching Towards Democratic Politics). New Jersey: Global Publishing Company.

Yan, Jiaqi. (1992a). Zhengzhi duome jiandan — liaojie zhengzhi zhilu (How Simple is Politics — the Way of Understanding Politics). Taipei: Ching Chung Bookstore.

Yan, Jiaqi. (1992b). Lianbang zhongguo de gouxiang (The Idea of a Federal China). Hong Kong: Ming Pao Publishing Co.

Yan, Jiaqi and Gao Gao. (1986). Wenhua dageming shinianshi (A Ten-Year History of the Cultural Revolution). Hong Kong: *Ta Kung Pao.*

Yang, Deguang.(Ed.) (1991). Xifang sichao yu dangdai zhongguo daxuesheng (Western Thoughts and Contemporary Chinese University Students). Zhengzhou: Henan Renmin Chubanshe.

Yang, L.Y. and Ma Yiyang. (1991). *After the thunderstorm: Tiananmen and its aftermath and impact.* Hong Kong: Pai Shing Cultural Enterprise Ltd.

Yao, Wenyuan. (1975). Lun Lin Biao fandang jituan de shehui jichu (On the Social Basis of the Lin Biao Anti-Party Clique). *Historical Studies,* (2),12-21.

Yau, Shing-mu. (1988). Paper on voting for president, and vice-chairmen. *Hong Kong Standard,* 9 April.

Ye, Jianying. (1979). Zai qingzhu zhonghua renmin gongheguo chengli sanshi zhounian dahuishang de jianghua (Speech Commemorating the Thirtieth Anniversary of the Establishment of People's Republic of China), Hong Kong: *Wen Wei Po,* 13 September.

Ye, Yonglie. (1992). Chenzhong de 1957 (The Heavy 1957). Nanchang: Baihuazhou Wenyi Chubanshe.

Yong, Jimin et als.(1996). Yu zongshuji tanxin (Heart to heart talk with the general secretary). Beijing: Zhongguo Shehui Chubanshe.

Zhang, Chunqiao. (1975). Lun dui zichan jieji quanmian zhuanzheng (On Exercising All-Round Dictatorship over the Bourgeoisie). *Historical studies,* (2),3-11.

Zhang, Zhabin and Song, Yifu.(Eds.) (1991). Zhongguo: Mao Zedong re (China: Mao Zedong Fever). Taiyuan: Beiyue Wenyi Chubabshe.

Zhao, Suisheng. (2000). *China and Democracy — Reconsidering the prospects for a democratic China.* New York: Routledge.

Zhao, Ziyang. (1981). *Government Work Report.* Hong Kong: *Ta Kung Pao,* 14 December.

Zhao, Ziyang. (1982), *China's economy and development principles.* Beijing: Foreign Languages Press.

Zhao, Ziyang. (1983). *Government Work Report.* Hong Kong: *Wen Wei Po,* 24 June.

Zhao, Ziyang. (1984). *Government Work Report. Remin Ribao*, 2 June.

Zhao, Ziyang. (1985). *Government Work Report.* Hong Kong: *Wen Wei Po*, 12 April.

Zhao, Ziyang. (1987a). *Government Work Report.* Hong Kong: *Wen Wei Po*, 26 March

Zhao, Ziyang. (1987b). Yanzhe you zhongguo tese de shehui zhuyi daolu qianjin (Advancing Along the Road of Building Socialism with Chinese Characteristics). Report delivered at the Thirteenth Party Congress of the CCP. *Renmin Ribao* (overseas edition), 4 November.

Zhao, Ziyang. (1988). *Government Work Report.* Hong Kong: *Wen Wei Po,* 28 March.

Zhao, Ziyang. (1994). A self-defense on handling 4 June   turmoil. *Economic Journal*, 4 June.

Zhengzhi gaige ziliao xuanpian bianxiezu (ZGZXP).(Ed.) (1987). Zhengzhi tizhi gaige ziliao xuanpian (Selected Documents of the Political Reform). Naijing: Naijing Daxue Chubanshe.

Zhonggong dangshi jiaoyanshi (ZDJ). (Ed.) (1990). Sishinian de huigu (Reflections on Forty Years of the PRC). Beijing: Zhonggong Zhongyang Dangxiao Chubanshe.

Zhonggong zhongyang wenxian yanjiushi (ZZWY).(Ed.) (1987). Shiyijie sanzhong quanhui yilai zhongyao wenxian xuandu, two volumes, (Selected Important Documents since the Third Plenum of the Eleventh Party Congress of the CCP). Beijing: Renmin Chubanshe.

Zhonggong zhongyang xuanchuanbu (ZZX).(Ed.) (1987).   Sixiang jiben yuanze he zichanjieji ziyouhua de duili (The Contradictions between Four Fundamental Principles and Bougeois Liberalization). Beijing: Renmin Chubanshe.

Zhongguo Shehui Kexueshe (ZSK). (1986). Woguo de zhengzhi tizhi gaige yu zhengzhixue de fazhan (Political Reform in Our Country and the Development of the Political Science), *Chinese Social Sciences*, (4),3-14.

Zhongguo Tongji Nianjian (ZTN), (China Statistical Yearbook), various years,

Zhongguo Tongji Zhaiyao (ZTZ), (A Statistical Survey of China), various years.

Zhou, Enlai. (1976). *Selected works.* Hong Kong: Yat San Publishing Compang

Zhou, Yang. (1979). Sanci weida de sixiang jiefang yundong (Three Thought-Liberation Movements). *Renmin Ribao,* 7 May.

Zhou, Yang. (1983). Guanyu makesizhuyi de jige lilun wenti de tantao (A Discussion Concerning Some Theoretical Problems of Marxism). *Renmin Ribao*, 16 March.

Zhu, Jiamin. (1995). Zhao Ziyang de zhinangtuan he zhongguo de shinian de jingji gaige (The Think Tanks of Zhao Ziyang and China's Ten Years of Economic Reform). *Ming Pao Monthly*, March, (351),40-3; April, (352),96-100; July, (355),72-77.

Zhu, Jianhua, Zhao Xinshu, and Li Hairong. (1990). Public political consciousness in China. *Asian Survey*, October, 30(10),992-1006.

Zhu Rongji. (1995). Guanyu zhongguo zhengzhi he jingji xingshi (Concerning the 1995 Political and Economic Situation in China), *Open*, February, (98),24-29.

Zhu Rongji. (1999). *Government Work Report. Wen Wei Po*, 6 March.

Zhu Rongji. (2000). *Government Work Report. Ta Kung Pao*, 6 March

Zhu Rongji. (2002). *Government Work Report. Wen Wei Po*, 6 March

Zhu Rongji. (2003). *Government Work Report.* Ta Kung Pao, 6 March

INDEX